Studies in Economic Transition

General Editors: **Jens Hölscher**, Reader in Economics, University of Brighton; and **Horst Tomann**, Professor of Economics, Free University Berlin

This series has been established in response to a growing demand for a greater understanding of the transformation of economic systems. It brings together theoretical and empirical studies on economic transition and economic development. The post-communist transition from planned to market economies is one of the main areas of applied theory because in this field the most dramatic examples of change and economic dynamics can be found. The series aims to contribute to the understanding of specific major economic changes as well as to advance the theory of economic development. The implications of economic policy will be a major point of focus.

Titles include:

Lucian Cernat
EUROPEANIZATION, VARIETIES OF CAPITALISM AND ECONOMIC PERFORMANCE IN CENTRAL AND EASTERN EUROPE

Irwin Collier, Herwig Roggemann, Oliver Scholz and Horst Tomann (*editors*)
WELFARE STATES IN TRANSITION
East and West

Bruno Dallago (*editor*)
TRANSFORMATION AND EUROPEAN INTEGRATION
The Local Dimension

Bruno Dallago and Ichiro Iwasaki (*editors*)
CORPORATE RESTRUCTURING AND GOVERNANCE IN TRANSITION ECONOMIES

Hella Engerer
PRIVATIZATION AND ITS LIMITS IN CENTRAL AND EASTERN EUROPE
Property Rights in Transition

Saul Estrin, Grzegorz W. Kolodko and Milica Uvalic (*editors*)
TRANSITION AND BEYOND

Hubert Gabrisch and Rüdiger Pohi (*editors*)
EU ENLARGEMENT AND ITS MACROECONOMIC EFFECTS IN EASTERN EUROPE
Currencies, Prices, Investment and Competitiveness

Oleh Havrylyshyn
DIVERGENT PATHS IN POST-COMMUNIST TRANSFORMATION
Capitalism for All or Capitalism for the Few?

Jens Hölscher (*editor*)
FINANCIAL TURBULENCE AND CAPITAL MARKETS IN TRANSITION COUNTRIES

Jens Hölscher and Anja Hochberg (*editors*)
EAST GERMANY'S ECONOMIC DEVELOPMENT SINCE UNIFICATION
Domestic and Global Aspects

Iraj Hoshi, Paul J.J. Welfens and Anna Wziątek-Kubiak (*editors*)
INDUSTRIAL COMPETITIVENESS AND RESTRUCTURING IN ENLARGED EUROPE
How Accession Countries Catch Up and Integrate in the European Union

Mihaela Kelemen and Monika Kostera (*editors*)
CRITICAL MANAGEMENT RESEARCH IN EASTERN EUROPE
Managing the Transition

Emil J. Kirchner (*editor*)
DECENTRALIZATION AND TRANSITION IN THE VISEGRAD
Poland, Hungary, the Czech Republic and Slovakia

David Lane and Martin Myant (*editors*)
VARIETIES OF CAPITALISM IN POST-COMMUNIST COUNTRIES

Tomasz Mickiewicz (*editor*)
CORPORATE GOVERNANCE AND FINANCE IN POLAND AND RUSSIA

Tomasz Mickiewicz
ECONOMIC TRANSITION IN CENTRAL EUROPE AND THE COMMONWEALTH
OF INDEPENDENT STATES

Milan Nikolic
MONETARY POLICY IN TRANSITION
Inflation Nexus Money Supply in Postcommunist Russia

Julie Pellegrin
THE POLITICAL ECONOMY OF COMPETITIVENESS IN AN ENLARGED EUROPE

Stanislav Poloucek (*editor*)
REFORMING THE FINANCIAL SECTOR IN CENTRAL EUROPEAN COUNTRIES

Gregg S. Robins
BANKING IN TRANSITION
East Germany after Unification

Johannes Stephan
ECONOMIC TRANSITION IN HUNGARY AND EAST GERMANY
Gradualism and Shock Therapy in Catch-up Development

Johannes Stephan (*editor*)
TECHNOLOGY TRANSFER VIA FOREIGN DIRECT INVESTMENT IN CENTRAL
AND EASTERN EUROPE

Hans van Zon
THE POLITICAL ECONOMY OF INDEPENDENT UKRAINE

Studies in Economic Transition
Series Standing Order ISBN 0–333–73353–3
(*outside North America only*)

You can receive future titles in this series as they are published by placing a standing order. Please contact your bookseller or, in case of difficulty, write to us at the address below with your name and address, the title of the series and the ISBN quoted above.

Customer Services Department, Macmillan Distribution Ltd, Houndmills, Basingstoke, Hampshire RG21 6XS, England

Industrial Competitiveness and Restructuring in Enlarged Europe

How Accession Countries Catch Up and Integrate in the European Union

Edited by

Iraj Hoshi
Staffordshire University, UK

Paul J.J. Welfens
University of Wuppertal, Germany

and

Anna Wziątek-Kubiak
Polish Academy of Sciences and Dąbrowa Górnicza Business School, Poland

First published 2007 by
PALGRAVE MACMILLAN
Houndmills, Basingstoke, Hampshire RG21 6XS and
175 Fifth Avenue, New York, N.Y. 10010
Companies and representatives throughout the world

PALGRAVE MACMILLAN is the global academic imprint of the Palgrave Macmillan division of St. Martin's Press, LLC and of Palgrave Macmillan Ltd. Macmillan® is a registered trademark in the United States, United Kingdom and other countries. Palgrave is a registered trademark in the European Union and other countries.

ISBN-13: 978-0-230-52156-8
ISBN-10: 0-230-52156-8

This book is printed on paper suitable for recycling and made from fully managed and sustained forest sources. Logging, pulping and manufacturing processes are expected to conform to the environmental regulations of the country of origin.

A catalogue record for this book is available from the British Library.

A catalog record for this book is available from the Library of Congress.

10   9   8   7   6   5   4   3   2   1
16   15   14   13   12   11   10   09   08   07

Printed and bound in Great Britain by Antony Rowe Ltd,
Chippenham and Eastbourne

Contents

List of Tables

List of Figures

Preface

This book is a result of the research project 'Changes in Industrial Competitiveness as a Factor of Integration: Identifying the Challenges of the Enlarged Single European Market' which was conducted under the European Commission's Fifth Framework Programme (Ref. HPSE-CT-2002-00148). The project investigated the factors and mechanisms influencing the competitiveness of the manufacturing industries of three accession countries – the Czech Republic, Hungary and Poland – on the eve of the European Union's Eastern enlargement. It was coordinated by Professor Anna Wziątek-Kubiak and the Center for Social and Economic Research (CASE Foundation), Warsaw. The 11 papers selected here focus on a limited number of issues; outputs representing other aspects of the project have been published elsewhere and can be found on the project's website (www.compete.case.com.pl).

Many people and organizations were involved and contributed to the project's success; we are grateful to all of them. A few, however, must be mentioned by name. We acknowledge financial support from the European Commission's Fifth Framework Programme without which this project would not have been possible. We thank the Commission's staff associated with the research: Mr Peter Fisch, Head of Unit in the Directorate-General for Research, and the two scientific officers of the project, Ms Andrea Schmolzern and Dr Heiko Prange-Gstöehl, for their advice and continuous support. Mr P. Fisch provided the initial stimulus for this research at a meeting on the Commission's Fifth Framework Programme in Warsaw in 2002 by encouraging applications from Polish scholars and institutions. We also thank CASE Foundation for supporting and facilitating the management and administration of this project, in particular Dr Ewa Balcerowicz, the President of CASE Foundation for her encouragement and active involvement from the application stage to the publication of this book; Krzysztof Szczygielski and Iga Magda, the two scientific assistants of the project for invaluable support to all our research partners; and Tomek Kubiak for his meticulous work on the preparation of the manuscript for publication. Krzysztof Szczygielski's involvement in the preparation and coordination of the project is also acknowledged.

Finally, we would like to acknowledge the debt of gratitude to our friends, partners, children and grandchildren who endured our neglect during the course of this research and the preparation of this book, without them, too, this book would not have been written.

Stoke on Trent   IRAJ HOSHI
Wuppertal   PAUL J.J. WELFENS
Warsaw   ANNA WZIĄTEK-KUBIAK

Notes on the Contributors

Dora Borbély works at the Economic Research Department of DekaBank in Frankfurt am Main, Germany.

Michael Brandmeier is a senior economist at the Institute for Economic Policy Research, Division of Money and Banking, University of Karlsruhe (TH), Germany.

Darko Hajdukovic is a researcher at Royal Holloway, University of London and at Staffordshire University, Stoke on Trent, United Kingdom.

Iraj Hoshi is Professor of Economics and Director of the Centre for Research on Emerging Economies, Staffordshire University Business School, Stoke on Trent, United Kingdom.

David Kernohan is a Head of Economics and Statistics at Middlesex University Business School, Hendon, United Kingdom.

Erjon Luci is an economist at the World Bank office in Tirana, Albania. Up to 2006 he was Head of the Research Department at the Bank of Albania.

Iga Magda is completing her PhD at the Warsaw School of Economics (SGH) and works as an economist at CASE – the Center for Social and Economic Research – Poland.

Krzysztof Marczewski is Professor of Economics at the Warsaw School of Economics (SGH) and Deputy Director for scientific research in the Warsaw-based Foreign Trade Research Institute.

Jorge Núñez Ferrer is an Associate Research Fellow at the Centre for European Policy Research in Brussels, Belgium.

Mary O'Donnell is a Lecturer in Economics at the University of Limerick, Ireland.

Krzysztof Szczygielski is a researcher at CASE – Center for Social and Economic Research (Warsaw) and a PhD candidate at the Warsaw School of Economics, Poland.

Paul J.J. Welfens is Professor of Economics and Director of the European Institute for International Relations at the University of Wuppertal, Germany.

Piotr Wójcik is completing a doctorate at the Faculty of Economic Sciences, Warsaw University, Poland.

Richard Woodward is an economist at CASE – the Center for Social and Economic Research – and a Lecturer in the Management School, Edinburgh University, Scotland.

Anna Wziątek-Kubiak is a Professor of Economics and Head of Department at the Institute of Economics, Polish Academy of Sciences, and at Dąbrowa Górnicza Business School, Poland. She also cooperates with the CASE Foundation.

List of Abbreviations

AC	Accession countries
AC3	Three accession countries: the Czech Republic, Hungary and Poland
AC10	Ten new member states
B-S	Balassa–Samuelson Effect
CE	Central Europe
CEECs	Central and Eastern European Countries
EC	European Community
EE	Eastern Europe
ERM II	European Exchange Rate Mechanism II
ESF	European Social Fund
FDI	Foreign direct investment
GMM	General Methods of Moments
HOS-Model	Heckscher–Ohlin–Samuelson Model
NMS	New EU member states
NMS3	Three new member states: the Czech Republic, Hungary and Poland (same as AC3)
OPT	Outward processing trade
RCA	Revealed comparative advantage
REER	Real effective exchange rate
RER	Real exchange rate
RUEV	Relative unit export value
RULC	Relative unit labour costs
SEZs	Special economic zones
SITC	Standard Industrial Trade Classification
UV	Unit value
UEV	Unit export value
ULC	Unit labour costs

1
Introduction and Overview

Anna Wziątek-Kubiak and Iraj Hoshi

This book is about the changes in the industrial competitiveness and restructuring in the three leading reforming countries of Central and Eastern Europe in the pre-accession period. It aims to analyse and provide answers to the following questions: Can Central and East European economies integrate in the European Single Market, become internationally competitive and catch up with older member states of the European Union after having been insulated from international competition and operated in a non-market system on the periphery of Europe for such a long time? What are the preconditions for successful integration and the catching-up of former planned economies and what are the obstacles to their integration? What aspects of the development path of these countries facilitate or hinder their integration?

The collapse of the central planning system revealed the sharp division of Europe into the former socialist Central and East European Countries (CEECs) – a kind of periphery model in economics of geography – and the market economies of the European Union (EU) – a kind of centre. The division was a result of the long-term isolation of CEECs from the world economy, brought about by system-specific institutional characteristics such as the structure of incentives which discouraged technological change, innovation and improvements in efficiency, informational asymmetries within planning, and inconsistent policy-making procedures. On the one hand, the emphasis of the system of incentives for enterprises on achieving 'volume' of production at the cost of 'quality' of output resulted in high unit costs, low competitiveness, technological obsolescence, anti-innovation bias and very low quality of goods (Winiecki, 2002). On the other hand, the incentive system adversely affected the resource allocation mechanism and the structure of production and trade, resulting in distorted development (Lipowski, 2000). Consequently, in all these countries, extractive and heavy industries were over-extended at the expense of light and consumer goods industries and the share of industry in GDP was much higher than in countries at similar levels of development (or GDP per capita).

The micro and macro-economic characteristics of socialist economies also influenced their involvement in international trade and in trade specialisation. The very low share of exports in GDP accompanied a dualistic pattern of trade – the structure of CMEA-bound exports being very different to that of West-bound exports. Engineering goods that were 'competitive' in CMEA countries and uncompetitive in Western markets dominated the CMEA-bound exports, while less sophisticated standardized intermediate inputs and light-industry products and consumer goods were dominant in West-bound exports. Much higher shares of raw materials, agricultural goods and fuels constituted a much higher share of their exports to the EU than that of market economies at similar level of development. At the same time, under-specialization was accompanied by a very low and deteriorating quality of exported goods. The unit export value of goods exported to the EU in 1988 was about one-third of the EU level, indicating not only distorted prices but also low quality (Winiecki, 2002, p. 26). The absence of proper (market-determined) domestic relative prices and a realistic exchange rate brought about losses rather than gains from trade.

As the former socialist countries 'under-traded' with the EU countries and 'over-traded' with each other, a natural consequence of the demise of socialism in the 1989–91 period was the readjustment of these countries' trade and the start of a process of integration into the EU. The foreign policy of CEECs was aimed at EU membership, an idea which was also promoted by the EU as part of its response to the collapse of communism (Baldwin, 1995). Given the specific, and distorted, nature of the development of former socialist economies, a major question posed at the start of the transition process was: what were the implications of the radical opening of these economies for their competitiveness and the structure of production and trade, which did not reflect competitive advantages, and for the economic growth of the integrating blocks – not only CEECs but also the EU countries? Although they produced and exported low quality goods for which the EU demand was limited, their factors endowments were different from countries with similar income levels and developing countries. CEECs were much better endowed with human capital and skilled labour (Halpern, 1995; Gros and Suhrcke, 2001) which was not fully reflected in their trade flows and trade specialization (Tajoli, 1998). They produced and demanded low quality goods not only because they could not spend enough on quality improvements. The high share of inter-CMEA-trade and the weak incentive for innovation and technological change strengthened specialization in low quality goods.

Linder's (1961) 'preference for similarity' theory of trade in final manufactured goods stating that similar countries trade more with each other than with very different countries suggested that CEECs could not radically increase their trade with the EU unless they substantially upgraded the quality of their goods (Murphy and Shleifer, 1991). In other words, in order to break out of the cycle of trade in low-quality goods with other CEECs, they had to upgrade the quality of their products. The improvement in quality was, of course, only one dimension of the challenge facing those CEECs who aspired to become accession countries (ACs) and its success depended also on whether or not they could increase their productive efficiency. An improvement in overall efficiency would be possible if resources shift from the less efficient to more efficient employment and from less competitive to more competitive sectors; that is, if the structure of the economy changes. The restructuring process would be facilitated if there is also a shift in the demand for goods with higher quality to encourage an increase in the production of these goods to meet the increased demand of the EU markets and thus also force changes in the composition and pattern of exports. The restructuring process would also result in an increase in aggregate productivity, economic growth and integration into the EU.

Although the abundance of skilled labour is conducive to structural change and integration, as it is an important source of innovation, other characteristics of CEECs such as the inherited specialization, institutional features, the shortage of capital and the obsolescence of capital stock could have accentuated the differences in industrial structure between these countries and enhance their 'peripheralness'. It was possible to avoid this possibility by changing the institutional characteristics, encouraging the inflow of foreign direct investment (FDI) and move towards the re-direction of their trade with EU states. Given that the institutional environment of these countries played a crucial role in shaping the transition process, establishing a well-functioning set of market institution was seen as essential for economic performance and integration – as was later confirmed by Bevan, et al. (2004). The inflow of FDI can open up new possibilities for the location of economic activity. Foreign companies can transfer more up-to-date technology to production facilities in new locations. Being better prepared to reduce X-inefficiency these companies can narrow the productivity gap and help to incorporate CEECs production into the global production network. The more so given that the CEECs were endowed with relatively cheap human capital resources which would allow a more effective use of modern capital and produce goods with higher quality. However the institutional environment and the long term character of some of the necessary change, the inherited behaviour of the labour force, political instability and strong turbulence of the economy may hinder the inflow of FDI to CEECs. They may also increase the differences in terms of economic growth and in integration from country to country. Many observers were pessimistic about the possibility of the expansion of CEECs' exports because of the low competitiveness of their industries, low quality of their products and their distorted production and trade structures. However, for the accession countries at least, the pessimism was misplaced.

The integration into the EU was a policy priority of CEECs. Although theoretical models showed that integration will result in the expansion of trade especially among similar countries and that adjustment costs will be smaller when countries are similar, integration was also promoted by the EU. Since the effects of integration depends closely on the similarity of costs, economic structures and economic institutions of the integrating units, the EU provided the ACs with a clear direction of reform in laws, politics, economics and administration to help bring about this similarity in a short period of time. This took the form of the EU's *acquis communautaire*, the comprehensive body of laws, rules and regulations that govern the Union and which should be met by new members before accession. Negotiations for accession were guided by the Copenhagen criteria (1993) which required that candidates reach an economic, political and institutional level comparable to the one of the EU members. Not only they had to become 'functioning market economies', they also had to show 'the capacity to cope with competitive pressure and market forces within the Union' (European Council, 1993). The conditions for CEECs' accessions were aimed at ensuring that the institutions in these countries will change and that the institutional and economic convergence will facilitate the integration process and diminish risk of weakening the EU.

Negotiations for accession influenced the process of industrial restructuring and institution-building in the accession countries (Kamiński, 2001). It speeded up the process of establishing the institutional framework of a market system in these countries through 'not only ...the greater probability of having "good laws" and having them faster, but also...inheriting in most cases already established routines' (Winiecki, 2002, p. 130). The obligation to introduce and keep EU regulations helped to stabilize the institutional environment and was conducive to the inflow of FDI and the working of economic agents. It raised economic efficiency and economic performance and accelerated the growth of new member states. Not only did new economic actors emerge and compete successfully with the state owned and foreign enterprises, the role of the state in the economy also radically changed.

The experience of accession countries (ACs) shows that their gradual integration into the European Single Market did not foster their 'peripheralness' in terms of the volume and structure of trade flows and GDP per capita. 'Peripherialness' did not materialize and, indeed, the opposite happened. Technical efficiency of firms in ACs has been converging towards the EU average (De Loecker, 2004), resulting in their convergence in terms of GDP per capita – this is a 'catching up' process. Their exchange rate regime shifted from an adjustable peg or peg to a floating rate. The structure of their trade across industries and within segments in terms of quality range converged towards the pattern of trade in the incumbent EU member states. Contrary to predictions, the growth of trade between the 'core' (EU-15) and the 'periphery' (ACs) of Europe was stronger than within the 'core' itself. The continuing institutional reforms, decreasing productivity gaps and structural changes in the ACs (Raiser *et al.*, 2004), indicate the increasing similarity of the new and incumbent member states as host countries for FDI and the growing substitutability of the two groups of countries in the eyes of foreign investors (Disdier and Mayer, 2004). The clear trend of converging GDP per capita to the EU level, continuing structural changes, and growing exports and market shares are all evidences of ACs' economies becoming competitive.

Meeting the Copenhagen criteria, that is achieving the capacity to compete and expand in the presence of rivalry on the EU market, eight CEECs became members of the EU on 1 May 2004. This suggests that at least some of the industries in these countries were seen to be able to cope with the competitive pressure on the EU market. The membership, in turn, enabled these industries not only to compete with and put pressure on the industries of 'old' EU members, but also cause substantial disruption in some sectors of the EU-15 member states. The important question, to which this book attempts to provide an answer, is: what are the factors that explain the improvements in industrial competitiveness of the new versus the 'old' EU members? Is it the labour cost advantage or other factors such as the quality of human capital, the inflow of FDI, improvements in the quality of capital stock, innovations, structural changes and the new emerging networking, or government policies that have resulted in improving competitiveness? Changes in competitiveness impact the catching-up process both directly and indirectly, through structural change. The latter depends not only on changes in competitiveness but also changes in demand and the development of higher value-added industries, that is, a shift in resources to these industries and a change in the structure of value added in manufacturing and in the pattern of trade specialization. The second set of questions to which the book responds concerns the determinants of the restructuring process in production, employment, specialisation patterns, and their impact on overall productivity of the manufacturing sector.

The opinion that the competitiveness of ACs had improved considerably did prevail in the end (European Commission, 1997) and has since been supported by numerous publications on the progress of the new member states. Most of the analyses deal with specific issues of competitiveness such as changes in the dynamics of trade, specialization, potential and actual trade and thus the level of trade, FDI flows, efficiency of enterprises and nominal and real convergence. But, surprisingly, only few of these have addressed the analysis of the determinants, factors and differentiation of changes in industrial competitiveness and in structural change in the manufacturing sectors of these countries. What is missing are contributions aiming at generalizing the determinants of changes in competitiveness and the structure of manufacturing in the new member states against the incumbent EU countries, at disaggregated industry level.

Competitiveness, of course, is a complex and rather ambiguous concept with many meanings. In the literature, there are at least two main approaches to competitiveness – microeconomic and macroeconomic.

In the microeconomic approach competitiveness is derived from rivalry and competition; it reflects the ability to compete. Competitiveness and its determinants are related to and derived from forms, factors and the effect of competition. This includes rivalry in price and non-price factors. In this approach the term 'competition' is used in the sense of rivalry among actual and potential competitors, a rivalrous competition (Nelson, 1996). It is synonymous with terms such as 'struggle' and 'conflict' (Martin, 2004), that is the situations in which parties producing substitutes end up in conflict. It encompasses the process of some firms pushing others out of the market and replace the goods produced by them. The micro approach to competitiveness concentrates on determinants of changes in competitiveness and its effects. This approach, focusing on technical efficiency, does not consider allocative efficiency, structural changes and the related shifts in resources between industries which influence aggregate productivity as well as the dynamics of growth.

In contrast, the macroeconomic approach to competitiveness focuses on the national level and on the 'the ability of an economy to provide its population with high and rising standards of living and high rates of employment on a sustainable basis' (European Commission, 2001–04).[1] In this approach the structural characteristics of the economy[2] are taken into consideration and are treated as the main factors determining the living standards and competitiveness *per se*. This approach extends the meaning of competitiveness to economic conditions for medium-term growth. However it does not show the mechanism of transmission of changes in the ability to compete at micro level into macro, national level, for example economic growth. The EU bodies and policies, of course, use both approaches to competitiveness. Although the term competitiveness was not used in the Copenhagen criteria for accession, the focus on the ability of the ACs to cope with competitive pressure suggests that these criteria referred to the microeconomic approach to competitiveness. On the other hand, focusing on policy implications, the European Commission (2001) uses the economy wide approach to competitiveness underlying 'the high rates of employment on a sustainable basis'.

This book, too, considers both approaches and provides an assessment of the determinants of changes in industrial competitiveness and the development of structural change in the three new member states during pre-accession period (1996–2003) which constituted the basis for catching up and the integration of these economies into the European Single Market. In our opinion enough time has passed to allow the identification of trends and the assessment of the importance of the determining factors behind these trends. The book focuses exclusively on the manufacturing sectors of the three accession countries – the Czech Republic, Hungary and Poland. It also considers the policy implications of changes in competitiveness and in the structure of manufacturing production of the ACs for them and for EU-15.

1.1 Overview of the book

Following this introductory chapter, the book is divided into three parts. The first part, covering five chapters, presents the differentiation in changes in competitiveness across the manufacturing industries of the three countries and highlights the importance of factors such as relative wages, productivity, the quality of goods, innovation, human capital, FDI, exchange rates, government policies and networking. Different approaches, assumptions and methodologies are employed to facilitate a better understanding of the catching up process and the integration of the new member states into the European Single Market.

The evaluation of changes in competitive pressure facing the manufacturing industries (at the disaggregated 3-digit level) of the three new member states on the enlarged EU-25 market and the main factors underlying this process – such as relative unit labour costs, relative quality, investment, FDI and productivity gap – are analysed in the first chapter. Looking at competitiveness from the point of view of the effect of rivalry and competition (i.e., performance competitiveness and competitive pressure) and factors influencing it, Wziątek-Kubiak and Magda analyse the measures of change in competitiveness at industry level. They identify factors which were conducive to the improvement in competitiveness of manufacturing industries of the three accession countries compared to the incumbent EU members and changes in their role over time. The analysis also considers the determinants of changes in competitiveness of those industries which increased the competitive pressure on the EU market the most, and those whose competitive position was the strongest and also rising. The authors show that adjustment in structure of production between the AC-3 and the EU was driven by differences in productivity growth and changes in the relative unit labour cost.

Chapter 3 focuses on one of the crucial aspects of the institutional change in the three accession states; that is, the role of government policy. Hashi, Hajdukovic and Luci examine the role of government in the context of the literature on public choice and rent-seeking behaviour and question the received wisdom that government interventions in the form of taxes and subsidies can lead to improvements in the competitiveness of industries. Using the microeconomic approach to competitiveness, that is treating competitiveness as the ability of an industry to expand its domestic and/or EU market shares, they use panel-data econometrics to investigate the impact of taxes and subsidies on the domestic and foreign competitiveness of the manufacturing industries (disaggregated to 3-digit level) in the three countries under consideration. They show that contrary to the views widely held in transition economies, and in most cases, government intervention has little impact on competitiveness. This leads them to argue that such interventions have been, most of the time, motivated by political pressure.

Chapters 4 and 5 present two different versions of a modified neo-classical model with endogenous growth, incorporating FDI. The focus of both papers is the impact of the real exchange rate (RER) on trade and growth. Using different scopes of analysis, assumptions and models, they offer alternative explanations for the geographic distribution of FDI inflows in transition economies and the divergent balanced growth path in these countries. In Chapter 4, on the 'Interdependency of Real Exchange Rate, Trade, Innovation, Structural Change and Growth', Welfens provides alternative explanations for changes in RER and shows their impact on trade, structural change and growth in the long-term equilibrium. Introducing a new approach to monetary growth policy in an open economy, he demonstrates that a real appreciation of the currency in the new member states follows from an increase in the premium factor reflecting the impact of the relative market size on RER and depends on the size of the demand shift between tradable and non-tradable sectors. The advantage of this model is that it can be used to track fiscal and monetary policy supply shocks simultaneously. Focusing on the RER dynamics and its economic effects, Welfens also presents a new structural model incorporating links between process and product innovation and price levels and thus extending the Hansen-Roger model. He shows that the appreciation of the domestic currency can act as an incentive to upgrade the quality of export products whereby such goods become less price sensitive. It results in changes in the structure of production, trade pattern and growth, and also generates pressure for structural change in the EU-15. The chapter ends with extended policy conclusion for the new and incumbent EU member states.

Following Foot and Stein (1991), Welfens assumes a negative relationship between RER and the volume of FDI inflow into the new EU member states and analyses the impact of RER on capital flows which influence growth. Commenting on Chapter 4 by Welfens, Brandmeier in Chapter 5 extends this analysis by using an extension of Romer (1990) and incorporating additional features based on the assumption that level of FDI inflows depends on the level of human capital stock. He introduces an alternative explanation for the divergent growth rates in CEECs by including the impact of human capita and the relationship between labour costs and productivity as a more important factor determining FDI inflows. The argument put forward is that the more human capital needed to realize an increase in labour productivity, the more spill-over impact will the FDI have on industrial sector. The availability of human capital which can be employed at comparatively lower costs than at other production sites in Europe is of crucial importance for the effective use and the modernisation of the capital stock. He also presents some empirical evidence on the positive relationship between the human capital endowment, growth rates and FDI shares, underlining the crucial role of FDI in the catching up process.

In Chapter 6, 'Networking and Competitiveness', Woodward and Wójcik analyse how the relationships between firms and other organizations (including other firms) affect their competitiveness and what kinds of networking are dominant in the Czech Republic, Hungary, Poland and Spain (looking in particular for country-specific or industry-specific patterns). They also compare the networking patterns of foreign-owned firms with those of domestic firms. This analysis includes both hierarchical (equity-based) and arm's-length relationships as well as networks understood in the classic sense (for example cooperative relationships which are neither hierarchical nor purely market-based). They use a sample of over 600 firms in four manufacturing industries (electronics, pharmaceuticals, food and automotive) in the three accession countries under consideration and one EU member state (Spain) described as peripheral in terms of technology-intensive production. The analysis demonstrates that the strategic use of networking and business partnerships to improve competitiveness is still in an early stage of development in the three accession countries, with much remaining to be learned. Foreign ownership remains an important determinant of at least some aspects of competitiveness (such as export activity), but investors in accession countries are distinguished from domestic firms more by the rate of growth than by the pattern of linkages.

The second part of the book is concerned with the 'catching-up' of the ACs and their integration in the EU which can be achieved through a deep restructuring of their industries and changes in their trade patterns, demand and the allocation of resources. These processes have been accompanied by uneven changes in competitiveness across industries, notably in productivity – which is the fundamental determinant of differences in living standards across countries. This part of the book presents the characteristics, trends and determinants of changes in structure of manufacturing and in trade patterns of the three ACs under consideration as compared to the incumbent EU countries and their links with the performance of manufacturing, trade patterns and catching-up.

This part starts with the analysis of structural change in Polish manufacturing and its determinants, and the Polish experience is especially relevant to the discussion of 'catching-up'. Poland's GDP is higher than the total of the Czech, Slovak and Hungarian GDP taken together. At the beginning of transition Poland was not only less developed but also much more closed and less integrated into the EU economy than Czechoslovakia and Hungary. The excessive industrial employment and the distorted structure of production characterized the Polish economy. The process of catching-up in Poland was accompanied by high unemployment rates, changes in the allocation of labour and other resources across industries and changes in structure of manufacturing output. The specific features of the structural change in Polish manufacturing, factors influencing this process as well as the impact of structural change on the aggregate productivity and on labour market developments are presented in Chapter 7, 'The Process of Structural Change and its Determinants in Polish Manufacturing, 1995–2003'. After presenting the scale and volatility of structural changes in Polish manufacturing as compared to that in the EU, Marczewski and Szczygielski analyse the role of various determinants of structural change – that is, domestic and EU demand, factor competitiveness and performance competitiveness. The in-depth analysis of the impact of the characteristics of industries such as the type of technology, skill-intensity, factor-intensity, concentration, internationalization of production, import penetration and FDI involvement on changes in employment and value added in the whole period (1995–2003) and two subperiods provide the basis for a better understanding of nature of structural change in the new member states and their effects. The chapter also includes the analysis of the impact of changes in the structure of manufacturing production on the growth of labour productivity and its development over time.

As the chapter on Poland focuses on structural change in manufacturing before accession, Chapter 8, 'Structural Change, Productivity and Performance: Some Evidence from Irish Manufacturing', draws on the Irish experience, comparing changes in the structure of manufacturing in the period before Ireland's accession to the EC in 1973 (namely 1968–73) with the post-accession period (1973–83) as well as the more recent period (1995–2002). Presenting the crucial role of structural change in the catching-up process in Ireland and dynamic nature of the relationship, O'Donnell focuses on different dimensions of the relationship between structural change and productivity in the pre- and post-accession period. The chapter starts with the analysis of the relationship between structural change and labour productivity growth at industry level (similar to the analysis undertaken in Chapter 7 for Poland), demonstrating the extent to which structural change and the reallocation of resources within manufacturing have contributed to labour productivity growth over time. The author then analyses the relationship between structural change in terms of output, value added, employment, turnover and exports and changes in performance, measured by profitability, value added and labour productivity over time. She shows that growth of various structural variables does not have a uniform impact on the performance of Irish manufacturing.

Chapters 8 and 9 concentrate on changes in the trade patterns of the new EU member states as compared to that of the incumbent states and discuss their determinants and their role in trade performance. In Chapter 9, aiming at answering the question 'What Drives Specialisation in the New EU Member States?', Borbely shows the change in the pattern of trade specialization in new member states in different types of industries, classified in terms of their quality and factor intensity, and analyses the determinants of these changes: lagged production, unit value of exports, relative wages, labour productivity, unit labour costs, FDI and the expenditure on research and development.

She shows that the impact of these factors on trade performance varies across industries according to their factor intensity. For example the unit value of exports plays an important role in explaining the comparative advantage in science-based and differentiated goods industries and hardly any role in labour intensive industries. FDI and relative wages, on the other hand, impact the comparative advantage in labour intensive industries.

In Chapter 10 Brandmeier comments on Borbely's analysis and, based on the example of Germany, extends and deepens the analysis by focusing on outsourcing and a number of other related issues as an alternative explanation for trade specialization. He shows that the strong competition in labour and resource-intensive industries takes place not only between CEECs and cohesion countries but also with the West European and Far Eastern countries. Although the comparative advantage of the EU-15 in human-capital-intensive and high-technology goods is still positive it is also eroding. Commenting on the determinants of changes in the pattern of exports of CEECs and the volume of outsourcing, he confirms the crucial role of FDI in this process. However although lower wages in CEECs are important in location decision by German companies, Brandmeier did not find a significant relation between the relative wage and the volume of outsourcing to CEECs from Germany. The outsourcing volume is strongly explained by differences in the sectoral labour productivity and not by the wage levels. This suggests that productivity gap and its changes as well as the type and quality of human capital influence this type of trade.

Although most chapters include the relevant policy implications, the third part of the book focuses exclusively on policy matters, employing an economy-wide approach to competitiveness. In Chapter 11, 'Enlargement and Industrial Competitiveness: Policy Implications for New and Old Member States of the EU', Ferrer and Kernohan draw on the results of the previous chapters and the project as a whole to assess policy implications for the new and old member countries. They argue that EU industries can take advantage of the lower costs and high education of the AC labour force and increase their competitiveness on the world market. As in the short run the new member states can become strong competitors in particular sectors or geographical areas, this improvement is not universally welcome in the older members. They recommend policies aimed at improving investment climate and the general economic and institutional conditions for extending competition (for example in the services market) but discourage specific industrial policies which may be thought to improve industrial competitiveness.

Notes

1 The *World Competitiveness Report* (IMD, 1996) uses a similar approach to competitiveness, that is 'the ability of a nation's economy to make rapid and sustained gains in living standards'.

2   Examples of such characteristics are: 'openness to international trade and finance, role of the government budget and regulation, development of financial markets, quality of infrastructure, quality of technology, quality of business management, labour market flexibility and quality of judicial and political institutions'.

References

Baldwin, R.E. (1995) 'The Eastern Enlargement of the European Union', *European Economic Review*, 39: 474–81.

Bevan, A.A., S. Estrin and K. Meyer (2004) 'Foreign Investment Location and Institutional Development in Transition Economies', *International Business Review*, 1: 43–64.

De Loecker, J. (2004) 'Comparing Performance of Firms in EU Accession Countries with an EU Benchmark', LICOS Discussion Papers. LICOS Centre für Transition Economics, Katholieke Universiteit Leuven, Leuven, http://ww.econ.kuleuven.av.be/licos.

Disdier, A.C. and T. Mayer (2004) 'How Different is Eastern Europe? Structure and Determinants of Location Choices by French Firms in Eastern and Western Europe', *Journal of Comparative Economics*, 32: 280–96.

European Commission (2001–04) *European Competitiveness Reports 2001–4*. Brussels: EC.

Gros, D. and M. Suhrcke (2001) 'Ten Years After: What is Special about Transition Countries', *Aussenwirschaft*, 56(2), June: 201–24.

Halpern, L. (1995) 'Comparative Advantage and Likely Trade Pattern of the CEECs', in R. Faini and R. Porters (eds), *European Trade with Eastern Europe*. London: CEPR.

Institute for Management Development (1996) *World Competitiveness Report 1996*. Geneva: IMD.

Kamiński, B. (2001) 'How Accession to the European Union Has Affected External Trade and Foreign Direct Investment in Central European Economies', World Bank Working Paper no. 2578. Washington, DC: Work Bank.

Lipowski, A. (2000) 'Zmiany w strukturze wytwarzania PKB w latach 1990–1998 (Changes in structure of GDP in 1990–1998: agriculture, industry and services)', in A. Lipowski (ed.), *Struktura gospodarki transformującej się. Polska 1990–1998 i projekcja do roku 2010 (Structure of an Economy Under Transition. Poland in 1990–1998 and a Forecast until 2010)*. Warsaw: Ziggurat.

Linder, S. (1961) *An Essay on Trade and Transformation*. Uppsala: Almquist & Wicksells.

Martin, S. (2004) 'Globalization and the Natural Limits of Competition', in M. Neumann and J. Weigand (eds), *The International Handbook of Competition*. Cheltenham, UK & Northampton, MA, USA: Edward Elgar.

Murphy, K.M. and A. Shleifer (1991) 'Quality and Trade', NBER Working Paper no. 3622, February.

Nelson, R. (1996) *The Sources of Economic Growth*. London, England & Cambridge, Mass: Harvard University Press.

Raiser, M., M. Schaffer and J. Schuchhardt (2004) 'Benchmarking Structural Change in Transition', *Structural Change and Economic Dynamics*, 15: 47–71.

Romer, P. (1990) 'Endogenous Technological Change', *Journal of Political Economy*, 98: 71–102.

Tajoli, L. (1998) 'The Economic Integration between the European Union and CEECs: Can We Learn from the Past?' CEPS Discussion Paper no. 31.

Winiecki, J. (2002) *Transition Economies and Foreign Trade*. London & New York: Routledge.

2
How Do New Member States Cope with Competition in the EU Market?

Anna Wziątek-Kubiak and Iga Magda

2.1 Introduction

The three accession countries (AC3) – the Czech Republic, Hungary and Poland – signed the Europe Agreement establishing association with the European Union and their member countries in 1991. This Agreement contributed to tangible changes in the three countries' economies, although it is not clear to what extent these were due to the Agreement itself or to other factors. It did, undoubtedly, result in the adjustment of the AC3 economies to the mechanisms and provisions in force in the European Union. However, this process was uneven in the manufacturing sector. Some industries adjusted relatively smoothly and increased competitive pressure on EU producers, while others have not and were, in effect, 'competed out'.

The central theme of this chapter is the differentiation in changes in the competitiveness of the AC3 industries – which are the most important players on the EU market[1] among the new member states (NMS) – and the factors that explain this. Deploying a Schumpeterian approach to competition and defining competitiveness as the ability to compete, the focus of the analysis is on the effects and factors of competition between the AC3 and the incumbent EU countries in the enlarged EU market. Studying the varied processes of selecting manufacturing industries in the EU market, this chapter demonstrates that the AC3 manufacturing industries increased competitive pressure on the EU market and the determinants conducive to this process. It concentrates on three groups of AC3 industries: those whose share of the EU market was diminishing, those whose share was large and increasing, as well as those whose share of the EU market was small but increasing. The comparison of these groups of industries across the three countries, and between them and the incumbent EU countries, allows us to determine the characteristics of the process of integration of the NMS into the Single Market. The analysis covers the manufacturing industries (at the three digit level of NACE Rev. 1.1 classification) of the Czech Republic, Hungary and Poland as compared to the incumbent EU countries. It focuses on the pre-accession period

13

(1998–2003) which was characterized by intensive adjustments in AC3 manufacturing industries to EU market conditions. This included a period (up to 2000) of intensive liberalization of trade with the EU and a short period just before accession when trade with the EU was almost fully liberalized.[2] Although our analysis here does not cover the whole period of liberalization, its effects had become mostly visible in the years discussed here.

The chapter is organized as follows: section 2.1 presents three approaches to competitiveness which are predominant in the literature: economy-wide, micro and trade. Section 2.2 presents diverging view on competitiveness which predominates in the literature; section 2.3 analyses the notion of competitiveness as the ability to compete and integrate into the European Single Market and discusses measurement problems; section 2.4 describes the methodology and model used; and section 2.5 provides a picture of changes in the competitiveness of the AC3 and their determinants. Section 2.6 identifies and characterizes the losers and two types of winners of the integration process, while conclusions stemming from this analysis are presented at the end of the chapter.

2.2   Diverging views on competitiveness

Virtually all debates on competitiveness have been conducted using measures of competitiveness rather than definitions. The application of different measures is the result of different ways of understanding this notion. This owes to the fact that competitiveness has not been defined as rigorously as, for example, comparative advantage. Some authors treat the concept as synonymous with comparative advantage while others conceive of it as a microeconomic or economy-wide characteristic. In contrast to the comparative advantage which is tied to the framework of trade theory, competitiveness is implicitly included in many theories, although none of these theories have ever used competitiveness as an explanatory variable (Gomory and Baumol, 2000). Each of these theories marks the boundaries of analysis which are reflected in ways of understanding and measurements of competitiveness. They are so strikingly diverse that it often seems that the subject of analysis is entirely different, though related by name. The different purposes for which competitiveness is used, for example for the analysis and design of policy or for ranking countries, further increases the differentiation of meaning of competitiveness and its measurement.

We distinguish between three concepts of competitiveness: microeconomic, macroeconomic and trade. The most controversial concept of competitiveness is the macroeconomic one, which applies to the characteristics of whole economies and countries. This concept is less meaningful than the micro concept because its theoretical base and aggregation method are problematic. As Krugman (1994) pointed out, economies and countries do not compete against each other in trade. They may in some sense compete with each other in attracting production resources, including foreign direct investment (FDI), but attributes for attracting FDI are not identical to strong performance in exports.

There are many versions of the macroeconomic concept of competitiveness. Perhaps the best–known version is the World Competitiveness Index (WEF/IMD, 1995) which is an international ranking of countries in terms of their business climate and may serve a useful purpose to international investors. However, its theoretical basis and the aggregation method are problematic, to say the least. This approach limits competitiveness to economic conditions for medium-term growth.

Another interpretation of macroeconomic competitiveness is more in line with the original meaning of the term. It follows from the microeconomic concept by aggregation. An economy is competitive if it has a large number of internationally competitive industries or firms. Dollar and Wolffs (1993) propose to measure this in terms of the productivity of the whole economy which determines the standard of living. This approach is also used by the European Commission (2001) which defines competitiveness as 'the ability of an economy to provide its population with high and rising standards of living and high rates of employment on a sustainable basis' thus covering a selection of EC's objectives. The question arises, however, as to whether competitiveness is in fact the same as economic growth/development, or whether it is just one of several variables influencing economic growth. If both are the same, that raises the question of whether there is any value in using two different-sounding terms to identify and assess growth factors, when they do not introduce anything new but only serve to perpetrate confusion. Our doubts, then, concern the very notion of competitiveness.

Microeconomic concepts and indicators of competitiveness have a more solid theoretical basis as they are based on standard microeconomics. Since they derive competitiveness from competition or from Schumpeterian rivalrous competition, they focus on the essential characteristics of producers in competition for market share. However, the ability to compete is evaluated by different measures reflecting effect and forms of competition such as changes in market share, price and non-price competitiveness, respectively unit cost. Since these indicators differ from each other in terms of various characteristics, the results of analysis differ considerably.

The trade approach to competitiveness is based on the classical theories of international trade – the Ricardian and Heckscher–Ohlin trade models. The subject of research is foreign trade performance. In this approach, competitiveness is synonymous with comparative advantage, that is patterns, sources and advantages of specialization. The concept of 'Revealed Comparative Advantage' (RCA), created by Balassa to measure specialization, is used and factor intensities are examined.

There are serious objections regarding the use of the RCA index as a measure of competitiveness. First, these estimates concern exclusively that part of domestic production that participates in international trade. However, changes in RCA are influenced by changes in domestic and foreign demand. Declining RCA can be the result of increased supply on the domestic market, which in turn can result from the high dynamics of growth in domestic demand. A rapid rise in domestic demand aids the 'suction' of not only imports, but also of exportable production and exports by domestic producers. If it is accompanied by a rapid rise in overall domestic production and an increase in its share of global production, then we are dealing with an improvement, rather than deterioration, of competitiveness (Dlugosch *et al.*, 1996, p. 75).

Secondly, Balassa formulated this index to assess specialization, not competitiveness. According to Balassa, 'competitiveness means the ability to sell, to compete on the market. But since international trade is determined by relative rather than absolute advantages, this concept does not fit well into classical comparative-cost theory' (Balassa, 1963, p. 29). Balassa, similar to Porter (1986, p. 15 and 17–18), rejects the validity of using the theory of international trade to assess competitiveness. The notion of comparative advantage is derived from the theory of international trade which does not consider the competition processes. Therefore this theory should be modified (Gomory and Baumol, 2000, p. 4). In an attempt to modify the classical theory of trade, Gomory and Baumol stress, 'there are in fact inherent conflicts in international trade. An improvement in the productive capacity of a trading partner that allows it to compete effectively with a home country industry, instead of benefiting the public as a whole, may come at the expense of the home country overall' (p. 4).

Thirdly, government policies influence inconsistencies between changes in export performance and competitiveness. They differentiate the activities of domestic and foreign companies both on domestic and foreign markets. Using trade indicators to assess competitiveness, one forgets that it is possible to export at a loss. Tolerating loss-making exports allows the company to retain specialization, but that does not mean that it upholds its level of competitiveness. Any distortions incorporated into trade flow and trade balance are also incorporated into the RCA index.

2.3 Competitiveness as the ability to compete

It is widely acknowledged that an improvement in competitiveness to a large extent determines the process of real convergence between the new and old member states (Tumpel-Gugerell, 2003) and their integration into the Single Market. However, the ambiguity of competitiveness tends to encounter persistent miscommunication in discussing its impact on economic growth and integration into the Single Market.

In this Chapter, we deploy a Schumpeterian approach to competitiveness. We presume that competitiveness, or competitive advantage (Krafft, 2000), derives from competition in the sense of 'struggle', 'rivalry' and 'conflict' among actual and potential competitors (Martin, 2004). This includes rivalry in prices, in improved techniques of productions and products for a given market or for productive resources. Competition is understood in terms of situations in which parties producing substitutes – aiming to achieve simultaneously the same and opposite goals – end up in conflict. However, there is also a broader approach to competition, which covers the struggle between actual and potential rivals and implies another definition of competition: the absence of entry barriers for new competitors and exiting from an industry in the longer-term (Stigler, 1965, pp. 264–5). A lowering of entry barriers impacts the evaluation of changes in the competitiveness of competitors operating and entering a given market as it reveals the real level of competitiveness of the protected agents.

Competition in the sense of rivalry also includes the notion of competition as selection of the fittest and elimination of the least fit. As a never-ending struggle (Porter, 1990), competition results in the selection of producers of a given product. It encompasses the process of some firms pushing others out of the market (and therefore also the goods produced by them). Changes in the competitiveness of a given firm's products result in changes in its market position (Frischtak, 1999). As a consequence, throughout the literature one often finds 'market share' treated as a performance indicator for competitiveness (Meeusen and Rayp, 2000).

Market participants aim at improving their position on markets in which their goods are sold. Changes in the competitiveness of exported products are therefore reflected in changes in foreign (export) market share. Changes in the competitiveness of domestic-based products competing against imports are reflected in changes in domestic market share. It follows that any evaluation of the competitiveness of domestic production based solely on exports has limited research capabilities (Casson, 1999).

The Schumpeterian concept of competition is grounded in cost and quality advantages which Schumpeter regarded to be much more important than the price competition of the traditional theory. It is one of the key elements of the 'creative destruction' of the capitalist economic process, as he puts it. Competition is a source of internal efficiency within a firm and plays a crucial role in its economic welfare. On the other hand, the issue of quality, incorporated into economic theory, has become an economic variable at least as important as price, along with sales methods and demand-creation methods that necessarily go hand-in-hand with product differentiation (Clark, 1963, p. 38; Abbott, 1955, p. 108). It is also 'the single most important force leading to the economic growth of companies in international markets' (Feigenbaum, 1988, p. 22).

The theoretical importance of products differentiation of and its determinants in explaining the evolution of foreign trade is based on the recent trade and endogenous growth theories expounded by Grossman and Helpman (1991a, b). Their models incorporate the concepts of quality ladders and vertical product differentiation. High-income consumers tend to buy higher quality product variants and the number of variants produced within vertical product differentiation depends on the income spread. Differences in consumers' disposable incomes and their changes have an impact on the scope of competition between producers.

Higher quality makes higher price possible without the loss of market share. Consequently, in the framework of monopolistic competition, by increasing the quality of goods produced for the domestic market a country can at the same time shift its import demand curve inwards and its export demand curve outwards. It follows from this that increases in market share may reflect not only improvements in the relative productivity but also an upward shift in the quality ladder. Firms challenge not only those consumers already present on their product market but also others, and their disposable incomes. Firms want consumers to buy their products instead of other goods. Competition occurs not only within a quality segment of a single branch or product groups, but also across branches and goods.

As has been widely recognized, richer countries tend to produce higher quality goods leading to the hypothesis that countries with similar levels of development trade with one another more often than with very different countries (Linder, 1961). This implies that the potential for exports from the latter countries to the former is limited (Murphy and Schleifer, 1991). Specialization at low quality levels and in labour-intensive products impacts on production and export opportunities of countries and their growth potential and may hamper growth opportunities in the long run. This process is significant for countries in the catching-up process as they also experience a rapid change in the structure of demand towards goods of higher quality and higher price. If the process of catching-up is not accompanied by improvements in quality but only by improvements in productivity, demand factors will restrain the high-growth dynamics of production that enhanced competitiveness. In effect, as Dullock (2002) shows, 'catching-up countries' may find themselves in the low quality trap and may generate 'path dependence where industrialised countries have the advantage of already having the capacity to produce high quality' (p.15). Therefore, in the catching-up process production dynamics will tend to be higher if accompanied by improvements in quality.

Deriving competitiveness from competition as a process of natural selection is the rationale behind using changes in market share as a measure of changes in the competitiveness. However, this can be distorted by changes in product quality, market (domestic or foreign) orientation of the output, differences in dynamics between domestic and foreign markets and in the dynamics of exports and imports compared to production dynamics.

An increase in domestic market share may be the result of a shift in the orientation of production from foreign to domestic. If both markets are open this shift does not reflect changes in the competitiveness of production. A higher rate of growth in foreign trade than in domestic production tends to result in a fall in the share of domestic production on the domestic market. This change does not necessarily have to mean the worsening competitiveness of domestic production. It may be accompanied by a rising share of exports on foreign markets which would in turn suggest an improvement in competitiveness. The rapid growth in domestic demand tends to encourage local producers to develop sales in this market. In such a situation, the acceleration of growth dynamics of deliveries to the local market may be accompanied by decelerating export growth dynamics, implying the stabilisation or even a reduction in the share of exports. However, a country's share in world production may increase quicker than its share in international trade.

Intuitively, any improvement in the competitiveness of domestic production should reflect in a rise in the share of domestic products on both domestic and foreign markets. A falling market share on both domestic and foreign markets suggests that the competitiveness of production is worsening. A more ambiguous situation arises is when changes in domestic and foreign market shares are in opposite direction when increase in the share of one market (e.g. domestic) is accompanied by a decrease in the share of the other (foreign) market. Deficiencies in using market share measures to gauge changes in competitiveness oblige one to consider other factors that may impact on the effects of competition.

2.4 Methodology and model

In this section we focus on the effects and determinants of competition between the industries of AC3 and EU15 in the enlarged EU25 market.[3] The share of AC exports to EU15 out of the EU25's internal exports is used as a measure of the effect of competition at AC3 manufacturing industries and those of the EU15 in the enlarged EU market. This means that we do not take into account the operation of AC3 industries and those of EU15 on non-EU markets on the one hand and that of non-EU industries on the EU markets on the other.

The indicator deployed has its advantages and disadvantages. It is narrower than the share of AC3 industries in EU25 demand. However, it reflects not only the effects of competition of AC3 producers and EU25 internal exporters, but also the effects of competition with EU products sold on their domestic markets.

The following arguments support the decision to use the share of AC3 exports to the EU15 in EU25 internal exports rather than their share in EU apparent consumption. Firstly, changes in the share of AC3 exports to the EU15 in the EU25's apparent consumption are influenced by changes in the dynamics of EU external trade. If the dynamics of EU15 external exports, for example, is higher than the rate of growth of its production, then the share of EU15 production in its apparent consumption falls. But this does not mean that the competitiveness of its products has deteriorated.

Secondly, changes in the share of EU15 turnover in its market may also reflect differentiation of the dynamics between EU and non-EU demand. Faster growth in EU15 demand may encourage EU15 producers to sell their products in EU15 rather than non-EU markets. In this way, EU15 producers turning to the European market may lose their share of the extra-EU markets, but not necessarily their competitiveness.

Thirdly, there is a lack of data on AC-10 domestic demand. Last, but not least, the high correlation (exceeding 0.94) between the level of, and changes in, the share of AC3 in the internal exports of the EU25 and its share in EU25 apparent consumption suggests that changes in the share of AC3 exports in EU25 internal exports to a large extent reflects changes in the competitive pressure of AC3 products on European markets.

Deriving the notion of competitiveness from rivalrous competition (Nelson, 1996, p. 52), and exploring market share as a measure of changes in competitiveness implies, firstly, that it is a relative term. Any assessment of the competitiveness of a given product manufactured by a company by measuring its productivity must be compared to the productivity of its rivals on the market where competition takes place. Improving productivity alone does not necessarily imply a rise in the company's micro-competitiveness, since other companies, foreign or domestic, may also increase their productivity by larger amount. In such a case, a drop in its international competitiveness level may accompany an improvement in its productivity. This is why, when analysing the factors influencing changes in the competitiveness of AC3 manufacturing, relative measures (as compared to the EU15 average) such as relative labour productivity, relative product quality and investment rate are used. As potential factors influencing competitiveness, the following indicators have been chosen: changes in Relative Unit Labour Costs (RULC), Relative Unit Export Value (RUEV), Relative Unit Intermediate Costs (RUIC) and Investment Rate (IR). Their impact on changes in market shares is estimated with the use of two logit models, described below.

We discuss the above variables and the rationale behind them. Unit Labour Costs (ULC) are calculated as the labour compensation (LC) (wages and salaries plus social contributions) of a particular industry i (three-digit level) relative to its turnover T. This shows whether changes in productivity counterbalance increases in wages and salaries. A relatively high productivity growth (resulting, to a certain extent, from a significant gap to the EU15 productivity levels) may have been accompanied by even higher wage increases. In such a situation, despite productivity growth, ULC would have worsened. Deriving competitiveness from rivalry we have applied a relative approach to competitiveness and examined industries' RULC, that's the ULC in AC3 in relation to the EU15.[4] We also analyse disaggregated changes in RULC between changes in its components' parts wages per employee and labour productivity.

RULC is derived by dividing the ULC in j country by the ULC in EU15 for industry i (at the three-digit level). The advantage of disaggregated data is that it shows the diversity of industry performance within countries. When RULC is above one (ULC in AC higher than in the EU), it means that the efficiency of the use of labour in the AC3 is lower than in the EU:

$$ULC_i^j = \frac{LC_i^j}{T_i^j}$$

$$RULC_i^j = \frac{ULC_i^j}{ULC_i^{EU15}}$$

The competition approach to competitiveness discourages us from using value added per employee as a measure of labour productivity, as firms do not compete via value added but by lowering their costs and/or improving the efficiency of production. Such measures can lead to lower prices (price competition), expansion of and the attraction of resources to finance quality enhancement necessary to win the competition battle via horizontal and vertical differentiation. This also enables higher dynamics of production growth.

A number of studies have introduced a variable reflecting unit labour cost and technology to explain the export performance of advanced countries. The wide variety of approaches taken have yielded little consensus about whether RULC matters for or affects market shares. The results depend not only on the approach used but also on the level of aggregation of data (Carlin *et al.*, 1999). Very few studies have considered the role of RULC in explaining the export performance of accession countries. As these countries compete mainly through prices, the question on the role of RULC for the evaluation of their competitive performance is relevant.

Unit Export Value (UEV) is used as a proxy for product quality.[5] The concept of UEV is not new, having been used in several empirical studies (Abd-el-Rachman, 1985; Lemoine, 1994; and Aiginger, 1997). It is defined as euro value of the export of a given industry i divided by its physical weight, usually a kilogram (OECD Proceedings, 1998). Its changes reflect changes in quality, shifts to higher product segments and to other value-enhancing features (service components, design and advertising). An important advantage of this measure is also its availability at a very detailed level of disaggregation for most countries:

$$UEV_i^j = \frac{Exports\_value_i^j}{Export\_weight_i^j}$$

$$RUEV_i^j = \frac{UEV_i^j}{UEV_i^{EU15}}$$

However, there are certain methodological problems using unit export values as measure of product quality. Firstly, changes in unit export values for a given product category may reflect both changes in product quality and changes in product characteristics bundle (Aw and Roberts, 1986). The more aggregated the product, the more serious the problem becomes. Secondly, it may be different from unit prices since it represents a unit of weight rather than the price of any unit (Rosati, 1998).

In addition to UEV, we also use Relative Unit Export Value (RUEV) as a measure of the quality position of j country's exports to the EU15 as compared to EU15 intra exports for each of the manufacturing industries (i). We take a drop in RUEV a sign of a fall in prices and often reflects increasing price competition. It indicates that AC firms have not improved the quality of their products as much as their EU15 counterparts and have not shifted to a higher quality segment of a given product market. An increase in RUEV suggests an improvement in the quality of products or a widening of the range of exported commodities within the more sophisticated industries.

Based on RUEV, the manufacturing industries of each of the AC3 were divided into three quality segments. The first covered industries whose UEV was similar to the EU15 average (RUEV >0.85). The second covered industries whose RUEV was between 0.45 and 0.85 (middle quality), while the third segment covered the lowest quality products RUEV < 0.45. The chosen levels of RUEV were based on their distribution across countries and industries, corresponding on average to the 1st and 3rd quartiles.

Investment rates are calculated as the investment in fixed capital in industry i in j country related to its turnover T and are used as a proxy for embodied technological change. As technology improves measured productivity, so it will affect RULC directly. This implies that the influence of technology variables has already been included. Nevertheless, there may also be some industry-specific factors, shifts across industries and changes in country-specific factors that are not reflected in measured productivity. The investment variable is therefore added to the model, covering both domestic and EU market shares.

Unit Intermediate Costs (UIC) reflected the share of industry i expenditures on intermediate costs in its turnover. We have applied a relative approach and examined industries' RUIC, that is the UIC in AC3 in relation to the EU15.

We have conducted our analysis based on two models (logit and multinomial logit), aiming at identifying the determinants of changes in market shares of the AC3. In the first model, because of the lack of reliable data on domestic shares in Hungary, we use as a proxy for changes in the competitive pressure of the AC3 only changes in EU market shares. In the second model (multinomial logit), using as proxies for competitiveness changes in both EU and domestic market shares, we have to narrow our analysis to Poland and the Czech Republic. For the first model, changes in RUIC, RULC and RUEV were chosen as potential variables influencing industries' competitiveness.

The investment rate could not be included due to the lack of data for Hungary (a break in the time series in 2001). It has been added in the second model.

In the first model a variable describing the market performance of a particular industry at the three digit level was chosen as the dependent variable. By '0' we denote a group of industries whose position on the European market deteriorated in the period of analysis while '1' denotes those industries that improved their position. The '0' group has been chosen as the reference group in the model.

Values of relative indicators for a given product group were chosen as a vector of exogenous variables (x). The multinomial logit model, where the probability that i th industry falls into a distinguishable kth category (where $k = 1, 2, 3$ in our case), was specified by the equations below:

$$p_{ik} = \frac{\exp(x_i'\beta_k)}{1 + \sum_{k=1}^{3} \exp(x_i'\beta_k)}$$

and

$$p_{i0} = \frac{1}{1 + \sum_{k=1}^{3} \exp(x_i'\beta_k)}$$

The analysis of the first model was performed for three sub-periods (1998–2003, 1998–2001, and 2001–03) for all industries in the three ACs. This allows us to see how robust the results are over time and to verify whether the factors influencing the market positions change over time.

As Table 2.1 shows, the estimated models are statistically significant (at a 10% level) for all of the three sub-periods and the goodness-of-fit tests proved they adequately fit the data. However, out of the three variables chosen as potential factors influencing changes in competitiveness, only RULC turned out to be significant regardless of the chosen time period. It significantly improves the odds of shifting into category 1 and its negative coefficients show that a decline in RULC increases the probability of achieving a better market position in the EU market by a given industry in each of the countries. The coefficients of the other variables included in the analysis – RUIC and RUEV – are not statistically significant. Therefore, these variables cannot be interpreted as a factor important for changes in market performance in the analysed period.

In the second model (a multinomial logit), changes in competitiveness were proxied by changes in both EU and domestic market shares and a new explanatory variable was added, that's the investment rate (*IR*). The model was performed for three sub-periods for Poland (1996–2003, 1998–2001, 2001–03) and for the years 1998–2003 in the case of the Czech Republic. The '0' group includes industries whose competitive position on both the European and domestic market deteriorated in the analysed period, while

Table 2.1 Results of the logit model for 1998–2003, 1998–2001 and 2001–03 for AC3 (dependent variable: changes in EU market shares–increase or decrease)

		1998–2003	1998–2001	2001–2003
Intercept	Coefficient	1.04	1.00	0.16
	Std. error	0.15	0.15	0.13
	p-value	0.00	0.00	0.23
RUIC	Coefficient	0.57	0.50	0.71
	Std. error	0.76	0.84	0.68
	p-value	0.46	0.55	0.30
RUEV	Coefficient	0.02	0.00	0.00
	Std. error	0.02	0.01	0.01
	p-value	0.51	0.69	0.76
RULC	Coefficient	−0.83*	−0.96*	−1.06*
	Std. error	0.40	0.54	0.58
	p-value	0.10	0.08	0.06
No of observations		272	272	272
In the reference group '0'		71	76	121
Log-likelihood		351.25	324.17	332.31

Note: * significant at the 10% level.

group '3' includes industries that improved their position on both the domestic and European markets. Group '1' includes industries that improved their position on the domestic market though diminished their share on the European one, while group '2' include, industries whose position on the domestic market worsened but improved on the EU market. The '0' group has been chosen as a reference group in the model. Table 2.2 summarizes the results.

As shown in the table, RULC remains a significant variable in Poland and the Czech Republic in most cases. Furthermore, IR turns out to be a significant factor in determining competitiveness too. Higher investments increased the probability of shifting into a higher group in the Czech Republic throughout the analysed period and in the years 2001—2003 in Poland. RUEV and RUIC in most cases did not influence changes in the market position of manufacturing industries in both countries.

We can conclude that during the pre-accession period, changes in market shares follow changes in RULC in the AC3. Much higher labour intensity of production, as compared to EU15, and a lower quality of goods, explain the role of RULC in competitive performance of the AC3. This also confirms that the AC3 compete mainly on cost, rather than on differentiation of goods and hence increased competitive pressure on those EU markets where cost competition prevails. RULC was also a crucial determinant of FDI inflows (Bevan and Estrin, 2004) and their increase. The increase of the share of foreign owned firms in the AC3 manufacturing production and exports strengthen

Table 2.2 Results of the multinomial logit for Poland and the Czech Republic (dependent variable: changes in EU and domestic market shares)

		Poland									Czech Rep.		
		1996–2003 Group		1998–2001 Group			2001–2003 Group			1998–2003 Group		
		2	3	1	2	3	1	2	3	1	2	3
Intercept	Coefficient	0.7	3.4	1.90	0.41	2.91	4.34	1.56	1.79	−0.35	1.53	1.33
	Std. error	2.8	3.6	5.38	2.60	2.97	4.91	3.04	3.31	0.7	0.50	.52
	p-value	0.8	0.3	0.72	0.87	0.33	0.38	0.61	0.59	0.62	0.00	0.01
RUIC	Coefficient	0.03	0.00	−0.03	0.02	−0.01	−0.11*	0.00	−0.02	−0.07*	−0.06**	−0.06**
	Std. error	0.03	0.04	0.06	0.03	0.03	0.07	0.03	0.04	0.04	0.03	0.03
	p-value	0.39	0.97	0.66	0.47	0.86	0.10	0.94	0.59	0.08	0.05	0.04
IR	Coefficient	0.51	0.16	1.16	0.94	1.02	2.61*	2.69***	2.92***	2.64**	2.29**	2.15*
	Std. error	0.66	0.81	1.26	0.65	0.74	1.24	0.96	0.99	1.14	1.12	1.13
	p-value	0.44	0.84	0.35	0.14	0.17	0.06	0.01	0.00	0.02	0.04	0.06
RULC	Coefficient	−0.02	−0.04**	−0.03	−0.02*	−0.03***	−0.04	−0.04***	−0.04***	−0.06*	−0.04***	−0.05**
	Std. error	0.01	0.02	0.03	0.01	0.01	0.03	0.01	0.02	0.04	0.02	0.02
	p-value	0.12	0.03	0.28	0.08	0.01	0.14	0.01	0.01	0.07	0.01	0.03
RUEV	Coefficient	0.00	0.01	−0.01	0.00	0.00	0.02	0.00	0.00	−0.42	0.21	0.1
	Std. error	0.01	0.02	0.03	0.01	0.01	0.02	0.01	0.01	1.27	0.68	0.74
	p-value	0.76	0.54	0.73	0.77	0.96	0.50	0.69	0.76	0.74	0.76	0.9
No of observations in the group		61/87	15/87	3/90	49/90	22/90	4/90	50/90	19/90	7/80	38/80	27/80
In the reference group												
Log-likelihood		117.9		159.7			144.10			163.4		

Notes: +Group '1' has been excluded from this analysis as it contained only one industry within this period of analysis; * significant at 10% level; ** at 5 %; *** at 1 % level.

the role of RULC in the changes in the EU market shares of these countries. An increase in the role of investment in competitive performance suggests a drop in the role of RULC in changes in the competitiveness of the AC3. Three questions, which will be addressed in the next section, arise. First, were the AC3 manufacturing industries winning the competition with EU counterparts? Second, how did their RULC change and what were the sources of these changes? Third, in which quality segment did the AC3 compete with EU15 the most and what changes took place in this field?

2.5   Changes in the competitiveness of the AC3 and their determinants

Between 1996 and 2003 the dynamics of exports of the AC3 to the EU15 was much higher than rate of growth of EU15 internal exports. It resulted not only in an increase in the role of trade in their economy[6] but also in an increase of the three countries' share of the EU market (Table 2.3). As the share of AC3 exports to the EU15 in the EU15 external imports and EU25 internal exports increased by over 80 per cent in 1996–2003, the AC3 took over a part of the increase in EU demand for both EU and non-EU goods. Given also the slow-down in EU GDP growth (2000–03) and in the EU15 intra-export dynamics, the improvement in the share of AC3 in the EU market demonstrates that they were pushing out some EU producers from the EU market. This, there-fore, suggests an improvement in ACs' product competitiveness as compared to its EU15 counterparts. Thus the catching up of the AC3 accompanied their integration into the EU market in terms of trade.

However, these improvements were highly differentiated in time and across countries. Hungary experienced the highest increase in its EU market share till 1999. In the subsequent years, the increase has been much more modest, especially when compared to that in Poland and the Czech Republic. The latter countries intensified their exports to the EU15 only after

Table 2.3   Changes in the share of AC3 exports to EU15 in the EU25 internal exports (per cent)

Share of AC3	1996	1997	1998	1999	2000	2001	2002	2003
In EU15 external imports	6.2	6.6	7.2	7.7	7.8	9.0	9.8	10.6
In AC-10 exports to EU15	70.8	72.7	73.6	74.6	75.0	76.6	75.9	74.9
In EU25 internal exports (AC3)	2.7	3.0	3.3	3.6	4.0	4.5	4.7	5.1
(PL)	1.0	1.1	1.2	1.2	1.4	1.5	1.6	1.8
(CZ)	0.9	1.0	1.1	1.2	1.3	1.5	1.6	1.8
(H)	0.8	1.0	1.1	1.3	1.3	1.5	1.5	1.5

Source: Comext database, own calculations.

1998. This observation is crucial for our analysis, which, due to data availability (for Hungary and the Czech Republic) concentrates on the 1998–2003 period, when Poland and the Czech Republic were catching up, whereas Hungary experienced a slowdown in its export dynamics, even though it made progress in productivity improvement and the quality of exported goods. Table 2.4 shows that improvements in market share accompanied the product upgrading of AC3 manufacturing. The quality of goods exported was much lower than the EU15 counterparts, implying that the analysed countries put competitive pressure on the lower quality segment of the market. However, the quality of exported goods was differentiated among the three countries and their industries, and over time. Hungary's exports to a large degree were composed of products with a quality corresponding to the EU15 level. In contrast, Poland and the Czech Republic tended to export products of a much lower quality. However, the share of high quality products in Poland's and the Czech Republic's exports increased significantly, from 27 per cent (Poland) and 22 per cent (Czech Rep.) to 42 per cent.[7] These changes reflected not only the dynamic increase in the exports of high quality goods, but also the visible increase in the quality of most goods. The latter was reflected in shifts between the three quality segments, mainly moving to higher quality segments.[8] It is worth mentioning that although the number of industries exporting high quality goods in Hungary increased, their

Table 2.4 RUEV, RULC and investment in AC3, 1996–2003

		1996	*1997*	*1998*	*1999*	*2000*	*2001*	*2002*	*2003*
RUEV	PL	0.55	0.57	0.59	0.59	0.61	0.66	0.66	0.68
	CZ	0.65	0.66	0.68	0.68	0.66	0.71	0.70	0.76
	H	0.76	0.77	0.81	0.82	0.87	0.76	0.97	0.97
RULC	PL	0.77	0.79	0.81	0.79	0.75	0.77	0.71	0.62
	CZ		0.80	0.81	0.82	0.79	0.77	0.79	0.73
	H			0.61	0.59	0.59	0.57	0.59	0.55
IR(%)	PL	6.8	7.2	8.2	7.1	5.7	5.0	4.9	5.0
	CZ		9.4	8.1	9.0	8.1	8.2	6.7	6.5
	H				7.4	6.6	12.6		
FDI stock	PL	297	377	281	675	870	1010		
per capita	CZ	832	897	1397	1708	2108	2604		
US	H	1470	1587	1835	1922	1942	2311		
Cumulative	PL	12.9	17.8	24.2	31.4	40.8	46.5	50.1	54.8
FDI inflows	CZ	5.5	6.8	10.5	16.9	21.8	27.5	36	38.6
from 1990	H	15.3	19.4	22.8	26.1	28.8	32.8	35.6	38.1
US$ bill.									

Note: Data on FDI relates to the whole economy.
Sources: Eurostat, OECD and national statistics, own calculations.

share in total Hungarian exports throughout the period diminished from 58 to 54 per cent. Either some of the highest quality products, in order to out-compete EU goods, had to lower prices or by maintaining prices they saw turnover and exports falling. Increasing productivity and falling RULC allow for such a strategy of maintaining EU market share. Low RULC in Hungary (Table 2.4) suggests further that improvements in competitive pressure on the EU market depend on the ability to shift into active, aggressive innovation and investment-based strategies at the firm level and product differentiation.

Changes in RULC and exports market share of the AC3 were differentiated between Hungary on the one hand and the Czech Republic and Poland on the other, and over time. The deterioration of RULC of the latter countries up to 1999 (see Table 2.4) accompanied a small improvement in the quality of exported goods and a small increase in EU25 export share. The expansion of Polish domestic demand, rather than improvements in efficiency, determined Poland's economic growth up to 1999 and resulted in a small improvement of Poland's export share. Afterwards, the quite considerable improvement in RULC and quality of exported goods (manifested in the increase in RUEV) of Polish and Czech manufacturing was in line with considerable improvements in both countries' export shares. This accompanied a drop in the investment rate and continuous large inflows of FDI into both countries (Table 2.4).

Our method of constructing RULC allows us to disaggregate changes in RULC into changes in the average wage per employee and labour productivity. It shows whether a decrease in RULC of the AC3 was the effect of a drop in the productivity gap against the EU15 or an increase in wage differentiation between them. Table 2.5 summarizes changes in wages, productivity and employment of AC3 versus EU15 over the period of analysis.

A drop in the RULC of AC3 manufacturing resulted from the combination of a drop in the productivity gap against EU15 and a slower rate of growth of

Table 2.5 Average changes in wages, productivity, turnover and employment of AC3 and EU manufacturing, 1998–2003 (in current prices)

Country	Wages per employee	Turnover per employee	Turnover	Employment	Differences between changes in wages and productivity (in percentage points)
	1	2	3	4	5
Hungary	93%	94%	82%	−6%	1
Czech Rep.	56%	69%	58%	−6%	13
Poland	38%	82%	48%	−19%	44
EU15	30%	20%	16%	−6%	−10

Source: Own estimation based on national statistics of the AC3 and Eurostat.

wages than that of productivity, especially in Poland. The labour force of the AC3 did not absorb all of the productivity gains as higher wages. The opposite was the case in the EU15. The EU15 unit labour cost increase was primarily the result of a reluctance to adjust changes in wages to that of productivity and to not react quickly or fully to cut total labour costs in the face of low rate of growth of production and productivity. Higher dynamics of growth in wages than in productivity in the EU15 support improvement in RULC in the AC3 and serve to increase the competitive pressure of their goods on EU goods. A drop in the productivity gap of the AC3 against the EU was brought about by rising output and – in the case of Poland – by a considerable fall in labour input, and a higher investment rate than in the EU15, although this is diminishing over time.

Among the analysed countries, the highest rates of growth in productivity were found in Hungary and the lowest in the Czech Republic. The considerable increase in wages in Hungary resulted in small improvements in RULC. However, the RULC in Hungary was still the lowest, reflecting the lowest productivity gap of the three countries against the EU15.

The pattern of employment shedding and wage changes was differentiated among the AC3. In Poland, in opposition to the Czech Republic and Hungary, increases in productivity were brought about by a considerable fall in labour input. This could mean that firms in Polish manufacturing are still more engaged in terms of defensive, shallow restructuring based on shedding of the labour force. However, according to estimates, not only labour-shedding but also innovation (Kolasa, 2005) and investment (Sztautynger, 2003) played a strong and positive effect on labour productivity growth. It may be that the quite high level of education of the Polish labour force (Wziątek-Kubiak *et al.*, 2004), resulting in high managerial efficiency, is a part of the explanation of the significant role played by innovation in productivity improvements. The main sources of innovation in Poland were investment, imports of new technologies and equipment as well as managerial efficiency of firms.

Aggregate data for manufacturing as a whole hide the differentiation in the kind of restructuring introduced, which accompanied changes in competitiveness across industries. In Poland, industries that increased market share the most, also started defensive restructuring earlier and then shifted to strategic, active restructuring based on innovation and higher investment intensity (Wziątek-Kubiak and Magda, 2005). In 1998–2003 they have less defensive and more strategic restructuring. The expansion of their production and exports accompanied job creation. The opposite was the case of industries which started defensive restructuring later. The simultaneous creation and destruction of jobs in Polish manufacturing suggests that a process of Schumpeterian competition was at work. It also means that unproductive labour force are being replace by productive workers and inefficient firms are shrinking while efficient ones are expanding.

The appreciation of national currency results in the increase of wages (in euro) and prices. If these increases are not offset by an increase in productivity, the result is an increase in RULC, and a drop in production and market share. But the appreciation of the AC3 currencies against the euro during the 1990s did not result in a worsening of export performance and RULC. This appreciation of the exchange rate was counterbalanced by a bigger drop in the productivity gap, allowing for improvements in the competitiveness of the AC3 exports to the EU15. This also created an incentive to upgrade export products in terms of quality and technological sophistication, which is a strategy to offset the upward pressure on prices arising from the appreciation of the currency. However, it is unrealistic to assume that domestic firms in the AC3 can quickly upgrade export products in terms of quality of product or innovativeness. The adjustment time or learning phase required depends on the general ability of firms to adjust, the share of skilled workers available and the level of sophistication already acquired, hence the presence of foreign investors. The fact that most FDI inflows to transition economies have been into the analysed countries has led to further improvements in their competitiveness and quality of goods.

FDI inflows were uneven across the three countries, their industries and over time (Table 2.4). Until 1997 the biggest FDI inflows was to Hungary and accompanied a considerable improvement in their EU market shares. The high dynamics of growth of the Polish economy since 1992 has encouraged an increase in FDI inflows since 1994, as decisions regarding FDI rely on past rather than contemporaneous information about the receiving countries (Bevan and Estrin, 2004). The considerable increase in FDI inflows into Poland and the Czech Republic since the mid-1990s, have caught up with low FDI inflows in the earlier period (Table 2.4).[9] Although FDI per capita has remained much lower in Poland than in the other two countries, the role of foreign owned firms in the Polish economy has increased considerably. In 2003, their share in Polish manufacturing accounted for 52.2 per cent of sales, 58 per cent of exports, 32 per cent of employment, and 47.2 per cent in investment in fixed assets (Chojna, 2005). The fact that the profitability and productivity of foreign owned firms was higher than domestic ones confirms their role in the improvement in competitiveness of AC3 manufacturing. On the other hand, the ownership advantage of foreign investors not only allows them to achieve better market position compared with local firms but also brings intangible assets and contributes to technological and quality upgrading. These were the major drivers of changes in the structure of Polish production in terms of the level of technology. The share of low-technology goods dropped from 67.9 per cent in 1995 to 34.4 per cent in 2005, while that of high-technology increased from 21.8 per cent to 46.8 per cent.

In summary, the increase in the competitive pressure of the AC3 on the EU market was driven by an improvement in RULC, which reflects a decrease in the productivity gap against the EU15 supported by a high investment rate, slower rate of growth of wages than that of productivity, an improvement in quality and the inflows of FDI.

2.6 Differentiation in competitive pressure across the AC3 industries: winners and losers of AC3 manufacturing industries in EU25 internal exports

Most AC3 industries increased their EU market shares. However this improvement varies across industries of the analysed countries. Three questions arise. Firstly, in which industries was the increasing competitive pressure of the AC3 on the EU markets strongest? Were they industries with high or low EU15 export share? Secondly, what were the causes of increasing pressure of these industries onto the EU market? Was it the slow progress in productivity improvements of the EU15 producers or the rapid improvements made by the AC3? Thirdly, which AC3 industries were pushed out of the EU market and what were the reasons for this? The answers to these questions allow us to highlight the impact of changes in competitiveness of the AC3 against the incumbent EU members on the restructuring of the enlarged EU market, trade flows and their determinants.

The focus will be on three groups of AC3 industries amongst which selection was based on changes of their EU internal exports shares: with two types of winners and losers:

- Large winners: those AC3 industries whose competitive pressure on the EU market was the strongest and increased over time. Their share of EU25 internal exports was large (at least double the manufacturing exports average) and increasing.
- Small winners: industries whose share of the EU market in 1998 was smaller than the average of EU25 internal exports' shares and at least double the growth of EU25 internal exports' share in each AC3 in a given period. This means that we focus on these AC3 industries which increased competitive pressure on EU market the most.
- Losers: industries whose share in EU25 internal exports diminished by at least 10 per cent and were possibly pushed out of the EU25 markets.

Winners cover 20 industries in Hungarian manufacturing (9 large winners), 28 Czech (20 large winners) and 43 Polish (20 large winners); while losers coves 15 industries in Hungarian and Czech manufacturing each and 11 Polish manufacturing out of 96 industries. The large number of Polish winner industries reflects the shift from inward to outward orientation of the Polish economy since 1998. Table 2.6 summarizes changes in the EU share of the three groups of industries for each country over the period of analysis.

The table shows the variation in changes in the shares of the three groups in EU exports between Hungary on the one hand and the Czech Republic and

Table 2.6 Average weighted share of large winners, small winners, losers and manufacturing average of AC3 in EU25 internal exports, 1996–2003

Year	Hungary				Czech Republic				Poland			
	1996	*1998*	*2001*	*2003*	*1996*	*1998*	*2001*	*2003*	*1996*	*1998*	*2001*	*2003*
Large	1.9	2.8	4.2	5.4	1.9	2.5	3.8	4.3	4.5	5.1	6.5	7.1
Small	0.3	0.7	0.9	1.1	0.3	0.4	1.2	1.9	0.5	0.7	1.5	1.9
Losers	1.3	1.3	1.2	0.9	1.0	1.0	0.8	0.8	2.3	1.9	1.5	1.1
Manufacturing	0.8	1.1	1.5	1.5	0.9	1.1	1.5	1.8	1.0	1.2	1.5	1.8

Source: Comext, own calculations.

Poland on the other. Among the group of large winners in the three countries, Hungary increased its share in the European market the most, whereas among the small winners it was Poland and the Czech Republic. Throughout the analysed period Hungary deepened its specialization. Poland and the Czech Republic's relatively slower increases in the large winners' share of the European market was accompanied by a high rate of their share's growth among the small winners. This suggests a change in the specialization model in the two countries and a rise of new competitors for European products in the analysed period.

Large winners

In the 1998–2003 period, the EU export share of the large winners of the AC3 increased considerably (see Table 2.6); with few exceptions,[10] these shares ranged from 3 per cent to 8 per cent. If the large winners in the AC3 were the same and their quality similar, one could expect some of them to dominate EU markets and push out EU15 products. However, the composition of the group of large winners in each AC3 and the quality of their products were different (cf. Appendix). Half of the Polish and Czech large winners overlap. Given that the quality of the Czech products was better than that of Polish products it can be deduced that they operated in different markets in terms of quality and were not rivals on the EU market. This was similar the case of Hungarian and Czech large winners. The differentiation of large winner industries across the three countries and the high differentiation in terms of the quality of exported goods (see Figure 2.2) meant that the AC3 exporters of these goods were targeting different EU markets. It also means that the cumulative pressure of the AC3 industries in question on the respective EU15 industry counterparts did not take place. Therefore, despite a relatively high and increasing share of large winners in the EU25 intra exports, their sales did not constitute a threat to the respective industries in the EU incumbent countries. Such a threat may arise only in particular industries of a handful of EU15 countries and across various quality segments of the European market.

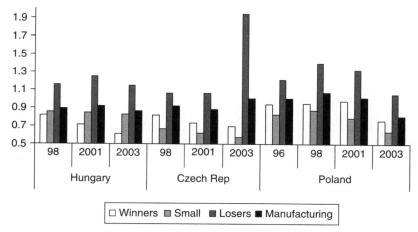

Figure 2.1 Relative unit labour costs of large winners, small winners, losers and manufacturing average of AC3, 1996–2003
Source: Comext database, own calculations.

In the period of analysis EU exports' share (Table 2.6) was high and rapidly increasing, whereas the RULC of the AC3 large winner industries was lower than that of the whole of manufacturing and rapidly diminishing (see Figure 2.1). However, it was differentiated across the three countries. In 1998, the RULC of Hungarian large winner industries was the lowest and decreased the most. This had an impact on the higher improvement (in terms of EU market share) of Hungarian large winner industries than of the Czech and Polish ones.

There were also some rather large differences in terms of quality of large winners' products across the three countries (see Figure 2.2). The RUEV of Polish goods was the lowest[11] and increased the least, while Hungarian and the Czech goods were closer to the EU level and increased quite considerably. The high quality of Hungarian products suggests increasing competition with the EU incumbent countries' manufacturers in this segment of market, thus augmenting the possibilities of them pushing the latter out of the EU market. The improvement of quality among the Hungarian large winners supported the increase of their share of European market. The Czech manufacturing goods were improving their quality rapidly, however, in the higher quality segment of the market they were facing strong competition from their EU counterparts, which hampered their increase in EU market shares. The price competition, which was possible owing to a decrease in RULC, resulted in a relatively slower increase in EU market shares among the Czech large winners compared to Hungarian ones. At the same time, Polish goods remained in the

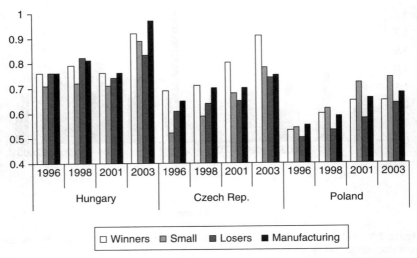

Figure 2.2   RUEV of Hungarian, Czech and Polish of large winners, small winners, losers and manufacturing average of AC3, 1996–2003
Source: Comext database, own calculations.

same segment of the market; their position improved as a result of a decrease in RULC and some improvement in quality.

Surprisingly, although RULC in Poland and the Czech Republic were quite low in 1998, labour productivity of large winners of both countries and their EU15 counterparts was lower than the average for manufacturing in these countries (Table 2.7), while the quality of employees (proxy by relative wages) was higher than the manufacturing average. The low productivity of Polish and Czech large winner industries was neutralized by low wages, which resulted in low RULC. The Hungarian large winners, dominated by foreign-owned firms, experienced a different situation and different changes in the analysed period. Both in Hungary and the EU15 these industries were distinguished by a comparatively high labour productivity and high qualification of employees which contributed to high labour productivity (Table 2.7) and lower RULC.

Within the analysed period the gap in productivity between these industries and the average of manufacturing either increased to the disadvantage of the former (in the Polish and EU cases) or did not change (the Czech Republic). The opposite was the case for Hungary. Considering the above facts, the question arises as to why the share of Polish and Czech large-winners industries in EU25 internal exports was high and increased strongly?

The low rate of growth of production in the analysed industries in the EU15, which accompanied a lack of adequate adjustments in employment

Table 2.7 Level of wages and labour productivity of the large winners of the AC3 and their EU15 counterparts, 1998 and 2003 (in national currency or euro)

		Wages		*Labour productivity*	
		1998	*2003*	*1998*	*2003*
Hungary	Large winners	1,269	2,438	45.8	130.1
(1,000 HUF)	in Hungary				
	Manufacturing average	1,179	2,272	41.5	80.4
	EU15 counterparts*	33	46	176	202
Czech Rep.	Large winners in Czech Rep.	5.3	8.3	28.6	53.0
(1,000 EUR)	Manufacturing average	5.4	8.4	34.6	58.5
	EU15 counterparts*	26	34	115	135
Poland	Large winners in Poland	22.0	29.5	121	211
(1,000 PLN)	Manufacturing average	24.1	33.3	155	282
	EU15 counterparts*	22	29	109	123
EU15	Manufacturing average	28	37	159	191
(1,000 EUR)					

Note: * EU15 counterparts are same 3-digit industries as the large winner industries in each AC.
Source: Eurostat, own calculations.

and wages (see Table 2.8), resulted from a slower productivity growth in the EU15 than the AC3 winner industries and contributed to the closing of the productivity gap between AC3 and EU15 and the decline in the RULC of the former countries. It also contributed to the high rate of export growth of the AC3 large winners industries to the EU15 which was the main factor behind the boost in their production. The growth of exports significantly exceeded the growth of manufacturing production in the analysed countries and was five to twelve times higher than the growth in manufacturing production in the respective EU15 counterparts. The share of large AC3 winners in AC3 total manufacturing production increased, while that of their EU15 counterparts in total EU15 manufacturing dropped. The obvious result of this was an increase in these industries' share of EU25's internal export.

All in all, Poland and to a lesser degree the Czech Republic increased their competitive pressure on the EU market in those industries whose productivity was comparatively low in both countries and this gap increased. Opposite was in case of Hungary. However, since their productivity increased faster than their EU15 counterpart industries, their EU export shares increased.

The adjustment processes which took place within the enlarged EU market were based on differential progress in relative (among countries) productivity. The improvement in the EU market shares of both Polish and Czech large winners stemmed from narrowing the labour productivity gap vis-à-vis the EU15 and not from the comparative advantage of the Polish and Czech

Table 2.8   Changes in wages, productivity, turnover and employment of the AC3 large winners and their EU15 counterparts, 1998 and 2003

		Wages per employee	Turnover per employee	Turnover	Employment	Differences between changes in wages and productivity (in percentage pts)
Hungary	Large winners in Hungary	92%	184%	281%	34%	92
	Manufacturing	93%	94%	82%	−6%	1
	EU15 counterparts	39%	15%	5%	−9%	−24
Czech	Large winners in Czech Rep.	56%	86%	103%	10%	29
	Manufacturing	56%	69%	58%	−6%	13
	EU15 counterparts	29%	17%	15%	−1%	−12
Poland	Large winners in Poland	34%	75%	78%	−1%	41
	Manufacturing	38%	82%	48%	−19%	44
	EU15 counterparts	30%	12%	11%	−1%	−18
EU15	Manufacturing	32%	20%	16%	−9%	−12

Source: Eurostat, own calculations.

industries in question over other industries in both countries. The weakness of the European counterparts of the Polish and Czech large winners was the basis for the latter's strength on the European market and determined changes in their EU market shares.

The liberalization of access to the EU market for the AC3 during the 1990s accelerated the structural changes taking place in the manufacturing sector of some of the EU incumbent countries, but did not instigate them. It impacted on improvements in Polish and Czech large winners' shares of the EU market. This liberalization was, therefore, not the source of economic problems in the manufacturing sector in the EU, though it revealed the weakness of economic performance and progress in various EU industries. However, one must keep in mind the relatively low quality level of Polish large winners' goods. They mostly pushed out of the EU25 market the producers of low quality goods and only to a small degree higher quality products.

Summing up, Hungarian export specialization in a relatively small number of large-winner industries reflected its comparative advantage over other Hungarian industries, as well as its competitive advantage over EU goods. The latter, operating in the same quality segment as Hungarian industries, faced increasingly strong competitive pressure.

Table 2.9 Levels of wages and productivity in small winners of AC3 and their EU counterparts, 1998 and 2003

		Wages		Turnover per employee	
		1998	*2003*	*1998*	*2003*
Hungary	Small winners in Hungary	1,461	2,710	59.1	71.3
(1,000 HUF)	EU15 counterparts	33	43	171	211
	Manufacturing	1,179	2,272	41.5	80.4
Czech	Small winners in Czech Rep.	5.3	8.2	35.3	74.7
(1,000 EUR)	EU15 counterparts	27	39	150	192
	Manufacturing	5.4	8.4	34.6	58.5
Poland	Small winners in Poland	27.6	38.0	210	368
(1,000 PLN)	EU15 counterparts	32	41	177	210
	Manufacturing	24.1	33.3	155	282
EU15	Manufacturing	28	37	159	191

Source: Eurostat, own calculations.

Large Polish winners operated in a lower quality segment of the EU25 market than their EU15 counterparts. The increase in their competitive pressure on the EU markets stemmed mainly from the weak progress made by the incumbent EU countries' counterpart industries rather than from strong progress made in Polish industries in question. The productivity of these industries was smaller and increased less than the average for manufacturing. In other words, Polish and Czech large-winner industries made a larger step forward in terms of improvement in competitiveness than their European counterparts. Improvements in the competitive advantage of these industries over the EU15 resulted from a weakness in EU15 progress.

Small winners

The industries grouped under the title 'small winners'[12] differed in many aspects from the 'large winners' discussed above. This was observed in terms of levels (in 1998) and changes over the analysed period in productivity, qualifications of the labour force, the quality of exported goods, RULC and EU market shares. On the other hand, small winners from Poland and the Czech Republic differ quite considerably from those in Hungary.

Surprisingly, although the EU exports share of small-winner industries was quite low in 1998[13] (Table 2.6), the RULC of Polish and Czech small-winner industries was much lower than the average for each manufacturing industry and of the large winners in both countries, while the productivity of these goods and the quality of the labour force in both countries and the EU counterparts was higher (see Table 2.9). To a large extent the low EU market share of

Table 2.10   Changes in wages, productivity, turnover and employment of the AC3 small winners and their EU15 counterparts, 1998–2003

		Wages per employee	Turnover per employee	Turnover	Employment	Differences between changes in wages and productivity (% points)
Hungary	Small winners in Hungary	85%	21%	16%	−4%	−65
	EU15 counterparts	31%	24%	20%	−3%	−7
	Manufacturing	93%	94%	82%	−6%	1
Czech	Small winners in Czech Rep.	56%	111%	111%	0%	56
	EU15 counterparts	43%	28%	15%	−10%	−14
	Manufacturing	56%	69%	58%	−6%	13
Poland	Small winners in Poland	37%	75%	55%	−11%	37
	EU15 counterparts	28%	19%	17%	−2%	−9
	Manufacturing	38%	82%	48%	−19%	44
EU15	Manufacturing	32%	20%	16%	−9%	−12

Source: Eurostat, own calculations.

small-winner industries in both countries reflected the lower than the average for manfuacturing quality of exported goods (see Figure 2.2) and the relatively low and slowly growing demand for them in the EU15. The low quality implies that the range of competition with the EU products was limited to the low quality segment of the market. However this was accompanied by quite high quality of employees (Table 2.9) which supported higher productivity and served its further improvement in the analysed period (Table 2.10).

Apart from the high level of qualifications of the labour force, the small-winner industries of the AC3 and EU15 counterparts were also characterized by high productivity: higher than the manufacturing average and the level of large winners (except for Hungarian). However, the high labour productivity of their European counterparts suggests a significant productivity gap between the AC3 and EU15 counterparts, which together with quality differentials was reflected in their low market shares.

During the period of analysis the AC3 small-winner industries increased their EU market shares quite considerably (Table 2.6). This was accompanied by a drop in their RULC (see Figure 2.1) and considerable improvements in quality of goods (see Figure 2.2). In the case of Poland and the Czech Republic, the drop in RULC and increase in RUEV were higher than that of the large winners. In terms of RULC, the competitiveness of small winners from

Poland and the Czech Republic increased, while that of those from Hungary did not improve

The changes in RULC were influenced by interdependencies between wages and productivity changes in AC3 compared to the EU15 (Table 2.10). Except for Hungary, the increase in wages and in productivity of AC3 small-winner industries and their EU counterparts was higher than the average for manufacturing and the large-winners' industries (Table 2.8 and 2.10). The much smaller drop in employment than the average for manufacturing implies that the drop in labour input did not play the key role in productivity improvement. The latter was supported by a high investment rate and in some industries also by inflows of FDI.

The rate of growth of productivity of small winners from Poland and the Czech Republic exceeded that of their EU15 counterpart industries. The increase in the productivity gap between small winners and the average for manufacturing to the advantage of the former was accompanied by a drop in the productivity gap between the small winners of both countries and their EU15 counterparts. Competition via labour productivity was crucial for changes of Polish and Czech small-winner industries in the EU market share. Significantly higher productivity than wage growth in Poland and the Czech Republic (Table 2.10) led to a decrease in RULC. It also contributed to the high rate of export growth of both countries' small-winner industries to the EU15 which stimulated a very high rate of growth of production (Table 2.10) – three to eight times higher than the growth in manufacturing production in respective EU15 counterparts. The share of small AC3 winners in AC3 total manufacturing production increased, while that of their EU15 counterparts in total EU15 manufacturing dropped. The obvious result of this was an increase in these industries' share of EU25's internal export.

This process was accompanied by a more rapid improvement in the quality of Polish and Czech small–winner industries compared to both countries' large winners, and to Hungarian ones, and led to a decrease in the quality gap *vis-à-vis* Hungary and all three countries' EU15 counterpart (see Figure 2.2). It also revealed new possibilities for export expansion into the EU market, acquiring new markets in terms of quality and contributed to the growth of the EU export market share.

The changes in Hungary were in contrast to changes in Czech and Polish small winner industries. In Hungary in 1998 the level of labour productivity of the analysed industries was 40 per cent higher than for average manufacturing (Table 2.9). However, during the analysed period the rate of growth was lower than the average – and worse than its EU15 counterparts (Table 2.10). As a result, in 2003 the level of labour productivity of the industries in question in Hungary was lower than the average for Hungarian manufacturing, while wages were quite high. The competitiveness of Hungarian small winners was deteriorating at the same time.

Table 2.11   Levels of wages and productivity in the losers of the AC3 and their EU counterparts, 1998 and 2003

		Wages		Turnover per employee	
		1998	*2003*	*1998*	*2003*
Hungary	Losers in Hungary	1,015	1,800	34.0	70.6
(1,000 HUF)	EU15 counterparts	20	28	152	195
	Manufacturing	1,179	2,272	41.5	80.4
Czech	Losers in Czech Rep.	5.3	8.8	39.8	71.8
(1,000 EUR)	EU15 counterparts	32	41	208	273
	Manufacturing	5.4	8.4	34.6	58.5
Poland	Losers in Poland	20.9	31.5	86	155
(1,000 PLN)	EU15 counterparts	26	34	134	181
	Manufacturing	24.1	33.3	155	282
EU15	Manufacturing	28	37	159	191

Source: Eurostat, own calculations.

Summing up, in the analysed period a group of dynamic exporters distinguished themselves among Polish and Czech manufacturing industries. Its labour productivity was high and increased more rapidly than average of manufacturing and the EU15 counterparts. These Polish and the Czech industries were in effect gaining competitive advantage on the EU market. Furthermore, significant increases in the quality of exported goods contributed to the shifts towards more dynamic EU markets and an improvement in market shares. This reflects the improvement in the ability of small winners from both countries to compete in the higher quality segment of EU market and also reflects new change which took place in specialisation of both countries.

Losers

In our analysis we have also identified a group of industries called the 'losers'. The decrease in their share of EU25 internal exports reflected the lower rate of growth of their production and their exports to the EU15 if compared to average manufacturing in AC3 (Table 2.11).

AC3 losers could be distinguished by the highest level of RULC, higher than the country's manufacturing average, and also improving the least (Figure 2.1). In terms of RULC they possessed no competitive advantages over their EU counterparts. The level of quality of exported goods was also decidedly the lowest also improved relatively the least. Similar to the case of other industries discussed above, Hungarian loser industries had the highest quality among the three ACs, and Polish losers the lowest. This indicates that mostly low quality goods were being pushed out of the market. Low quality

Table 2.12   Changes in wages, productivity, turnover and employment of AC3 losers and their EU counterparts, 1998–2003

		Wages per employee	Turnover per employee	Turnover	Employment	Difference between changes in wages and productivity (% points)
Hungary	Losers in Hungary	77%	108%	64%	−21%	30
	EU15 counterparts	39%	29%	12%	−13%	−10
	Manufacturing	93%	94%	82%	−6%	1
Czech	Losers in Czech Rep.	64%	81%	32%	−27%	17
	EU15 counterparts	31%	31%	20%	−9%	0
	Manufacturing	56%	69%	58%	−6%	13
Poland	losers in Poland	51%	80%	15%	−36%	29
	EU15 counterparts	30%	35%	14%	−15%	5
	Manufacturing	38%	82%	48%	−19%	44
EU15	Manufacturing	32%	20%	16%	−9%	−12

Source: Eurostat, own calculations.

of goods and its poor improvement hampered the growth of their production and exports.

In 1998 loser industries in Hungary and Poland had the lowest levels of labour productivity, below the average for manufacturing (Table 2.11). Much higher productivity of the EU15 counterpart industries than the average of EU15 manufacturing implies a high productivity gap between the AC3 losers and their EU15 counterparts. On the other hand, in 1998 the level of wages in the loser industries was lower than the country's manufacturing average in each of the AC3 and the EU15 counterparts (except for Czech counterparts), indicating a low level of qualifications among employees (Table 2.11).

The rapid increase in productivity, much higher than that in the EU15 counterparts, contributed to some decrease in the productivity gap which remained high. The main source of the improvement in labour productivity was a larger fall in employment than in EU counterparts, and also a several-fold higher than the average decrease in employment in the AC3 manufacturing (Table 2.12). However, the wage growth in these industries was more rapid than for the manufacturing average of AC3 and EU15 (Table 2.12), meaning that the wage policy of firms was hampering improvements in competitiveness. Depending on the changes in wages related to productivity, RULC of these industries either increased (the Czech Republic) or diminished (Hungary and Poland) and remained much higher than manufacturing average of the AC3 in 2003. The restructuring of the analysed industries based on employment shedding which accompanied the increase in wages was rather shallow, though it brought about growth in labour productivity. A strong fall in employment, despite relatively high increases in wages, resulted in the growth of labour productivity. However opposite to the EU15 counterparts productivity level (except for Czech) remained much lower than average of manufacturing of the analysed countries. Very low quality of the exported goods, its small improvement and high productivity gap and high RULC were hampering the possibilities of their production growth and expansion on EU markets.

The rate of growth for Polish losers' turnover and exports was threefold lower than the manufacturing average. In the Czech Republic this ratio was twofold whereas in Hungary the dynamics were 30 per cent lower than the average, although still higher than in the EU15. As a result, the share of these industries in manufacturing's output of the AC3 diminished. The rise of exports was even slower than for outputs. The decrease in the share of these industries in AC3 manufacturing turnover and exports contributed to their fall in EU25 internal export share.

Summing up, a high productivity gap and relatively high wages resulted in high RULC and hampered cost competition of the AC3 loser industries with that of the EU15. Very low quality and its relatively small improvement (apart from Poland) together with a relatively small demand for these goods accounted for the fall of their shares in the European market.

2.7   Conclusions

In the pre-accession period (1998–2003) the AC3 industries increased their competitive pressure on most of the manufacturing industries on the EU25 market. The growth in their share of the EU25 market, the drop in RULC, the narrowing of the productivity gap and the increase in the quality of exported goods all confirm the improvement in the competitiveness of AC3 manufacturing industries. The increase in competitive pressure during the slowdown in the incumbent EU15 countries also confirms the progress made by the AC3.

Improvements in the competitiveness of AC3 manufacturing industries was differentiated across time, among the three countries (Hungary versus the Czech Republic and Poland), across manufacturing industries and quality segments of the EU15 market. The average quality of Hungarian industries, although highly differentiated among industries, was higher than Polish or Czech industries. However the share of exports of Polish and Czech high-quality goods in their total exports to the EU15 increased quite considerably. The opposite was the case for Hungary. This suggests increasing difficulty in exporting Hungarian high-quality goods to the EU15.

The major source of improvement in the competitiveness of the manufacturing industries of the three countries was a drop in the productivity gap in relation to the EU15. The productivity rate of growth of the AC3 overtook those of wages, resulting in a drop in their RULC. The opposite was the case for the incumbent EU countries.

Although the share of the AC3 large winner industries of EU25 internal exports was quite large the cumulative competitive pressure on the EU market was not strong. The specialization of Hungarian exports on a few large winners, dominated by foreign-owned firms, reflected both their comparative advantage over other Hungarian manufacturing industries and their competitive advantage over EU15 industries. The latter, operating in the same quality segments as their Hungarian counterparts, felt the increased competitive pressure of Hungarian industries. The growth in the competitive pressure of Czech and Polish large winners on the EU market was also reflected in the small progress in productivity made by the EU counterparts and their weaknesses. The level and improvement in productivity of the above-mentioned Polish and the Czech industries was lower than the manufacturing average. The specialization of Polish and Czech exports to the EU in relatively less productive industries (large winners) implies that the expansion of these exports to the EU results in lower-than-potential economic growth in both countries. The further external liberalisation of the EU market will hamper the further dynamic growth of some Polish and Czech large winners.

In the period of analysis a number of new dynamic industries (small winners) emerged among Polish and Czech exporters. They were characterized by higher and dynamically increasing productivity compared to their manufacturing average and to their incumbent EU counterparts. The improvement in the quality of their goods helped to improve their position on the EU market.

All in all, the increase in the EU market share of both large and small winners from the AC3 was the outcome not only of improvements in their productivity but also the poor performance of their EU15 counterparts in this respect.

The analysis shows that, firstly, changes in the competitive pressure of a particular industry of a given country on external markets reflect changes in relative (i.e. domestic related to foreign) labour productivity and not differences in labour productivity across industries within the country. Secondly, the analysis of market quality segments verifies the estimates of changes in the competitive pressure of AC3 on EU15 industries based on changes in relative productivity or market share. The increase in the EU market shares of a particular industry may be accompanied by differentiation in competitive pressure across market quality segments. Thirdly, competition by productivity – and not by wages – was the main factor of competition among the AC3 and the EU15 industries. The reason for a decrease in the RULC of the AC3 countries was the high dynamics of productivity growth, exceeding the growth of wages. This led to an increase in employment and resulted in high growth dynamics of production and an increase in EU export shares. The opposite was the case in changes in the incumbent EU countries.

2.8 Appendix

Table 2.A1   Large winners in AC3

Hungary

157	Manufacture of prepared animal feeds
204	Manufacture of wooden containers
311	Manufacture of electric motors, generators and transformers
312	Manufacture of electricity distribution and control apparatus
313	Manufacture of insulated wire and cable
315	Manufacture of lighting equipment and electric lamps
316	Manufacture of electrical equipment n.e.c.
322	Manufacture of television and radio transmitters and apparatus for line telephony and line telegraphy
323	Manufacture of television and radio receivers, sound or video recording or reproducing apparatus and associated goods

Czech Republic

171	Preparation and spinning of textile fibres
174	Manufacture of made-up textile articles, except apparel
203	Manufacture of builders' carpentry and joinery
222	Printing and service activities related to printing
251	Manufacture of rubber products
261	Manufacture of glass and glass products
262	Manufacture of non-refractory ceramic goods other than for construction purposes; manufacture of refractory ceramic products
266	Manufacture of articles of concrete, plaster, cement
281	Manufacture of structural metal products
282	Manufacture of tanks, reservoirs and containers of metal; manufacture of central heating radiators and boilers
283	Manufacture of steam generators, except central heating hot water boilers
287	Manufacture of other fabricated metal products
311	Manufacture of electric motors, generators and transformers
312	Manufacture of electricity distribution and control apparatus
313	Manufacture of insulated wire and cable
316	Manufacture of electrical equipment n.e.c.
343	Manufacture of parts, accessories for motor vehicles
352	Manufacture of railway, tramway locomotives, rolling stock
355	Manufacture of other transport equipment n.e.c.
361	Manufacture of furniture

Poland

153	Processing and preserving of fruit and vegetables
174	Manufacture of made-up textile articles, except apparel
182	Manufacture of other wearing apparel and accessories
183	Dressing and dyeing of fur; manufacture of articles of fur
203	Manufacture of builders' carpentry and joinery
204	Manufacture of wooden containers

(Continued)

Table 2.A1   (Continued)

205	Manufacture of other products of wood; manufacture of articles of cork, straw and plaiting materials
231	Manufacture of coke oven products
262	Manufacture of non-refractory ceramic goods other than for construction purposes; manufacture of refractory ceramic products
281	Manufacture of structural metal products
282	Manufacture of tanks, reservoirs and containers of metal; manufacture of central heating radiators and boilers
283	Manufacture of steam generators, except central heating hot water boilers
313	Manufacture of insulated wire and cable
314	Manufacture of accumulators, primary cells and primary batteries
315	Manufacture of lighting equipment and electric lamps
316	Manufacture of electrical equipment n.e.c.
323	Manufacture of television and radio receivers, sound or video recording or reproducing apparatus and associated goods
352	Manufacture of railway, tramway locomotives, rolling stock
355	Manufacture of other transport equipment n.e.c.
361	Manufacture of furniture

Table 2.A2   Small winners in AC3

Hungary

155	Manufacture of dairy products
175	Manufacture of other textiles
212	Manufacture of articles of paper and paperboard
222	Printing and service activities related to printing
244	Manufacture of pharmaceuticals, medicinal chemicals and botanical products
245	Manufacture of soap, detergents, cleaning, polishing
291	Manufacture of machinery for the production and use of mechanical power, except aircraft, vehicle and cycle engines
300	Manufacture of office machinery and computers
332	Manufacture of instruments and appliances for measuring, checking, testing, navigating and other purposes, except industrial process control equipment
334	Manufacture of optical instruments,photographic equipement
353	Manufacture of aircraft and spacecraft

Czech Republic

158	Manufacture of other food products
175	Manufacture of other textiles
233	Processing of nuclear fuel
245	Manufacture of soap, detergents, cleaning, polishing
247	Manufacture of man-made fibres

(*Continued*)

Table 2.A2   (Continued)

291	Manufacture of machinery for the production and use of mechanical power, except aircraft, vehicle and cycle engines
300	Manufacture of office machinery and computers
322	Manufacture of television and radio transmitters and apparatus for line telephony and line telegraphy
323	Manufacture of television and radio receivers, sound or video recording or reproducing apparatus and associated goods

Poland

156	Manufacture of grain mill products, starches and starch products
157	Manufacture of prepared animal feeds
171	Preparation and spinning of textile fibres
175	Manufacture of other textiles
211	Manufacture of pulp, paper and paperboard
212	Manufacture of articles of paper and paperboard
221	Publishing
222	Printing and service activities related to printing
243	Manufacture of paints, varnishes and similar coatings, printing ink and mastics
245	Manufacture of soap, detergents, cleaning, polishing
247	Manufacture of man-made fibres
251	Manufacture of rubber products
252	Manufacture of plastic products
263	Manufacture of ceramic tiles and flags
268	Manufacture of other non-metallic mineral products
286	Manufacture of cutlery, tools and general hardware
297	Manufacture of domestic appliances n.e.c.
312	Manufacture of electricity distribution and control apparatus
331	Manufacture of medical and surgical equipment and orthopaedic appliances
333	Manufacture of industrial process control equipment
341	Manufacture of motor vehicles
343	Manufacture of parts, accessories for motor vehicles

Table 2.A3   Losers in AC3

Hungary

151	Production, processing, preserving of meat, meat products
158	Manufacture of other food products
174	Manufacture of made-up textile articles, except apparel
181	Manufacture of leather clothes
182	Manufacture of other wearing apparel and accessories
191	Tanning and dressing of leather
193	Manufacture of footwear
202	Manufacture of veneer sheets; manufacture of plywood, laminboard, particle board, fibre board and other panels and boards

(Continued)

Table 2.A3   (Continued)

205	Manufacture of other products of wood; manufacture of articles of cork, straw and plaiting materials
232	Manufacture of refined petroleum products
242	Manufacture of pesticides and other agro-chemical products
243	Manufacture of paints, varnishes and similar coatings, printing ink and mastics
264	Manufacture of bricks, tiles and construction products
271	Manufacture of basic iron and steel and of ferro-alloys (ECSC)
365	Manufacture of games and toys

Czech Republic

154	Manufacture of vegetable and animal oils and fats
181	Manufacture of leather clothes
191	Tanning and dressing of leather
192	Manufacture of luggage, handbags and the like, saddler
193	Manufacture of footwear
201	Sawmilling and planing of wood, impregnation of wood
204	Manufacture of wooden containers
241	Manufacture of basic chemicals
242	Manufacture of pesticides and other agro-chemical products
244	Manufacture of pharmaceuticals, medicinal chemicals and botanical products
264	Manufacture of bricks, tiles and construction products
265	Manufacture of cement, lime and plaster
267	Cutting, shaping and finishing of stone
354	Manufacture of motorcycles and bicycles
363	Manufacture of musical instruments

Poland

154	Manufacture of vegetable and animal oils and fats
182	Manufacture of other wearing apparel and accessories
192	Manufacture of luggage, handbags and the like, saddler
193	Manufacture of footwear
244	Manufacture of pharmaceuticals, medicinal chemicals and botanical products
265	Manufacture of cement, lime and plaster
273	Other first processing of iron and steel and production of non-ECSC ferro-alloys
296	Manufacture of weapons and ammunition
321	Manufacture of electronic valves and tubes and other electronic components
351	Building and repairing of ships and boats
363	Manufacture of musical instruments

Notes

1   Among the new member states (NMS), AC3 are the most important players as they constitute 75% of NMS trade with the EU.
2   Most tariffs were lifted by 2000.
3   15 EU members and 10 new member states.

4   In the literature, relative labour productivity is often determined as the relation of an industry's productivity to total manufacturing's productivity.

5   However, in the literature there are several different proxies for product quality e.g. patents, R&D expenditure, investments; see Muscatelli (1995).

6   It also concerns the traditionally domestic-oriented Polish economy. The share of exports in GDP increased from 23.7% in 1995 to 34.7% in 2003, while of imports from 21.5% to 36.9% respectively.

7   However, the share of low quality goods (RUEV < 0.45) in Polish exports to EU15 remained very high, although it diminished from 28 to 22 per cent. The share of these goods in Czech exports was much lower (drop from 18 to 5 per cent) and in Hungary extremely low (7 to 1 per cent).

8   In Poland the number of industries in the highest quality segment increased from 13 to 27, in the Czech Republic from 22 to 32 and in Hungary from 24 to 47 (own calculations based on Comext database).

9   The increase in cumulative FDI from 1996 till 2003) reached $42 billion in Poland, $33 billion in the Czech Republic, and $23 billion in Hungary.

10 The share of five Polish industries in EU intra exports exceeded 9%.

11 There was quite a considerable variation in terms of the level of quality within the Polish group of industries.

12 These consist of 10 industries in Hungary, 23 in Poland and 8 in the Czech Republic.

13 It varied from 0.15% to 3.5%.

References

Abbott, L. (1955) *Quality and Competition*. New York: Columbia University Press.

Aiginger, K. (1997) 'The Use of Unit Values to Discriminate between Price and Quality Competition', *Cambridge Journal of Economics*, 21: 571–592.

Aw, B.Y. and M.J. Roberts (1986) 'Measuring Quality Change in Quota-Constrained Imports Market. The Case of US Footwear', *Journal of International Economics*, 21: 45–60.

Balassa, B. (1963) 'Recent Developments in the Competitiveness of American Industry and Prospects for the Future', Yale University Economic Growth Center, Center Paper no. 12.

Bevan, A.A. and S. Estrin (2004) 'The Determinants of Foreign Direct Investment into European Transition Economies', *Journal of Comparative Economics*, 32: 775–787.

Carlin, W., A. Glyn and J. van Reenen (1997) 'Quantifying a Dangerous Obsession? Competitiveness and Export Performance in an OECD Panel of Industries', CEPR Discussion Papers no. 1628. London: CEPR.

Casson, M. (ed.) (1999) *International Competitiveness*. London: Routledge.

Clark, J.M. (1963) *Competition as a Dynamic Process*. Washington, DC: The Brookings Institution.

Dlugosch, B., A. Freitag and M. Kruger (1996) *International Competitiveness and the Balance of Payments. Do Current Account Deficits and Surpluses Matter?* Cheltenham, UK: Edward Elgar.

Dollar, D. and E.N. Wolff, (1993) *Competitiveness, Convergence and International Specialization*. Cambridge, Mass. & London, England: The MIT Press.

Dullock, U. (2002) 'Trade and Transition – Is there a low quality trap?' Vienna: WIFO, mimeo.

Feigenbaum, A.V. (1988) 'Quality and business growth today', *Quality Progress*, 15(11): 22–25.

Gomory, R.E. and W. Baumol (2000) *Global Trade and Conflicting National Interests*. Cambridge, Mass. & London, England: The MIT Press.

Grossman, G.M. and E. Helpman (1991a) 'Quality ladder in the theory of growth', *Review of Economic Studies*, 59: 43–61.

Grossman, G.M. and E. Helpman. (1991b) 'Quality ladders and product cycles', *Quarterly Journal of Economics*, 425: 557–586.

Krafft, J. (2000) 'Introduction' in J. Krafft (ed.), *The Process of Competition*. Cheltenham, UK & Northampton, MA: Edward Elgar.

Kolasa, M. (2005) 'What drives productivity growth in the new EU member states? The case of Poland', ECB Working Paper Series no. 486, Frankfurt am Main, Germany.

Krugman, P. (1994) 'Competitiveness: A Dangerous Obsession', *Foreign Affairs*, 73(2) (March/April): 28–44.

Linder, S. (1961) *An Essay on Trade and Transformation*. Uppsala: Almquist & Wicksells.

Martin, S. (2004) 'Globalization and the natural limits of competition', in M. Neumann and J. Weigand (eds), *The International Handbook of Competition*. Cheltenham, UK & Northampton, MA: Edward Elgar.

Meeusen, W. and G. Rayp (2000), 'Patents and Trademarks as Indication of International Competitiveness', in P. Buigues, A. Jacquemin, and J.F. Marchipont (eds), *Competitiveness and Value of Intangible Assets*. Cheltenham: Edward Elgar.

Murphy, K.M. and A. Schleifer (1991) 'Quality and trade', NBER Working Paper no. 3622.

Muscatelli, V.A.(1995) 'NIE export performance revisited: the estimation of export demand elasticities and the role of product differentiation and growth', in D. Vines and D. Currie (eds), *North-South Linkages and International Macroeconomic Policy*. New York & Melbourne: Cambridge University Press.

Nelson, R. (1996) *The sources of economic growth*. Cambridge, Mass. & London England: Harvard University Press.

OECD (1998) *The Competitiveness of Transition Economies*. Paris: OECD.

Rosati, D. (1998) 'Emerging trade patterns of transition countries. Some observations from the analysis of unit values', MOCT-MOST 8, 51–67.

Stigler, G.J. (1965) *Essays in the History of Economics*. Chicago and London: The University of Chicago Press.

Sztaudynger, J.J. (2003) 'Nieliniowość wpływu inwestycji na wzrost gospodarczy' (The nonlinear impact of investment on economic growth), in E. Kwiatkowski and T. Tokarski (eds), *Wzrost gospodarczy, restrukturyzacja i rynek pracy w Polsce. Ujęcie teoretyczne i empiryczne* (Economic growth, restructuring and labour market in Poland. Theoretical and empirical approach). Łódź: University of Łódź.

Tumpel-Gugerell, G. (2003) 'Introduction', in G. Tumpel-Gugerell and P. Mooslechner (eds), *Economic Convergence and Divergence in Europe. Growth and Regional Development in an Enlarged European Union*. Cheltenham, UK, & Northampton, MA, USA: Edward Elgar.

WEF/IMD (1995) The World Competitiveness Report. Geneve and Lausanne: World Economic Forum and Institute for Management Development.

Wziątek-Kubiak, A. and I. Magda (2005) 'Differentiation of changes in competitiveness among Polish manufacturing industries', CASE Foundation Studies and Analysis no. 314. http://www.case.com.pl/upload/publikacja_plik/ 9939339_sa314.pdf

Wziątek-Kubiak, A., M. Jakubiak and M. Antczak (2004) 'Differences in productivity and its determinants among firms from the Czech Republic, Hungary, Poland and Germany. The case of the cosmetics industry', CASE Foundation Studies and Analysis no. 284.

3

Can Government Policy Influence Industrial Competitiveness? Evidence from Poland, Hungary and the Czech Republic

Iraj Hoshi, Darko Hajdukovic and Erjon Luci

3.1 Introduction

One of the major economic debates of the past four or five decades has been whether government intervention in support of a particular firm or industry will have a positive effect on the performance of that unit. Intervention has always been justified on the grounds of market failure, with taxes and subsidies as devices that can be used to ameliorate the impact of market failure. Markets fail because of the presence of monopoly power, increasing returns, activities involving externalities or spillovers, information asymmetry, and so on. It is often claimed that intervention through anti-trust laws, regulation, taxes and subsidies can reduce the impact of these market failures.

However, over the past twenty years there have been a number of developments in the literature which have seriously weakened, if not totally undermined, the case for government intervention. Firstly, it has been shown that most cases of market failure may be dealt with through market-based solutions operating through the price system. Secondly, the contributors to the notion of 'government failure' have demonstrated that government intervention, instead of reducing the impact of market failure, often results in further inefficiencies in resource allocation. Thirdly, the notion of 'inter-governmental competition' has established that government support, in the form of lower taxes, higher subsidies or other incentives designed to attract investors to a particular area or country leads to sub-optimal outcomes when several governments, or regions, are competing with each other for the attraction of investors.

In the European Union (EU), state intervention which affects competition between firms in different member states has been prohibited under the European Community (EC) Treaty, though this has not stopped members to continue their support for national firms and industries – risking the occasional criticism or censure by the Commission and having to reverse the particular policy. The Lisbon declaration that member states will work towards creating the most competitive knowledge-based economy in the world provided some governments new opportunities to increase certain types of intervention in the hope of contributing to the achievement of this goal, that is increasing the competitiveness of their firms and industries. This is particularly the case in the new member states of the EU (especially the three countries under consideration here) where the level of government intervention in the form of state aid has been above the EU average and its composition more distortionary than that in the EU (Hashi and Balcerowicz, 2006). Moreover, the general philosophy and direction of policy in these countries do not appear to have changed fundamentally since the accession either. Consequently, the need for the analysis of the impact of government intervention remains as important as ever.

This chapter is divided into four sections. The theoretical framework for the analysis of government intervention, in particular the potential distortions caused by, and the sub-optimal consequences of, such interventions are discussed in the second section. The third section concentrates on one of the important forms of state intervention in the three new member states, that is state aid, and discusses the potential impact of different types of state aid on industrial competitiveness. Empirical work on the impact of various government policy instruments on industrial competitiveness is presented in section four and concluding remarks are offered in section five.

3.2 Theoretical background

The arguments in favour of state intervention go back to the early days of the development of modern economics and will not be repeated here. The critics of state intervention, however, maintain that such intervention is most often counterproductive, with suboptimal outcomes when compared to the non-intervention alternative. Here, we shall briefly review these arguments.

Market failure

The instances of market failure commonly discussed in the literature were mentioned earlier. The traditional solutions to market failure (for example, using taxes and subsidies), however, have been the subject of much debate and discussion in the literature. It has been argued that government intervention, or collective action, is not necessarily the best way of dealing with market failure. Monopolies, especially natural monopolies arising from the presence of increasing returns, can be regulated through independent regulatory agencies which push them toward linking prices to average costs and price increases to average increases in costs.[1] Furthermore, in cases where price discrimination between customers are possible, the natural monopolist will have an incentive to set prices for the marginal customer according to its marginal cost, thus making regulation rather ineffective (Khan, 1988).

The literature on natural monopoly regulation (dating back to Averch and Johnson, 1962) have also shown the inefficiencies and distortions caused by the attempt to impose a ceiling on the rate of return earned by natural monopolies.[2] Much of the problem arises from the presence of information asymmetry regarding cost structure, technology, and expected changes in prices between the regulator itself and the firms it is meant to regulate. Alternative arrangements involving greater competition (actual or potential) and auctions for the right to supply the final products of a natural monopoly, that is policies which do not require direct intervention by the state, may involve less inefficiency (Demsetz, 1968; Stigler, 1971; Joskow and Noll, 1981).

The treatment of spillover effects, or externalities, has been no less controversial. On the one hand, it has been shown that the legal enforcement of property rights through courts will in some cases (though not always) make it possible to internalise the cost of externalities (Coase, 1960). The imposition of technical specification on equipment used in economic activities causing negative spill-over effects (electricity generation, chemical industry and similar activities), and their enforcement have been seen as equally effective methods. Tradable pollution rights, an attempt to reduce the impact of externalities through the price system, has been another substitute to direct government intervention.

The important point highlighted by these contributions is that because of the government's own insufficient information and the lack of knowledge of how the regulated agents will behave in the face of regulation or other forms of intervention, the outcome of policies aimed at reducing the inefficiencies caused by market failure, may be even less efficient than if the government did not act at all.

Public choice

The proponents of government intervention assume that the government has the incentive and the willingness to pursue a policy designed to improve the net social welfare (the sum of producer and consumer surplus). However, the literature on public choice, regulatory capture, interest groups, and rent-seeking has seriously questioned this assumption and weakened the case for government intervention. This literature broadly demonstrates that state intervention, far from resulting in Pareto improvement, may often be welfare reducing (Tullock, 1965; Bennett and Orzechowski, 1983; Migue and Balaguer, 1974; Olson, 1965; Pelzman, 1976, Kruger, 1974; Buchanan *et al.*, 1980).

Politicians aim to maximize their utility function which is affected by their chances of getting re-elected, retaining their jobs and promotion, expand the size of their departments, increase their perks of the job, and so on (Tullock, 1965). The consequence is that large bureaucracies tend to get larger and despite loud pronouncements about waste in government, the volume of resources handled through governments grows regularly and significantly

(Migue and Beleaguer, 1974; Bennett and Orzechowski, 1983). The voting system in Western democracies create a fertile ground in which politicians thrive by passing legislation which contains compromises designed to attract votes of other legislators and striking deals with other groups to ensure the passage of their bills. In the process, they are subject to influence from organized interest groups (association of producers, trade unions, farmers, steel producers, oil men, environmentalists, religious groups and others). Politicians and government officials who implement policies are also subject to 'capture' by those industries they are expected to regulate (Pelzman, 1976).

Given the uncertainty and incomplete information, it is often not easy to separate interventions based on a desire to reduce the impact of market failure from interventions motivated by political and electoral considerations and lobbying. As many observers have argued, the pitfalls of state support not only include the difficulty of identifying the costs and benefits of the externality targeted but also unearthing the underlying lobbying and political capture (Carliner, 1986; Neven and Roller, 2000). Once support for a firm or industry starts, it is very difficult to stop it even when the original aim of the programme is met – the argument to support infant industries or less developed regions often falls in this category.

The deregulation movement of the 1980s which starting with air transport and telecommunications, was one of the outcomes of the debates of the earlier period and produced huge welfare gains (Winston, 1993). It was recognized that in most cases, resources will be allocated more efficiently by improvements in the competitive environment such as the removal of barriers to entry and exit and facilitating the establishment of new firms, setting technical standards and minimum information requirements, improving the legal framework for property rights and law enforcement, and contracting out some of the functions of the government (Baumol, 1982).

Intergovernmental competition

When several governments (local, regional or national) compete for a new entrant's investment by offering various incentives (lower taxes, subsidies, investment in infrastructure, etc.), the outcome may be a downward spiral of taxes with adverse effects on all governments involved. The initial model of this type of industrial policy was concerned with how governments attract firms to their area through lower taxes only in order to 'lock' them into the new location and raise taxes at a later point to recoup the tax advantages given to the firms (Doyle and van Wijnbergen, 1984). The model was later extended to cover a variety of different conditions, including the existence of more than one locality in a country competing with each other for the new entrant (King *et al.*, 1993). They showed that if the inducements for new investors are financed by the federal government, the targeted locality would obtain a higher expected pay-off but the improvement would be at the expense of other localities which bear the cost of the inducement.

The supporters of industrial policy have generally highlighted the benefits of investment attraction policies for the receiving region but not considered its impact on other, particularly surrounding, regions. They have ignored the negative externalities imposed on other locations (the movement of resources, especially skilled labour, away from the neighbouring locations, the lost rent, and the lost benefits of the potential for economies of scope). There is also the fact that the cost of the subsidy falls on residents of all regions. In an important paper on the impact of the European Airbus project on the world welfare, Neven and Seabright (1995) identified several sources of negative externalities generated by this project. They showed that while the Airbus project has had a definite positive impact on the European welfare, estimated at around $50 billion over a fifty year period, its impact on the world welfare was strikingly negative, with the loss to rivals estimated at over $100 billion.[3]

The notion of intergovernmental competition was further developed by Besley and Seabright (1999) using an auction framework with governments as bidders trying to attract investment to their region or country. They showed that in a dynamic multi-period setting, intergovernmental competition may generate inefficient outcomes. This point has much relevance when members of an international grouping (such as the European Union) resort to investment incentives to attract firms to their regions in competition with each other. They show that the inefficient outcomes, resulting from negative externalities and government failures, can only be dealt with when the group as a whole impose guidelines on individual countries to regulate their support policies. The establishment of a set of rules on granting state aid to enterprises in the EU is an example of such guidelines.

To sum up: there are serious concerns about the impact or effectiveness of state intervention aimed at dealing with the impact of market failure. Government intervention may produce sub-optimal outcomes because:

- The intervention may be motivated by political and electoral considerations of politicians, or under pressure from lobbyists working for special interest groups and be devoid of economic justification. Political decisions are often the result of compromises made by politicians in bringing different interest groups together to form a coalition so that they can pass the relevant legislation through the parliamentary process.
- Intervention may be difficult to stop even when it has achieved its initial aims because of the coalition of interest groups formed around the policy. Once a policy is established and group interest created, it is difficult to withdraw it.
- Firms receiving government support are shielded from competition and lack the incentive to restructure themselves in order to face competition – as long as they continue to receive government support.

3.3   State aid and competitiveness

In order to highlight the types of state intervention corresponding to the preceding discussion, we use the example of 'state aid', common in all EU member states. In the EU, there is a general agreement that state intervention should be kept to the very minimum and that it should not have a distorting effect on competition between firms. For this reason, those activities of the state which may distort or threaten to distort competition between firms from different member states are prohibited under Article 87 (1) of the EC Treaty. However, under Articles 87(2) and 87(3), exceptions have been allowed to enable national governments to intervene in certain areas where the policy may have significant positive effects.[4] The argument here focuses on the need to correct for market failure, particularly in the financing of long term investment in human capital, research and development and technological innovation, that is activities which may not be financed to the desirable level by the market system because of the existence of externalities and spill-over effects. It is argued that, in these specific circumstances, the benefits derived from intervention are greater than the costs they impose (though this has never been clearly demonstrated).

While, in overall terms, the scale of intervention has been generally limited, though not insignificant (around 1 per cent of GDP in EU15 and around 1.5–4 per cent in the new member states), its composition has been the cause of much concern as some elements of state aid have greater potential for distortion than others. Generally, state aid falls into one of the following categories:

- Broad, or generic, support to all firms (or firms in specific industries) to enhance R&D, training, environmental improvement projects, and so on.
- Direct support to industries, or even firms, in financial distress caused either by the systemic change or by their inability to face domestic or more importantly international competition.
- Incentives to attract investment to regions suffering from social and economic deprivation or one of the many special economic zones established by (mostly new) member states.

The first type of support falls in the so-called 'horizontal' policy group, where all firms meeting certain criteria qualify for support and therefore the intervention does not have a direct and adverse effect on competition between firms. It is also the type of support with beneficial externalities and spillover effects which may enhance a country's long-term competitiveness. The other two types of support are different and have the potential to distort competition significantly. Support for individual firms or industries (usually referred to as either 'rescue and restructuring' aid or 'sectoral' aid) and to regions (referred to as 'regional' aid) are, without doubt, distorting: they favour one firm, industry or region against their competitors in the same country or in other EU states. In the context of the debate on 'market failure versus government failure', the important question is whether the magnitude of distortions is significant or not, or whether the beneficial effect of the policy outweighs its adverse consequences.[5]

The important point to note is that the composition of state aid in Poland, Hungary and the Czech Republic (as with most other new member states from Central and Eastern Europe) has been very different than those in the older member states. On the whole, the bulk of state aid has been spent on policies (such as 'rescue and restructuring', sectoral and regional) which have greater distorting consequences and only a much smaller fraction allocated to horizontal aid schemes with least distorting effects. This is in sharp contrast to the situation in older EU states where the bulk of aid has been allocated to horizontal objectives – in the majority of EU15, this has been over 75 per cent with some countries such as Belgium reaching 99 per cent (see Hashi and Balcerowicz, 2006 for details).

Given the aim of this chapter, we are interested in finding out whether or not these policies have resulted in positive outcomes, particularly in terms of improving the competitiveness of the recipients on home and EU markets. Of course, these policies may have been successful in the sense of having improved the level of training, research and development and thus benefited all or many firms in the economy or the industry (that is benefiting all competitors). They may have saved some enterprises from certain bankruptcy or attracted foreign investment into a region or a country. But they may also have involved negative externalities for other industries, regions or countries. Furthermore, state support is sometimes also used to simply cover the running cost of loss making firms (with powerful political backing), or to attract investors from another region of the country (or another member state), in which case benefits will be transitory with little, if any, effect on competitiveness. It is the overall impact of these policies on competitiveness that we are concerned with here.

There are two ways in which the impact of these interventions can be assessed. One is to investigate individual industries in detail, through case studies, identifying the specific forms of intervention and their (at least direct) impact. It is much more difficult to measure the impact of negative externalities (the impact on other industries, regions or countries). The investigations into the impact subsidies to iron and steel and coal industries in Poland (Supreme Chamber of Control 2002a and 2002b) showing that the policy had largely failed in bringing these industries to profitability and speed up their restructuring, are examples of this approach. Studies of special economic zones (SEZs) in Poland by Kryńska (2000) and Jensen and Winiarczyk (2004) are other examples.[6] Here, the authors analyse the impact of policies designed to attract investors to these regions and conclude that (i) the main reason for firms locating their business to SEZs was the tax relief offered to investors, (ii) firms moving to SEZs had closed down or substantially decreased their activity in their previous location, (iii) the policy had distorted local competition by offering incentives to large (often foreign) firms, and (iv) the policy had failed to achieve its main stated objective of fighting unemployment in Poland. It, therefore, seems quite likely that any benefit to the new location was at the expense of other localities, confirming the views of King *et al.* (1993) and Besley and Seabright (1999).

An alternative approach to the study of the impact of state intervention is to consider the population of industries as a whole and develop an econometric model in which an industry's competitiveness is affected by a range of factors including government policies. Such a model will be useful in identifying the simultaneous impact of different factors on the competitiveness of industries. It will also be more generalizable as it will look at the whole population of industries. In order to undertake this study, ideally, it would be necessary to have the data on sectoral and regional types of state aid at industry level which, unfortunately, is not available (state aid data is published at aggregate level). The only available option, though not ideal, is to use the total taxes imposed, and subsidies granted, to each industry as proxies. This is done in the following section.

3.4 Empirical results

A model of industrial competitiveness

There are many approaches to the definition and measurement of industrial competitiveness. Following Arrto (1987) and Wziatek-Kubiak (2003a), we consider competitiveness as the ability to sell a product on a market in competition with other producers.[7] More specifically, it is the ability of producers from the three accession countries to sell on their domestic and EU markets (where they compete with EU and non-EU competitors) that demonstrates their competitiveness (Dobrinsky, 1995). Therefore, we measure an industry's competitiveness by its performance on the home and EU markets – its share on the domestic market and on the EU market during the period of analysis. We expect competitiveness to be influenced by two types of factors: the commonly known factors such as productivity and cost structure (labour cost, material cost, energy cost, and so on) and, in the context of the present chapter, the government policy instruments (such as taxes, subsidies, and rules governing depreciation, environmental regulations, permits, and so on). Furthermore, given that we are concerned with competition on the EU market, the industry's cost structure will only be relevant when they are compared with those of the EU producers. Government policy instruments influence the firms' incentive system and the environment in which they operate. They will, therefore, affect the behaviour of firms and their managers, and their performance in the process of competition.

The general model used in our analysis is as follows:

$$COMPET = \alpha_0 + \beta_1 SUBSIDIES + \beta_2 TAXES + \beta_3 LOWERVAT + \delta_i X_i + + \sum_{j=1}^{m} \phi_j YR_j + \varepsilon$$

where *COMPET* represents competitiveness of an industry measured by the share of that industry's sales on (i) the domestic market and (ii) the EU apparent consumption (output plus imports less exports); *SUBSIDIES* is the total subsidy received by firms in the industry as a proportion of industry sales; *TAXES* is the total tax paid by firms in the industry (profit tax, social insurance and health contributions, local taxes, etc.), also as a proportion of sales; *LOWERVAT* is the proportion of sales subject to lower or zero VAT. The information on the proportion of sales subject to lower VAT is available only for Poland. In the Czech Republic, instead of this variable, we have information an additional dimension of state policy, namely the proportion of industry sales accounted for by publicly owned enterprises in each industry (*STATESHARE*). These three variables are instruments of government interaction. Other regulatory mechanisms (such as environmental rules) are less quantifiable and are therefore left out of the model. *X* is a vector of variables measuring the inputs or the impact of inputs of firms (and by definition those of the industry); *YR* shows the year dummies (8 for Poland and 6 for Hungary and the Czech Republic), and ε is the error term.

The unit of analysis in this model is industry at '3-digit' level, as defined by NACE classification. The model should enable us to trace the impact of taxes and subsidies (and other measures of government intervention) on the performance of industries in terms of their share of home and EU markets. The vector *X* consists of factors other than taxes and subsidies which directly or indirectly influence industrial competitiveness and, therefore, have to be controlled for. They include: unit labour cost (*ULC*), measured by the labour cost/sales ratio, or, unit labour cost relative to the EU (*RULC*), measured by the ratio of unit labour cost divided by the EU unit labour cost (*RULC* is used in the estimation of the first measure of competitiveness while *ULC* is used in the estimation of the second measure); unit material cost (*UMC*), measured by the material cost/sales ratio; labour productivity (*LABPROD*), measured by the sales/employment ratio; unit export value of the industry relative to the EU unit export value (*RUEV*), measured by the euro value of one ton of exports of each industry relative to the EU level; investment intensity (*INVEMP*), measured by investment per employee; and the restructuring efforts of firms in each industry (*RESTRUC*) measured by the change in the share of industry *i* in the manufacturing sector's employment.[8] In order to reduce the potential feedback effect of these two variables on competitiveness, we use their lagged values.[9] The actual model estimated is:

$$COMPET = \alpha_0 + \beta_1 SUBSIDIES + \beta_2 TAXES + \beta_3 LOWERVAT + \delta_1 RULC + \delta_2 UMC$$

$$+ \delta_3 LABPROD + \delta_4 RUEV + \delta_5 INVEMP + \delta_6 RESTRUC + \sum_{j=1}^{8} \phi_j YR_j + \varepsilon$$

Estimation methodology

Given that the sample covers almost all of the 3-digit industries in the three countries under consideration over a 6–8-year period, the panel-data technique is the obvious choice for empirical work. However, the presence of heteroskedasticity and autocorrelation problems (which are quite likely in this type of data-set) means that a more efficient method than OLS should be considered. Furthermore, there are also indications that some of the independent variables in the model may be endogenous. Subsidies and competitiveness, for example, are likely to be dependent on one another: if industries receive specific types of subsidies (such as the horizontal-type state aid), they may become more competitive while, at the same time, more competitive industries may have spend more resources on lobbying and attract more subsidies.[10] The use of normal OLS or panel data in the presence of endogeneity produces biased estimates (Green, 1997; Maddala, 2001). The endogeneity problem can be dealt with by instrumenting the endogenous variable (though finding appropriate instruments may be quite difficult).[11] It is of course possible to deal with some forms of endogeneity by using lagged values of a variable – and indeed this is done with some independent variables such as 'restructuring' or 'investment intensity' but this was not possible with subsidies because lags may just be part of an underlying process.

The introduction of instruments and the presence of heteroskedasticity and autocorrelation problems may be handled by the use of the General Method of Moments (GMM) technique, in particular the 'GMM with kernel-based estimation' variant. A user-written programme, IVREG2 (developed by Baum *et al.*, 2003), available in the STATA package, enables us to produce heteroskedasticity and autocorrelation consistent statistics – which are essential for efficient parameter estimation (Cushing and McGarvey, 1999).

The 'IVREG2' programme also generates three diagnostic tests for the appropriateness of instruments used: 'Hansen J1' statistic (the Lagrange multiplier test of excluded instruments), 'Hansen J2' statistic (the statistic obtained from the regression where excluded instruments are included)[12] and 'C statistic' (exogeneity/orthogonality of suspected instruments). The first two are calculated as tests of overidentifying conditions. The first Hansen J statistic is calculated from a regression with excluded instruments and the second from a regression with full set of instruments used. The joint null hypothesis of these tests is that the instruments are valid instruments (they are uncorrelated with error term) and that they are rightly excluded from original equation and thus should not be rejected. These statistics, under the null hypothesis, have Chi-sq distribution. The 'difference-in-Sargan' or the C statistic is calculated as the difference between the two J statistics. In effect it tests if the instrument should be in the full specification, that is if they belong in the second stage of the regression rather than in the first one. Failing to reject it 'requires that the full set of orthogonality conditions be valid' (Baum *et al.*, 2003), which we suspect may not be the case in our example. This null hypothesis should therefore be rejected.

The precise definition of all variables and their measurement methods are shown in Table 3.1. The summary statistics for variables used in regressions are presented in the Appendix.

Data

There are 102 three-digit industries in NACE classification system (Rev. 3) though a few of them are excluded from the study because of the lack of data (arising from the small number of constituent firms and the possibility of identifying the individual firm, thus violating the confidentiality requirement). The empirical work is based on the data for around 90 three-digit industries in the manufacturing sector of the three countries under consideration. The period of analysis depends on the availability of data, 1996–2003 (for Poland), and 1998–2003 (for Hungary and the Czech Republic).

Although the data used for this study have been obtained from a variety of sources, the main source has been the statistical returns from enterprises to the national statistical offices (form F-01 in Poland, P-501 in the Czech Republic and the information from the Tax Office in Hungary). These were supplemented by Eurostat's New CRONOS and COMEXT data bases and other information from the National Banks and Central Statistical Offices of the three countries. Although the data used in this study come from reliable sources, the method of collection and the coverage of data are somewhat different in different countries, with some including all firms and others including only firms with over 20 employees. Moreover, the foreign trade data are generally collected according to 'trade classification' and then converted to 'industrial classification', thus introducing some element of inaccuracy in the process. The foreign trade data sometime include 're-exports' which, if large, can distort the calculations. Indeed, the Hungarian data base contains a very large number of industries where the export figures are larger than the figures for domestic production – an indication of

Table 3.1 Definition of variables and their measurement

Variables	Definition and measurement
COMPET1	Competitiveness on the EU market; measured by an industry's share of EU market – the industry's exports to EU divided by EU apparent consumption (EU sales plus EU imports less EU exports).
COMPET2	Competitiveness on the domestic market; measured by an industry's share of domestic market – the industry's sales less its exports divided by the total domestic market (total sales plus imports less exports).
SUBSIDIES	Subsided received by firms in an industry divided by the industry's sales, lagged by one year in Poland and the Czech Republic; in Hungary this refers to tax allowance received by firms on certain investments.
TAXES	Total taxes paid by firms in an industry, including profit tax, social and health contributions, local taxes, etc, as a proportion of the industry's sales.
LOWERVAT	Proportion of industry's sales subject to lower or zero rate of VAT (for Poland only).
STATESHARE	Sales in publicly owned enterprises (those with a majority state ownership) in each industry as a proportion of total sales in that industry (for the Czech Republic only).
ULC	Unit labour cost; calculated as total cost related to labour (gross wages and salaries plus social and health contributions paid by employers) divided by sales.
RULC	Unit labour cost relative to the EU; calculated as unit labour cost in an industry divided by unit labour cost of that industry in the EU.
UMC	Unit material cost; calculated as total cost of material used in production divided by sales in Poland and the Czech Republic; in Hungary this variable is unit intermediate costs, including all intermediate inputs.
LABPROD	Labour productivity; calculated as the total sales of the industry divided by employment in the industry.
RUEV	Unit export value of each industry divided by the unit export value of that industry in the EU (the value of exports divided by the volume of exports in euro per kilogram).
INVEMP	Investment to employment ratio; the value of investment divided by the number of employee.
RESTRUC	Restructuring efforts in each industry; the absolute value of the annual change in the share of each industry in manufacturing employment, lagged by one year.
EMP	Employment in the industry.

(Continued)

Table 3.1   (Continued)

Variables	Definition and measurement
EMPSALE	Employment/sales ratio.
EMPSALEIndex	Employment/sales ratio in index form (its value in year t divided by its value in year $t-1$).
SOCCONT	Social contribution/sales ratio.
SOCCONTIndex	Social contribution/sales ratio in index form (its value in year t divided by its value in year $t-1$)
PROFSAL	Profit/sales ratio (industry profit is the sum of profits and losses of all firms in the industry)
YR	Year dummies

much re-exporting and inaccurate conversion of trade statistics to industrial statistics. For this reason, the domestic competitiveness variable (*COMPET2*) is not estimated for Hungary.

Results

We will discuss the results of the investigation for the two indicators of competitiveness separately. Tables 3.2 summarizes the results of the application of the GMM with kernel-based estimator for competitiveness on the EU market of the industries in the three countries. The table illustrates the impact of taxes and subsidies and a number of control variables on the share of the EU market accounted for by industries from Poland, Hungary and the Czech Republic.

The main feature of the table is that, in general, government instruments have no or negatively significant impact on competitiveness on the EU market. In Poland and the Czech Republic, subsidies are negative and significant; Taxes are negative and significant in Poland and insignificant in Hungary and the Czech Republic. The only exception to the general pattern is the subsidies in Hungary. But, here, it should be noted that the data for total subsidies is unavailable in Hungary and the figures used in the regression refer only to the tax allowances offered to firms on certain investment activities (that is, the data cover only a part of total subsidies).

The preferential treatment of industries through lower VAT (in Poland) is also negative and significant. This kind of treatment encourages firms to concentrate on the domestic market (where they perceive to have an advantage) and diverts their attention away from the EU markets (more on this later). The share of the state in each industry's sales, that is the sale of enterprises with a majority state ownership in total sales, an indicator of the extent of

Table 3.2   Government policy and competitiveness on the EU market, 1996–2003

	Dependent variable: *COMPET*1 (share of EU market)		
	Poland	*Hungary*	*Czech Republic*
SUBSIDIES	−33.333**	0.114***	−0.138***
	(0.018)	(0.001)	(0.000)
TAXES	−0.242***	0.025	−0.108
	(0.000)	(0.684)	(0.543)
LOWERVAT	−1.455***	nd	nd
	(0.000)		
STATESHARE	nd	nd	−1.621***
			(0.000)
RULC	−1.075***	−0.335	−0.755*
	(0.005)	(0.292)	(0.070)
UMC	1.394***	0.681	1.140***
	(0.000)	(0.372)	(0.000)
LABPROD	−0.728***	−0.354**	−1.804***
	(0.000)	(0.021)	(0.000)
RUEV	0.176	nd	nd
	(0.151)		
INVEMP	0.245**	nd	0.385***
	(0.038)		(0.001)
RESTRUC	−0.016	0.251***	0.089*
	(0.653)	(0.000)	(0.075)
Model specification	Semi-log	Semi-log	Semi-log
No. of observations	578	332	421
Instruments	EMPSALEIndex SOCCONTIndex	EMPSALEIndex SOCCONTIndex	EMP SOCCONTIndex
DIAGNOSTICS			
R2 (centred)	0.413	0.177	0.423
Hans J1 statistic	3.285	5.289	5.259
	(0.193)	(0.072)	
Hans J2 statistic	0.435	0.000	0.722
	(0.510)	(0.993)	(4.536)
C statistic	2.851	5.289	4.536
	(0.091)	(0.022)	(0.033)
White/Koenker nR2 test (*p*-value)	78.494 (0.000)	32.356 (0.000)	122.434 (0.000)
Hausman test (*p*-value)	305.52 (0.000)	81.91 (0.000)	238.76 (0.000)

Notes: All equations include a constant term; *p*-values are shown in brackets. For the full list of variables, see Table 3.1; for the explanation of diagnostics, see the text. * Significant at 10%; ** significant at 5%; and *** significant at 1%; nd: no data; in the semi-log specification, dependent variable is in log form but one or more of the independent variables are in non-log form.

state's direct influence (available in the Czech Republic only) also seems to have a negative and significant effect.

In terms of the control variables, the interesting feature of the table is the impact of labour and material cost on the EU competitiveness. Normally we expect unit costs (or unit costs relative to EU unit costs) to have a negative impact on competitiveness. The impact of the 'relative unit labour cost' is negative and significant in Poland and the Czech Republic and insignificant in Hungary. Unit material cost, however, is negative in the former two countries and insignificant in the latter. The positive sign seem to indicate a different process. As in some other studies, unit material cost may embody better quality and more expensive intermediate products and may therefore indicate higher quality of goods exported (Wziątek-Kubiak and Winek, 2004, p. 18).

The investment intensity seems to have the expected positive effect on competitiveness in both Poland and the Czech Republic (no data on investment is available for Hungary). The restructuring indicator either has the expected sign (positive effect) as in Hungary and the Czech Republic, or is insignificant as in Poland. The one unexpected sign in Table 3.2 is that of 'labour productivity' which is negative and significant in all three countries. The only possible justification is that firms which improve their productivity may suffer from inertia and may tend to become lax, reducing their focus on competitiveness.

The diagnostics of the model are, generally, satisfactory. The statistics produced by the IVREG2 procedure are heteroskedasticity and autocorrelation consistent. The three statistics produced by the instrumental variable procedure are generally of the correct magnitude (or nearly so). J1 and J2 are usually large enough (p-values around or more than 10%) so that the null hypotheses can not be rejected. The null hypothesis underlying the C statistic is rejected for all three regressions, supporting the validity of instruments. The final statistical issue that needs to be resolved is to check whether the use of GMM is an appropriate research strategy, as it implies loss of efficiency compared to the OLS. A variant of the Hausman test can be used to investigate this issue. Here, as Baum *et al.* (2003) point out, Hausman should not be interpreted as 'a test of endogeneity or exogeneity of regressors *per se*, but rather as a test of the consequence of employing different estimation methods on the same equation.' It is nevertheless useful to report this test as well, which we refer to as Hausman. The null hypothesis of this test is that the OLS is an appropriate estimation technique. The Hausman test confirms that the 'subsidies' variable has been correctly treated as endogenous in our analysis. It is true that although the industries under consideration all belong to the manufacturing sector, they are considerably different from each other (compare, for example, meat processing industries with car manufacturing). It is, therefore, rational to expect the presence of heteroskedasticity. The

White/Koenker statistic,[13] a variant of the Pagan and Hall (1983) test for the heteroskedasticity can be used to confirm this. The test is readily available in STATA software and is reported in Tables 3.2 and 3.3 – and is satisfactory in all cases. The underlying null hypothesis is that the model does not suffer from heteroskedasticity. Note that this test is very robust and performs well in cases where heteroskedasticity is present not only in one equation but in the entire system.

We can now consider the results of the estimation procedures for the competitiveness on the domestic market, shown in Table 3.3. As already mentioned, the data for domestic market shares in Hungary is unavailable due to discrepancies between trade statistics and industrial statistics and, therefore, we can only run the estimation procedure for Poland and the Czech Republic.

For the domestic market competitiveness regressions we have used the same tax and subsidy variables as before but for control variables are slightly different. Instead of the unit labour cost relative to the EU labour cost, we have used the simple unit labour cost. We have also omitted the relative unit export value and labour productivity (the latter is very closely related to unit labour cost). The RULC and RUEV are particularly relevant when competition on foreign markets is being studies and are less relevant to domestic competition. In both countries, taxes are insignificant; subsidies are insignificant in Poland; the share of public sector in industries' sales is also insignificant. The preferential treatment of some industries by means of lower VAT seems to have a positive effect on domestic competitiveness. Lower VAT rates encourage firms to focus on their domestic markets where they have an advantage (compared to their foreign markets). As a result, while their share of domestic market improves, their share of EU market declines. Subsidies in Poland are insignificant but in the Czech Republic they seem to have a positive effect on domestic competitiveness. It is possible that over time, subsidies in this country have changed in nature and gradually become of the less distorting type (horizontal) and therefore play a positive role.

As for the control variables, the results are generally as expected. The unit labour cost and unit material cost are both negative; investment intensity is insignificant in both countries and the restructuring efforts of firms seem to have a positive impact on their share of the domestic market.

As far as the diagnostics are concerned, the three statistics relating to the instrumental variable procedures are appropriate in the Czech regressions but not quite satisfactory in the case of the Polish case, implying that the instruments do not meet all the required conditions. It has to be noted that finding appropriate instruments is a hard task and one may not always be able to instruments that satisfy all conditions. This is the case in the Polish dataset, for example, where the J1 and J2 statistics are such that the null hypothesis can be rejected at 5% level of significance.

Table 3.3 Government policy and competitiveness on the domestic market, 1996–2003

	Dependent variable: COMPET2 (share of domestic market)	
	Poland	*Czech Republic*
SUBSIDIES	−0.025	0.048*
	(0.127)	(0.057)
TAXES	−0.034	−0.060
	(0.307)	(0.549)
LOWERVAT	0.345***	nd
	(0.000)	
STATESHARE	nd	0.066
		(0.727)
ULC	−0.419***	−0.563***
	(0.000)	(0.000)
UMC	−0.190**	−0.579***
	(0.017)	(0.000)
INVEMP	0.003	−0.002
	(0.932)	(0.978)
RESTRUC	0.102***	0.064**
	(0.000)	(0.017)
Model specification	Semi-log	Semi-log
No. of observations	431	390
Instruments	EMPSALE	EMPSALE
	PROFSALE	SOCCONT
DIAGNOSTICS		
R2 (centred)	0.291	0.115
Hans J1 statistic	5.698	4.474
	(0.058)	(0.107)
Hans J2 statistic	2.824	0.372
	(0.093)	(0.542)
C statistic	2.875	4.103
	(0.090)	(0.043)
White/Koenker nR2	25.367	12.588
test (*p*-value)	(0.000)	(0.000)
Hausman test (*p*-value)	82.04	93.50
	(0.000)	(0.000)

Notes: All equations include a constant term; *p*-values are shown in brackets. For the full list of variables, see Table 3.1; for the explanation of diagnostics, see the text. * Significant at 10%; ** significant at 5%; and *** significant at 1%; nd: no data; in the semi-log specification, dependent variable is in log form but one or more of the independent variables are in non-log form.

3.5 Concluding remarks

There is general agreement amongst economists about the existence of market failure in certain circumstances, but there is no agreement about the impact or the effectiveness of state intervention aimed at dealing with such instances. The literature on government failure, particularly in the areas of public choice and rent seeking have demonstrated that governments (and government officials) may engage in maximising their own objective functions which are different from that of the society. 'Collective action' may produce a variety of outcomes – some involving net welfare gain and, others, net welfare loss.

While there is some empirical evidence on specific areas of government intervention such as the regulation of utilities, there is little empirical evidence on the effectiveness of state aid policies, in particular the impact of taxes and subsidies. The impact of government policy in specific areas such as the banking sector, the energy sector, special economic zones, etc., has been highlighted elsewhere. This chapter attempts to provide more general evidence on the impact of taxes, subsidies and other means of state intervention on the competitiveness of industries. As an alternative to the case study approach, we have opted for the econometric approach, trying to obtain broader results by using the information on all three-digit industries in the manufacturing sector of the three countries. Although regression analysis may suffer from problems such as the representativeness of the sample, accuracy of data, comparability across countries, measurement errors, endogeneity, specification and functional form problems, it has the advantage of using a large volume of data and taking into account most of the relevant features of the competitiveness process. In other words, it can provide a good complement to the case study method.

The empirical work presented in this chapter shows that in the period before the accession of Poland, Hungary and the Czech Republic to the European Union, taxes and subsidies in these countries often had either a significant and negative impact, or no significant effect at all, on industrial competitiveness and, as such, were counterproductive. This result, to some extent, undermines the case made by the proponents of 'industrial policy' as well as 'state aid' who believe taxes and subsidies can be used to bolster a country's industrial competitiveness – at home and abroad. The situation is likely to have been the same in the latest accession countries and the present candidate countries. Further research aimed at improving the model specification and the quality and coverage of data is needed to general these results in a broader context. But the main lesson is that industrial competitiveness in these countries is improved not by government intervention but by the efforts of firms themselves.

Appendix: Summary statistics for variables used in regressions

Table 3.A1   Summary statistics for variables used in regressions for different countries

Variables	No. of observ.	Mean	Std. dev.	Min.	Max.
Poland					
COMPET1	736	0.009	0.029	2.020E−05	0.317
COMPET2	722	0.567	0.245	0.031	0.996
SUBSIDIES	778	0.003	0.014	0.000E+00	0.243
TAXES	773	0.017	0.012	2.060E−05	0.085
LOWERVAT	794	0.259	0.282	0.000	0.944
ULC	778	0.232	0.101	0.027	0.534
RULC	759	1.181	0.754	0.357	18.388
UMC	778	0.503	0.130	0.134	0.908
LABPROD	778	177.701	233.677	21.300	2708.570
RUEV	685	0.616	0.342	0.054	1.863
INVEMP	778	11.249	12.791	0.000	118.991
RESTRUC	800	0.001	0.001	0.000	0.006
Hungary					
COMPET1	594	0.004	0.007	0.000	0.059
SUBSIDIES	580	0.008	0.055	0.000	0.983
TAXES	578	0.011	0.026	0.000	0.398
ULC	574	0.175	0.085	0.022	0.531
RULC	527	0.923	0.442	0.146	3.579
UMC	545	0.703	0.108	0.206	0.984
LABPROD	573	60000	75000	5000	692000
RESTRUC	505	0.001	0.002	0.000	0.012
Czech Republic					
COMPET1	658	0.007	0.011	0.000	0.132
COMPET2	566	0.473	0.253	0.018	0.986
SUBSIDIES	712	0.001	0.002	0.000	0.030
TAXES	673	0.379	0.278	0.000	0.995
STATESHARE	673	0.379	0.278	0.000	0.995
ULC	698	0.172	0.072	0.013	0.490
RULC	669	0.881	0.527	0.303	11.289
UMC	698	0.477	0.124	0.130	0.941
LABPROD	712	53.926	73.804	10.122	1093.939
INVEMP	698	3.473	4.233	0.163	53.448
RESTRUC	606	0.001	0.001	0.000	0.021

Notes

1   A major subject of discussion has been the identification of the exact segment of a production process which is a 'natural monopoly' and its separation from other parts of the activity (for example, the recognition that only the transmission of electricity through a national grid – and not the whole of electricity supply

industry, that is production, distribution and sale – is characterized by natural monopoly).

2 It was the recognition of these inefficiencies that eventually led to the formulation of 'price-capping' as an alternative method of regulation in the 1980s.

3 The Airbus project was aimed at establishing a European aircraft company capable of producing a wide range of commercial aircraft and of competing with the American rivals Boeing and McDonnell-Douglas (MDD). The arguments in favour of state support ranged from beneficial externalities, technological spillovers and improving consumer welfare through lower prices resulting from increased market competition and reduced market power of Boeing. Using a computable partial equilibrium model and simulation procedures to analyse the production and price behaviour of the three rivals, Neven and Seabright compared the profit and consumer surplus in the industry with and without the entry of Airbus. They showed that the entry of Airbus forced its rivals to reduce their production levels, increased their unit production cost by denying them the full benefits economies of scale and scope, reduced Boeing's market power and enabled MDD to increase its range of products and compete more effectively with Boeing.

4 Article 87(1) states that 'any aid granted by a Member State or through State resources in any form whatsoever which distorts or threatens to distort competition by favouring certain undertakings or the production of certain goods shall, in so far as it affects trade between Member States, be incompatible with the common market.' Article 87(2) allows aid with a social nature which is given to all consumers meeting certain criteria (older people, for sample). Article 87(3) allows aid to regions with very low living standards, aid to help the development of certain activities, and aid in some exceptional circumstances provided such aids do not have an overall adverse effect on trade.

5 For a detailed report on the distortionary impact of subsidies in the UK, see Office of Fair Trading (2004).

6 The former study focused on 4 of the 17 SEZs and considered the motives and operations of 56 enterprises (3/4 of investors in these areas) involved in these areas. The second study, involved over 250 firms located in all SEZs.

7 This is the 'change in market share' notion of competitiveness. Competitiveness can also be analysed by changes in productivity, relative prices, balance of trade, and so on. For a discussion of various approaches to competitiveness, see Wziatek-Kubiak (2003b).

8 Restructuring involves, more than anything else, a change in employment. Successful firms increase their employment while struggling firms try to reduce their work force – the extent to which firms can change their employment is an indicator of their restructuring efforts. For this reason, the absolute value of a change in employment share of each industry in total manufacturing employment is taken into account.

9 We believe that investment and restructuring will affect competitiveness by improving and modernising production technology, changing the input and output mix (and possibly other channels too). But it is also possible to think that more competitive firms will also invest more and embark on more restructuring. The lagged values of these two variables will reduce the feedback effect as competitiveness in this period is unlikely to affect investment or restructuring efforts in the previous period.

10 See Hajdukovic (2007) for a more detailed analysis of the relationship between subsidies and competitiveness.

11   It is essential to report not only the precise instruments used in a regression but to provide the economic rationale for the use of such instruments too. It is also necessary to show that the instruments are exogenous with respect to the main dependent variable but related to the endogenous variable. The estimation method used in this chapter enable us to do these.

12   For a discussion of the Hansen J-statistic, see Hansen (1982) and Hayashi (2000).

13   This statistic is reported as 'White/Koenker $nR2$' in Tables 3.2 and 3.3. The letter n refers to the number of observations.

References

Arrto, E.W. (1987) 'Industrial Policy and International Competitiveness, The Case of Eastern Europe', in K.S. Hughes (ed.), *European Competitiveness*. Cambridge: Cambridge University Press.

Averch, H. and L.L. Johnson (1962) 'Behavior of the Firm under Regulatory Constraints', *American Economic Review*, 52, December: 1052–69.

Baum, C.F., M.E. Schaffer and S. Stillman (2003) 'Instrumental Variables and GMM: Estimation and Testing', *The Stata Journal*, 3(1): 1–31.

Baumol, W.J. (1982) 'Contestable Markets: An Uprising in the Theory of Industrial Structure', *American Economic Review*, 72(1), March: 1–15.

Bennett, J.T. and W.P. Orzechowski (1983) 'The Voting Behavior of Bureaucrats: Some Empirical Evidence', *Public Choice*, 41(2): 271–84.

Besley, T. and P. Seabright (1999) 'The Effects and Policy Implications of State Aids to Industry: An Economic Analysis', *Economic Policy*, 28, April: 15–53.

Buchanan, J., R. Tollinson and G. Tullock (1980) *Towards a Theory of the Rent Seeking Society*. College Station, Texas: Texas A & M University Press.

Carliner, G. (1986) 'Industrial Policy for Emerging Industries', in P.R. Krugman (ed.), *Strategic Trade Policy and the New International Economics*. Cambridge, Mass.: The MIT Press.

Coase, R.W. (1960) 'The Problem of Social Cost', *Journal of Law and Economics*, 3(1), October: 1–44.

Cushing, M.J. and M.G. McGarvey (1999) 'Covariance Matrix Estimation', in L. Matyas (ed.), *Generalised Methods of Moments Estimation*. Cambridge: Cambridge University Press.

Demsetz, H. (1968) 'Why Regulate Utilities?', *Journal of Law and Economics*, 11, April: 55–65.

Dobrinksy, R. (1995) 'Economic Transformation and Changing Patterns of European East-West Trade', in R. Dobrinksy and M. Landesmann (eds), *Transforming Economies and European Integration*. Aldershot: Edward Elgar.

Doyle, C. and S. van Wijnbergen (1984) 'Taxation of Foreign Multinationals: A Sequential Bargaining Approach to Tax Holidays', CEPR Discussion Paper no. 25, August, London.

Green, H.G. (1997) *Econometric Analysis*, 3rd edn. London: Prentice-Hall International.

Hajdukovic, D. (2007) Government policies in transition countries: the case of state aid. Empirical evidence from Czech Republic, Hungary and Poland, Royal Holloway University of London, mimeo.

Hansen, L.P. (1982) 'Large Sample Properties of Generalised Methods of Moments Estimators', *Econometrica*, 50(4) (July).

Hashi, I. and E. Balcerowicz (2006) 'The comparative analysis of state aid in Poland, Hungary and the Czech Republic prior to accession', *International Journal of Economic Research* 3(1): 17–38.

Hayashi, F. (2000) *Econometrics*. Princeton, Princeton University Press.

Jensen, C. and M. Winiarczyk (2004) Location Choice and Employment Allocation of Foreign Investors in Poland – Are the Special Economic Zones successful?, Copenhagen Business School, mimeo (December).

Joskow, P.L. and R. Noll (1981) 'Regulation in Theory and Practice: An Overview', in G. Fromm (1981), *Studies in Public Regulation*. Cambridge, Mass.: MIT Press.

Khan, A. (1988) *The Economics of Regulation*. Cambridge, Mass.: MIT Press.

King, I., R.P. McAfee and L. Welling (1993) 'Industrial Blackmail: Dynamic Tax Competition and Public Investment', *Canadian Journal of Economics*, xxvi (3), August: 590–608.

Kruger, A. (1974) 'The Political Economy of the Rent-Seeking Society', *American Economic Review*, 64: 291–303.

Kryńska, E. (ed.) (2000) *Polskie Specjalne Strefy Ekonomiczne* (Polish Special Economic Zones). Warsaw: *Wydawnictwo Naukowe Scholar*.

Maddala, S.G. (2001) *Introduction to Econometrics*. 3rd edn, New York: John Wiley & Sons.

Migue, J.L. and G. Balaguer (1974) 'Towards a General Theory of Managerial Discretion', *Public Choice*, 17, Spring: 27–43.

Neven, D. (1994) 'The Political Economy of State Aids in the European Community: Some Econometric Evidence', CEPR Discussion Paper no. 945, April, London.

Neven, D. and L.H. Roller (2000) 'The Political Economy of State Aid: Econometric Evidence for the Member States', in D. Neven and L.H. Roller (eds). *The Political Economy of Industrial Policy in Europe and the Member States*. Berlin: Sigma.

Neven, D. and P. Seabright (1995) 'European Industrial Policy: The Airbus Case', *Economic Policy*, 24, October: 313–58.

Office of Fair Trading, OFT (2004) *Public Subsidies, A Report by the Office of Fair Trading*, OFT750 (November), London: OFT.

Olson, M.L. (1965) *The Logic of Collective Action*. Cambridge, Mass.: Harvard University Press.

Pagan, A.R. and D. Hall (1983) 'Diagnostic tests as residual analysis', *Econometric Review*, 2(2): 159–218.

Pelzman, S. (1976) 'Towards a General Theory of Regulation', *Journal of Law and Economics*, 19(2), August: 211–48

Stigler, G. J. (1971) 'The Theory of Economic Regulation', *Bell Journal of Economics*, 2(1), Spring: 3–21.

Supreme Chamber of Control (2002a) Informacja o wynikach kontroli restrukturyzacji finansowej i organizacyjnej górnictwa węgla kamiennego w latach 1990–2001 (Report on the results of audit on financial and organisational restructuring of hard coal mining between 1990–2001) 178/2002, Warsaw.

Supreme Chamber of Control (2002b) Informacja o wynikach kontroli restrukturyzacji i przekształceń własnościowych w hutnictwie żelaza i stali (Report on the results of audit on restructuring and ownership changes of iron and steel sector), 169/2002, Warsaw.

Tullock, G. (1965) *The Politics of Bureaucracy*. Washington, DC: Public Affairs Press.

Winston, C. (1993) 'Economic Deregulation: Days of Reckoning for Microeconomists', *Journal of Economic Literature*, 31(3), September: 1263–89.

Wziątek-Kubiak, A. (2003b) On Essence and Measurement of Changes in Competitiveness of the Accession Countries. Critical Review of Literature, 'Studies and Analysis' CASE Foundation no. 321, http://www.case.com.pl/upload/publikacja_plik/9939339_sa314.pdf.

Wziątek-Kubiak, A. and D. Winek (2004) 'Are changes in market shares a relevant indicator of changes in competitiveness? A Case of Poland', *Opere et Studio Oeconomia*, 1(2), May: 1–19.

4
Interdependency of Real Exchange Rate, Trade, Innovation, Structural Change and Growth

Paul J.J. Welfens

4.1 Introduction

One can observe that transition countries, including the accession countries, have recorded long term real appreciation *vis-à-vis* the euro and other currencies. Long-term appreciation does not rule out considerable short-term real exchange rate (RER) fluctuations, where stages of temporary nominal and real currency depreciation may be an element of a long-term real appreciation process. On the one hand one must ask therefore what role does volatility – including potential overshooting – play and on the other the focus should be on the impact of the RER trend on economic development.

The RER q^* is defined here as eP^*/P (e is the nominal exchange rate in price notation, P the price level, $*$ denotes foreign variables, q is real exchange rate), while the relative price of non-tradables (N goods; T is tradables) is denoted as $\phi = P^N/P^T$. It is clear that the international law of one price will not hold strictly for tradables if we take into account transportation costs, tariffs and other trade impediments. However, even without these physical and political impediments, the law of one price does not hold universally across countries – at least not in a Schumpeterian world, with product innovations and process innovations. Subsequently, we will take a closer look at potential explanations and the implications. The competitiveness of EU15 and Central and East European (CEE) accession countries, as well as of the EU25, will be affected by dynamic structural change and the newly emerging regional division of labour and innovation.

From a theoretical perspective, the RER affects trade, structural change and economic growth in an interdependent way. In the short run a change in the RER will influence portfolio capital flows since the interest parity says that the domestic interest rate $i = i^* + \mathrm{d}\ln e/\mathrm{d}t$ (i^* is the interest rate; note that within a medium-term perspective $i = r + \pi$ and $i^* = r^* + \pi^* - \pi$ is the inflation rate and r the real interest rate – so that we get the equation $r = r^* + \mathrm{d}\ln q^*/\mathrm{d}t$). Overshooting in this respect could be a problem, that is, the medium depreciation rate could diverge from the short-term depreciation rate. In the medium term

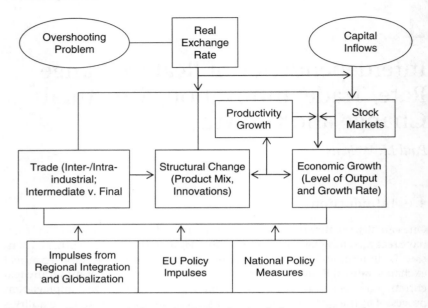

Figure 4.1   Exchange rate dynamics, trade, structural change and growth

the RER rate also will affect the trade volume, the product mix of exports and imports plus the current account position. Moreover, the structure of output will be affected. This will partly be linked to sectoral productivity growth. In the medium and long term there will be direct and indirect effects on national income and per capita income. These changes will in turn affect structural change and trade. In an open economy the picture would be incomplete without considering the effects of exchange rate dynamics on capital inflows as well as the stockmarket.

To the extent that there is an increase of capital inflows and in particular foreign direct investment (FDI) inflows there will be effects on production potential and productivity growth (see Figure 4.1). From a policy perspective, one must ask which impulses arise from regional integration and economic globalization. Moreover, the questions as to which EU policy impulses are relevant and which national policy measures could spur growth must be asked. It is clear that one should expect considerable structural change in the initial transition stage in CEECs and possibly also once high foreign direct investment inflows occur. This occurred early on in Hungary and the Slovak Republic, but only with a considerable delay in Poland. The various subsequent indicators show different intensities of structural change and the intensity of change is not equal across the various indices. On theoretical grounds (see Appendix) one should focus mainly on the Lilien index and the modified Lilien index as they both take into

Table 4.1 Various indicators measuring structural change based on production data at the NACE 2-digit level

	Period	LI	MLI
Germany	1993–2002	0.1097	0.0327
Greece	1995–2002	0.1222	0.0318
Hungary	1993–2001	0.4124	0.0814
Poland	1993–2001	0.1427	0.0282
Portugal	1995–2001	0.0820	0.0177
Slovak Rep.	1993–1999	0.2766	0.0442
USA	1993–1998	0.0497	0.0096

Notes: LI = Lilien Index; MLI = modified LI, see Appendix.
Sources: OECD STAN Database; own calculations.

consideration each sectors' relative weights and also meet other standard requirements.

As one can see in Table 4.1, of the various indicators showing the intensity of structural change in the period from 1993 to 2001/02, all point to a quite strong structural change in several ACs. Ideally, workers move out of sectors with low productivity growth towards sectors with high productivity growth, the latter often being found in sectors with high foreign direct investment inflows. FDI and investment by domestic firms will increase capital intensity and this, along with improved technology, will raise productivity. A positive gap between the growth rate of wages and sectoral productivity growth will reinforce sectoral profit rates, which in turn should stimulate sectoral FDI inflows. Given that economic catching-up and modernization are associated with high cumulated FDI inflows, one should expect that a considerable part of trade is shaped by FDI. Intra-company trade accounts for roughly one-third of trade in OECD countries.

In contrast, the degree of structural change in Germany was rather low, though this might be related to rather rough sectoral decomposition. For example, if international outsourcing to CEECs takes place this will probably be associated with considerable structural change, although at the two-digital level one should note that no fewer automotive parts are produced in Germany in the early twenty-first century than a decade earlier.

As regards structural change, this is partly related to technologies while also partly to other factors – including real exchange rate (RER) changes. There are two alternative definitions of the RER $q = P/(eP*)$ – with $*$ denoting a foreign variable and P and e representing the price level and the nominal exchange rate, respectively; P represents a basket of goods which is composed of tradables and non-tradables. An alternative for defining the RER is $\lambda' = P^T/(eP^{T*})$, where T stands for tradables. A rise in q or in λ' can be identified with real appreciation. Subsequently, we take a closer look at alternative explanations for RER changes which must include an analysis of the links between nominal exchange rate dynamics and the RER (section 4.2).

We demonstrate within a monetary growth model that real money demand does not depend on the real interest rate unless the savings rate is a function of the real interest rate. Section 4.3 is on the RER and economic development, trade, structural change and growth, where we also focus on a new structural model with product and process innovations but also on various aspects of the more complex Hansen–Röger model. Our analysis also takes a look at the links between the RER and economic growth. In the final section, we present some basic policy conclusions. The Appendix presents some innovative modelling related to the topic of exchange rate dynamics and macroeconomic analysis (including smooth linking of supply-side effects and demand-side impulses). Underpinning the paper, there is strong emphasis on the fact that the dynamics of exchange rate development and growth should simultaneously take into consideration trade and FDI.

With reference to all OECD countries and CEECs, and Asian countries in particular, a considerable share of trade is intra-company trade. The perspective adopted here is a mixture of Schumpter's and Dunning's, namely in the sense that innovation and FDI are emphasized. Both trade and FDI depend on the RER, although as the FDI stock contributes to the overall capital stock in the host country the net trade position – more precisely the current account – depends on cumulated FDI: the difference between output produced and domestic absorption (the sum of consumption, government consumption and investment, including FDI inflows) is equal to net exports. There also is a geographical coincidence in the sense that the gravity equation for FDI and trade typically shows similar patterns. This applies to CEECs, for which Western Europe represents the main export market and also the main source of FDI inflows. Such inflows contribute to product upgrading over time. The analytical focus has various time horizons and brings some new insights, including the fact that in a non-inflationary economy the demand for money does not depend on the (long-term) real interest rate. Indeed, ambiguous results from empirical analysis in this field are well known. We also develop a rather convenient graphical model to focus on the issues of structural change and competitiveness and we propose new ways of how to include the optimum growth literature in the analysis of Schumpeterian economic dynamics.

From a policy perspective, it becomes clear that analysing macroeconomic topics can hardly be done adequately without taking into account structural change and innovation dynamics. While innovation and structural adjustment are a natural element of EU Eastern enlargement both in Western Europe and CEECs (or in a North-South perspective), not much is known about the adjustment costs of firms and countries when moving up the technology ladder.

4.2 Exchange rate dynamics, relative prices, employment and growth

Technological progress and the long-term price level

Process innovations and the price level

In modern economies, process innovations are an important element of economic development. It is surprising that the role of process innovations has not been much considered in medium term macro models. Only in long-term growth models have they played a role. However, the dominant neoclassical growth models are non-monetary models in the sense that money-market equilibrium is not considered. In this chapter we will show that combining a growth model with money-market equilibrium is quite useful. The following analysis is not only relevant for Schumpeterian innovation dynamics in a monetary economy (and every modern economic system is a monetary economy), we also can state that the role of monetary policy cannot be fully assessed if we do not include the role of technology. As regards the role of monetary policy, it has been emphasized (Ball, 2001) that income elasticity of the demand for money of less than unity has crucial implications for monetary policy, for example that the Friedman rule of monetary policy is not optimal and the growth rate of money should be below the growth rate of output in order to achieve price stability.

Moreover, monetary aggregates are still important in the new era of inflation targeting (Hayo, 1999). Recent empirical work – based on co-integration analysis and error correction models – for broad money in Australia (Valandkhani, 2005), Germany (Beyer, 1998), the Eurozone (Coenen and Vega, 2001) and the UK (Ericsson, 1998), namely for narrow money, have all shown that long-term income elasticity is quite close to unity, which is consistent with the quantity theory of money (if the elasticity were 0.5 the implication is that the Baumol–Tobin transaction approach is applicable, if the elasticity is above unity money is a luxury good). As regards the growth of demand for money relative to income, Lambsdorff (2005) has presented empirical evidence for a cross-country approach. We will show that the income elasticity of demand for money points to important long term implications in the context of technological progress. Process innovations which amount to the cutting of costs typically are expected to lead to a fall of the price level. The expansion of the digital economy is often considered as a case where process innovations have played a strong role (Audretsch and Welfens, 2002; Welfens, 2002). This represents a typical perspective for an economy in which all sectors are subject to process innovations.

However, this apparently convincing insight from microeconomics has one pitfall, as we will show in a simple long-term approach to the quantity theory of money. We will combine money-market equilibrium with the condition of profit maximization; namely showing that the real interest rate r

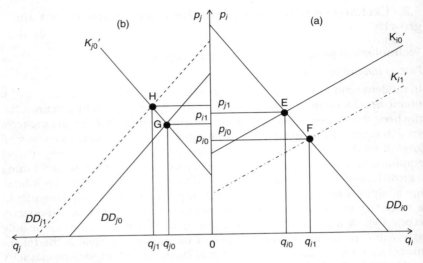

Figure 4.2 Ambiguous effect of technological progress on price level

should be equal to the marginal product of capital. We will demonstrate that, in the case of the income elasticity of demand for money between 0 and 1, there will be an increase in the equilibrium price level. Let us start the analysis with a standard microeconomic perspective of process innovations. Assuming there is a process innovation in market i (see in the following graph the downward shift of the marginal cost curve K_i' where i could represent the tradable sector) and an unchanged supply condition in market j. At first sight this will lead to a fall of price pi and hence (with b denoting the share of income spent on good i) a decline of the aggregate price level $P = (p_i)^b p_j^{(1-b)}$. One may introduce some refinement to the argument, namely that a real income effect associated with higher output in the i-market and the (potentially transitory) fall of pi, would shift the demand curve in the j-market upwards so that the price pj would rise as a consequence of technological progress in sector i; thus the effect on the price level is ambiguous (see Figure 4.2).

However, we can prove, within a macroeconomic approach, that there is no ambiguity at all if the income elasticity of the demand for money is in the range between 0 and unity. If the income elasticity is above unity then the long-term equilibrium price level will fall as a consequence of process innovations. The relevant mechanism partly includes the macroeconomic money market: demand for money is affected by a rise in the technology level in two, offsetting, ways as we will see. In a consistent macro model with goods markets and a money market the relevant mechanism is related to the demand for money and this in turn suggests that there must be a real balance effect in the goods markets (or in the aggregate goods market).

True long-term equilibrium in the money market

Let us consider long-term money market equilibrium, namely, real money balances M/P equals the real demand for money m^d (Y, i) where M is the nominal money stock, Y aggregate output and i the nominal interest rate. As we will assume an expected inflation of zero, we will set $i = r$ (the real interest rate). Moreover, we will consider a Cobb–Douglas production function with a Harrod factor A:

$$Y = K^\beta (AL)^{1-\beta} \tag{4.1}$$

and impose the condition of profit maximization so that

$$r = Y_K = \beta Y/K \tag{4.2}$$

Here β is the output elasticity of capital and Y_K the marginal product of K. In this approach the marginal product of capital determines the real interest rate. Thus we are not following the optimum growth model, which leads to $f'(k') = \theta + n$ where k' is modified capital intensity $K/[AL]$, f' the marginal product of capital, θ is the time preference and n the growth rate of the population (modified golden-rule; alternatively the golden rule could be used $f'(k') = n$ (see Blanchard and Fischer, 1989). For an optimum growth approach one should rather take n to be endogenous here; one also could argue that the golden-rule approach assumes that utility maximizing consumers dominate the capital market, while our approach assumes that investors dominate capital markets (in reality both groups will have an influence so that $r = b'\theta + (1 - b')f'(k')$; b' represents the relative impact of consumers – we have a similar problem as with exchange rate determination in the presence of fundamental actors and speculators betting on present trends).

Next we follow the standard assumption that the real money demand m is a positive function of Y and a negative function of the nominal interest rate i. Money-market equilibrium is defined by

$$M/P = m(Y, i) \tag{4.3}$$

Taking a look at the long-term money-market equilibrium condition (defined by $M/P = m$ and the equality of the real interest rate and the marginal product of capital) brings an important and surprising insight. It is convenient to define real money demand as

$$m = Y^\sigma \sigma'/I \tag{4.4}$$

Let us point out that with a real money demand function $m = Y^\sigma \sigma'/i$ (or a similar specification; $\sigma > 0$; $\sigma' > 0$) and zero expected inflation (hence the nominal interest rate $i = r$), we get in an economy with profit maximization and a

Cobb–Douglas production function $Y = K^\beta(AL)^{1-\beta}$ the somewhat surprising result that an irreversible rise of the level of technology A could raise the price level P. This can be seen from the money market equilibrium condition $M/P = m^d(Y, i)$, which is solved here for the steady state price level $P\#$:

$$P\# = MY^{1-\sigma}\text{ß}[Y/K]/\sigma' = [\beta MY^{1-\sigma}/K]/\sigma' \qquad (4.5)$$

It is obvious that a rise of M will raise the equilibrium price level, while for a given real interest rate and hence a constant ratio Y/K a rise of output will reduce the price level. If the international law of one price holds, namely $P = eP^*$, the nominal exchange rate is given (assuming an exogenous P^*) by $P\#/P$. Now let us consider the equation for the price level (the true monetary long-term equilibrium condition) in more detail:

$$P = (\beta/\sigma')M(AL)^{(1-\beta)(1-\sigma)}K^{\beta(1-\sigma)-1} \qquad (4.6)$$

We can see that a rise in the capital stock will reduce the price level, which corresponds to standard results from a model with two markets (or one aggregate goods market) in which there has been an increase in production capacity:

$$\partial P/\partial K < 0 \qquad (4.7)$$

Indeed, this condition is obviously fulfilled given $\beta(1-\sigma)-1 < 0$ and $s(1-\sigma) < 1$; and $1-(1/\beta) < \sigma$. Since the expression $1-(1/\beta)$ is negative and σ is positive, the multiplier for K is always negative. As regards the impact of process innovations ($dA > 0$) (and similarly for dL) we find a rather paradoxical result (one should recall that the monetary approach to the balance of payments is also paradoxical as the Mundell–Johnson argument emphasizes that in a small open economy with a fixed exchange rate a rise of the foreign price level will raise, via arbitrage, the domestic price level and hence in turn raise the demand for money; the excess demand for money translates into a current account surplus which leads to a rise in the money supply which is consistent with the initial rise of P). We can indeed see:

$$\partial P/\partial A > 0 \text{ if } 0 < \sigma < 1 \qquad (4.8)$$

If the income elasticity of the demand for money is slightly below unity, a rise of the technology level (A) will raise the price level. If this elasticity were above unity, process innovations will lead to a lower price level. As is well-known from the literature, there has been (at least since Milton Friedman's argument that money is a luxury good: hence the income elasticity should be above unity) a long debate about the income elasticity of money and the empirical evidence is not always conclusive as to whether the elasticity is below or above unity. Returning to the true long term equilibrium condition in the money market, one may want to describe labour market equilibrium in a very simple way, namely labour supply $L^s = L^d$. We assume labour supply as exogenous, while labour demand is determined by the real wage equation (profit maximization) $W/P = \beta Y/L = \beta k^\beta = \beta A^{-\beta} k'^\beta$ where k is capital intensity and $k' =: K/(AL)$ and W the nominal wage rate ($w =: W/P$) is the real wage rate). Thus $P = W/[\beta k^\beta]$, which determines the nominal wage rate W.

In an open economy one additionally would have to consider real interest rate parity, namely $r = r^* + d\ln q^{E*}/dt$; here q^E is the expected RER. In our long-term approach the level of technology has an impact both on real income and on the real interest rate: the reason for the interesting paradox presented is the role which the level of technology has on the marginal product of capital and hence on the interest rate; a rise of A amounts to raising the marginal product of capital and hence the interest rate so that the demand for money is reduced. Therefore money market equilibrium (at a given nominal money supply and a given capital stock) can only be restored if the price level is rising (this might be interpreted in a way that the real income effects of technological progress can overcompensate for the direct price effect of falling marginal costs). If $\sigma = 1$, the price level would remain stable and the positive real output effect associated with the rise of A would generate exactly sufficient additional demand for money to restore the equilibrium. If $\sigma > 1$, the income-induced rise in real demand for money would be so large that it would require a fall in the price level for equilibrium in the money market to be restored.

Whatever the specification of the demand for money, there will always be a critical value of the income elasticity below which a rise in A has to be accompanied by a rise in the price level if a new equilibrium is to be achieved in the money market. Basically, we have an interesting empirical question, on the one hand, and on the other the idea presented reinforces any natural scepticism one might have when simple analogies from microeconomics are drawn to derive macroeconomic conclusions. Even parallel process innovation in both markets could ultimately lead to a rise of the price level, that is to say if the real income effect in both markets is strong enough to outweigh the productivity/cost effect related to process innovations.

Long-term growth perspective

Next we recall that $k' =: K/[AL]$. Let us rewrite the true long-term monetary equilibrium condition in the following way, where we observe that in the following equation the elasticity of P with respect to AL is apparently negative (this seems to contradict the initial equation for true long term monetary equilibrium, although one must take into account that the variable k' contains AL in the denominator!):

$$P = (\beta/\sigma')M(AL)^{-\sigma}k'^{\beta(1-\sigma)-1} \tag{4.9}$$

Assume that savings $S = sY$, reinvestment is proportionate to K (parameter δ) and that overall investment $I = dK/dt + \delta K = S$. From the standard neoclassical growth model we know that the equilibrium value $k'\#$ is expressed for the case of a given L and a given A by $k'\# = (s/\delta)^{1/1-\beta}$. Thus we get:

$$P = (\beta/\sigma')M(AL)^{-\sigma}[s/\delta]^{[\beta(1-\sigma)-1]/[1-\beta]} \qquad (4.10)$$

One should note, however, that the assumption that there is profit maximization imposes a restriction on the parameter sets since we have $\beta k'^{\beta-1} = r$ and hence $k'\# = (\beta/r)^{1/1-\beta}$; and we have $k'\# = [s/\delta]^{1/[1-\beta]}$. This requires a specific savings rate, namely $s = (\beta/r)\delta$, which could be fulfilled by choice of a specific β. We can state that a rise of M raises the long-term equilibrium price level while a rise of the savings rate will reduce it. An increase in the depreciation rate δ will raise the price level. In a stationary, non-growing, economy inflation is always a monetary phenomenon. Next we consider an economy with population growth and sustained progress so that (with e' denoting the Euler number, n the growth rate of population and a the growth rate of the technology level A) $L = L_o e'^{nt}$ and $A = A_o e'^{at}$. We therefore get the following equation, which offers some non-monetarist insights about inflation:

$$P(t) = (\beta/\sigma')M[s/(a + n + \delta)]^{[\beta(1-\sigma)-1]/[1-\beta]}(L_o A_o e'^{(a+n)t})^{-\sigma} \qquad (4.11)$$

Obviously in a growing economy there could be sustained deflation, namely to the extent that $a + n$ exceeds zero. A rise of the progress rate a will lead to both a rise of the level of P and of the deflation rate, respectively, (the expression $\beta(1 - \sigma) - 1$ is always negative, so that the impact for the level of P is unambiguous). We now return to the true condition of long term monetary equilibrium. Let us briefly focus on the case of an open economy, which suggests an additional potential paradox. A paradox in an open economy in which there is parallel technological progress in country 1 and country 2 ($dA > 0$, $dA^* > 0$; and $dA = dA^*$) will occur if the income elasticity of the demand for money is below unity (in the interval 0,1) in the home country and above unity in country 2. The consequence of global technological progress is that the price level in country 1 will rise, while it will fall in country 2; implicitly one has to assume downward wage flexibility if unemployment is to be avoided. If the nominal exchange rate is constant the effect is a real appreciation of the home country's currency and this has to be taken into account in the context of the interest parity which reads, in the absence of inflation, $r = r^* + d\ln q^*/dt$, where q^* is defined as eP^*/P (e is the nominal exchange rate); hence technological progress will affect capital flows through the logic of the interest parity. While some observers analysing country 1 might argue that process innovations (or rises in labour productivity) lead to a real appreciation, the true story is that process innovations *per se* do not lead to this appreciation, rather it is a mechanism which is related to the money market. Our approach suggests that analysing long term price level dynamics in open economies with technological progress should be done in a careful way and must include analysis of the money market. The common analytical split between pure trade theory (which never looks at the money market) and the monetary theory of international economic relations is not adequate in certain cases.

If one considers the case of flexible nominal exchange rates and process innovations (again with σ in the interval 0.1 in country 1 and above unity in country 2) one may assume that the nominal exchange rate is rising, so that there is a nominal depreciation of the currency. Speculators and scientists, therefore, should be interested in the size of the income elasticity of the demand for money. It seems likely that in poor countries this is below unity, while in countries with a high per capita income it is above unity as the demand for real balances and other wealth assets rises more than proportionately as income rises. Economic catching up of poor countries, and thus international real income convergence, could thus help to avoid the above paradox. To learn more about the role of this paradox from an empirical perspective one should in particular study the link between progress and the price level in those countries where the income elasticity of the demand for money is below unity in a certain period and above unity in the following period.

Next we take a look at the RER eP^*/P, assuming that the above equilibrium equation holds in a similar way abroad:

$$P^* = (\beta^*/\sigma'^*)M^*(L_o^*A_o^*e'^{(a^*+n^*)t})^{-\sigma^*}[s^*/(a^* + n^* + \delta^*)]^{[\beta^*(1-\sigma^*)-1]/[1-\beta^*]} \qquad (4.12)$$

Now we get a much better understanding of the long-term RER, which is given (denoting $s/(a+n+\delta) =: s''$, $L_oA_o =: Z'$ and $[\beta(1-\sigma)-1]/[1-\beta] =: \beta'$) by the following expression:

$$q^* = e(\beta^*/\beta)(\sigma'/\sigma'^*)(M^*/M)(Z'^*e'^{(a^*+n^*)t})^{-\sigma^*}[s''^*]^{\beta'^*}/(Z'e'^{(a+n)t})^{-\sigma}[s'']^{\beta'} \qquad (4.13)$$

If $\beta' = \beta'^*$ we can state that a rise in the foreign savings rate relative to the domestic savings rate will raise the real long-term equilibrium exchange rate; a relative rise in the domestic savings rate will bring about a real appreciation; as $-\sigma < 0$ we can add that a relative rise in the sum of the domestic progress rate and the population growth rate will also bring about a real appreciation (both a relative rise in the savings rate and a relative rise in the domestic progress rate are typical of economic-technological catching up (with Japan being a prominent example in the 1970s and 1980s). One should note that the world real income in terms of country 1 (home country) is $Y^W = Y + q^*Y^*$.

Process innovations are a standard phenomenon of economic analysis. In a monetary economy one cannot, however, neglect the impact of the money market on the price level. Since process innovations not only affect real output but also the marginal product of capital and therefore the real interest rate, one has a principal ambiguity with respect to the impact of technology on the price level. There is a critical size of the income elasticity below which a rise in the level of technology implies a rise in the price level; with an elasticity above the critical value, process innovations will bring about a fall in the price level. The impact of technology on the price level, in turn, will have an impact on capital flows since a change in the real interest rate is part of interest parity. Our analysis suggests that analysing technological progress requires combining analysis of the real sphere and of the monetary sphere of the economy. As we have shown, monetary policy can be used to avoid inflation by an adequate choice of the growth rate of the money supply.

The nominal exchange rate, real exchange rate and long-term equilibrium

Naturally, there is a link between the nominal exchange rate and the RER q^*. It holds that $E(\ln e) + E(\ln P^*) = E(\ln P)$. As regards the variance VAR, it holds that $VAR(\ln e + \ln P^*) = VAR(\ln e) + VAR(\ln P^*) + 2cov \ln e, \ln P^* = VAR \ln P$. If one were to assume that $VAR \ln P = VAR \ln P^*$, it is clear that for any variance of $\ln e$ and of $\ln P^*$, there must be negative $cov \ln e, \ln P^*$. It is indeed plausible that a depreciation of country 1's currency will go along with a fall in country 2's price level as goods imported from country 1 will become cheaper in country 2.

From the perspective of a small open economy, the short-term nominal exchange rate e is determined by the interest rate parity $i = i^* + a^E$ where a^E denotes the expected depreciation rate and i the nominal interest rate. In the long term the interest rate at home and abroad is given by $i = r + \pi$ (the sum of the real interest rate r and the inflation rate π) and $i^* = r^* + \pi^*$, which implies, with profit maximization $r = Y_K$ and $r^* = Y_K^*$, respectively: $(r - r^*) + (\pi - \pi^*) = a^E$. If there is free capital mobility and domestic and foreign bonds are perfect substitutes – but no free movement of foreign direct investment – it holds that $r = r^*$, which makes the interest parity fully consistent with long term purchasing power parity $P = eP^*$ if there is no (systematic) difference between expected and actual devaluation rate. The RER $q^* =: eP^*/P$ is determined in the short term by nominal exchange rate dynamics and in the long term P and P^* play a role as well. Overshooting phenomena of the short term nominal exchange rate thus will affect the RER temporarily.

If domestic and foreign bonds are not perfect substitutes, while there is full mobility of foreign direct investment, the marginal products at home and abroad will be equal in the long run: $Y_K = Y_K^*$. Hence profit maximization in both countries will indirectly bring about the condition $r = r^*$ in the long run. However, there is not really a long term in the strict sense if one does not take a growth model and various other aspects into consideration. One specific aspect will refer to the fact that foreign direct investment flows will be a function of the RER, as Froot and Stein (1991) argue. We will turn to this later and firstly focus on the issue of a long term equilibrium RER.

If we are to make a prediction about the domestic price level we could use a model that predicts the nominal exchange rate (Welfens and Borbely, 2004) and combine this with a model which explains the foreign price level P^*. As regards the latter one may consider a rather simple approach based on four elements:

- Money-market equilibrium: this must be considered in the long-term growth modelling of a monetary economy;
- Profit maximization: in the long term the real rate of interest must be equal to the marginal product of capital (with a standard Cobb–Douglas production function $Y = K^\beta (AL)^{1-\beta}$ the marginal product of capital $Y_K = \beta Y / K$ where K is capital, L is labour and A the level of labour-saving technology);
- A simple growth model: in a neoclassical growth model – with a growth rate $d\ln A/dt =: a$, a Cobb–Douglas production function (as above) and a savings function $S = sY$ – the steady-state solution for per capita output $y\# = A_0 e^{\prime at} (s/n)^{\beta/1-\beta}$; here e' denotes the Euler number. Hence the level of the growth path of y is a positive function of the initial level of technology A_0 and the savings rate s, and the growth rate a. We will show that in an open economy with trade and foreign direct investment – and monetary transactions – the equilibrium solution looks more complicated and suggests new empirical approaches;
- An assumption with respect to the strategy of monetary policy.

Initially we are interested in the level of P^*, which is not really exogenous here. One can show – as an innovative feature of the model – that the long-term demand for money is independent of the real interest rate unless the savings rate depends on the real interest rate. Money market equilibrium requires that real supply ($M/P; M$ is the nominal money stock) equals real money demand $m^*(\ldots)$:

$$M^*/P^* = m^*(Y^*, i^*) \tag{4.14}$$

The equilibrium condition for the money market is fairly general, as we will see. Indeed, it is reasonable both for a narrow definition of the money supply (M_1) and for broad money supply (M_3). If we consider M_1, cash balances plus deposits, one should expect a close medium term link with the price level. In an underemployed economy a rise in the money supply will raise output Y, and as the capacity utilization rate is increased the price level P will increase with a certain delay. If one wants to express (A.1) in a kind of a quantity-theoretical framework we can simply write: $M_1 = V'(i, Y)PY$, with V' denoting the inverse of the income velocity of money. While it often is claimed that M_3 (M_1 plus term deposits plus savings deposits) is linked with the price level, there are no serious arguments as to why a rise in broad money M_3 should raise the price level unless one argues that there is a strong real balance effect. A serious argument would look different: A rise in M_2' – here defined as M_3 minus M_1 – would increase within a portfolio-theoretical approach with the demand for stocks as real capital being complementary to money balances. Combining a higher stock of M_2' with a higher value of stocks $P'K$(P' is the stockmarket price level and K the capital stock) reduces the portfolio risk.

To the extent that P' is positively correlated with P, one may expect that empirical investigations into the long term demand for money come up with positive evidence for a link between M_3 and P. This point is easily understood if we assume that the fundamental value of stocks reflects discounted future profits, which are – in a very simple two-period perspective (with Ω denoting unit labour costs and E the expectations operator) – given by the straightforward expression: $(P_t - \Omega_t)Y_t + (E(P_{t+1}) - E(\Omega_{t+1}))Y_{t+1}/(1+i) = P'$. Assuming, for simplicity, that market participants expect $E(Y_{t+1}) = Y_t$, that unit labour costs are constant, that output $Y = K \ln L$ (we will, however, later switch to Cobb–Douglas) and that firms finance all investment through the stock market, we can state the following equation: $M_2' = V''(i, Y)P'K$ and – assuming that $\Omega = P\omega$ – thus $M_2' = V''(i, Y) \, (P(1-\omega))(1+(1+i)^{-1}) \, Y/\ln L$. We can then add M_1 and M_2' and state – with $\omega' =: 1 - \omega$ – the long-term money-market condition:

$$M_3 = V'(i, Y)PY + V''(i, Y)(P\omega'(1 + (1+i)^{-1})Y/\ln L$$
$$= PY[V'(..) + V''(..)\omega'(1 + (1+i)^{-1})]/\ln L \qquad (4.14')$$

This now looks more or less like the quantity theory of money $MV(Y,i) = \psi PY$. We can therefore indeed return to (4.14) while specifying for country 2 a specific money demand function:

$$M^*/P^* = Y^{*^{\sigma^*}} \sigma^*/i^* \qquad (4.14'')$$

Thus the real money demand m^* is specified as $Y^{*^{\sigma^*}} \sigma^*/i^*$ where Y^* is foreign real output and i^* the foreign nominal interest rate, which in turn is the sum of the expected inflation rate plus the real interest rate r. The parameters σ and σ' stand for the apparent income elasticity of the demand for money and the implicit interest responsiveness of the demand for money, respectively. However, we will show that in a long-term perspective, σ^* and $\sigma^{*'}$ are not really the income elasticity of the demand for money and the domestic real interest rate, respectively. Assuming (with K^*, A^*, and L^* denoting capital, the level of technology and labour input) a Cobb–Douglas production function abroad, we have:

$$Y^* = K^{*^{\beta^*}}(A^*L^*)^{1-\beta^*} \qquad (4.15)$$

Moreover, as we assume that factors are rewarded in accordance with the marginal product rule, it holds that:

$$r^* = \beta^* Y^*/K^* \tag{4.16}$$

In the absence of inflation/deflation, we can thus write that the money market equilibrium for country 2 is as follows:

$$M^*/P^* = Y^{*\sigma^*}\sigma^*/(\beta^* Y^*/K^*) = K^* Y^{*\sigma^*-1}\sigma^{*\prime}/\beta^* \tag{4.17}$$

Here we have taken into consideration that $i = r$ and that under profit maximization $r = \beta Y/K$. Taking logarithms we get:

$$\ln P^* = \ln M^* - (\sigma^* - 1)\ln Y^* + (\ln \beta^*/\sigma^{*\prime}) - \ln K^* \tag{4.18}$$

As is obvious, the long-term income elasticity of the demand for money is not σ^* but $\sigma^* - 1$. We can rewrite the equation in per capita terms (actually in efficiency labour units AL) on the right-hand side, and this will be termed true long-term money market equilibrium:

$$\ln P^* = \ln (M^*/A^*L^*) - (\sigma^* - 1)\ln (Y^*/A^*L^*) + (\ln \beta^*/\sigma^{*\prime})$$
$$- \ln (K^*/A^*L^*) - (\sigma^* - 2)\ln (A^*L^*) \tag{4.19}$$

Note that in the case of flexible exchange rates the nominal money supply is exogenous. This is the main case we want to consider further below. The problem looks different under fixed exchange rates (in the case of the AC this largely corresponds to the situation of moving to the European Exchange Rate Mechanism II).

If we assume that savings $S = sY$, no population growth, a zero rate of capital depreciation and that technological progress rate $(dA/dt)/A = a$ is exogenous, we get – with $y' =: Y/(AL)$ and $k' =: K/(AL)$ and # for steady state – the standard neoclassical steady state solution, namely $y'\# = (s/a)^{\beta/1-\beta}$ and $K/(AL) = k'\# = (s/a)^{1/1-\beta}$. Thus it is obvious that in the long-term demand for money, the savings rate and the progress rate will enter into play. The interest elasticity of money should be zero. If empirical analysis on the long-term money demand finds a significant impact of r, it effectively confuses r^* and r, that is the condition $r = r^*$! (In an inflationary world one may, of course, have to consider the inflation rate as an additional variable determining the demand for money). Only in the case that one assumes that the savings rate depends on the interest rate would long-term money-market equilibrium depend on the interest rate.

In the case that monetary policy maintains a constant m''^*#(with $m''^* =: M^*/(A^*L^*)$), we get:

$$\ln P^* = \ln m''^*\# - \{[1 + (\sigma^* - 1)\beta]/(1 - \beta)\}\ln (s^*/a^*) + (\ln \beta^*/\sigma^{*\prime})$$
$$- (\sigma^* - 1)\ln (A^*L^*) + \ln (A^*L^*) \tag{4.20}$$

Long-term equilibrium is therefore a positive function of the central bank's target money stock m'. Assuming that the apparent income elasticity of the demand for money (σ) is smaller than unity, the price level is a negative function of the level of technology and of the size of the labour force. Moreover, it is a negative function of the ratio of the savings rate to the progress rate, provided that $((1 + (\sigma^* - 1)\beta^*)/(1 - \beta^*))$ is positive. Note that the price level is stationary only if labour input declines at the same growth rate as the level of technology rises or if the apparent income elasticity of the demand for money is unity. The long-term expected price level depends only on exogenous parameters, in particular the savings rate and the progress rate.

In an open economy we may assume – now considering the world from a country 1 perspective – that savings $S = s(Y + q^*r^*F^{n**}/P^*)$, where F^{n*} is nominal net claims on the rest of the world. Hence $q^*r^*F^{n**}/P^*$ is interest income accruing in terms of domestic goods. We assume that net real foreign assets q^*F^{n**}/P^* expressed in domestic goods are proportionate to Y. Defining $f^{**\prime} =: q^*F^{n**}/P^*AL = q^*F^{r**}/AL$, assuming that $f^{**\prime} = vy'$ and assuming a constant progress rate in country 1, namely a, and a production function:

$$Y = K^\beta (AL)^{1-\beta} \tag{4.21}$$

we get a steady state value:

$$y'\# = (s(1 + r^*v)/a)^{\beta/1-\beta} \tag{4.22}$$

If we define $F^{r**}/AL = v'$ and assume that households consider v' as a target ratio we can write:

$$y'\# = (s(1 + r^*q^*v')/a)^{\beta/1-\beta} \tag{4.22'}$$

Per capita income is therefore – denoting e' with the Euler number – given by:

$$y\# = A_o e^{\prime at} s(1 + r^*q^*v')/a)^{\beta/1-\beta} \tag{4.22''}$$

Hence the long-term steady-state value of $y'\#$ depends on the RER. Moreover, long-term money-market equilibrium will also depend on the RER, as is obvious if we plug in (4.22) into (4.19'); equation (4.19') is the corresponding equation for the domestic economy:

$$\ln P = \ln m'' - (\sigma - 1)\ln y' + \ln (\beta/\sigma') - \ln k' - (\sigma - 2)\ln (AL) \tag{4.19'}$$

$$\ln P = \ln m'' - \{[1 + (\sigma - 1)\beta]/(1 - \beta)\} \ln (s(1 + r^*q^*v')/a)$$
$$+ (\ln \beta/\sigma') - (\sigma - 2) \ln (AL) \qquad (4.19'')$$

If we assume for simplicity's sake that r^*q^*v'/a is close to zero we may use the approximation that $\ln (1 + r^*q^*v^*)/a) \approx r^*q^*v'/a$. A rise in the RER – hence a real depreciation – will increase the price level if $(1 + (\sigma - 1)\beta) < 0$. This now points to an empirical issue.

Real exchange rate, growth path and steady state

Let us get back to (4.22'). A real depreciation will raise the level of the growth path. This implication is, however, not robust if we assume that the progress rate depends negatively on q^*, for example, if we assume that imported licences or technology intensive intermediate products play an important role for the country being considered. Then we may state the hypothesis (with a_1 denoting the progress rate in a closed economy):

$$a = a_1 - B''q^*; \text{assumption: } a_1 \neq B''q^* \qquad (4.23)$$

where B'' is a positive parameter related to v'

We now also get an ambiguous result with respect to the impact of q^* on the price level (see 4.19''). It still holds that the level of the growth path is positively influenced by q^* (see 4.22'). However, the growth rate is negatively influenced and the sum of both effects on real per capita income will become negative after some critical time $t = t'$. We have a quasi-endogenization of growth and the progress rate, respectively, since from a traditional small-country perspective the RER – in a world in which only tradables exist – is exogenous. This, however, is no longer true if there are non-tradables and differentiated tradables. For every product variety sold in the world market, increasing exports will correspond to a fall in the price of the respective product; this problem will be neglected for now. Rather we turn to the accumulation dynamics of foreign assets, where an important aspect to consider is that $dF^{n**}/dt = r^*F^{n**} + PX/e - P^*J$ so that:

$$(dF^{n**}/dt)/P^* = r^*F^{r**} + X/q^* - J = r^*F^{r**} + xY/q^* - jY \qquad (4.24)$$

$$(dF^{r**}/dt)/F^{r**} = r^* + x(Y/q^*)/F^{r**} - jY/F^{r**} = r + x/v - jq^*/v \qquad (4.25)$$

In the next section we take a closer look at the RER from a medium-term perspective, where the link between the RER and investment will be considered. Before we turn to this aspect let us briefly consider the case of an open economy with foreign direct investment inflows and a production function where real money balances and the ratio of per capita imports $j' = J/(AL)$ and export intensity $x' = X/(AL)$ enter the production function:

$$Y = K^\beta (AL)^{1-\beta}(J/AL)^{\beta'}(X/AL)^{\beta''}(m/AL)^{\beta'''} \qquad (4.26)$$

The specific assumption here is that the output effect of imported intermediates/imported machinery and equipment – only those should be included in J here – is diluted if there are more workers in efficiency units. This mechanism could be associated with learning-by-doing in the sense that importing, say machinery, brings a one-off productivity increase for workers dealing with sophisticated imports. If one assumes that imported machinery and equipment is employed with a lag of one period, the current import J would also show up in a higher K. A similar reasoning holds with respect to $X/(AL)$ to the extent that one assumes that X/AL is a measure of the exposure of workers to world market dynamics. It is debatable whether or not m or $m' =: m/(AL)$ – or m/L – should enter the production function; only empirical analysis can solve the issue. Here we use m', as one may argue that liquidity on a per capita basis is relevant for saving transaction costs and actually contributing to labour productivity. Finally, note that in a model with both inward and outward foreign direct investment, one might also have to include the stock of outward FDI, namely to the extent that there is considerable asset-seeking investment, which implies international transfers of technology from subsidiaries to the parent company. Firms in technology-intensive industries which invest abroad – namely in technologically-leading countries so that new technologies can be picked up relatively easily – will benefit from a company wide technology transfer that is not just from the company head-quarters to the subsidiary but also from the subsidiary back to the parent company.

Instead of using $J/AL =: j'$ and $X/AL = x'$ in the production function, one might chose a production function with $1 + j'$ and $1 + x'$ so that zero imports and zero exports imply a consistent output for the case of a closed economy. However, we use j' in the production function on the basis of the assumption that the country considered has become so specialized that it requires indispensable foreign inputs (in empirical investigations only imports of intermediate products and capital goods should be considered). For the sake of simplicity, we also use x' and not $(1 + x')$.

One may assume that real money balances enter the production function through a positive external effect of households using money in all transactions in the goods market. Therefore,

$$y' = k'^\beta j'^{\beta'} x'^{\beta''} m'^{\beta'''} \qquad (4.27)$$

The accumulation dynamics is given by:

$$dk'/dt = s(1 - b\beta)k'^\beta j'^{\beta'} x'^{\beta''} m'^{\beta'''} - ak' \qquad (4.28)$$

Here we have assumed that foreign investors have share b of the capital stock; and as capital income is βY, the national income is GDP minus $b\beta Y$. Savings S is proportionate to national income and therefore we have $S = sY(1 - b\beta) = s'Y$. As we assume $J/AL = j(q^*)Y/AL$ and $X/AL = x'(q^*)Y^*/AL$ or more conveniently $X/AL = x'(q^*)y'^*A^*L^*/AL$ so that we get:

$$y'\# = s(1 - b\beta)j'^{\beta'}y'^{\beta'}x'^{\beta''}y'^{*^{\beta''}}(A^*L^*/AL)^{\beta''}m'^{\beta'''}/(n + \delta + a)^{\beta/1-\beta} \qquad (4.29)$$

If one were to impose a strict long-term trade balance requirement one might want to impose in (4.28) the long-term equilibrium condition that $X = q^*J$ so that $x' = q^*j'$, which, however, is not done here.

Taking into account the money market equilibrium condition (4.19') in an appropriate way, namely $m' = y'^{1/\beta+(\sigma-1)}(AL)^{\sigma-1} \ \sigma/\beta$, we obtain $\Omega' =: (A^*L^*/AL)$:

$$y'\# = s(1 - b\beta)j'^{\beta'}y'^{\beta'}x'^{\beta''}y'^{*^{\beta''}}\Omega'^{\beta''}y'^{(1/\beta+(\sigma-1))\beta'''}(AL)^{(\sigma-1)\beta'''}(\sigma/\beta)^{\beta'''}/$$
$$(n + \delta + a))^{\beta/1-\beta} \qquad (4.30)$$

The implicit solution for the steady-state output therefore is

$$y\#^{'1-(1/\beta+(\sigma-1))\beta'''-\beta''} = s(1 - b\beta)j'^{\beta'}x'^{\beta''}y'^{*^{\beta''}}\Omega'^{\beta''}(AL)^{(\sigma-1)\beta'''}(\sigma/\beta)^{\beta'''}/$$
$$(n + \delta + a)^{\beta/1-\beta} \qquad (4.31)$$

$$y\#' = \{s(1 - b\beta)j'^{\beta'}x'^{\beta''}y'^{*^{\beta''}}\Omega'^{\beta''}(AL)^{(\sigma-1)\beta'''}(\sigma/\beta)^{\beta'''}/$$
$$(n + \delta + a)^{\beta/1-\beta}\}^{1/1-(1/\beta+(\sigma-1))\beta'''-\beta''} \qquad (4.32)$$

We will assume that $b\beta$ is close to zero so that $\ln(1 - b\beta) \approx b\beta$. If we take logarithms and define $\beta\# := 1/(\beta/(1 - \beta))(1 - (1/\beta) + (\sigma - 1))\beta''' - \beta'')$ we have a testable production function, namely for per capita income $y =: Y/L$:

$$\ln y = \beta\# \ln s - \beta\# b\beta + \beta\#\beta' \ln j + \beta\#\beta'' \ln x + \beta\#\beta'' \ln y'^* + \beta\#\beta'' \ln(A^*L^*)$$
$$+ \beta\#((\sigma - 1)\beta''' - \beta'')\ln(AL) + \beta\#\beta''' \ln(\sigma/\beta) - \beta\#(n + \delta + a) + at \qquad (4.33)$$

Taking a look at (4.32) we can see that the level of the growth path positively depends on the effective savings rate s', x', y'^* and the relative technology level (A^*L^*/AL); note that the y'^* variable effectively reflects the impact of exports. The steady state equilibrium output per capita – in efficiency units – is therefore a positive function of the income elasticity of the demand for money provided that $\sigma < 0$. As regards the impact of q^* one has to consider $b(q^*)$, $x'(q^*)$ and $j'(q^*)$, which is not unambiguous. Only empirical research can give a clear answer. The growth rate per capita income $y = Y/L$ is a, and one could consider how foreign direct investment, government expenditures (consumption vs. R&D promotion) and trade will affect the progress rate, which raises many new interesting issues. We will pick up the issue of government expenditures and discuss its impact on the level of growth and growth itself.

An interesting refinement is to assume that $S = sY(1 - b\beta)(1 - u)(1 - \tau)$, where u is the structural unemployment rate and τ the income tax rate. Then for y' we get the following steady state:

$$y\#' = \{s(1 - b\beta)(1 - u)(1 - \tau)j'^{\beta'}x'^{\beta''}y'^{*\beta''}\Omega'^{\beta''}(AL)^{(\sigma-1)\beta'''}(\sigma/\beta)^{\beta'''}/$$

$$(n + \delta + a))^{\beta/1-\beta}\}^{1/1-(1/\beta+(\sigma-1))\beta'''-\beta''}$$ (4.34)

We can thus consider the impact of unemployment and the income tax rate – both a higher tax rate and a higher unemployment rate will reduce the level of the growth path – as well as that of j' and x' on the level of the growth path. Moreover, we can also discuss the effects of the unemployment rate and the tax rate – making specific assumptions as to how tax revenues are used (public consumption vs. R&D financing) – on the growth rate.

Finally, we should take into account the requirement that in the long term the current account must be balanced. For the simple case of no foreign direct investment we have:

$$XP = eP^*J$$ (4.35)

We will assume that:

$$X = j^*(q^*)Y^*$$ (4.36)

$$J = j(q^*)Y$$ (4.37)

Therefore we get – while multiplying the left-hand side of (4.35) by $A^*L^*/[A^*L^*]$ and the right-hand side by $AL/[AL]$ – the equation $XP = eP^*J$ or

$$j^*Y^*P = eP^*jY$$ (4.35')

Thus we obtain:

$$[A^*L^*]j^*Y^*P/[A^*L^*] = ALeP^*jY/[AL]$$ (4.35'')

$$[A^*L^*]/[AL] = q^*jy'/j^*y^*$$ (4.37)

Note that there is a relation between j' and j since $J/(AL) =: j' = jy'$; this applies in a similar way to the foreign country, namely $j'^* =: x' = j^*y'^*$.

Replacing in equation 4.17 the expression $\Omega' =: A^*L^*/AL$ from equation 4.23 we get:

$$y'\# = s(1 - b\beta)j^{\beta'}y'^{2\beta'}x'^{\beta''}y'^{*\beta''}[q^*jy'/j^*y^*]^{\beta''}y'^{(1/\beta+(\sigma-1))\beta'''}(AL)^{(\sigma-1)\beta'''}e'^{\beta'''\sigma/\beta}/$$
$$(n + \delta + a))^{\beta/1-\beta} \tag{4.30'}$$

Therefore we can write,

$$y'\# = s(1 - b\beta)j'^{\beta'}y'^{\beta'+\beta''}x'^{\beta''}y'^{*2\beta''}[q^*j/j^*]^{\beta''}y'^{(1/\beta+(\sigma-1))\beta'''}(AL)^{(\sigma-1)\beta'''}e'^{\beta'''\sigma/\beta}/$$
$$(n + \delta + a))^{\beta/1-\beta} \tag{4.30''}$$

We can thus derive a similar equation to equation 4.21 where the elasticity ψ' of y' with respect to the modified expression $\{...\}$ is higher than in equation 4.21; note that we make the assumption that y'^* actually is foreign steady state per capita income in efficiency units. Moreover, one can see that the elasticity of $y'\#$ with respect to the RER will also have to consider the expression $[q^*j(q^*)/j^*(q^*)]^{\beta''}$, which reflects a modified Marshall–Lerner impact. The overall effect of q^* on y' can, however, not be assessed without considering that b, j' and j' also are a function of q^*. The bottom line is that one may consider allowing for a permanent trade balance surplus in our model with asymmetric foreign direct investment and this leads to a minor modification:

$$j^*Y^*P = eP^*jY + b\beta YP \tag{4.35'}$$

On the right-hand side we have nominal imports plus nominal dividends accruing to the foreign parent companies. Obviously we can write:

$$j^*Y^* = [q^*j + b\beta]Y \tag{4.38}$$

It also is debatable whether or not an adequate import function should not read $J = jZ$ (with national income $Z =: Y - b\beta Y$); and an adequate export function $X = jZ^* = jY^* + b\beta Y/q^*$.

Investment, real exchange rate and employment

As is well-known, the RER ($q^* = eP^*/P$) has an impact upon the trade balance, although the RER will also affect foreign direct investment, as was emphasized for the case of imperfect capital market by Froot and Stein (1991). Foreign investment inflows in the recipient country – say an EU accession country or a newly industrializing economy – can be expressed as a share ψ in overall investment, where $\psi(q^*)$; the partial derivative of ψ with respect to q^* is positive since a depreciation of the host country's currency effectively makes it easier for foreign investors to be successful in mergers and acquisitions. We thus assume that the overall investment output ratio I/Y is a positive function of the RER (in empirical analysis a positive correlation between I/Y will also catch the impact of improving net export expectations on the side of investors). Assuming profit maximization in an open economy in the form that the marginal product of capital Y_K is equal to the foreign real interest rate r^* we can write for the growth rate of real output:

$$g_Y = (I/Y)r^* \tag{4.39}$$

Denoting the investment output ratio as $z = z(q^*)$ and recalling Verdoorn's Law, namely that the growth rate (g) of labour productivity Y/L is a positive function of the growth rate of output (Q and Q' are positive parameters), we have:

$$g_{Y/L} = Q' + Q''g_Y \tag{4.40}$$

According to Verdoorn's Law, the growth rate of employment will be a positive function of output growth:

$$g_L = -Q' + [1 - Q'']g_Y; \tag{4.41}$$

Hence

$$g_L = -Q' + [1 - Q'']z(q^*)r^* \tag{4.42}$$

If we assume that the parameter Q' is a positive function of the productivity-wage lag – meaning the time it takes for the real wage to fully catch up with marginal labour productivity Y_L (the long-term equilibrium values are denoted by #) – then the marginal product is proportionate ($1 - \beta$ is a parameter in the interval 0.1) to the average labour productivity ($Y_L = (1 - \beta)y$; β is the output elasticity of capital):

$$g_L = -Q' + Q''([y\#/w\#]/[y/w])z(q^*)r^* \tag{4.43}$$

The parameter $Q''' =: 1 - Q''$ thus depends positively on the steady state productivity–wage ratio relative to the current productivity–wage ratio. Hence outside the steady state – according to which $(1 - \beta)y$ would be equal to the real wage rate w – the growth rate of labour demand will be a negative function of the current real wage rate and a positive function of per capita income y. An interesting case is to assume that Q''' – we have assumed Q'' to be smaller than unity – follows an inverted logistical adjustment path as y/w approaches $y\#/w\#$.

Figures 4.3–4.7 show the growth rate of employment and the annual change of investment/GDP ratio for the EU15 countries, Germany, Hungary, Poland and the Czech Republic.

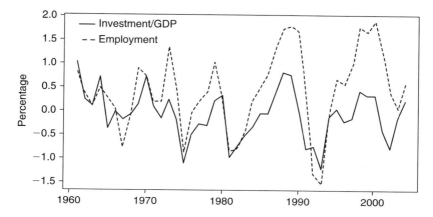

Figure 4.3 EU15: growth rate of employment and annual change of investment/GDP ratio

Notes: Until 1991 growth rates of Western Germany; since 1992 Unified Germany, also in E15 aggregates.

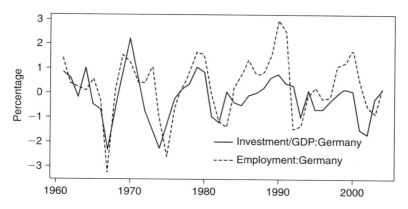

Figure 4.4 Germany: growth rate of employment and annual change of investment/ GDP ratio

Notes: Until 1991 growth rates of Western Germany; since 1992 Unified Germany, also in E15 aggregates.

Technology, exchange rate changes and the relative tradable price

In the following analysis we will take a closer look at the role of technological progress – while sectoral capital stocks are assumed to be given in the short term – which, for simplicity we assume to only occur in the tradables sector (T). Tradables and non-tradables are gross substitutes on the demand side and the supply side. There is a technology shift parameter in the tradables

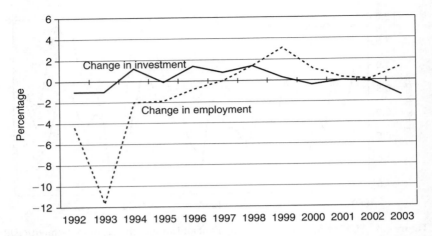

Figure 4.5 Hungary: growth rate of employment and annual change of investment/GDP ratio
Source: *Transition Report*, EBRD, various issues.

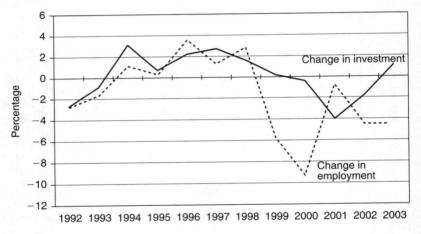

Figure 4.6 Poland: growth rate of employment and annual change of investment/GDP ratio
Source: *Transition Report*, EBRD, various issues.

market, namely A. In addition, the demand for tradables is assumed to negatively depend on the relative price of non-tradables ($P^N/P^T =: \phi$) and positively on the real money balances M/P – a proxy for wealth. M denotes the nominal money supply and P the price level. We assume that the quality of N-goods is given and does not change, but the quality index Q of tradables could change through product innovations in the tradables sector. Hence the

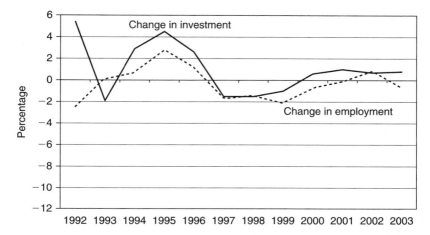

Figure 4.7 Czech Republic: growth rate of employment and annual change of investment/GDP ratio

Source: *Transition Report*, EBRD, various issues.

hedonic price index is given by $P = P^{N\alpha}P^{T1-\alpha}/Q = \phi^{1-\alpha}P^{T}/Q$; the parameter α is in the interval 0.1. Due to arbitrage, we have $P^{T} = e\lambda'P^{T*}$ where e is the nominal exchange rate, λ' is a parameter reflecting trading costs (before full regional integration $\lambda' > 1$, full integration $\lambda' = 1$). Supply in both sectors depends on ϕ and labour as well as on capital stocks.

We can state a straightforward equilibrium condition for the tradables sector, namely tradables supply $T = T'$ where T' denotes tradables demand. Any excess supply in the tradables sector is equivalent to a current account surplus since we are considering a small open economy. Equilibrium in the non-tradables market is given by the equality of non-tradables supply N' and non-tradables demand $N' = N''(\dots) + G$ where $N''(\phi, \tau, M/P)$ is the private sector demand for non-tradables and G government consumption of non-tradables; τ denotes the tax rate. Note that the nominal exchange rate e enters the demand for both goods since M/P can be written as $M/(\phi^{1-\alpha}e\lambda'P^{T*}/Q)$ (see Fig. 4.8). The initial equilibrium is determined by the intersection of the *NN* curve – which portrays equilibrium in the non-tradables markets – and the *TT* curve, which portrays equilibrium in the tradables sector – as well as a balanced current account. Technological progress in the tradables sector, that is a rise in the supply parameter A, will shift the *TT*-curve upwards (TT_1) so that there is a rise in the relative non-tradables price and a nominal depreciation. The price level remains constant if the nominal appreciation rate $-g_e = (1 - \alpha)g_\phi$ where g denotes growth rates. A given price level P_o is here indicated simply by the curve $\phi = (QP_o/P^{T*}e)^{1/(1-a)}$; the PP_o line indicates a given price level in ϕ-e space. Thus it depends on the slope of the *NN* curve whether or not technological progress in the T-sector brings about a fall or a rise in the price level. If the nominal wage is inflexible, a falling price level will bring about classical unemployment, which in the context of empirical analysis should not be misinterpreted as technological unemployment.

If there are no downward wage flexibility points below the PP line, an excess supply in the labour market is indicated. If the composition of tradables is increasingly characterized by product innovations, the tradables supply will become less price elastic as a higher share of product innovations typically will require more specialization and indeed higher sunk costs on the tradables supply side. Moreover, the demand for tradables becomes less price elastic; that is $\partial T'/\partial \phi$ will fall and the slope of the TT curve will rise. Hence a depreciation will bring about a higher current account than previously. This is somewhat surprising as one might think that a lower relative price elasticity makes the trade balance (or the current account) less price sensitive. However, one has to take into account that a rise in the relative price level of non-tradables will cause less supply-switching on the supply side of the economy.

An expansionary fiscal policy in the sense of raising G would shift the NN curve to the right and hence bring about a higher relative non-tradables price and a depreciation of the currency. A fall in trading costs would shift the NN curve upwards and the TT curve downwards, which in all cases would bring about a nominal depreciation, while the effect on the relative price of non-tradables is unclear. An expansionary fiscal policy in the form of a cut in the tax rate τ would bring about a rightward shift of TT and an upward shift of NN. In the lower part (b) of Figure 4.8 we have drawn – for an exogenous expected exchange rate $E(e_1)$ – the interest parity line according to $i = i^* + E(e_1) - e/e$.

The short-term impact of an expansionary monetary policy would be a fall in the nominal interest rate and hence a nominal and real depreciation. As prices are assumed to be sticky, there would be a price reaction only in the medium term. An expansionary monetary policy therefore moves the economy (see panel (a), from point E_o to point F' so that we have an excess supply in the tradables market – with a temporary current account improvement – and an excess supply in the N market. The rise in the real money stock shifts the NN curve and the TT curve to the right and finally will also raise the price level (which implies that the long-term rightward shift of NN and TT will be smaller than in the medium term). Hence we get a new real equilibrium point, which might be between E_o and F'. Assuming that money-market equilibrium can be written as $M = V'(i)PK$, a rise in M will shift the PP-line upwards; a rise in i dampens the shift.

The approach is more complex if we consider the Hansen and Röger (2000) model. In it, the RER is determined through the intersection point of the domestic equilibrium line and the foreign equilibrium line. Consumption is assumed to depend positively on real income Y and negatively on the gap between the desired stock of wealth (F) and actual real financial wealth f.

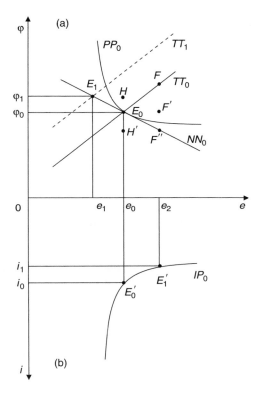

Figure 4.8 Equilibrium in the (a) tradables market (*TT*) and non-tradables market (*NN*) and interest parity (b); model can track fiscal and monetary policy and supply shocks

Tradables supply is T, demand T'; $T(\phi, A, K^T) = T'(\phi, \tau, M/P)$; with $P^N/P^T =: \phi$;
$M = PV(i)K$; $P = \phi^{1-\alpha}P^T/Q$
Non-tradables equilibrium : $N(\phi, K^N) = N''(\phi, \tau, M/P) + G$; arbitrage: $P^T = e\lambda P^{T*}$;
Interest parity $i = i^* + E_1(e) - e/e$

It also depends negatively on the real interest rate r relative to the long-term equilibrium level $r\#$ (in a small open economy equal to r^*). Interest parity together with the domestic equilibrium condition gives a differential equation in q. Setting $dq/dt = 0$ and $df/dt = 0$ gives two equilibrium lines which jointly determine the equilibrium solution.

There is one particular instability area in part (a) of Figure 4.8, namely between the *PP* curve and the *NN* curve (starting in point E_o: the area where NN_0 is written). We observe in this area both an excess supply in the goods market and an upward real wage pressure – at a given nominal wage – so that the risk of unemployment is quite high, unless workers who lost their jobs in the N-sector easily find new jobs in the T-sector, which in turn would have to generate a rather high trade balance surplus. If there is product innovation in the tradables sector both the TT curve and the NN curve will become steeper.

4.3   Real exchange rate dynamics and economic effects

Real exchange rate and trade

The rise in the RER has effects in transition countries. It affects:

- The volume of imports whose growth is reinforced as imported goods become cheaper.
- The volume of exports whose dynamics are dampened – this does not exclude high export growth to the extent that domestic firms show a rising export orientation or that subsidiaries of foreign multinationals increase exports.
- With standard price elasticity assumptions there will be a deterioration of the trade balance, which could be reinforced by relatively high growth over time; as one can write, net exports (X') of goods and services as a function of the RER (with $\partial X'/\partial q < 0$), domestic demand Y (with $\partial X'/\partial Y < 0$), foreign demand Y^* (with $\partial X'/\partial Y^* > 0$), the domestic production potential Y'(with $\partial X'/\partial Y' > 0$) and the foreign production potential $Y^{*'}$ (with $\partial X'/\partial Y^{*'} < 0$), it is clear that demand side effects as well as supply side effects have to be taken into account.
- There is an incentive to upgrade export products in terms of quality and technological sophistication, which is a strategy to offset the upward price pressure from the appreciation of the currency.

A real appreciation – according to Froot and Stein (1991) – will reduce the influx of foreign direct investment, which implies a long-term deterioration of the current account since the increase in production potential will slow down. This holds at least if one assumes that foreign direct inflows mainly affect the tradables sector; typically FDI inflows will transitorily lead to a current account deficit since there will be major imports of machinery and intermediate produces; often the subsidiary will use the same equipment as the parent company. In the long term FDI inflows in the tradables sector should raise net exports of goods and services as firms will increasingly sell products not only in the host country market but in world markets as well.

Real exchange rate and growth: standard and new growth theory

In all industrialized countries, achieving sustained economic growth in the sense of a long-term increase in output or output per capita is a crucial goal.

From a neoclassical perspective, the basic growth models of Solow (1970) emphasize the role of the production function – and the respective input factors of capital and labour – as well as the savings rate. Growth is modelled as a steady-state equilibrium phenomenon characterized by accumulation dynamics for capital and certain parameters of the utility function (Dixit, 1976). Modern growth theory has to some extent added emphasis on the role of human capital formation (Lucas, 1988), but the mechanics of the basic neoclassical growth model can be retained if one interprets capital as human capital or skilled labour.

Technological progress

If one assumes that savings $S = sY$, a stationary population and that savings S equals investment $I = dK/dt$ while there is labour-augmenting Harrod-neutral progress in the production function so that output $Y = K^\beta [AL]^{(1-\beta)}$, we obtain – with a denoting of the exogenous growth rate of $A(t)$ – a slightly modified equation for the accumulation dynamics of $k' =: K/[AL]$ where k' is dubbed capital per efficiency unit of labour:

$$dk'/dt = sk'^\beta - ak' \tag{4.44}$$

We might further refine this equation by introducing population growth (growth rate n), which leads to $[a + n]k'$ as the second right-hand side term in the equation for the accumulation dynamics:

$$dk'/dt = sk'^\beta - [a + n]k' \tag{4.45}$$

The solution of this Bernoullian differential equation is (with C_o to be determined from the initial conditions and e' denoting the Euler number; see Appendix):

$$k'(t) = \left\{ C_o e'^{-[a+n](1-\beta)t} + [s/[a + n]] \right\}^{1/1-\beta} \tag{4.46}$$

Clearly, there is a convergence for k' as long as $\beta < 1$. Here, it should be added that this applies as long as the growth rate n is not critically negative, that is the shrinkage speed of the population must not exceed a – obviously a problem which a priori cannot be dismissed in the case of ageing societies with declining populations.

The steady state value for k' is:

$$k'\# = [s/[a + n]]^{1/1-\beta} \tag{4.47}$$

Per capita consumption in the steady state is given by the difference of per capita output and investment per capita (I/L), that is $C/[AL] = f(k') - [I/L]\#$;

as [I/L]# is equal to $(n + a)k$ maximizing per capita consumption requires –
with $c' =: C/[AL]$ as a necessary condition:

$$dc'/dk' = f'(k') - (n + a) = 0 \qquad (4.48)$$

$$f'(k'\#) = n + a \qquad (4.49)$$

Let us point out one important aspect: in the case of a Cobb–Douglas production function the marginal product of capital is given by $f'(k') = \beta k'^{\beta-1}$. If one
assumes that firms also maximize profits and hence $f'(k') = r$, the optimum
growth policy is defined by the condition:

$$r = \beta k'^{\beta-1} = a + n \qquad (4.50)$$

Therefore,

$$k'^{opt} = \{\beta/[a + n]\}^{1/1-\beta} \qquad (4.50')$$

Obviously this coincides with (47) only if $s = \beta$. Since β in industrialized countries is roughly 1/3 and since savings ratios in most OECD countries are only
around 20 it seems that the major challenge for a government interested in
maximizing long-term per capita consumption is indeed to raise the national
savings rate. From an empirical perspective it is, however, unclear the extent
to which β changes in the course of technological development. As regards
the expansion of the digital 'New Economy', one may anticipate that the β,
the production elasticity of capital, will increase.

We can also add capital depreciation at rate δ so that the second right-
hand term in the above equation becomes $[a + n + \delta]k'$. This will not affect
the mechanics of the model in any critical way. All this is in the framework
of standard textbook growth analysis (see for example Jones, 1998), and is
indeed a good starting point for some theoretical progress and certain refine-
ments and theoretical innovations. Before we take a look at those it is useful
to briefly recall some key insights from the optimum growth theory in the
traditional sense, namely of neoclassical growth models that have been used
to derive optimum growth policies (Phelps, 1961; Weizsäcker, 1962). In those
models, government can achieve maximum per capita consumption if the
savings rate is manipulated in a certain way. In an economy with a constant population growth rate (n), profit-maximizing firms, no technological
progress and zero capital depreciation, the optimum growth policy is characterized by the equality of n and the real interest rate r. Since output growth
in the steady state is equal to n, the implication is that the growth rate of
output is equal to r. Grossman and Helpman (1991) have made broad analytical progress in growth modelling, although the issue of optimum growth
was not picked up on. Aghion and Howitt (1998) presented new ideas about
endogenous (new) growth, emphasizing in particular the role of innovation.

The result in a model in which consumers discount utility – thus going beyond the traditional approach – is not much different since maximizing the welfare function F (with U denoting Utility relevant for an integral from to infinity, per capita consumption c', e' the Euler number and ρ the rate of time preference) to be maximized is:

$$F = \int U(c_t')e'^{-\rho t}dt \tag{4.51}$$

subject to $dk'/dt = f(k') - c' - (n+a)k'$ which gives – with denoting the current-value shadow price – the Hamiltonian:

$$H = \int U(c_t')e'^{-\rho t}dt + \lambda\left[f(k') - c' - (n+a)k'\right] \tag{4.52}$$

The optimality conditions ($\partial H/\partial c' = 0$ and $\partial H/\partial k' = -d\lambda/dt$) give the Ramsey rule:

$$r = -d\ln U'(c')/dt + \rho + n + a \tag{4.53}$$

In the steady state – where c' is constant and hence the growth rate of the marginal utility U' is zero – we thus get:

$$r = \rho + n + a \tag{4.54}$$

As we are not so much interested in the role of the time preference we will not rely on the complex Hamiltonian approach. Rather, a simple graphical model is sufficient for bringing out the main critical results. The reader interested in the role of time preference can replace n in the relevant steady-state condition through $n + \rho$ if he wants to highlight the role of ρ. One may also note that adjusting the utility function in a way which contains both c' and k' – or more generally wealth – gives only a minor modification. The optimum steady state $k#$ rises in comparison with traditional optimum growth approaches.

In the subsequent analysis, we are initially interested in endogenizing technological progress. The following section takes a closer look at some key issues of endogenous growth and proceeds with combining optimum growth approaches and endogenous growth modelling. We will also consider the role of long-term relative price changes in the context of technological progress. The analysis presented then leads to several interesting policy conclusions related both to growth and innovation policy. The main conclusions clearly go beyond the standard analysis in the literature and basically suggest considerable changes in economic policy in both advanced and catching-up countries.

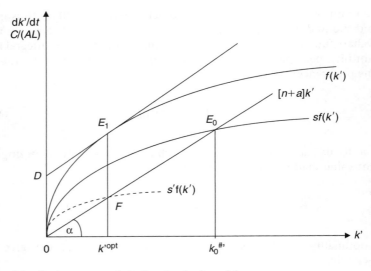

Figure 4.9   Optimum growth in the standard model

Optimum endogenous growth

The standard optimum growth literature of Phelps (1961) and Weizsäcker (1962) has established for the case of a closed economy that within a neoclassical growth model, optimum growth – defined by maximization of steady state per capita consumption C/L – is determined by the condition that in the absence of technological progress, the growth rate of the population n is equal to the marginal product of capital Y_K. Moreover, in a world of implicit profit maximization and zero capital depreciation, this also implies that the real interest rate $r = F'(k) = n$, where $F'(k)$ is the marginal product of capital (alternatively we denote the marginal product of capital as Y_K); the function $y = F(k)$ is linear homogenous, $y = Y/L$ is per capita output and $k =: K/L$ capital intensity. From an optimum growth perspective, a government's growth policy should aim to manipulate the savings rate s – establishing a new adequate savings rate s' – in such a way that the intersection point of the curve nk with $sF(k)$ is such that for the respective $k\#$ the slope of the $F(k)$ curve is equal to n. Similarly, if there is Harrod-neutral technological progress, we have a production function $Y/[AL] = f(k')$ where $k' = K/[AL]$.

Graphically, the steady state value $k'\#$ is determined by the intersection of $[n + a]k'$ and the curve $sf(k')$ as shown in point E_0 (Figure 4.9). In the steady state output, Y will grow at the rate $n + a$. Again, governments could consider the topic of optimum growth, namely maximizing consumption per capita in the steady state. As $y = C/[AL] + I/[AL]$, it is clear that point k'^{opt} is the optimum (DE_1 is parallel to the curve $[n + a]k'$), and it will be achieved – see Figure 4.9 – if the government reduces the savings rate to s'. In the implicit case of profit maximization, the optimum is characterized by the equality of r and the marginal product of capital $f'(k')$ and hence by $r = f'(k') = a + n$. Note that in the model profit maximization is introduced here in an *ex post* fashion with no endogenous mechanism driving the economy towards k'^{opt}.

The standard optimum growth approach takes the population growth rate n as given and suggests that governments should adjust the aggregate savings rate s. Indeed governments could do so by adjusting the government budget deficit–GDP ratio in an appropriate way.

Role of government consumption

In the case of a constant Harrod-neutral progress rate a, the mechanics of the neoclassical growth model remain the same as in the basic model. An interesting refinement suggested here is to analyse the role of government consumption G under the simple assumption that $G = \gamma Y$ and that private consumption as well as government consumption are full substitutes while γ negatively affects the progress rate, as we assume:

$$a = a_1(1 - b'\gamma) \tag{4.55}$$

where a_1 is the progress rate that would hold without government consumption and b' is a positive parameter in the interval 0,1. Progress is still exogenous here as γ is exogenous. Ruling out government deficits and therefore taking into account that $\gamma = \tau$ (where τ is the income tax rate), the accumulation dynamics are now given by:

$$dk'/dt = s[1 - \gamma]k'^{\beta} - [a_1(1 - b'\gamma)]k' \tag{4.56}$$

The effect of government consumption on long-term growth and technological progress is negative. However, the effect of γ on the level of the growth path is ambiguous since the steady-state solution is given by:

$$k'\# = \{s[1 - \gamma]/[a_1(1 - b'\gamma)]\}^{1/1-\beta} \tag{4.57}$$

The numerator in the above expression is reduced by rising government consumption so that the $s[1 - \gamma]k'^{\beta}$ curve – in $dk'/dt - k'$ space – bends all the more downward the higher γ is. However, the ray OF (for $\gamma = 0$) showing $[a_1(1 - b'\gamma)]k'$ also rotates downward (see OF' for a certain γ in the interval 0,1), so that $k'\#$ could rise or fall as the consequence of relatively higher government consumption. Our analysis thus raises some interesting questions about the role of government in a neoclassical growth model. For the sake of simplicity, we will assume that the optimum capital intensity is not affected (see Figure 4.10). However, it is clear that the optimum capital stock has increased, as the curve ak' has become flatter (we assume zero population growth). The gap between the natural steady-state capital intensity and optimum capital intensity has narrowed. If narrowing this gap is considered an element of optimal policy, one has an interesting avenue of research. From a political economy perspective, the final outcome will depend on the use of tax revenues. If government spends those revenues in a way which helps to attract more foreign direct investment, in turn leading to a rise in the long-term progress rate, one could not simply argue that introducing taxes has negative economic effects.

Politically optimal growth obviously can diverge considerably from what is optimal in a situation in which perfectly informed rational economic agents are interacting. If governments, in an economy with profit maximization, wants to maximize long-term per capita consumption while ignoring the link between γ and the progress rate the optimum k' is given by the condition:

$$r = [a_1(1 - b'\gamma)] \qquad (4.57')$$

If government expenditures represented pure R&D promotion expenditures, the impact of γ on the progress rate would not be negative, and a positive impact would be expected, which leads (here b'' is the parameter indicating the impact of R&D promotion on the progress rate, and b'' in turn will be linked with FDI, and FDI is a function of the RER) to the following modified optimum growth condition:

$$r = [a_1(1 + b''\gamma)] \qquad (4.57'')$$

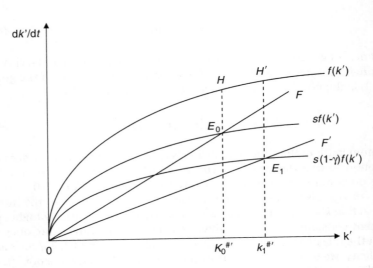

Figure 4.10 Government consumption and the steady state in a neoclassical growth model

he implication obviously is that the optimum steady-state value of k' is educed so that there is a stronger case for government intervention, namely in the following sense. The increased gap between the 'natural' steady state apital intensity and the optimum capital intensity has widened – remember that it still holds that $\gamma = \tau$. Hence, there are good reasons that the overnment intervenes in such a way as to reduce the long-term savings atio. In a short-term Keynesian perspective, a transitory impact of such a neasure would be a rise in output, provided that there is some unemployment in the initial situation. However, these short-term aspects are of minor importance here. It must, however, be emphasized that both in AC and in the EU15 it would be important to focus the policy debate on the issue of optimum growth.

4 Conclusions

heoretical analysis has shown that a real appreciation of the currency – in country catching up economically – can have several major effects (see 'igure 4.11):

- It reduces the costs of capital.
- It reduces foreign direct investment inflows, but has an ambiguous effect on output per capita.
- It stimulates product upgrading in the tradables sectors. However, it is unrealistic to assume that firms can quickly upgrade export products in terms of quality or product innovativeness. The adjustment time or learning phase required typically depends on the general ability of firms to adjust, the level of technological sophistication already acquired (and

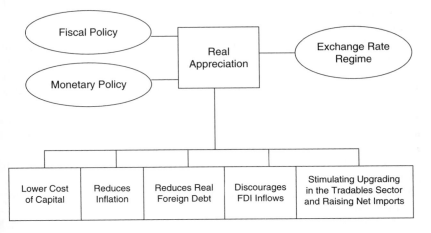

Figure 4.11 Effects of a real appreciation

hence the presence of foreign investors) and the share of skilled work
ers available. A sudden strong real appreciation should be avoided, as th
supply-side responsiveness of firms can cope only with limited exchang
rate pressure. Moreover, as real appreciation tends to reduce foreign direc
investment inflows, phases of sudden and strong real appreciation coul
become a problem for an accession country (and all the more so the highe
initial trade balance deficit is).

- It raises net imports of goods and services in the medium term – after th
  initial negative *J*-curve effect.
- It could affect the price level and the inflation rate, respectively.
- It reduces net foreign debt.

Among the policy implications, governments in poor countries – such a
AC – should stimulate savings and encourage foreign direct investment. I
would also be wise to avoid early fixing of the nominal exchange rate, sinc
a normal rise in the relative price of non-tradables can no longer be achieve
through nominal and real appreciation but only through an increase of th
non-tradables price, which must be stronger than the price increase of th
tradables. That is, combining low inflation rates and the long term increas
of non-tradables prices is difficult to achieve unless one has flexible exchang
rates. There is, however, some risk that flexible exchange rate regimes coul
be associated with temporary overshooting. Since the exchange rate is ar
international relative price, the reason for overshooting dynamics could b
internal or external. Strong and sudden real appreciations should be avoided
If the real appreciation comes not through a fall in the nominal exchange rat
but through a very low inflation rate, this could create serious problems ir
an economy with insufficient downward wage flexibility. Moreover, the rel
ative rise in the non-tradables price to normally expected prices, along witl
a process of economic catching-up, requires a fall in the non-tradables price
which could be difficult to achieve. While foreign direct investment inflow:
are basically a welcome ingredient for economic catching up, government:
in host countries should be careful to avoid unnecessary concentration ten
dencies which could undermine the flexibility and innovativeness needed ir
an open economy exposed to temporary or permanent real appreciation o
its currency.

The EU Eastern enlargement will bring medium-term real appreciation for
the ACs, which will affect foreign direct investment, trade and the current
account. From an EU15 perspective, the CEECs generate pressure for structural change and international outsourcing, on the one hand, while driving
high-wage countries to increasingly specialize in technology-intensive goods
on the other. For the governments of EU15 countries, this could encourage promotion of technological progress through R&D subsidies. From an
optimum growth perspective, both national governments and supranational
EU policy should consider opportunities to bring about optimum growth.

There is clearly a special challenge for the Eurozone due to uniform interest rates The long-term dynamics of the current account, FDI growth and structural change require further analysis. It is not easy to design a consistent economic policy which stimulates the overall growth of EU25 while maintaining economic stability.

The EU would be well-advised to seriously consider the implications of endogenous growth theory and of optimum growth theory. National governments in leading EU countries could indeed try to influence the progress rate, and in the Eurozone achieving optimum growth could be a challenge for cooperation between the national governments of the Eurozone's member countries – adjusting R&D promotion policy adequately – and the ECB with its opportunities to adjust the interest rate. AC should also carefully study the options of an optimum growth policy.

A major challenge for the EU25 is that an efficient modernization and innovation process requires that adjustments in the EU15 – especially in high wage countries – should be structural change towards skill-upgrading and product innovation, which normally go along with a relative rise in relative unit export values (UEV) 'relative' means in comparison to the USA, which is the leading OECD country. In a triangular economic perspective, rising EU15 outsourcing towards AC should strengthen global competitiveness so that EU15 RCAs in the global market should improve in particular in sectors in which EU15 countries have rising imports from AC. Whether the overall development of the EU25's terms of trade will be positive in the medium term is unclear. As regards Germany, it is remarkable that the weighted average unit export value for industrial products stayed flat in the 1990s while that of the USA strongly increased. Hence, the relative German UEV fell considerably (Figure 4.12).

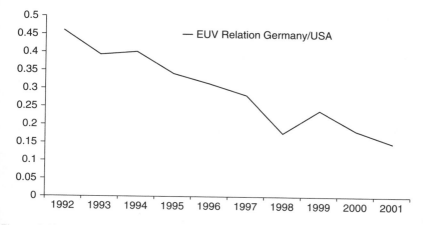

Figure 4.12 Relative unit export value of German industry (Germany relative to USA)
Source: OECD STAN and Comext Database – US Data without NACE 36.

The developments in Germany suggest that it is facing declining profit rates in world markets and might therefore faces an intensified struggle for income (in another words social conflicts between workers and capital owners). If Germany is forced by the interplay of domestic dynamics and global structure change to move more towards less profitable sectors, the German current account balance might improve if import demand is sufficiently elastic. It will in any case be important to conduct further research on European and global economic dynamics in the future.

Appendix

Statistical measures of structural change

According to Stamer (1999), the degree of structural change between the time points or time periods, 1 and 2, can be measured by several indicators, including the following indicators (for output X) if we distinguish sectors $i = 1 \ldots n$:

LILIEN Index (*LI*) (see LILIEN, 1982a, b):

$$LI_{1,2} = \sqrt{\sum_{I=1}^{n} x_{i2} \left(\ln \frac{x_{i2}}{x_{i1}} \right)^2}, \quad x_{i1} > 0, \quad x_{i2} > 0. \tag{4.58}$$

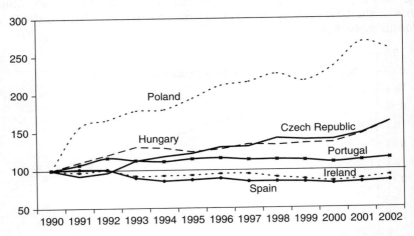

Figure 4.A1 Real effective exchange rate (P/eP^*) dynamics in selected EU countries: Poland, Hungary, Czech Republic, Portugal, Spain and Ireland, 1990–2002

Source: *World Development Indicators*, 2004.

* denote a foreign variable, i.e. price.

The modified LILIEN Index (*MLI*) (see Stamer, 1999, pp. 42–4):

$$MLI_{1,2} = \sqrt{\sum_{I=1}^{n} x_{i1}x_{i2}\left(\ln \frac{x_{i2}}{x_{i1}}\right)^2}, \quad x_{i1} > 0, \quad x_{i2} > 0. \tag{4.59}$$

All indicators mentioned above have advantages and drawbacks. The choice of an indicator has to be made on the basis of the goals of the respective research. For many purposes, the norm of absolute values and/or the Euclidean norm are frequently used measures. A useful indicator as a measure of diversification is the index proposed by LILIEN (1982a). Some drawbacks of this indicator are remedied by the Modified LILIEN Index of Stamer (1999). This, however, comes at the cost of a more complex interpretation.

References

Aghion, P. and P. Howitt (1998) *Endogenous Growth Theory*. Cambridge, Mass.: MIT Press.

Audretsch, D. and P.J.J. Welfens (2002) *Economic Growth and the New Economy in the US and Europe*. Heidelberg and New York: Springer.

Ball, L. (2001) 'Another Look at Long-Run Money Demand', *Journal of Monetary Economics*, 47: 31–44.

Beyer, A. (1998) 'Modelling Money Demand in Germany', *Journal of Applied Econometrics*, 13: 57–76.

Blanchard, O.J. and S. Fischer (1989) *Lectures on Macroeconomics*. Cambridge, Mass.: MIT Press.

Coenen, G. and J.L. Vega (2001) 'The Demand for M3 in the Euro Area', *Journal of Applied Econometrics*, 16: 727–48.

Dixit, A.K. (1976) *The Theory of Equilibrium Growth*. Oxford: Oxford University Press.

Ericsson, N.R. (1998) 'Empirical Modelling of Money Demand', *Empirical Economics*, 23: 295–315.

Jones, C.I. (1998) *Introduction to Economic Growth*. New York: Norton.

Froot, K.A. and J.C. Stein (1991) 'Exchange Rates and Foreign Direct Investment: An Imperfect Capital Markets Approach', *Quarterly Journal of Economics*, 106: 191–217.

Grossman, G.M. and E. Helpman (1991) *Innovation and Growth in the Global Economy*. Cambridge, Mass.: MIT Press.

Hansen, J. and W. Roeger (2000) 'Estimation of Real Equilibrium Exchange Rates', European Commission Economic Papers no. 144, Brussels.

Hayo, B. (1999) 'Estimating a European Money Demand Function', *Scottish Journal of Political Economy*, 46: 221–44.

Lambsdorff, J. (2005) 'The Puzzle with Increasing Money Demand – Evidence from a Cross-Section of Countries', *Kredit und Kapital*, 38: 155–76.

Lilien, D.M. (1982a) 'Sectoral Shifts and Cyclical Unemployment', *Journal of Political Economy*, 90: 777–93.

Lilien, D.M. (1982b) A Sectoral Model of the Business Cycle. Modelling Research Group (mimeo).

Lucas, R.E. (1988) 'On the Mechanics of Economic Development', *Journal of Monetary Economics*, 22: 3–42.

Phelps, E.S. (1961) 'The Golden Rule of Accumulation: A Fable for Growth Man', *American Economic Review*, 51: 638–43.

Solow, R.M. (1970) *Growth Theory: An Exposition*. Oxford: Oxford University Press.

Stamer, M. (1999) *Strukturwandel und Wirtschaftliche Entwicklung in Deutschland, den USA und Japan*, (Structural Change and Economic Development in Germany, the USA and Japan). Aachen: Shaker.

Weizsäcker, C. von (1962) *Wachstum, Zins und optimale Investitionsquote*, (Growth, Interest Rate and Optimal Investment Ratio). Tübingen: Mohr.

Welfens, P.J.J. (1997) 'Privatization, Structural Change and Productivity: Toward Convergence in Europe?' in S. Black (ed.), *Europe's Economy Looks East*. Cambridge: Cambridge University Press, pp. 212–57.

Welfens, P.J.J. (2002) *Interneteconomics.net*. Heidelberg and New York: Springer, 2nd edn forthcoming 2006.

Welfens, P.J.J. and D.Borbèly (2004) 'Exchange Rate Developments and Stock Market Dynamics in Transition Countries: Theory and Empirical Analysis,' Paper presented at CEPS, Brussels, 18–20 November, EIIW Working Paper no. 126.

World Bank (2004) World Development Indicators, CD-Rom.

5
Divergent Growth Rates in Central and Eastern European Countries: An Alternative View

Michael Brandmeier

5.1 Introduction

In Chapter 4, Welfens performs a thorough theoretical analysis of real exchange rates (RER) and their impact on trade, structural change and growth. He also considers aspects of optimum growth. In this commentary we do not focus on his new approach to monetary growth policy in an open economy environment and thus skip the link between process innovation and price level. In this chapter, instead of dipping into a theoretical analysis of RER and its long-term equilibrium (Chapter 4, section 4.2), we focus on the impact of RER on trade, growth and relative tradable prices (section 4.3) and on the assumed relationship between RER and foreign direct investment (FDI) (section 4.2). In section 5.1 we briefly summarize the effects of productivity change on the tradable sector and its effects on the equilibrium combinations of relative prices and nominal exchange rates, and the effects of a real appreciation on the trade balance. We then discuss, in a simple growth model, the argument of Froot and Stein (1991), that an increase in RER (real appreciation of the currency) will tend to discourage FDI. In section 5.2 we develop a model explaining the economic growth of a small open economy, while in section 5.3 we show empirically that there is no clear evidence that the RER plays a significant role in the influx of FDI into Central Europe. Section 5.5 concludes.

5.2 Inflows of foreign direct investment, endogenous growth and real exchange rate dynamics in Central and East European countries

In the model presented in Chapter 4, Welfens assumes that technological progress in the tradable sector occurs through an exogenous increase in the total factor productivity (parameter *A* of a Cobb–Douglas production function). In Figure 4.8 in Welfens the *TT* curve stands for a balanced trade balance and describes the equilibrium combinations of relative prices $\Phi = P^N/P^T$ and the nominal exchange rate e (in price notation) of the tradable goods market. The *TT* curve shifts upwards if A increases exogenously. The positive slope of the *TT* curve in Figure 4.8 results from lower tradable prices P^T if the productivity parameter A increases. The nominal exchange rate e has to increase to create higher foreign demand, to reduce the excess supply of tradables.

The slope of the *TT* curve becomes steeper if the composition of tradable goods production contains more technologically sophisticated products, because the demand for tradable goods of a higher quality is assumed to be less price sensitive.[1]

One can conclude from this model that product innovations in the tradable sector increase the relative price of non-tradables for a given nominal exchange rate e. Secondly, a fall in the trading costs reduces the unstable area (below the *PP* curve and above the *NN* curve for all $e > e_0$), which is signified by excess supply in both goods markets and by upward real wage pressure. One advantage of this model is that it could be used to track fiscal and monetary policy supply shocks simultaneously, if positive trading costs ($\lambda' > 0$), an exogenous technology shift parameter in the tradable sector A and sticky prices are assumed.

In section 4.3, Welfens summarizes the effects of the RER on trade in transition countries: appreciation leads to a deterioration of the trade balance, because import goods become cheaper and export goods more expensive.[2] An appreciation of the domestic currency is an incentive to upgrade export products in terms of quality and thus the exported goods become less price-sensitive. However, it is not empirically confirmed that an appreciation of the currency in transforming countries reduces significantly the amount of influx of FDI, because foreign investors probably do not pay too much attention to recent real exchange rate fluctuations, but look closely either at cheaper locations to set up in business in Central Europe (CE) or seek to increase sales through local production facilities (see section 5.3).

Economic growth textbooks include chapters on alternative theories of endogenous growth (Jones, 2002; Barro and Sala-i-Martin, 2003), focusing on the role of human capital and infrastructure of an economy and the production of intermediate capital goods such as sources for economic growth.

Welfens (2005, pp. 20–34) presents a model explaining the growth impact of RER dynamics in transition countries by including FDI in a growth model that is embedded in a modified neoclassical framework. In this simple two-country model inflows of FDI depend on the RER according to Froot and Stein (1991). Asymmetric FDI will lead to sustained differences in per capita income across countries (Welfens, 1997). Barro *et al.* (1995, p. 104) developed a growth model with partially mobile capital in an open-economy version to explain evidence on conditional convergence at a rate of about 2 per cent per year (Mankiw *et al.*, 1992; Barro, 1991; Levine and Renelt, 1992).

Capital is only partially mobile because borrowing is limited to finance accumulation of physical capital. The accumulation of human capital is not included. Empirically, capital mobility has to be imperfect, because otherwise the predicted rates of convergence for output and capital are infinite. Therefore, small open economies in the transition countries would jump immediately to steady state levels of output, physical capital and human capital per effective worker, if households can borrow and lend at the going interest rate on world capital markets and if goods are tradable internationally, but the labour factor cannot migrate (Barro *et al.*, 1995, p. 109). To avoid this result Barro *et al.* (1995) proposed the introduction of adjustment costs and irreversibility conditions for physical and human capital. The authors restricted borrowing on world markets to finance physical capital accumulation. Instead of introducing assumptions about international financing of human capital formation, Welfens (2005) assumes, following Froot and Stein (1991), that an appreciation of the RER discourages FDI inflows to the former transition countries in Central and Eastern Europe.

In recently published papers on the spillover effects of FDI there is evidence that such spillover appears to be much stronger in relatively high-technology than in relatively low-technology sectors (Keller and Yeaple, 2003, p. 34). To explain this empirical fact one must take into account that FDI inflows, which boost physical capital accumulation in transition countries, are not uniformly distributed across sectors and countries because human capital formation is positively correlated with the technology requirements of production in manufacturing: The more human capital formation is needed for production in one sector to realize an increase in labour productivity, the more spillover impact the FDI has on this industrial sector. Secondly, FDI inflows are almost motivated by labour cost advantages on one hand and by a labour force with sufficient human capital stock on the other side, able to produce a greater variety of human capital-intensive intermediate goods, which fulfil sufficiently high quality standards (Brandmeier, 2005, p. 381).

Endogenous growth models focus on human capital as an important factor for economic growth. The Augmented Solow Model (ASM), of Mankiw *et al.* (1992), asserts that a high level of human capital leads to a higher level of per capita income by assuming exogenous technological progress. Opposing the ASM and the Lucas (1988) Model, which focus on the rate of human capital accumulation as an engine for economic growth, Romer (1990) presented a model which places the locus of long-term growth of economies on the stock of human capital. The Romer model seems to be more appropriate than the other two models because it focuses firstly on human capital as an input factor for the production of an homogenous output good and, secondly, the number of different intermediate capital goods in an economy depends on technology being a non-rival good.

By introducing the FDI inflows as a channel for technology transfers to the new member states (NMS) it seems reasonable to assume monopolistic competition in the production of intermediate goods so that their prices exceed their costs. In extending the Romer Model foreign trade should also be included.[3]

In contrast to the model of Welfens (2005, pp. 21–5), we do not concentrate on the negative relationship between the RER and the volume of FDI inflows into the NMS. Instead of the RER we focus on the relationship between labour costs relative to the labour productivity of the labour force as a more important factor determining FDI inflows into the NMS. Therefore, the variety of balanced growth paths in CEECs can be explained – according to the New Growth Theory – by the differential levels of stock of human capital in these countries. A lower level of human capital means a lower percentage of the labour force that is capable of making use of modern production technologies. Recently published empirical literature on the spillover effects of FDI and R&D on economic growth in transition countries shows that 'regions with a large technology gap would only benefit from technology diffusion [via FDI and R&D channel to increase total factor productivity], if there is a sufficient higher level of educational attainment' (Tondl and Voksic, 2003, p. 22). Furthermore, the FDI stock has the strongest impact on regional growth in Eastern Europe. Tondl and Voksic (2003, p. 22) calculated that double FDI than others leads to 'almost 6 times higher (economic) growth rates (per capita), while general investment has a much lesser impact on growth'.

Resmini (2004, p. 18) confirmed that the impact of Eastern enlargement of the EU is not uniform across regions and sectors. Those sectors with increasing returns to scale, such as chemicals, transport equipment and motor vehicles are those which are most involved in relocation processes. This empirical evidence on where industries relocate and which sectors are most affected by the relocation process shows that the determinants of FDI inflows into CEECs and changes in the trade patterns of manufactured goods have to be taken into account when locating the engines of economic growth.

The traditional Balassa–Samuelson effect (BS-effect) implies that the RER will increase because the ratio of the relative price of non-tradables increases along with a rising per capita income. Frensch (2005, pp. 4–5) presented a monopolistic competition model of trade with product differentiation to show the different behaviour of prices and productivities when tradable goods are differentiated. The author finds that there is a terms of trade effect that is absent in the classic Balassa–Samuelson model with homogenous tradables and non-tradables. Secondly, this terms of trade effect depends negatively on the elasticity of substitution between any pair of industrial products. A higher elasticity of substitution strengthens the BS-effect.

Welfens (2005, p. 17) came up with other reasons for a real appreciation of the currency in the NMS:

- The premium factor h increases, which reflects the impact of relative market size and the size of relatively affluent people in the society.
- The relative price of non-tradables between countries (P^N/P^{N*}) rises more than the relative price of tradables (P^T/P^{T*}) falls in the case of a relatively strong demand shift in favour of the non-tradables sector in the new EU member states.[4]
- The relative price of non-tradables falls less than the relative price of tradables rises, when the relative productivity growth of the non-tradables sector could be stronger in the NMS.

The growth model including FDI in Welfens (2005) consists of a Cobb–Douglas production function with capital K, labour L and a Harrod-neutral progress factor for two countries. Welfens (2005, p. 22) assumed that asymmetric FDI will lead to sustained differences in per capita income across countries. In the model the national income in both countries depends on production Y (respective Y^*) and the share of the capital stock owned by foreign companies. The profits of these foreign companies in one country increase the income of the other country. The savings depend on income Z. Movements in the interest rate r, after the closed and planned economy in CEECs becomes an open market economy, were not addressed in this model.

After deriving a steady state for national income and capital intensity per efficient worker, Welfens (2005) obtained the following condition:

$$\frac{b''}{2b(q)} < s < \frac{b''}{b(q)}$$

with s denoting the savings rate and b'' an exogenous parameter denoting the share of FDI on profits of foreign companies in the NMS. The share of the capital stock owned by foreign companies, which negatively depends on q (which is the RER in price definition of the currency of the new EU member states) is given by $b(q)$. This equation sums up the growth model including FDI and shows that the savings rate in the NMS has to be at a certain interval. Then the economy obtains a higher steady value of capital intensity and national income per capita.

As noted above, the FDI share b of the capital stock is assumed to depend negatively on RER. In this paper we present a similar growth model, which includes the factor intensity of foreign trade patterns and the FDI share in relation to GDP. The model shows that the FDI share corresponds with an increased diversity of foreign trade pattern. The foreign trade pattern of a country with a high FDI share of GDP has the distinction of having a high share of human capital intensive exports to total export volume. It is assumed that the bulk of FDI inflows serves to improve production possibilities in a representative small open economy. The level of FDI inflows does not depend on RER, but on the level of human capital stock in the economy, as in the Romer (1990) model. It is an extension of this model because it incorporates additional features, like the variety of intermediate goods produced in CEECs. Following Frensch and Gaucaite-Wittich (2005, p. 11), the variety of intermediate goods can be measured by product variety, which is 'designed to reflect product differentiation by the country of origin of imports'. We do not use the classification of broad economic categories (BEC), because the BEC distinguishes only between capital and consumer goods. This classification provides no information about the factor intensity of the production of manufactured export and import goods.

Observing the trade pattern of countries with a relatively high FDI share in GDP we also confirm that increasing intra-firm trade often leads to improved quality of export goods, which can be measured by unit values (Borbely, 2005). Assuming that the law of one price does not always hold, a premium factor $h < 1$ explains gaps in product innovativeness between countries (Welfens, 2005, p. 16):

$$P^T = h \cdot eP^T *$$

with p^T = price for tradable goods (the foreign price level is denoted with an asterisk.). The nominal currency rate e is noted in price definition.

Country I shows such a deficit relative to the foreign country II, if it produces a smaller variety and obtains lower unit values for its export goods. The reason for this lies in the fact that the inclusion of a country in CEE in an international production network begins with FDI. The effects of FDI on prices depend on the sector in which the huge bulk of investments are realized: the Balassa–Samuelson effect works if FDI increases labour productivity in the tradable sectors and later on higher wages beyond their labour productivity are also paid in the non-tradable sectors. Welfens (2005, p. 17) showed that the impact of relative market size and income distribution have been influential in the course of economic catching up.

In the next section we present the outline of a simple growth model including FDI inflows into CEECs and the different amounts of export variety patterns in these countries. We derive the equation for a steady state of economic growth of the economy that depends on both variables.

5.3   An endogenous growth model with foreign direct investment and intermediate capital goods production in CEECs

Following Jones (2002, p. 116), the factor capital K can be interpreted as the sum of intermediate capital goods z together with factor labour L

to produce a homogenous good Y:

$$\int_0^{h(t)} z_j(t)dj = K(t) \tag{5.1}$$

The range 0 to $h(t)$ determines the number of intermediate capital goods z, which could be produced in a small open economy. The intermediate capital goods z are partly imported from the EU15. The production function of country i is defined as follows:[5]

$$Y_i = L_i^{1-\alpha} \cdot \int_0^H z_{ij}^\alpha dj \tag{5.2}$$

To include trade in the growth model we assume that the time in accumulating skills is higher in countries that are open to trade (Jones, 2002, p. 136). Therefore, the range of intermediate capital goods expands the larger the export variety pattern of this country is. This assumption takes into account learning effects from imitations of invented new designs or new intermediate goods variety. To keep the model simple we assume that the learning effects are proportional to an increased export variety pattern.

The export variety pattern could be defined as the relative share of human capital intensive exports in the total exports of one country to approximate the relative employment of human capital as an important factor in production of homogenous good Y (Feenstra, 1999). The imported intermediate capital goods z are mainly used for supplying the factor capital for the export industry in small open economies in CEE. Therefore Y_i could be interpreted as the export volume that country i in CEE exports to EU15 countries.[6] The intermediate capital goods z are classified by factor intensities. Therefore, the number of intermediate capital goods h could be approximated empirically by the share of human capital intensively produced exports in CEECs.

By integrating FDI inflows into the model we determine that the number of intermediate capital goods $h(t)$ not only depends on the previous level of human capital h, the years of schooling u, but also on the ability of the small country to attract FDI. We assume, further, a positive spillover impact of FDI on human capital formation through learning skills outside of formal education:

$$\dot{h} = \mu \cdot e^{vu}b^\gamma h^{1-\gamma} \tag{5.3}$$

Following Jones (2002, p. 117), we assume the parameter $\mu > 0$ and $0 < \gamma < 1$. The FDI inflows b are positive and a higher b increases the derivative of h with respect to time. Dividing both sides by h leads to the growth rate of human capital depending on FDI inflows:

$$\frac{\dot{h}}{h} = \mu \cdot e^{vu}\left(\frac{b}{h}\right)^\gamma \tag{5.4}$$

The capital accumulation equation is standard:

$$\dot{k} = s_K y - dk \tag{5.5}$$

with s_k as marginal saving rate and the parameter d taking into account the amount of depreciation of capital. Solving for $\dot{k} = 0$ and the steady state conditions for y (if y is defined as $y = Y/HL$), g_b represents the growth rate of FDI inflows b and n is the growth rate of the labour force L:

$$y^*(t) = \left(\frac{s_K}{n + g_b + d} \right)^{\frac{\alpha}{1-\alpha}} \cdot h^*(t) \tag{5.6}$$

Substituting $\left(\dfrac{h}{b} \right)^* = \left(\dfrac{\mu}{g} \cdot e^{vu} \right)^{1/\gamma}$ in equation (5.6) lead to an equation in which the steady state of economic growth of the economy depends on the steady state of foreign capital inflows into the economy:

$$y^*(t) = \left(\frac{s_K}{n + g + d} \right)^{\frac{\alpha}{1-\alpha}} \cdot \left(\frac{\mu}{g} \cdot e^{vu} \right)^{1/\gamma} \cdot b^*(t) \tag{5.7}$$

In closing the model one needs to explain which factors determine the optimal time path of FDI inflows $b^*(t)$. Instead of arguing that FDI inflows depend on RER, we assume a correlation between FDI stock in several economic sectors and the corresponding unit labour costs, and a significant relationship between the outsourcing volume and the FDI stock. We assume the following unit cost function, which is additive separable:[7]

$$\underset{m,v}{Min} \left[\begin{array}{l} (c_1 - m)(x_1 + v) + (c_2 - m)(x_2 - v) + \tau \cdot v + \theta(x_2 - v) + K(m) + \\ + \lambda(x_2 - v) + T(v) - F \end{array} \right]$$

The parameters c_1 and c_2 denote the unit costs for the production of good Y in EU15 and in a location in CEECs. The turnovers in country 1 or 2 are denoted by x_1 and x_2. The variable v describes intra-firm exports, with $T(v) = tv^2/2$ as transportation costs, depending on intra-firm exports v. The fixed costs are denoted by F. The volume of manager capacity is denoted by m, $\theta(x_2)$, a subvention for production locally in CEECs and $\tau(x_1)$. We assume a linear demand function: $p_i = a_i - x_i$, $i = 1$ (EU15), $i = 2$ (CEECs).

After deriving the total unit cost function of the multinational firm we get the following condition for the profitability of foreign investment:

$$x_1 < \frac{1}{t}(c_1 - c_2 - \theta - \tau)$$

This condition can be interpreted as follows: transportation costs must be equal to the unit cost difference, if the production takes place in CEECs. With an increasing sales potential in CEECs the convex transportation costs are rising. When we adopt this equation, the FDI inflows $b^*(t)$ depend mainly on the unit cost difference, if the import duty or subvention revenues are not decisive for the investment decision:

$$b^*(t) = B(c_2 - c_1; x_2)$$

Besides the inflow of FDI $b(t)$, the value of human capital is decisive for the balanced growth path of the economy. In the next section we explain why the share of FDI in GDP may vary between countries in CEECs and why the FDI inflows are mainly into four countries in CE.

5.4 Motives for foreign direct investment and their impact on economic growth in CEECs

In the previous section we assumed a positive relationship between the balanced economic growth rate, human capital and foreign direct investment. Following Jones (1998, pp. 128–9), the basic business investment problem could be posed by calculating the expected present discounted value of the profit stream of an investment, because this value is exactly the sum a (foreign) investor is willing to pay to purchase the subsidiary. Welfens (2005) made use of this reasoning to explain why an increase of the RER in the FDI host country will discourage foreign investment: because the purchase then became more expensive for the foreign investor. The RER might have an impact on FDI if the investment decision is mainly taken with portfolio considerations in mind. Then the foreign investors would probably search for new investment opportunities, if movements of the currency lead to higher costs, to hedge against currency risk.

We focus on FDI decisions which require medium and long-term investment duration and the 'lasting interest by a resident entity in one economy ('foreign investor') in an entity resident in an economy other than that of the investor ('direct investment enterprise')' (OECD, 1999, pp. 7–8). Therefore, portfolio considerations can be ruled out if the foreign investor aims to directly influence the operations and the strategy of the management of the direct investment enterprise by acquiring a share of more than 10 per cent of votes at its shareholders' general meeting.

Enterprise surveys on motives of foreign investors in CEECs until 1995 tended to show that potential investors in CEECs mostly wanted to serve the new market in CEECs (Bamberger *et al.*, 1997; Beyfuss, 1995; Kaufmann and Menke, 1997). Up to 1995 enterprise surveys showed different results because the labour-cost advantages of CEECs became increasingly relevant for FDI decisions. Resmini (1999) discovered that (especially German) investors were looking for opportunities to invest in CEECs to decrease their labour costs.

There is a lot of evidence that labour productivity increased in CEECs when multinational enterprises realised investment projects there and started to expect increasingly close supplier linkages. A German automotive supplier, for example, employs on average relatively more trained workers and researchers working on discovering and developing more complex product solutions aimed at improving their intermediate goods. These improved intermediate goods in turn serve to increase the value and quality of the final good. When the small supplier followed the big multinational firm in building new factories in CEECs labour productivity in certain sectors rose. A higher labour productivity is reflected in higher wages and subsequently by higher prices for tradable goods in comparison to the labour productivity in non-tradables sectors (such as services: hairdressing, rubbish collection, security services). This therefore confirms the fact that the observed appreciation trend in some CEECs can be explained by the classical Balassa–Samuelson effect.

In the growth model in section 5.2 we derived the equation that FDI inflows and human capital formation positively explain the balanced economic growth rates in the CEECs. Therefore, the observable differences in economic growth rates can be probably explained by these variables. Next we pose the question: what has driven foreign direct investment decisions in Central Europe in recent years? This could also answer the question: why do the former transition countries have different balanced growth paths? Figure 5.1 plots the different economic growth rates in the CEECs.

Behind the acceding countries' frontrunners – Hungary and Poland – come the Czech Republic and Slovakia, which have both attracted huge volumes of FDI recently. Figure 5.1 shows convergent growth rates for the last two years.

Figure 5.2 presents the geographic distribution of FDI stocks in CE relative to GDP. This indicator approximates the attractiveness of the host country for foreign investors.

In Figure 5.3 the effect of FDI inflows on total employment is considerably higher for a small country like Hungary. More than 8 per cent of employees in Hungarian manufacturing have worked for an enterprise with foreign ownership.

Enterprise surveys named wage differentials as one of the major influences for FDI decisions in CEECs (DIHK, 2004), and from Table 5.1 we see that the wage gap become greater the more eastwards the country is located. For example, labour costs per hour in the Czech Republic and Poland are a fifth of the corresponding EU15 values.

Table 5.2 shows that the labour costs per hour diverge across sectors. In sectors where foreign investors have purchased a relatively large share of the capital stock (electricity, gas and water supply, financial intermediation) relatively high wages were paid.

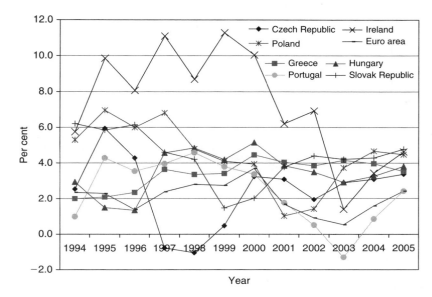

Figure 5.1 Economic growth rates of cohesion and several NMS
Source: OECD (2003b), Annex, table 1.

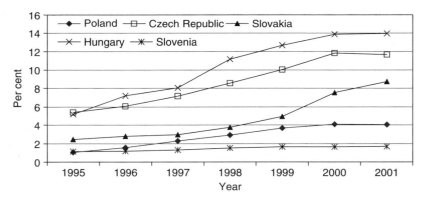

Figure 5.2 FDI shares on GDP in CE acceding countries*
Note: *FDI stocks.
Source: Deutsche Bundesbank, *Special Statistical Publications*, no. 10, International Capital links, April 2005.

To assess the competitiveness of industrial sectors in different countries one has to take into account labour productivity differences. Figure 5.4 shows that, besides Slovakia, all countries showed convergent unit labour costs (ULC). ULC are based on figures from 1996 (ULC equal to 100 per cent);

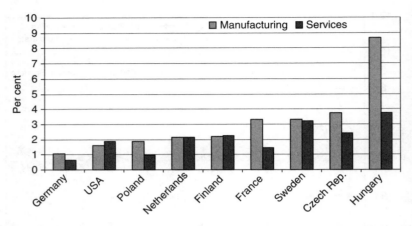

Figure 5.3 Share of foreigner-owned enterprises in total employment in the sector, average for the 1990s in per cent
Source: OECD (2003a, p. 200).

Table 5.1 Labour cost per hour in manufacturing in euro

EU and acceding countries	1996	1997	1998	1999	2000	2001	2002
EU25 European Union	16.75	17.17	17.64	18.26	19.33	19.62	20.02
EU15 European Union	20.07	20.63	21.13	21.78	22.94	22.6	23.68
Euro area	21.58	21.41	21.51	21.87	22.5	21.98	–
Austria	22.96	22.55	22.77	23.54	23.85	24.26	24.9
Germany	26.01	25.7	26.07	26.7	27.63	28.19	28.74
Spain	15.04	14.89	14.93	15.05	15.12	14.15	14.86
Finland	20.11	–	–	21.08	22.02	23.5	24.5
France	22.63	22.52	22.36	23.3	24	24.6	–
Greece	8.64	9.15	9.18	10	10.38	11	11.8
Portugal	5.97	6.17	6.37	6.72	7.05	7.29	7.69
Sweden	23.34	24.07	24.43	25.37	28.3	27	28.33
United Kingdom	14.56	17.45	19.17	20.71	23.33	24.02	24.87
10 new EU member states	2.7	2.97	3.24	3.41	3.81	4.36	4.43
Czech Republic	2.63	2.79	3.06	3.17	3.57	4.3	5.03
Estonia	1.78	2.05	2.33	2.43	2.7	3.01	3.33
Hungary	2.76	3.03	3.1	3.3	3.68	4.04	–
Lithuania	1.29	1.64	1.88	2.09	2.54	2.63	2.74
Latvia	–	1.61	1.71	1.84	2.09	2.18	2.24
Poland	2.66	3.04	3.35	3.57	3.95	4.66	4.59
Slovenia	6.65	7.14	7.57	7.89	8.19	8.7	–
Slovakia	2.25	2.51	2.82	2.59	3.05	3.14	3.46
Bulgaria	–	–	–	–	1.18	1.2	1.23
Romania	–	–	–	–	1.26	1.37	1.46

Source: Eurostat Luxembourg, database.

Table 5.2 Labour cost per hour in euro in 2000

Sector	Germany	Poland	Czech Rep.	EU13*	CEE**
Mining and quarrying	31.57	7.36	4.91	22.79	4.96
	138.5	*32.3*	*21.5*	*100.0*	*21.8*
Manufacturing	28.48	3.95	3.58	23.50	3.09
	121.2	*16.8*	*15.2*	*100.0*	*13.1*
Electricity, gas and water supply	35.94	5.73	4.78	30.48	4.18
	117.9	*18.8*	*15.7*	*100.0*	*13.7*
Construction	21.19	4.01	3.60	19.39	2.95
	109.3	*20.7*	*18.6*	*100.0*	*15.2*
Motor vehicle trade and services	21.45	4.03	3.89	19.11	3.20
	112.2	*21.1*	*20.4*	*100.0*	*16.7*
Hotels and restaurants	13.94	3.00	2.94	14.81	2.62
	94.1	*20.3*	*19.9*	*100.0*	*17.7*
Transport, storage and communication	24.40	4.98	4.08	21.30	3.93
	114.6	*23.4*	*19.2*	*100.0*	*18.5*
Financial intermediation	35.87	6.66	6.89	34.85	6.45
	102.9	*19.1*	*19.8*	*100.0*	*18.5*
Real estate, renting and business affairs	22.20	4.83	4.18	24.20	3.89
	91.7	*20.0*	*17.3*	*100.0*	*16.1*
Mean value	26.12	4.95	4.32	23.38	3.92
Standard deviation	14.34	4.47	2.14	0.00	2.67

Notes: Labour costs are defined as gross wages and salaries including social security contributions by the employer. Figures in italics represent values in per cent; *Average labour costs per hour of EU15 without Belgium and Ireland; **Average labour costs per hour of EU accessing countries and of the new EU member states without Turkey and Malta.
Sources: Paternoster (2003); Clare and Paternoster (2003).

therefore, the graphs could only be interpreted as a device to assess the development of ULC in the period from 1997 until 2003.

Since 2001, Poland has improved its competitiveness: for example, its ULC fell to 83.2 per cent in 2003. Ireland showed consistently low ULC and received both considerably high FDI shares of GDP and high economic growth rates (see Figure 5.1).

The outsourcing variable is defined as:[8]

$$Outs - CE_{i,t} = \frac{z_{i,t} \cdot 100}{\sum_{j}^{n} y_{ij,t} + m_{i,t}}$$

where $Z_{i,t}$ = an indicator for imports of intermediate goods from five countries of Central Europe (CE = Czech Republic, Hungary, Poland, Slovakia, Slovenia) of a single output branch i at time t; $y_{ij,t}$ = in Germany produced intermediate goods for each input sector j being destined for the output

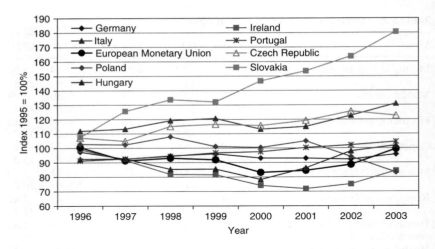

Figure 5.4   Relative unit labour costs in the European Union

Notes: Competitiveness-weighted relative unit labour costs in the manufacturing sector in dollar terms; competitiveness weight takes into account the structure of competition in both export and import markets of the manufacturing sector of 42 countries. An increase in the index indicates a real effective appreciation and a corresponding deterioration of the competitive position. For details on the method of calculation see Durand *et al.* (1998) and OECD *Economic Outlook, Sources and Methods* (http://www.oecd.org/eco/sources-and-methods).

Source: OECD (2003b), Annex, table 44.

branch *i* at time *t*; $m_{i,t}$ = total German imports of intermediate goods being destined for the output branch *i* at time *t*; and *t* = 1995, 1996, ..., 2000.

From Table 5.3a we see that unit labour costs and FDI stock are significantly correlated only for the Czech Republic. In Table 5.3b there is a significant coefficient between FDI stock and value added for Hungary and Poland and between FDI stock and outsourcing volume for Poland.

Table 5.4 shows the R&D effect and the quantity of human resources in several CE countries: Slovakia, Czech Republic, Slovenia and Poland were the four countries with the highest youth education attainment (the share of 20 to 24-year-olds with completed formal upper secondary education in 2004). The seventh column shows the percentage of graduates in science and technology studies in 2003. Ireland obtained the highest values with 24.2 per cent of graduates, followed by Finland and Sweden. Germany (ranked 11) and the five CEECs showed the lowest shares of graduates studying technology and science.

The considerable and sustained high real economic growth rates of 7.5 per cent per year on average in the last 10 years in Ireland can be explained. Human capital formation in Ireland is one of the driving forces for steady economic growth; the indicators in Table 5.4 show chat especially the relatively

Table 5.3 Pearson correlation coefficients

(a) Between unit labour costs and FDI stock

	Unit labour costs CR	*FDI stock CR*
Unit labour costs CR	1	−0.608**
FDI stock CR	−0.608**	1
	Unit labour costs Poland	*FDI stock Poland*
Unit labour costs Poland	1	−0.162
FDI stock Poland	−0.162	1
	Unit labour costs Hungary	*FDI stock Hungary*
Unit labour costs Hungary	1	−0.127
FDI stock Hungary	−0.127	1

(b) Between value added and FDI stock

	Value added HU	*FDI stock HU*	*Outsourcing volume HU*
Value added HU	1	0.791**	−0.064
FDI stock HU	0.791**	1	−0.265
	Value added PL	*FDI stock PL*	*Outsourcing volume PL*
Value added PL	1	0.466**	−0.234
FDI stock PL	0.466**	1	−0.268*
Outsourcing volume PL	0.466**	1	1

Notes: 6 observations from 1997 to 2000, 14 economic sectors; ** correlation is significant at a 1% level (two-sided test); * correlation is significant at a 5% level (two-sided test).

high public expenditure on education has contributed to the success of a high percentage of graduates with successfully completed courses in technology and science-based studies. The coincidence of decreasing unit labour costs, as shown in Figure 5.4, and a well-trained labour force may only be a rough confirmation of the theoretical assertion in section 5.2, but it also explains the fact that FDI from Germany in CEECs is concentrated mainly in only five countries (Czech Republic, Poland, Hungary, Slovakia and Slovenia), although wage costs per hour are considerably lower in Eastern Europe (without the Baltic states) than in Central Europe.[9]

5.5   Summary and conclusions

The aim of this chapter has been to comment on Chapter 4 and Welfens' (2005) model, discussing the impact of the RER on trade, structural change

Table 5.4 Indicators for human capital resources in EU

| | R&D effort; total R&D expenditure as percentage of GDP, 2003 | | Quantity of human resources | | | | | |
| | | | Youth education attainment level[c], 2004 | | Public expenditure on education as percentage of GDP, 2002 | | Science and technology graduates[d], 2003 | |
	%	Rank	%	Rank	%	Rank	%	Rank
EU 25	1.95[pe]		76.4[p]		5.23[e]		11.0[a]	
EU 15	2.00[p]		73.5[p]		5.12[e]		11.9[a]	
Belgium	2.33[p]	7	82.1	9	6.26	4	11	7
Czech Republic	1.35	10	90.9	2	4.41	13	6.4	14
Denmark	2.6[p]	5	76.1	11	8.51	1	12.5	6
Germany	2.5[e]	6	72.5[p]	12	4.78	11	8.4	11
Greece	0.64[a]	15	81.7[p]	10	3.96	16		
Spain	1.11	12	62.5	13	4.44	12	12.6	5
Ireland	1.12[p]	11	85.3[p]	6	4.32	15	24.2	1
Hungary	0.97	13	83.4	8	5.51	9	4.8	15
Austria	2.19	8	85.3	6	5.67	7	8.2	13
Poland	0.59	16	89.5	4	5.6	8	9	9
Portugal	0.79[p]	14	49	14	5.83	6	8.2	13
Slovenia	1.53[e]	9	89.7	3	6.02	5	8.7	10
Slovakia	0.57	17	91.3	1	4.35	14	8.3	12
Finland	3.51[p]	2	84.6	7	6.39	3	17.4[b]	2
Sweden	4.27[a]	1	86.3	5	7.66	2	13.9	3

Notes: [a] 2001; [b] 2002; [c] Total percentage of the population aged 20 to 24 having completed at least upper secondary education; [d] Tertiary graduates in science and technology per 1000 of population aged 20–29 years; [e] estimated value; [p] provisional value.
Source: Zeman (2005, p. 21) Annex, table 1.

and growth and present alternative explanations for the divergent growth rates in CEE. There is no dispute that sustained ups and downs in RER have influenced the volume of trade. It is widely confirmed in the literature that the RER can be seen as an indicator of the competitiveness of export industries struggling to win a higher market share for their products on the world market. Empirically, the relationship between a higher variety in export manufactured goods and a structural change in an economy is proven, especially for small open economies like those in CEE. Recently published papers on economic integration and industry location (Resmini, 2004, p. 18) and the role of FDI and human resources in the CEECs (Tondl and Voksic, 2003, p. 27) indicate that FDI has played a crucial role for catching-up countries – like the NMS – in gaining a sustained and higher balanced growth path.

In the previous section stylized facts about the geographic distribution of FDI and human capital underline the theoretically underpinned assertion that both variables explain a good deal of the divergence in economic growth between CEECs in the last 12 years.

Welfens (2005) presented a modified neoclassical model with endogenous growth. Endogenous growth of output rose in this model by the share of FDI in overall capital stock, which increases the growth rate of output (Welfens, 2005, p. 23). The share of FDI in the overall capital stock depends on the RER and therefore Welfens assumed that appreciation of the currency would discourage FDI. The FDI share as a function of the RER has the following impact on the growth rate: it accelerates the adjustment process towards a steady state. Probably, an important determinant of the growth rate is the share of FDI in overall capital stock, which has two major consequences for trade patterns and prices: it increases the growth rate of GNP per capita and leads to sustained differences in per capita income across countries (Welfens, 2005, pp. 22–3) measuring the capital.

We have focused on the determinants of the share of the capital stock owned by foreign companies. Due to empirical problems in stock in section 5.3 we used the share of FDI in GDP and excluded portfolio considerations by foreign investments in CE. With these limitations we present some stylized facts about growth, FDI and their determinants. The empirical coincidence between higher average growth rates, higher FDI shares and the higher human capital endowment of the labour force underlines the crucial role of FDI in the catch up process. To assure an optimum endogenous growth rate the gap between natural steady-state capital intensity and optimum capital intensity has to be narrowed. Welfens (2005, p. 30) proposed the use of tax revenues in attracting more foreign direct investment in order to raise the long-term economic progress rate of the economy.[10]

Theoretical and empirical analysis also reinforced the assertion that sufficient human capital stock of the labour force could, on the one hand, explain divergent economic growth rates because the spillover effects of FDI can only be realized if foreign investors outsource production sequences with a relatively high value added. Modernization of the capital stock of the economy could only be used effectively if the human capital resources of the labour force were sufficient and available to be employed at comparatively cheaper costs than at other production sites in Europe.

In the final concluding remarks on the impact of RER on trade, structural change and growth we confirm the assertion that a small and gradual appreciation of the currencies in CE would assist governments by decreasing the foreign debt burden and stimulating the capability of export industries to qualitatively upgrade their products. Therefore, governments should invest in human capital formation and aim to encourage the upgrading of human capital and cross-sectoral labour mobility.

Each of the EU25 countries is in intense competition with each other to attract new product lines at existing and recently established production sites. Countries with relatively high wages on average have to create sufficient downward wage flexibility to minimise employment losses because of this increased competition and have to invest in sufficient human capital formation. On both conditions, Germany – like other high-wage countries – may remain attractive for industrial production and assure relatively high employment levels in manufacturing.

Notes

1   Let us assume that the relative prices Φ do not change at the beginning. A depreciation of the nominal exchange rate e increases the foreign demand of tradable goods. The excess demand decreases when the price of tradables P^T rises. The relative price Φ moves down when the price of non-tradables remains unchanged. Analogous to TT, the slope of NN is negative.

2   This 'normal' reaction of the current account occurs if the absolute value of the sum of export and import demand elasticities is greater than unity and the export and import supply elasticities are infinitely high (Marshall–Lerner condition).

3   The Romer model (1990) indigenizes technological progress by introducing the search for new ideas from researchers interested in profiting from their inventions. It explains why and how the advanced countries of the world as a whole exhibit sustained growth. Therefore the model has to be adapted to explain why some countries in Central Europe grow faster than others, when in the 1990s all countries in Central and Eastern Europe started to transform their economies towards the market.

4   The symbol asterisk denotes the foreign price level or the price level in country II representing the EU15.

5   A similar production function was used by Barro and Sala-i-Martin (2004, p. 286) to build an endogenous growth model with an expanding variety of products. Technical progress takes place in this model by an expansion in N the number of varieties of intermediate goods available at finite prices at the current time. The index i for the countries is suppressed in the following equations, being the same for all countries in CEE.

6   In 2003 the share of exports to EU15 countries varies from 71 (Hungary) to 81 per cent of total exports (Brandmeier 2005, p. 115).

7   A complete exposition of the model of horizontal and vertical integration can be found in Brandmeier (2005, pp. 207–15).

8   We use the input–output tables of the German Federal Statistical Office to calculate the share of imported intermediate goods needed for the production process in each German manufacturing output sector.

9   The FDI inflow to the Baltic states mainly from Finland and Sweden were not taken into consideration in this commentary.

10   Some countries in CEE like Estonia and Slovakia have used tax exemptions for some years to attract foreign investments. They also have decreased the corporate tax rates to low levels or introduced a flat tax (Slovakia).

References

Bamberger, I. and M. Evers (1997) 'Internationalisierung', in H.C. Pfohl (ed.), *Betriebs-wirtschaftslehre der Mittel- und Kleinbetriebe* (Internationalization, Business

Management of small and medium-sized enterprises (SME). 3rd edn. Berlin: Erich-Schmidt-Verlag, pp. 377–417.

Barro, R.J. and X. Sala-i-Martin (2003) *Economic Growth*, 2nd edn. Cambridge, Mass.: MIT Press.

Barro, R.J., N.G. Mankiw and X. Sala-I-Martin (1995) 'Capital Mobility' in 'Neoclassical Models of Growth', *American Economic Review*, 85(1): 103–15.

Barro, R.J. (1991) 'Economic Growth in a Cross Section of Countries', *Quarterly Journal of Economics*, 106(2): 407–43.

Beyfuss, J. (1995) 'Standortqualitäten der Länder Mittel- und Osteuropas' (Location qualities of CEEC), in *IW-Trends*, Cologne: no. 2: 31–42.

Borbély, D. (2005) Foreign Trade Specialization on the EU Market: Dynamics, Determinants and Competitiveness, European Institute for International Economic Relations at the University of Wuppertal, November, mimeo.

Brandmeier, M. (2005) 'Die ökonomische Integration der mittelosteuropäischen Länder' (Economic Integration of CEEC), *Internationale Wirtschaft Globalised Economy*, 27, Köln-Lohmar.

Clare, R. and A. Paternoster (2003) 'Arbeitskostenerhebung 2000: Kandidatenländer, Statistik kurz gefasst' (Labour cost survey 2000: candidate countries, statistics in focus), theme 3-23/2003, Eurostat Luxembourg.

Deutsche Bundesbank (2005) Special Statistical Publication, *International Capital Links*, 10.

Deutsche Industrie und Handelstag (DIHK, German Chambers of Commerce) (2004) 'Envestitionen im Ausland – Studie auf Basis einer Unternehmensbefragung durch die Industrie- und Handelskammern'. Berlin: DIHK.

Durand, M., C. Madaschi and F. Terribile (1998) 'Trends in OECD Countries' International Competitiveness: The Influence of Emerging Market Economies', OECD Economics Department Working Paper no. 195.

Feenstra, R. (1999) 'The Impact of Outsourcing and High-Technology Capital on Wages: Estimates for the United States, 1979–1990', *Quarterly Journal of Economics*, August: 907–40.

Frensch, R. (2005) 'Balassa–Samuelson effects in the presence of product differentiation and trade barriers. Implications for transition and convergence', first draft, Department of Economics, Osteuropa-Institut München, July.

Frensch, R. and V. Gaucaite-Wittich (2005) 'Available product variety and technical change, first version', Department of Economics, Osteuropa-Institut München, April.

Frensch, R. and V. Gaucaite-Wittich, V. (2004) 'The Benefits from Product Differentiation in Modern Economics', Forost Working Paper no. 19.

Froot, K. and J. Stein (1991) 'Exchange Rates and Foreign Direct Investment: An Imperfect Capital Markets Approach', *Quarterly Journal of Economics*, 106: 191–217.

Jones, C.I. (2002) *Introduction to Economic Growth*, 2nd edn. New York: Norton.

Jones, C.I. (1998) *Introduction to Economic Growth*. New York: Norton.

Kaufmann, F. and A. Menke (1997) 'Standortverlagerungen mittelständischer Unternehmen nach Mittel- und Osteuropa – Eine empirische Untersuchung am Beispiel der vier Visegrád-Staaten (Relocation of middle-class enterprises (SME) to CEEC – empirical survey based on four Visegrád countries) *Schriften zur Mittelstandsforschung* no. 74, Bonn: NF Institut für Mittelstandsforschung' (Institute for Research on Middle Classes).

Keller, W. and S. Yeaple (2003) 'Multinational Enterprises, International Trade, and Productivity Growth: Firm Level Evidence from the United States', International Monetary Fund, Working Paper no. 248.

Levine, R. and D. Renelt (1992) 'A Sensitivity Analysis of Cross-Country Growth Regressions', *American Economic Review*, 82 (4): 942–63.

Lucas, R. (1988), 'On the mechanics of economic development', *Journal of Monetary Economics*, 22 (1): 3–42.

Mankiw, N., Romer, D. and Weil, D. (1992) 'A contribution to the Empirics of Economic Growth', *Quarterly Journal of Economics* 107 (2): 407–37.

OECD (2003a) '*OECD Economic Outlook*', edition 2003/1, no. 73, Paris.

OECD (2003b) '*OECD Economic Outlook*', edition 2003/2, no. 74, Paris.

OECD (1999) 'OECD Benchmark Definition of Foreign Direct Investment', 3rd edn, Paris.

Paternoster, A. (2003) 'Arbeitskostenerhebung 2000. Kandidatenländer, Statistik kurz gefasst', (Labour cost survey 2000: candidate countries, statistics in focus), Theme 3-7-2003, Luxembourg: Eurostat.

Resmini, L. (2004) 'Economic Integration and Industry Location in Transition Countries', Center for European Integration Studies, Bonn, Working Paper. B10-2004.

Romer, P. (1990) 'Endogenous technological change', *Journal of Political Economy* 98, 71–102.

Tondl, G. and G. Voksic (2003) 'What makes regions in Eastern Europe catch up? The role of foreign investment, human resources and geography', Center for European Integration Studies, Bonn: Working Paper B12–2003.

Welfens, P. J.J. (2005) 'Impact of the Real Exchange Rate on Trade, Structural Change and Growth', Paper presented at the final conference of 5th framework project: Changes in Industrial Competitiveness as a Factor of Integration. Identifying Challenges of the Enlarged Single European Market', Brussels: CEPS.

Welfens, P.J.J., J. Addison, D. Audretsch, T. Gries and H. Grupp (1999) *Globalization, Economic Growth and Innovation Dynamics*, Berlin: Springer.

Welfens, P.J.J. (1997) 'Privatization, Structural Change and Productivity: Toward Convergence in Europe?' in S. Black (ed.), *Europe's Economy Looks East*. Cambridge: Cambridge University Press, pp. 212–57.

Zeman, K. (2005) 'Conditions created for Knowledge-based Economy in the Czech Republic', Paper prepared for the Conference on Medium-Term Economic Assessment 29–30 September in Sofia, Institute of Integration of the Czech Republic into European and World Economy, University of Economics Prague.

6
Networking and Competitiveness
*Richard Woodward and Piotr Wójcik**

6.1 Introduction

The new members of the European Union from Central and Eastern Europe and the old 'cohesion' countries[1] (Greece, Ireland, Portugal and Spain) are united by their need to upgrade their industries *vis-à-vis* the more affluent member countries of the European Union. Examining the upgrading process at the firm level rather than the industry level, we analyse the ways in which various factors internal to, and actors external to, the enterprise affect the changes in its competitiveness. We are particularly interested in the relationships between an enterprise's competitiveness and its linkages with outside actors, and focus in this work on the roles of various partners (especially customers, suppliers, and various types of research institutions, but also, for example, investors and local governments) in their relationships with the firm. In other words, we are concerned with the effects of various kinds of networks on competitiveness.

What do we mean by a network? Much of the literature on networks interprets them as organizational forms which are neither market relationships (that is, an arm's length, contractual relationship) nor a hierarchy (for example a relationship based on equity, as in the case of the relationships of mother companies with their subsidiaries). Instead, it is a horizontal, cooperative relationship often evolving over time as trust among partners develops. An arm's-length relationship could evolve into a network relationship if, for example, a supplier relationship based on price alone and subject to change at any time were replaced by a long-term commitment to cooperate with that firm in increasing its quality and reducing costs. In this chapter we have adopted a broader focus, including not only the horizontal partnerships

* The authors would like to thank Anna Wziątek-Kubiak, Iraj Hoshi and Tomasz Mickiewicz for their comments and suggestions. The usual disclaimers apply.

commonly understood to constitute networks, but also hierarchical (equity-based) and arm's length relationships, in order to gain as complete a view as possible of how relationships with external actors affect competitiveness in a group of four cohesion countries: the Czech Republic, Hungary, Poland and Spain.

In the general literature on how networks affect enterprise performance, we find a consensus that in the process of enterprise upgrading, an important role is played not only by activities occurring within the enterprise, but also by its cooperation with other organizations and its ability to learn from such cooperation. The networks within which the firm pursues such cooperation and realizes gains there from are among its most important assets, and its skills in developing such networks and extracting gains from them are of crucial interest in studying the processes of firms' upgrading and their integration into the European and global economy.[2] In particular, a large literature exists on the subject of formal and informal firm networks and their role in innovation, one of the principal components of competitiveness (see Hägg and Johanson, 1983; von Hippel, 1988; Rothwell, 1991, 1992; Sabel, 1994; Mutinelli and Piscitello, 1998; Kogut, 2000). Their importance is due to the fact that they make it possible for the transfer of knowledge to a firm from other firms as well as from research institutions to take place. However, the literature on absorptive capacity also shows that firms must make some efforts of their own to generate knowledge in order to be able to absorb it from outside as well (Cohen and Levinthal, 1990). This is, in fact, the primary justification for analysing the role of certain internal factors in the improvement of competitiveness in a study that focuses primarily on the impact of linkages with external partners.

Little work has been done in this area in the post-Communist transition countries. The literature which does exist[3] describes the following, among other things: first, a severe adverse shock to network activity is observed at the beginning of the transition; the same is true of innovation activity. These countries remain peripheral with respect to world technology-intensive production. Foreign-owned firms generally dominate domestic firms clearly in terms of various measures of performance, particularly those most closely linked with upgrading, in spite of the fact that FDI appears to be usually market- and efficiency-seeking rather than knowledge-seeking. The literature also shows that the number of foreign-owned companies' backward linkages into the economies of the host countries increases over time. In the absence of firms' own R&D activity, technological upgrading is occurring through the import of machinery and use of licensing, and the East Asian experience indicates that this may indeed be the beginning of a long-term trajectory leading to world-class technological and innovative capabilities. This is also reflected in a gradual shift of exports to goods with higher levels of skilled labour inputs (the Czech Republic, in particular, has seen an increase in R&D-intensive production).

Using this background as a basis for further work, we provide in-depth descriptive information about the patterns of a wide variety of enterprise relationships in three transition countries (the comparison with Spain, a long-standing, albeit relatively less-developed, EU member country is an additional innovative feature of this chapter). Our primary concern is to identify the relationships between the enterprise linkage patterns identified and enterprise competitiveness. For example, we wish to examine with which partners firms cooperate most intensely for various types of activities (for example R&D, product innovation, improvements in product quality or inventory management, and so on), and what types of benefits are obtained from cooperation with given classes of partners (for example, customers, suppliers, universities and research institutes, and so on).

Additionally, we were interested in a comparison of the role of foreign investors with that of private domestic owners in the development of enterprise capabilities, as well as the importance of cooperation with foreign partners (for example, participation in the international production networks of multinational corporations; see Borrus, 1997; Ernst, 1997), and also sought to identify problems which are transition specific and distinguish them from those which are of a broader nature (this was made possible by studying countries with and without a socialist past).

We proceed as follows: In section 6.2 we provide a descriptive overview of the enterprises studied in the four countries, presenting information on the performance of the firms in a number of areas, including – among other things – sales, markets, financial indicators, R&D and patent activity, employment structure (skilled versus unskilled employees) and training, as well as on various forms of relationships. In section 6.3 we present a comparative empirical analysis carried out on a database compiled from the survey of enterprises in all four countries. Here we investigate the relationships between competitiveness on the one hand and the internal and external determinants of competitiveness, especially network activity on the other. In section 6.4 discuss the results, and in section 6.5 we provide conclusions and some reflections on policy issues.

6.2 Descriptive overview[4]

In this section, we begin with a brief look at the breakdown of the sample by country, industry and ownership. We follow this with an overview of the performance of the firms in the sample and a number of determinants of competitiveness which are internal to the firm (such as its investment spending and investment in training, R&D activity, and patents). Finally, we briefly examine the phenomena in which we are primarily concerned in this research: relationships with other actors (other firms, non-commercial entities, and so on) which may have an effect on competitiveness.

Table 6.1 Number of firms in the sample

Country	Industry				
	Food and beverages	*Pharmaceuticals*	*Electronics*	*Automotive*	*Total*
Czech Republic	40	5	52	21	118
Hungary	62	10	72	17	161
Poland	125	21	38	43	227
Spain	40	32*	36	26	134

Note: * Spain – chemicals.

The sample

Table 6.1 shows the breakdown of the sample of firms by industry and country. The four manufacturing industries represented in our sample – electronics, automotive and auto parts, pharmaceuticals, and food and beverages – were selected in order to achieve a mix of traditional and science-based industries as well as with a view to their presence in all the countries studied, allowing for a maximum degree of comparability across those countries. In selecting the companies in each country, an attempt was made to ensure that the weight of each industry relative to the other three would roughly reflect the situation in the population of firms in those industries in that country (exact proportions are not maintained, however, as a fully proportional representation of food companies would lead to their total domination of the sample, in some cases making up more than half of it; by the same token, the pharmaceuticals industry is overrepresented, as a representative number of pharmaceutical firms would be negligible). The other selection criterion for the companies studied was their size, with almost all companies having at least 50 employees (though a few exceptions had to be made in the pharmaceuticals industry in order to obtain a sufficient number of firms). Within these constraints, the selection of firms was random (subject, of course, to the additional constraint that the firm agreed to participate in the research). The enterprise surveys (interviews) were carried out in 2004 (with the exception of the Czech Republic, where the survey was undertaken at the beginning of 2005).

Table 6.2 shows the structure of the sample in terms of ownership forms and industrial and country origin. The classification of ownership is based on the type of owner identified by the respondent as the 'controlling owner' and is thus not defined strictly in terms of the percentage of shares actually held. We observe very few state-owned enterprises; the largest percentage, 7 per cent, is found in Poland. Domestically owned companies with a clearly identifiable owner are the largest group, constituting a majority of all the national samples except Hungary's (the figure for Spain is somewhat misleading as it also includes companies with no majority owner, which are usually publicly

Table 6.2 The structure of the sample by ownership and industry (%)

		Country			
		Poland	*Hungary*	*Czech Republic*	*Spain**
Type of owner	No response	1.3	1.9	0.8	0.0
	State	7.0	3.1	1.6	0.0
	Domestic individual	41.4	32.3	40.2	79.8
	Domestic industrial	9.7	8.7	14.8	
	Financial	1.3	8.1	2.5	NA
	Foreign individual	3.5	9.9	8.2	20.2
	Foreign industrial	14.5	30.4	26.2	
	No controlling owner	15.4	0.0	2.5	NA
	Other	5.7	5.6	3.3	NA
	Total	100	100	100	100
Industry	Food & beverages	46.8	37.3	32.8	28.0
	Automotive	10.6	8.7	17.2	16.8
	Pharmaceuticals	9.0	5.0	4.1	NA
	Chemicals	0.5	1.2	0.8	24.2
	Electronics	16.5	41.0	43.4	23.6
	Other	16.5	6.8	1.6	7.5
	Total	100.0	100.0	100.0	100.0

Notes: * In Spain, the data only distinguishes between domestic and foreign companies. For Spain, pharmaceuticals companies, if present in the sample, are included under the classification 'chemicals'.

traded). Foreign-owned companies constitute well over one-third of both the Czech and Hungarian samples, as opposed to about 20 per cent of the samples from the two larger countries, Poland and Spain.

Measures of competitiveness: performance

In this section we overview information on various areas of performance that reflect on the competitiveness of the enterprises surveyed. These include exports versus domestic market orientation and such financial indicators as revenue growth, costs and profitability.

Regarding export versus domestic market orientation, we collected data on percentages of the respondent firms' sales generated in domestic markets, EU export markets, and other export markets (see Table 6.A1 in the Appendix, which shows the percentage of firms in each country having sales to a given market within a certain range of shares in total sales). On this basis, measuring export intensity as the percentage of a firm's sales realized in export markets, we find Spain and Poland to be clearly less export-oriented than the smaller countries of Hungary and the Czech Republic, and export to the EU clearly dominates other export markets. (As one might expect, the rate of growth of exports to the EU is much higher for the new member states than for

Spain.) There is also a positive relation between size and export intensity, and between foreign ownership and export intensity (both export performance and export growth are vastly superior in foreign-owned companies). The automotive industry is clearly the most export-oriented (with electronics as a close second) and food the most strongly oriented toward the domestic market (it is interesting to note the frequency with which pharmaceutical exports are directed at other regions than the European Union).

Our examination of financial indicators of competitiveness included certain financial ratios, such as the ratio of total revenues to total costs, as well as dynamic measures indicating the percentage growth of a given indicator between a base year (usually 1998) and 2003, the year before the survey was carried out (see Table 6.A2 in the Appendix). In most cases, the median values seem to be more reliable indicators of the situation as a whole, due to the influence of outliers on means (extraordinary values of outliers, for example with respect to growth of certain indicators, are often due to the presence of start-up companies in the sample). The poorest revenue growth performance in the period studied was found in Poland, where the median is negative, and the highest in Hungary; the values for the Czech Republic and Spain are similar. Profits and profitability were generally unremarkable for all countries. Increases in labour costs were by far the highest in the Czech Republic, and the lowest (negative) in Spain. The Czech Republic and Poland had the greatest success in containing material and energy costs.

Reviewing the same indicators by industry, we found positive revenue growth in all of the four industries studied, with especially strong performance in electronics and the automotive industry. Profitability is by far the highest in pharmaceuticals, but falling for companies in all four industries. Labour costs are lowest in the food industry and highest in electronics (not including the chemical industry, which is specific here to Spain); they grew most strongly in the automotive and pharmaceutical industries. The share of materials and energy costs in total costs was generally falling – most strongly where its level was highest (in the food and automotive industries).

Finally, a comparison of financial indicators in domestic and foreign-owned companies shows revenue growth to be vastly superior in foreign-owned companies. However, in the areas of costs and profitability, the two groups are virtually indistinguishable.

Internal determinants of competitiveness: development activities

In this section, we overview data on company performance in various areas which we hypothesize to have important effects on competitiveness. These include the existence of R&D and design units and quality control labs in the firms, investment spending, and employee skills and training.

We find quality control labs to be nearly universal, with the lowest incidence in Hungary (see Table 6.A3 in the Appendix, which shows the percentage of firms in each country having a particular unit). Foreign-owned firms more frequently have R&D and quality control units. This may be seen as inconsistent with other studies documenting the tendency among foreign-owned companies for company headquarters in the home country to be responsible for R&D activity (for example, Gassmann and von Zedtwitz, 1999), as well as a study casting some doubt on the contribution of foreign-owned companies to total R&D in Poland (Górzynski *et al.*, 2006). As one would expect, the presence of R&D and quality control units shows a strong, positive relationship to size, although quality control units are found in an overwhelming majority of even small companies.

With regard to investment spending (see Table 6.A4 in the Appendix), the Polish companies seem to have had the highest investment intensity (measured by the ratio of investment spending to profits) in the analysed period (1998–2003), and the Czech companies the lowest; with respect to trends over time, however, investment seems to have been growing faster in Hungary and the Czech Republic than in Spain and Poland. By industry, in the analysed period the food industry (followed closely by pharmaceuticals) seems to have been both the most investment intensive and the one with the highest investment growth, and the automotive industry the least investment intensive. Pharmaceuticals saw a significant drop in investment. Domestically owned companies tend to be more investment intensive than foreign-owned ones, but the growth rate is similar in both groups.

Next, we consider the employment structure as a measure of the skill level of the company's work force. Because of the nature of the data, we had to proxy the share of highly-skilled employees in the work force by the share of white-collar and technical staff in total employment, and looked at both values for 2004 (that is, at the time of the interview) and growth during the analysed period, starting with the base year of 1998 in most cases (see Table 6.A5 in the Appendix). In general, we see healthy employment growth everywhere but in Poland (by contrast, all industries appear to be in decline by this measure, with electronics falling fastest and pharmaceuticals being the most stable). The share of white-collar staff in total employment is by far the lowest in Spain and similar in the other three countries. The discrepancies are smaller in the case of technical staff, but the same pattern exists. However, if increases in the share of white-collar and technical staff are a good measure of the growth of the human capital of the work force, the trend in Poland is much less favourable than in the other countries. Pharmaceuticals is the clear leader for white-collar and technical staff share, followed by electronics. Over time, electronics saw the most rapid employment growth (not including the chemical industry, which is specific to Spain), although automotive and pharmaceutical firms saw faster growth of white-collar and technical staff. Foreign-owned companies are clearly growing more dynamically, but seem less human-capital intensive with respect to work force share measures.

Continuing in this vein, we look at investment in human capital, examining companies' responses about the importance of managerial and employee training for raising the skill level of their work forces (see Table 6.A6 in the Appendix). Polish and Czech companies seem to evaluate the importance of training much higher than do Hungarian and Spanish companies. The level of differentiation across industries seems lower, though pharmaceuticals companies seem to value both managerial and employee training significantly more than others do. There is virtually no distinction between domestic and foreign ownership.

External determinants of competitiveness: forms of cooperation

We now turn our attention from the internal determinants of competitiveness to the question of various forms of cooperation, or network activity. First, we consider the markets from which companies acquire their supplies – domestic, EU and other foreign markets. Poland is by far the most autarkic country. In other respects, patterns seem fairly similar across countries, with a rough balance of imports and domestic supplies, and the EU as the dominant source of imports. The food industry is clearly more autarkic than others, but otherwise the patterns are very similar across industries. As one would expect, domestically-owned firms have a higher proportion of domestic supplies than foreign-owned firms.

Next, we consider various types of cooperation enumerated in the next section (see Tables 6.A7–10 in the Appendix). We observe the dominance of arm's length relationships (OEM,[5] subcontracting) over equity-based relationships in the Czech Republic and Poland (acquisitions are popular in Hungary); however, licensing is unpopular. Foreign-owned companies cooperate with foreign partners (including suppliers) more often than domestically owned companies do, but seem to have well-developed domestic supplier networks.[6]

We also asked about the benefits from various types of cooperation with various types of partners (this is described in more detail in the next section). In the Czech Republic, Hungary and Poland, the most important partners who, in the respondent firms' opinion, help to improve those firms' competitiveness were suppliers, followed by customers. The most frequently cited areas of benefits from cooperation are product quality and design, R&D, delivery terms and timeliness in the Czech Republic; delivery terms and timeliness in Poland, and quality and timeliness of deliveries in Hungary. Spain was very similar to the Czech Republic, with the four most frequently cited areas of benefits being product quality and design, R&D, and timeliness of deliveries.

6.3   Networks and their impact on competitiveness[7]

In this section we analyse the relationships between networking activity and the internal determinants of competitiveness on one hand and two measures of competitiveness on the other. In doing so, we will look for national and industry patterns as well as differences between domestically and foreign-owned companies.

Table 6.3   Descriptive statistics for competitiveness measures

Competitiveness measure	N	Minimum	Maximum	Median	Mean	Standard deviation
Ratio of EU export revenues to sales revenues	374	0.00	1.00	0.02	0.20	3.82
Gross profitability (2003)	472	−13.72	1.00	0.028	−0.10	1.22

The measures of competitiveness used as dependent variables in the regressions presented here were the percentage of the firm's sales realized in EU export markets (a measure of export intensity) and gross profitability (that is, the ratio of total revenues minus total costs to total revenues). Although we are aware of the imperfections of profitability as a competitiveness measure, we considered it desirable to examine more than one measure of competitiveness, as a one-size-fits-all measure simply does not exist; profitability in difficult times will not reflect the ability of the firm to survive and prosper in better times,[8] whereas export intensity is irrelevant for a firm operating primarily or exclusively on the domestic market (we also considered, and rejected, domestic market share as a competitiveness measure). The descriptive statistics for these two competitiveness measures are presented in Table 6.3.

The internal determinants of competitiveness used as independent variables in the regressions are:

- A dummy variable for the existence of an R&D lab or design unit.
- Product innovation (the percentage of sales attributed to products less than two years old).
- The number of R&D activities carried out in-house, and
- The percentage share of technical workers in workforce.[9]

Explanatory variables in the models also included:

- The number of years since the foundation of the company.
- A dummy variable for foreign ownership.
- The number of years since the controlling owner acquired its share.

With regard to enterprise linkages, we asked the surveyed firms about types of cooperation in which they were engaged. These could include any of the following relationships with customers, suppliers, or competitors (domestic or foreign):

- Acquisitions.
- Joint ventures.

- OEM.
- Subcontracting.
- Licensing.
- Strategic alliances.
- Cooperation with competitors.
- Secondments.
- Technical assistance.

We also asked about benefits obtained from cooperation in the following areas:

- Employee training; improvements in skills and knowledge of employees and management.
- Improvements in inventory management.
- Improved product quality.
- Product specification and design.
- Research and product development.
- Improved marketing.
- Timeliness of delivery.
- Terms of delivery.
- Improved access to finance.
- Improved access to modern technologies.
- Improvements in the production process.
- Modernization of production equipment (advice about choice of technology and so on).
- Increasing production opportunities (by purchase of licenses and so on).
- Access to new markets.
- Access to new distribution channels.
- Joint lobbying.
- Joint participation in trade fairs.
- Assistance with filling orders when own production capacity is fully utilized.

Respondent firms could indicate whether they had been obtained benefits from cooperation in any given area with a domestic partner, a foreign partner, or both (partners included customers, suppliers, investors, and other companies in the same industry). The scale used in this question was as follows: 0 if there is no such relationship (no benefit), 1 if the relationship is with a domestic partner in the case of a domestically-owned firm or with a foreign partner in the case of a foreign-owned firm, 2 if it is with a foreign partner in the case of a domestically-owned firm or with a domestic partner in the case of a foreign-owned firm, and 3 if there are relationships with both foreign and domestic partners. We treated this as an ordered scale, reasoning that domestic relationships of domestically-owned companies and foreign partnerships of foreign-owned companies could be presumed to demonstrate a lower level of networking capability than domestic relationships of foreign-owned companies (that is, backward linkages into the host economy) and foreign partnerships of domestically-owned companies.

Due to the very large number of networking-related variables contained in the data, we employed factor analysis for data reduction purposes. However, instead of using the factors generated as new variables, for each of the groupings of variables included in each component, the values of the variables contained in each component were added to obtain a value that can be interpreted as a measure of the enterprise's networking capabilities (specifically, the company's ability to extract benefits from various types of relationships with various types of partners) for a group of areas of benefit from cooperation that the factor analysis shows to be related. All resulting variables have ordered values, making it possible to include them in the linear regressions and interpret their coefficients. The variables constructed in this manner are as follows:

- Types of cooperation 1 – total number of the following relationships: joint ventures with customers (both foreign and domestic); licensing, strategic alliances, cooperation with competitors and secondments with domestic customers; strategic alliances and cooperation with competitors with foreign suppliers; joint ventures, OEM, licensing, strategic alliances, cooperation with competitors and secondments with domestic suppliers; all types of cooperation with domestic competitors.
- Types of cooperation 2 – total number of all types of cooperation with foreign competitors.
- Types of cooperation 3 – total number of OEM relationships with foreign and domestic customers and foreign suppliers.
- Benefits from cooperation 1 – benefits from cooperation with customers in the areas of: product quality, specification and design, research and development, marketing, and the terms and timeliness of delivery.
- Benefits from cooperation 2 – benefits from cooperation with customers in the areas of: access to finance, access to modern technologies, improvements in the production process, modernization of production equipment (advice about choice of technology and so on), increasing production opportunities (by purchase of licenses and so on), and assistance with filling orders when own production capacity is fully utilized.
- Benefits from cooperation 3 – benefits from cooperation with suppliers in the areas of: product specification and design, access to modern technologies, improvements in the production process, and modernization of production equipment (advice about choice of technology and so on).

- Benefits from cooperation 4 – benefits from cooperation with suppliers in the areas of: marketing, access to finance, increasing production opportunities (by purchase of licenses and so on), access to new markets and distribution channels, joint lobbying, and joint participation in trade fairs.
- Benefits from cooperation 5 – benefits from cooperation with other companies in the industry in the areas of: access to modern technologies, improvements in the production process, modernization of production equipment (advice about choice of technology and so on), increasing production opportunities (by purchase of licenses and so on).
- Benefits from cooperation 6 – benefits from cooperation with other companies in the industry in the areas of access to new markets and distribution channels.
- Benefits from cooperation 7 – benefits from cooperation with other companies in the industry in the areas of employee training and qualifications, product quality, research and development, and marketing.

Due to problems with missing data and the large number of variables (despite the use of data reduction based on factor analysis), we employed a number of OLS techniques allowing us to optimize both adjusted R^2 and the number of cases included. For each of the three dependent variables, we present two stepwise OLS regressions – backward and forward – used to identify significant variables; then, due to the well-known problems of biasedness in stepwise regressions, we present OLS estimates obtained without the use of stepwise regression methods. The results are found in Tables 6.4 and 6.5. However, we will mainly discuss the results of the non-stepwise regressions as these are the most reliable estimates.

We note, first of all, that we are more successful at explaining export performance than profitability, but on the other hand the number of usable observations for the latter is much higher than in the case of the former. What are our results?

For export performance (Table 6.4), we should first note that due to missing data Spanish firms are excluded from these regressions. That being said, we observe that the use of stepwise regression techniques did not result in the inclusion of country dummies. However, while country seems not to matter, industry does: electronics is found to be positively linked to export activity (the absence of the automotive industry here is surprising, given our results in section 6.2, and is presumably due to missing data). We see a positive relationship with foreign ownership and the use of supplies imported from EU member countries. This is what we would expect: foreign-owned companies tend to be exporters (as found in section 6.2. above), and exporters tend to import relatively more of their supplies than domestically-owned companies. Interestingly, both the share of technical staff in the work

Table 6.4 Networking and competitiveness (dependent variable: EU exports as a percentage of sales)

Variable	Stepwise: forward	Stepwise: backward	Non-stepwise
Foreign ownership	0.387***	0.399***	0.274***
	(6.002)	(6.173)	(5.773)
Electronics industry dummy	0.331***	0.344***	0.290***
	(4.923)	(5.277)	(5.694)
EU supplies as percentage of	0.178***	0.175***	0.292***
total supplies	(2.665)	(2.688)	(5.79)
Technical employees' share in	−0.283***	−0.315***	−0.264***
work force	(−4.540)	(-4.969)	(-5.720)
Number of R&D activities	−0.133**	−0.127**	−0.121***
done in-house	(−2.105)	(−1.996)	(−2.617)
Innovative products as	0.120**	0.114**	0.0125
% of sales	(2.098)	(2.036)	(0.287)
Types of cooperation 2	–	0.130**	
		(−2.132)	–
Types of cooperation 3	0.222***	0.202***	0.111**
	(3.638)	(3.395)	(2.380)
Benefits from cooperation 4	–	0.139*	
		(1.872)	–
Benefits from cooperation 7	−0.123**	−0.165**	−0.0424
	(−1.993)	(−2.583)	(−0.930)
Secondments with foreign	−0.118*		
customers	(−1.873)	–	–
Secondments with foreign		−0.146**	
suppliers	–	(−2.394)	
Subcontracting with foreign	0.134**	0.167***	0.146***
customers	(2.304)	(2.884)	(3.275)
Benefit from cooperation with		−0.118*	
suppliers in area of assistance			
with filling orders when own			
production capacity fully			
utilized	–	(−1.827)	–
Adjusted R^2	.585	.603	.522
N	262	260	263

Notes: * significant at 10% level of confidence; ** significant at 5% level of confidence; *** significant at 1% level of confidence; t-statistics are provided in brackets. For definition of types of cooperation and benefits of cooperation, see the text.

force and the in-house R&D activity are negatively related with exports (this result is made especially puzzling when we consider the facts that foreign-owned companies tend to be stronger exporters and, as we saw in section 6.2, foreign-owned companies tend to have R&D units more often than domestically-owned companies). The sign on the coefficient for the proportion of sales accounted for by innovative products is positive; however, the coefficient is not statistically significant.

Eight network variables are found in our regressions, though only three are found in all three regressions, and of these, only two are statistically significant in the non-stepwise regression, and these are related to export performance in ways that are practically pre-determined by definition. First, the variable types of cooperation 3 (that is, the total number of OEM relationships with foreign and domestic customers and foreign suppliers) is positively related to exports. Second, we see the positive role of subcontracting with foreign customers (thus, the role of outsourcing by foreign companies clearly extends beyond OEM in these economies). The sign on benefits from cooperation 7 (that is, benefits from cooperation with other companies in the industry in the areas of employee training and qualifications, product quality, research and development, and marketing) is negative but not statistically significant. In view of the results for the model with profitability as the dependent variable, to which we will now turn, it is worth emphasizing that no coefficients of networking variables in this model are both negative and statistically significant.

For profitability (Table 6.5), interestingly, we see fewer non-networking, and more networking, variables than in the case of EU export performance, but, as noted, the explanatory power of this model is lower than that of the one for exports (as one might expect given the aforementioned problems with profitability as a measure). The coefficient of the number of years since company foundation or acquisition is negative, which tends to indicate that older companies tend to have lower profitability (a result not particularly surprising for post-Communist countries, in which companies existing before 1989 or 1990 are burdened with the legacy of the central planning system). The sign for the dummy indicating the presence of an R&D unit is negative, which is a result similar (though not identical) to that found in the case of export performance.

Eighteen network-related variables are found in the regressions, though only ten are statistically significant, and these are mostly negative. Benefits from cooperation 2, benefits from cooperation 3 and benefits from cooperation 6 have negative signs. The signs are also negative for the following variables: secondments with foreign customers, benefits from cooperation with other companies in the industry in the form of assistance with filling orders when own production capacity is fully utilized, benefits from cooperation with other companies in the industry in the modernization of production equipment, and benefits from cooperation with other companies in industry in area of product specification and design. Only three network variables have positive signs: benefits from cooperation 4, benefits

Table 6.5 Networking and competitiveness (dependent variable: gross profitability 2003)

Variable	Stepwise: Forward	Stepwise: Backward	Non-stepwise
Number of years since foundation	−0.200*** (−3.527)	−0.203*** (−3.725)	−0.116*** (−2.673)
R&D unit (dummy)	–	−0.104* (−1.772)	−0.099** (−2.174)
Types of cooperation 1	0.047 (0.675)	–	0.108 (1.271)
Types of cooperation 3	–	−0.139** (-2.396)	−0.09 (−1.513)
Benefits from cooperation 1	–	0.189** (2.298)	0.081 (1.356)
Benefits from cooperation 2	−0.288*** (−4.434)	−0.374*** (−4.944)	−0.266*** (−4.556)
Benefits from cooperation 3	−0.282*** (−3.788)	−0.315*** (−4.266)	−0.166*** (−2.839)
Benefits from cooperation 4	0.343*** (4.180)	0.333*** (4.452)	0.237*** (4.033)
Benefits from cooperation 5	0.257** (2.133)	0.710*** (4.202)	0.402*** (2.910)
Benefits from cooperation 6	–	−0.156** (−2.539)	−0.099** (−2.000)
Benefits from cooperation 7	0.338*** (3.302)	0.298*** (2.996)	0.275*** (3.623)
Secondments with foreign customers	−0.287*** (−3.840)	−0.241*** (−3.221)	−0.139** (−2.002)
Secondments with foreign suppliers	0.168** (2.339)	0.177*** (2.607)	0.072 (0.961)
Technical assistance with domestic customers	0.121** (2.077)	0.119** (2.175)	0.072 (1.340)
Benefit from cooperation with other companies in industry in area of assistance with filling orders when own production capacity is fully utilized	−0.120* (−1.674)	–	−0.198*** (−4.114)
Benefit from cooperation with other companies in industry in area of modernization of production equipment (advice about choice of technology and so on)	−0.389*** (−3.567)	−0.497*** (−4.562)	−0.354*** (−3.842)

(Continued)

Table 6.5   (Continued)

Variable	Stepwise: Forward	Stepwise: Backward	Non-stepwise
Benefit from cooperation with other companies in industry in area of product specification and design	−0.404*** (−4.028)	−0.451*** (−4.832)	−0.371*** (−5.674)
Benefit from cooperation with suppliers in areas of employee training and improvements in skills and knowledge of employees and management	0.142** (2.287)	0.164*** (2.653)	0.096* (1.920)
Benefit from cooperation with suppliers in area of research and product development	–	−0.133** (−2.106)	−0.053 (−1.038)
Benefit from cooperation with other companies in industry in area of improvements in the production process	–	−0.297*** (−2.796)	−0.090 (−1.038)
Adjusted R^2	.429	.476	.273
N	419	414	412

Notes: * significant at 10% level of confidence; ** significant at 5% level of confidence; *** significant at 1% level of confidence-statistics are provided in bracket. For definition of types of cooperation and benefits of cooperation, see the text.

from cooperation 5, and benefits from cooperation 7.[10] It is difficult to discern any pattern with respect to which variables have positive signs, and which have negative ones. Among the various types of partners, both suppliers and other firms in the industry appear with both positive and negative coefficients, as do a number of types of cooperation (including access to finance, access to modern technologies, improvements in the production process, modernization of production equipment, access to new markets and distribution channels, and increasing production opportunities). One is tempted to ascribe this seeming lack of pattern, and perhaps the presence of networking coefficients which are both negative and significant, to the aforementioned noisiness of the dependent variable and the low explanatory power of the model (as evidenced by the low adjusted R^2) in comparison with the model with export intensity as the dependent variable, and simply discard the results. Moreover, the fact that the values of the variables reflect only the number of relationships and whether the partner is foreign or domestic, and not some measure of the duration or depth of the relationships, may be another reason for the lack of clarity of this picture. There might, for example, be an inverse relationship between the number of relationships on one hand and their duration and intensity on the other, which lack of data about the latter prevents us from exploring. Perhaps a more refined set of data about the quality of the relationships would yield clearer results.

However, a review of some relevant literature and closer examination of the variables which have only positive coefficients may shed some light on the issue. The networking variables which have only positive coefficients are related to cooperation in the areas of marketing, joint lobbying and participation in trade fairs, employee training and qualifications, product quality, and research and development. If we compare these variables with those that have both positive and negative signs in light of the upgrading hierarchy suggested by Kaplinsky and Readman (2001), we observe that, for the most part, the former correspond to lower-level forms of upgrading (process and product upgrading), related to improvements in the abilities necessary to achieve larger and more efficient output, whereas those with positive coefficients are mostly connected with a higher, or more advanced, form of upgrading – functional upgrading – in which the firm improves its capabilities in higher value added areas. This would suggest that firms that have reached the level of cooperating in the latter areas have attained higher levels of upgrading and, in turn, greater profitability. Further discussion of the possible implications of the negative signs will be found in the next section.

6.4 Discussion

It is clear that relations with customers and suppliers go beyond arm's length relationships based on price and quality parameters which respondent firms treat as 'exogenous'; instead, they work with their partners to improve and learn. Consciousness of quality is high and drives cooperative relationships with customers and suppliers. At least in the case of companies owned by foreign corporations, there is no evidence of a shortage of backward linkages developed by foreign-owned companies.

The regression results indicate that the effects of cooperative activity on competitiveness are still ambiguous: we observe both positive and negative impacts of various network variables on competitiveness. There is good reason to believe that this indicates that the strategic use of network activity and business partnerships to obtain competitiveness improvement is still in an early stage of development, with much remaining to be learned. As discussed in the previous section, a possible interpretation of variation in the signs of coefficients in the profitability model relates positive linkages between networking and profitability with cooperation in areas reflecting higher levels of upgrading.

The transition led to the disorganization of domestic enterprise networks existing under socialism (Blanchard and Kremer, 1997) and the process of building new ones under new, market-based economic conditions, given the specific constraints of the transition environment (including very weak rule of law, weak capacity of courts to enforce contracts, and so on), has been very difficult. In fact, as pointed out by Ickes *et al.* (1995), efforts to maintain enterprise networks inherited from the socialist system can act as a brake on upgrading activity. This could be at least a partial explanation of some of the negative coefficients on networking variables. Moreover, such results are corroborated by research showing that the relationship between productivity and innovation-related cooperation with other firms or with non-commercial organizations is negative in the five new German Länder, which share a Communist past with three of the four countries, while it is positive in the West German Länder (Brussig and Dreher, 2001; Brussig *et al.*, 2003; Günther, 2003, 2004). These authors believe the explanation for this discrepancy lies in the fact that the East German firms' cooperative efforts are young, and thus occurring in a phase in which they bring investment costs but not yet significant returns, which are expected to materialize in the future. This explanation would be equally valid in the case of the firms explored here.

A further explanation could be found in the literature on innovation networks, which gives us grounds to hypothesize that the low level of networking capabilities of firms in transition countries may lead to disappointing results when they do engage in various types of networking activities. Vinding (2002, cited in Powell and Grodal, 2005) finds that domestic partners have a stronger positive impact than foreign partners, which could explain a negative sign on variables whose values are higher the more relationships with foreign partners are observed. Godoe's (2000, cited in Powell and Grodal, 2005) results suggest that intimacy and duration of relationships are important determinants of their yields, whereas relationships in transition economies are likely to be young (and, as noted above, ones pre-dating the beginning of the transition may even be pathological). Powell *et al.* (2005) find that a firm's benefits from participation in a network depend on its centrality in that network. However, it is likely that the sampled firms in the peripheral economies studied in this chapter play rather peripheral roles in many of the networks in which they are involved, particularly those with foreign partners. Exploring whether these factors are indeed responsible for the results observed would in some cases require much deeper exploration of the data and in others data we do not have.

At least for the two measures of competitiveness used here, there is no relationship between competitiveness and country, although at least export performance seems strongly linked to industry. A number of other non-network factors seem to be important determinants of competitiveness. Some of the evidence here is surprising, in particular the negative effects we observed in the case of R&D and the share of technical staff in the work force.

In all of these countries foreign investors play an extremely important role in the economy, though this role is much smaller in the food industry, which is largely (though far from exclusively) domestically owned and domestic market oriented. In all of them, foreign ownership is still associated with much higher growth of key performance indicators than domestic ownership, indicating that domestic players still have a long way to go to become world players. (This does not mean that by all measures foreign-owned firms are more competitive than domestically owned firms. In terms of costs and profitability levels, they are indistinguishable. What really distinguishes the two groups is the rate of growth, although there are exceptions; for example, investment intensity is higher in domestic firms, and the growth of investment similar in the two groups.) What is interesting is that in all of these countries foreign investors have market- and efficiency-seeking motives rather than knowledge-seeking motives. None of these economies can be said to be knowledge-based. As noted, our results do not support claims of a low level of backward linkages of foreign-owned companies (suggesting a need for scepticism regarding calls for the creation of new, or extension of any existing, requirements regarding domestic content). In fact, the Hungarian results suggest that low numbers of local suppliers in industries dominated by foreign investors are not due to a lower propensity of foreign producers to utilise domestic sources, but rather to shortages of potential domestic suppliers.

6.5   Conclusions and policy implications

We believe our results provide evidence that 15 years after the beginning of the transformation, the socialist era legacy is now a much less important factor affecting the competitiveness of firms in these industries, with other factors – more specifically, world trends in various industries – having assumed much greater importance. It seems that there may be more that unites these four countries than divides them: all four can be described as 'peripheral' economies, with industrial production using factors such as unskilled labour and natural resources (and, to some extent, capital) relatively intensively, and using skilled labour relatively less intensively. In many ways, it is now country size rather than the socialist legacy that determines the differences among countries: Hungary and the Czech Republic, having small domestic markets, tend to have manufacturers which are export-oriented, while a country without a socialist past, Spain, and one with a socialist past, Poland, have more domestic market oriented producers, due to the much larger size of their domestic markets. However, our analysis does show that the number of years since the firm's foundation or acquisition may have a significant negative effect on competitiveness, indicating that newer firms tend to perform better.

As discussed in the introduction, the importance of network activity has been demonstrated in the substantial literature on the subject. Our results, however, show that firms in the countries studied have, on the whole, not yet begun to see returns from this source of competitive advantage; indeed, at least for the time being, it may result in more costs than benefits, at least for some aspects of performance. Network activity in these countries is still largely concentrated within value chain relationships and focuses on quality control and inventory management issues, not innovation. The paths for development in these areas have been very well-researched for at least two decades now, beginning with the literatures on Japanese management systems, total quality control, and so on, and the issues involved are very well-known in industry world-wide. Thus, market forces are currently sufficient to ensure that the post-Communist countries make positive adjustments in these spheres. The CEECs are currently far enough behind technologically that it usually pays for their firms to import technology rather than seeking to develop it.

Nevertheless, if these countries are to successfully evolve in the direction of knowledge-based economies as the newly industrialised countries of East Asia have done (and as the Lisbon Strategy would have them do), they will have to move beyond this stage and become innovators at some point. At that time it is clear that innovation-related cooperation will become an increasingly important issue, and that those firms which can master these capabilities earlier will acquire significant competitive advantage.

Our research seems to indicate that much work can and should be done to improve the absorption capacity of firms in these countries, concentrating on human capital development through the improvement of education from the pre-school to the postgraduate level as well as training and life-long learning initiatives. The evidence of negative relationships between competitiveness on the one hand and R&D activity and the share of technical staff in total employment on the other is disquieting. Perhaps the point here is that technical skills may be counterproductive if not used properly or coupled with certain other communicative or business skills. This is an important point in considering the education of engineers, as it is clear that the presence of technical and engineering skills unaccompanied by abilities to interact with personnel in non-technical departments such as marketing or to think about product development issues in purely technical categories, ignoring economic aspects, often fails to lead to effective innovation.

Appendix

Table 6.A1   Sales markets, by country (% of sales revenues)

Market	Share	Country			
		Poland	Hungary	Czech Republic	Spain
Domestic market	1–10%	16.5	23.5	13.7	6.3
	11–90%	34.9	48.7	59.0	60.3
	91–100%	48.6	27.7	27.4	33.3
Export to European Union	1–10%	58.9	29.8	18.8	40.4
	11–90%	37.4	45.2	76.0	59.6
	91–100%	3.7	25.0	5.2	0.0
Other export	1–10%	64.7	62.7	61.7	51.9
	11–90%	34.3	35.6	38.3	48.1
	91–100%	1.0	1.7	0.0	0.0

Table 6.A2   Financial indicators by country

Indicator	Statistic	Country			
		Poland	Hungary	Czech Republic	Spain
Increase of total	Mean	439.22	1,779.82	89.11	1,542.31
revenues (%)	Median	−4.65	67.38	24.39	23.19
	Minimum	−96.57	−82.94	−57.86	−74.68
	Maximum	59,238.07	129,900.00	2,676.29	105,714.79
Increase of sales	Mean	45.23	2,703.03	53.93	31.67
revenues (%)	Median	−0.35	50.95	34.38	22.22
	Minimum	−88.09	−99.99	−59.32	−74.68
	Maximum	2,170.08	209,900.00	313.10	322.30
Increase of export	Mean	479.47	223.39	676.66	78.89
revenues (%)	Median	35.46	40.81	52.21	17.09
	Minimum	−100.00	−100.00	−72.46	−99.95
	Maximum	8,227.17	3,550.00	20,566.67	1,227.35
Ratio of export	Mean	0.11	–*	0.40	0.29
revenues to sales	Median	0.00	0.28	0.32	0.21
revenues	Minimum	0.00	0.00	0.00	0.00
	Maximum	1.00	–*	0.98	0.99
Increase of EU	Mean	274.77	402.63	739.00	146.28
export	Median	35.46	50.00	23.53	4.63
revenues (%)	Minimum	−100.00	−100.00	−73.33	−99.95
	Maximum	2,807.70	5,500.00	15,733.33	3,615.00

(Continued)

Table 6.A2   (Continued)

Indicator	Statistic	Country			
		Poland	Hungary	Czech Republic	Spain
Ratio of EU export revenues to sales revenues	Mean	0.08	0.31	–*	0.23
	Median	0.00	0.06	0.17	0.13
	Minimum	0.00	0.00	0.00	0.00
	Maximum	1.00	1.00	–*	0.77
Ratio of total revenues to total costs	Mean	7.20	18.93	1.16	12,633.42
	Median	1.03	1.06	1.00	1.04
	Minimum	0.10	0.00	0.10	0.31
	Maximum	1,092.78	1,081.08	10.63	1,073,750.00
Increase of ratio of total revenues to total costs	Mean	675.11	1,223.37	21.06	–0.43
	Median	0.00	–1.21	0.40	–0.45
	Minimum	–92.22	–92.14	–90.11	–37.40
	Maximum	109,813.14	99,191.34	888.48	25.66
Ratio of gross wages and salaries to total costs	Mean	0.18	–*	0.25	0.55
	Median	0.15	0.19	0.19	0.55
	Minimum	0.00	0.00	0.02	0.04
	Maximum	0.65	–*	1.13	0.92
Increase of ratio of gross wages and salaries to total costs (%)	Mean	12.12	53.36	37.33	–2.01
	Median	4.50	5.49	12.34	–4.59
	Minimum	–92.00	–99.96	–90.88	–72.53
	Maximum	671.43	2,878.97	944.64	59.83
Ratio of materials and energy to total costs	Mean	0.49	0.66	0.58	–*
	Median	0.51	0.48	0.50	0.15
	Minimum	0.00	0.00	0.02	0.03
	Maximum	0.98	16.67	5.17	–*
Increase of ratio of materials and energy to total costs (%)	Mean	37.86	378.17	13.26	10.93
	Median	–0.77	2.55	–5.76	3.48
	Minimum	–92.00	–100.00	–93.51	–42.93
	Maximum	2,600.62	27,156.81	933.21	205.81
Increase of gross profit (%)	Mean	–713.09	–449.40	1,476.98	–5.03
	Median	–40.21	0.00	–34.58	–50.46
	Minimum	–102,465.35	–128,718.33	–5,100.00	–1,136.41
	Maximum	9,920.93	100,400.00	83,245.09	2,483.23
Gross profitability	Mean	–0.02	–0.32	–0.11	0.04
	Median	0.03	0.06	0.00	0.04
	Minimum	–8.64	–13.72	–9.45	–2.26
	Maximum	1.00	1.00	0.91	1.00
Increase of gross profitability (%)	Mean	–763.19	–1,127.48	114.27	–72.26
	Median	–45.89	–29.78	–44.17	–56.01
	Minimum	–71,334.76	–44,818.66	–2,006.42	–1,156.31
	Maximum	2,163.68	1,152.45	4,887.83	864.43

Notes: * Due to an impossible maximum value (in excess of 1.0), these figures are unavailable.

Table 6.A3   Firms with R&D and quality control units (%), by country

Type of unit	Country			
	Poland	*Hungary*	*Czech Republic*	*Spain*
R&D unit	35.7	35.4	56.9	64.1
Quality control lab	78.4	70.8	85.3	81.5

Table 6.A4   Investment spending statistics (%), by country

Investment indicator	Statistic	Country			
		Poland	*Hungary*	*Czech Republic*	*Spain*
Increase of investment spending	Mean	379.81	1,672,532.70	124.87	113.43
	Median	9.29	37.50	29.75	7.16
	Minimum	−100.00	−100.00	−100.00	−95.60
	Maximum	18,452.88	115,384,515.	908.50	1,687.60
Ratio of investments to gross profit	Mean	9.04	18.89	−8.60	0.77
	Median	0.45	0.25	−0.01	0.18
	Minimum	−25.81	−60.92	−807.26	−7.67
	Maximum	606.67	1,800.00	11.00	21.63

Table 6.A5   Employment structure, by country

Employment indicator	Statistic	Country			
		Poland	*Hungary*	*Czech Republic*	*Spain*
Growth of total employment (%)	Mean	2,032.68	146.20	32.98	14.92
	Median	−15.87	6.67	11.59	10.71
	Minimum	−82.38	−75.00	−89.59	−70.00
	Maximum	364,363.64	4,900	350	244.44
Share of white-collar staff in work force	Mean	27.19	26.63	30.19	13.35
	Median	22.73	20.55	25.40	10.91
	Minimum	0.02	2.86	2.44	0.63
	Maximum	100.00	100.00	95.76	61.40
Growth of white-collar employment (%)	Mean	23.75	83.81	53.57	26.94
	Median	−1.48	15.61	11.80	10.82
	Minimum	−92.50	−87.50	−83.89	−54.21
	Maximum	1240	1900	1950	800
Share of technical staff in work force	Mean	13.55	14.92	19.06	11.16
	Median	8.23	8.00	13.26	5.83
	Minimum	0.00	0.00	0.80	0.32
	Maximum	112.60	150.00	79.85	90.91
Growth of technical staff	Mean	30.67	96.45	57.69	52.60
	Median	0.00	6.92	20.00	1 4.08
	Minimum	−100	−87.10	−69.51	−40.00
	Maximum	600	3,344.44	1750	400

Table 6.A6   The importance of managerial and employee training, by country (% of firms giving indicated response)

Type of training	Degree of importance	Country			
		Poland	Hungary	Czech Republic	Spain
Managerial training	Little or no importance	3.6	19.3	1.7	18.2
	Important	39.9	67.1	36.1	52.6
	Very important	56.5	13.7	62.2	29.2
	Total	100	100	100	100
Employee training	Little or no importance	7.1	19.9	7.6	16.7
	Important	49.1	73.3	45.4	45.7
	Very important	43.8	6.8	47.1	37.7
	Total	100	100	100	100

Table 6.A7   Czech Republic: types of cooperation, by type of partner (% of country sample)

Type of cooperation	Foreign competitors	Customers	Suppliers	Domestic competitors	Customers	Suppliers
Acquisitions	0.0	1.1	0.0	1.1	2.1	0.0
Joint ventures	0.0	21.3	7.4	0.0	1.1	1.1
OEM	8.5	31.9	17.0	2.1	42.6	23.4
Subcontracting	3.2	29.8	13.8	2.1	30.9	27.7
Licensing	0.0	8.5	4.3	0.0	2.1	1.1
Strategic alliances	2.1	11.7	7.4	2.1	9.6	9.6
Cooperation with competitors	0.0	1.1	0.0	0.0	0.0	0.0
Secondments	9.6	11.7	2.1	6.4	8.5	1.1
Technical assistance	0.0	3.2	1.1	0.0	4.3	3.2
Other	0.0	0.0	0.0	0.0	0.0	0.0

Table 6.A8   Hungary: types of cooperation, by type of partner (% of country sample)

Type of cooperation	Foreign competitors	Customers	Suppliers	Domestic competitors	Customers	Suppliers
Acquisitions	6.0	1.3	11.4	10.7	17.4	20.0
Joint ventures	3.4	4.9	5.4	3.4	4.7	4.7
OEM	4.0	16.1	12.8	3.4	11.4	10.7
Subcontracting	2.7	5.4	8.7	4.7	12.8	11.4
Licensing	3.4	4.7	8.7	2.0	3.3	3.4

(*Continued*)

Table 6.A8 (Continued)

Type of cooperation	Competitors	Foreign customers	Suppliers	Competitors customers	Domestic	Suppliers
Strategic alliances	4.0	5.4	6.0	4.0	4.7	6.0
Cooperation with competitors	–	–	–	–	–	–
Secondments	2.7	3.3	4.7	1.3	4.0	4.7
Technical assistance	4.0	9.3	8.7	4.0	8.7	8.1
Other	2.0	4.7	3.4	2.7	2.7	4.0

Table 6.A9 Spain: types of cooperation, by type of partner (% of country sample)

Type of cooperation	Competitors	Foreign customers	Suppliers	Competitors customers	Domestic	Suppliers
Acquisitions	21.5	17.7	17.7	20.9	20.9	21.5
Joint ventures	19.0	15.8	16.5	18.4	18.4	19.6
OEM	17.7	18.4	17.7	18.4	20.3	19.6
Subcontracting	18.4	15.2	17.7	19.6	18.4	26.0
Licensing	17.1	15.2	17.1	19.0	17.1	19.6
Strategic alliances	20.9	17.7	17.7	22.2	20.9	22.2
Cooperation with competitors	20.3	15.8	15.2	20.9	19.6	18.4
Secondments	16.5	14.6	14.6	17.1	16.5	17.7
Technical assistance	17.1	17.1	17.1	18.4	21.5	23.4
Other	1.3	0.0	0.0	0.6	0.6	0.6

Table 6.A10 Poland: types of cooperation, by type of partner (% of country sample)

Type of cooperation	Competitors	Foreign customers	Suppliers	Competitors customers	Domestic	Suppliers
Acquisitions	0.4	1.8	0.9	1.3	4.4	1.8
Joint ventures	0.4	0.4	0.4	0.4	0.0	0.0
OEM	1.3	9.7	4.0	1.3	13.7	3.5
Subcontracting	1.3	8.4	9.3	4.0	19.8	22.9
Licensing	0.9	4.4	3.5	0.4	5.3	2.2
Strategic alliances	0.4	1.8	0.9	1.8	3.5	2.6
Cooperation with competitors Secondments	1.3	2.2	2.6	0.9	6.2	1.8
Technical assistance	0.9	5.3	13.7	3.1	15.4	22.0
Other	0.4	0.4	0.0	0.9	0.9	1.3

Notes

1 So called in the parlance of the European Union due to the perceived need for special action in poorer member countries to strengthen cohesion within the EU.
2 For a review of this literature see Woodward *et al.* (2005a).
3 A review of such work as has been done on enterprise linkages and their relationship to enterprise performance in two West European and three Central European countries (the Czech Republic, Hungary, Ireland, Poland and Spain) is contained in Woodward *et al.* (2005b).
4 The surveys were carried out by four country teams, whose separate reports can be found in: Álvarez *et al.* (2005) for Spain, Goldfajn *et al.* (2005) for the Czech Republic, Sass (2005) for Hungary, and Woodward *et al.* (2005a) for Poland.
5 Original Equipment Manufacturing.
6 More precisely, companies owned by foreign corporations have levels of domestic supplier relationships that are comparable to those of domestically-owned companies; however, companies owned by foreign individuals tend to have fewer domestic suppliers.
7 The authors would like to thank Tomasz Mickiewicz and Deniz Eylem Yoruk for their assistance in methodological matters, and Amelia Kalukiewicz for her assistance in the entry and cleaning of the data. Of course, the usual disclaimers apply.
8 Additional problems with the profitability measure are the fact that an elevated level may simply reflect the lack of competition on a monopolistic or oligopolistic markets and the fact that this variable is subject to many accounting conventions (as well as outright manipulation) in addition to purely economic factors and thus may be a particularly 'noisy' variable.
9 Other variables whose significance was explored included investment intensity (the ratio of investment expenditures to gross profit), the importance ascribed by the respondent to employee training, the ratio of R&D spending to total revenues, and two dummy variables for certification, one for ISO and one for other types of certification; however, stepwise regressions (see below) eliminated these variables from the models.
10 The insignificant variables include types of cooperation 1 (positive), types of cooperation 3 (negative), benefits from cooperation 1 (positive), secondments with foreign suppliers, technical assistance with domestic customers, benefits from cooperation with suppliers in the area of employee training and qualifications (positive), benefits from cooperation with suppliers in R&D and benefits from cooperation with other companies in the industry in improving the production process (negative).

References

Álvarez, I., M.A. Fonfría and R. Marín (2005) 'The Role of Networking in the Competitiveness Profile of Spanish Firms', Working Paper 04/05, Madrid: Instituto Complutense de Estudios Internacionales.

Blanchard, O. and M. Kremer (1997) 'Disorganization', *Quarterly Journal of Economics*, 112(4): 1091–26.

Borrus, M. (1997) 'Left for Dead: Asian Production Networks and the Revival of US Electronics', BRIE Working Paper no. 100, Berkeley: Berkeley Roundtable on the International Economy.

Brussig, M. and C. Dreher (2001) 'Wie erfolgreich sind Kooperationen? Neue Ergebnisse zur Kooperationspraxis in Ostdeutschland' (How successful is cooperation? New results on cooperative practice in East Germany), *WSI Mitteilungen*, 9: 566–72.

Brussig, M., S. Kinkel and G. Lay (2003) 'Verbreitung und Nutzen regionaler Netzwerke in der deutschen Investitionsgüterindustrie' (Extent and advantages of regional networks in the German investment goods industry), *Zeitschrift für Wirtschaftsgeographie*, 47(1): 9–41.

Cohen, W.M. and D.A. Levinthal (1990) 'Absorptive Capacity: A New Perspective on Learning and Innovation', *Administrative Science Quarterly*, 35: 128–52.

Ernst, D. (1997) 'From Partial to Systemic Globalization: International Production Networks in the Electronics Industry)', Working Paper no. 98, Berkeley: Berkeley Roundtable on the International Economy.

Gassmann, O. and M. von Zedtwitz (1999) 'New Concepts and Trends in International R&D Organisation', *Research Policy*, 28: 231–50.

Godoe, H. (2000) 'Innovation Regimes, R&D and Radical Innovations in Telecommunications', *Research Policy*, 29: 1033–46.

Goldfajn, K., A. Putzova and A. Zemplinerova (2005) 'The Importance of Foreign-owned Enterprises for the Competitiveness of Czech Manufacturing', Prague: Czech Institute for Applied Economics.

Gorzynski, M., M. Jakubiak and R. Woodward (2006) 'Key Challenges to the Development of the Knowledge-Based Economy in Poland', in K. Piech and R. Radosevic (eds), *The Knowledge-Based Economy in Central and East Europe: Countries and Industries in a Process of Change*. Basingstoke: Palgrave Macmillan.

Günther, J. (2003) 'Innovationskooperationen in Ost- und Westdeutschland: überraschende Unterschiede' (Innovation cooperation in East and West Germany: Surprising differences), *Wirtschaft im Wandel*, 9(4): 104–9.

Günther, J. (2004) 'Innovation Cooperation: Experiences from East and West Germany', *Science and Public Policy*, 31(2): 151–8.

Hägg, I. and J. Johanson (1983) 'Firms in Networks: A New Perspective on Competitive Power', Uppsala Business and Social Research Institute (SNS).

Ickes, B., R. Ryterman and S. Tenev (1995) 'On Your Marx, Get Set, Go: The Role of Competition in Enterprise Adjustment', University Park: Pennsylvania State University (mimeo).

Kaplinsky, R. and J. Readman (2001) 'How Can SME Producers Serve Global Markets and Sustain Income Growth?' Institute of Development Studies Papers, University of Sussex.

Kogut, B. (2000) 'The Network as Knowledge: Generative Rules and the Emergence of Structure,' *Strategic Management Journal*, 21: 405–25.

Mutinelli, M. and L. Piscitello (1998) 'The Entry Mode Choice of MNEs: An Evolutionary Approach', *Research Policy*, 27: 491–506.

Powell, W.W. and S. Grodal (2005), 'Networks of Innovators', in J. Fagerberg, D.C. Mowery and R.R. Nelson (eds), *The Oxford Handbook of Innovation*. Oxford: Oxford University Press.

Powell, W.W., D.R. White, K.W. Koput and J. Owen-Smith (2005) 'Network Dynamics and Field Evolution: The Growth of Inter-organizational Collaboration in the Life Sciences', *American Journal of Sociology*, 110(4): 1132–205.

Rothwell, R. (1991) 'External Networking and Innovation in Small and Medium-Sized Manufacturing Firms in Europe', *Technovation*, 11(2): 93–112.

Rothwell, R. (1992) 'Successful Industrial Innovation: Critical Factors for the 1990s', *R&D Management*, 22(3): 221–39.

Sabel, C.F. (1994) 'Learning by Monitoring: The Institutions of Economic Development', in N. Smelser and R. Swedberg (eds), *Handbook of Economic Sociology*. Princeton, NJ: Russell Sage and Princeton University Press.

Sass, M. (2005) 'Competitiveness and Networking – the Case of Hungary', Budapest: Institute of Economics of the Hungarian Academy of Sciences.

Vinding, A.L. (2002) 'Interorganizational Diffusion and Transformation of Knowledge in the Process of Product Innovation', PhD thesis, Aalborg University.

Von Hippel, E. (1988) *The Sources of Innovation*. New York, Oxford: Oxford University Press.

Woodward, R., M. Górzyñski and P. Wójcik (2005a) 'Networks and Competitiveness in Foreign and Domestic Firms: The Polish case', Warsaw: CASE – The Center for Social and Economic Research.

Woodward, R., D.E.Yoruk, M. Bohata, M.A. Fonfria, M. O'Donnell and M. Sass (2005b) 'The Role of Networks in Stimulating Innovation and Catching-up in European Enterprises: A Literature Review', *Opere et studia*, no. 3.

7
The Process of Structural Change in Polish Manufacturing in 1995–2003 and its Determinants

Krzysztof Marczewski and Krzysztof Szczygielski

7.1 Introduction

Although the terms 'economic structure' and 'structural change' are frequently used in the economic literature there are no universally accepted definitions of these notions. We argued in Marczewski and Szczygielski (2005) that two approaches can be distinguished:

- Structural change in the strict sense is a change in the distribution of a certain economic variable (e.g. employment, value added etc.) over a set of sectors or branches. This approach is present in the work of development economists and economic historians (e.g. Kuznets, 1971; Chenery and Taylor, 1968) and more recently in the studies of Aiginger (2000), Czyżewski and Orłowski (2000) or Wyżnikiewicz (1987).

- Structural change in the broad sense, or in other words change in structural characteristics, is a qualitative change in the whole economy or parts of it and the precise scope of change is defined by each author according to the scope and requirements of his/her study. The structural characteristics encountered in the literature are, among other things, the endowment of production factors and their distribution in the economy, the level of technology, institutional factors (such as inter-enterprise links, government-private sector relations, labour market regulations and others), the environmental sustainability of production and so on (see e.g. Lipowski, 1998). They tend to be supply-side changes. The EU's Lisbon Strategy, with its lists of 'structural indicators', is a good example of this perception of structural change (see Royuela-Mora, 2005; European Commission, 2004).

In empirical analysis both approaches are sometimes combined, as analysis of structural change in the strict sense may be helpful in analysis of changes in certain structural characteristics. In such studies (for example Fagerberg,

1999) one examines the relative growth of branches that one assumes represent a certain level of the structural characteristics under research (for example technology-intensity, productivity).

The focus of this study is slightly different (even if we employ similar analytical techniques): we first measure the structural change in the strict sense (i.e. the changes in the structure of employment, sales and value added) in Polish manufacturing industry in 1995–2003, and only then we seek to explain the observed developments and in particular draw conclusions about the structural change in the broad sense i.e. about structural characteristics. More generally, we will examine four types of factors of structural change in the strict sense (which will be explained further in this chapter):

- Changes in demand (domestic and foreign).

- Changes in the factor competitiveness of manufacturing branches.

- Changes in the competitive performance of the manufacturing branches.

- Structural characteristics of manufacturing industry: technology level, skill-intensity, factor-intensity, concentration, internationalization of production, import penetration and FDI involvement.

We will analyse changes in labour productivity separately.

As previous studies (Lipowski, 1998, 2000) show, Poland underwent considerable structural change (in the broad sense) in the first half of the 1990s, largely overcoming the legacy of the centrally planned economy, with its skewed structure of output, employment and foreign trade. Our study covers the period 1995–2003. Although the Polish economy was more advanced by then it still had several characteristics of a post-communist economy, for example the considerable number of state-owned enterprises. What is more, some of the structural effects of reforms implemented before 1995 took some time to become visible. This applies for instance to privatization agreements that often obliged foreign investors to maintain for a certain period of time the existing level of employment. Once that period had elapsed employment cuts were often initiated (at the beginning of 2000 a high number of such layoffs took place; see Boni, 2004, p. 36). These are the reasons why one would expect substantial structural changes also after 1995.

Our study is structured as follows. We start by discussing the macroeconomic situation in the analysed period, that is 1995–2003 (section 7.2). In section 7.3 we measure structural change in the strict sense, that is changes in the distribution of employment, value added and sales in Polish manufacturing industry in 1995–2003 on the 3-digit level of the NACE nomenclature. In section 7.4 we attempt to explain the observed changes. Firstly, we run an econometric analysis to examine the impact of the four kinds of factors explained above. Then we employ a 'shift and share' technique of labour productivity analysis to supplement the findings of the econometric analysis. The conclusions of the study are presented in section 7.5.

To avoid any ambiguity related to terminology we adopt the following convention. Whenever we refer to structural change we mean structural change in the strict sense. When we refer to structural characteristics we mean one of the seven features of manufacturing industry mentioned above.

We use the following data from the Polish Central Statistical Office: data on manufacturing branches (based on enterprise 'F-01' statistics), data on price indexes and data on international trade. Data on average exchange rates were taken from the National Bank of Poland. We have also used two Eurostat databases: Comext for international trade, and New Cronos, for data on industrial branches in the EU15.

7.2 Macroeconomic framework of the analysis

The basic time framework for analysis are the years 1995–2003; the period directly precedes Poland's accession to the European Union and is quite heterogeneous.

Three sub-periods can be easily identified: 1995–98, 1999–2001 and 2002–03. During the first a high GDP growth rate was maintained, underpinned by expanding import supplies and strong domestic demand (see Figure 7.1). The unemployment rate decreased considerably. Both monetary and fiscal policies were rather loose, so the pace of the reduction of the high inflation inherited from the early 1990s was slow. The current account deficit fell continuously in this period.

The Russian crisis in August 1998 and the subsequent turbulence on European markets opened the second stage in 1999. The safety margin of the

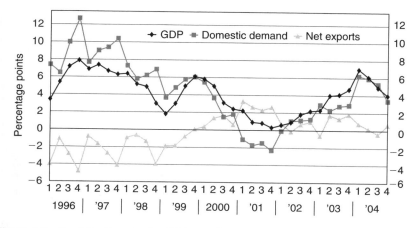

Figure 7.1 Contributions to the GDP growth in 1996–2004 (in percentage points)

current account to GDP ratio was surpassed at the end of 1999 and in response monetary policy was considerably tightened. The restoration of external equilibrium was accompanied by a severe slowdown in economic activity and a significant rise in the unemployment rate. High interest rates and massive inflows of foreign direct investment (see Figure 7.2), stimulated by the second wave of privatization, contributed to a strong appreciation of the zloty and rapid disinflation.

Simultaneously, the shelter for domestic producers that high tariff and non-tariff protection offered in the first sub-period was considerably reduced during the second sub-period.

Figure 7.3 illustrates these developments. Exchange rate protection (ER protection) is the protection delivered by real effective exchange rate (REER, which is based on CPI deflators) defined as the real domestic price of a foreign currency unit (see for example Corden, 1997). Total protection comprises

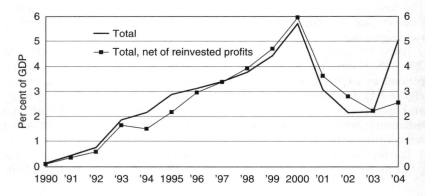

Figure 7.2   Inflow of foreign investments to Poland in 1990–2004

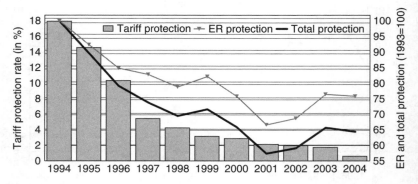

Figure 7.3   The level of tariff protection (left hand scale) and the dynamics of foreign exchange rate (ER) protection and of total protection (right-hand scale) in 1994–2004

both the exchange rate protection and the tariff protection. It is interpreted as the real domestic price a foreign currency unit spent on imports.[1]

As a result of these developments the profitability of many manufacturing branches, including traditional exporters, was seriously affected. Facing deterioration of their financial position enterprises intensified their restructuring efforts, cutting excessive employment, freezing wages and reducing investments in fixed assets. Interestingly, at the same time overall exports accelerated as new capacities built into factories created by foreign investors were put into operation, especially in the motor car parts and accessories sector.

The minimum rate of the GDP growth was reached in 2001, and from that time on the economy entered a period of a modest recovery. Monetary policy was considerably eased and the zloty depreciated. Employment started to increase only in late 2003. FDI inflows stabilized relative to GDP at a level half as low as in the second sub-period. Given that the three intervals were so different we decided to prioritize our analysis where possible.

7.3 Structural change in Polish manufacturing industry, 1995–2003: scale and volatility of the process

Methodology

A useful way to analyse structural change is to treat the structure of manufacturing industry in a given year t as a point in the R^n space: $x^t = (x_1^t, x_2^t, K x_n^t)$, where x_i^t is the share of the industry i in total manufacturing employment (or sales, value added and so on) and

$$\sum_i x_i^t = 1$$

Structural change between years t and s can then be defined as the distance between the two points measured by a given metrics d. The most natural concept is to adopt the Euclidean metrics:

$$d_E(x^t, x^s) = \sqrt{\sum_i (x_i^t - x_i^s)^2}$$

The advantage of this measure is that it corresponds to the intuitive perception of distance. Thus it can be interpreted as the 'total structural shift' in manufacturing industry in a given period; see Figure 7.4 for a graphical illustration of structural change in an industry consisting of 3 branches, for example $x^t = (x_1^t, x_2^t, x_3^t)$).[2]

However most authors prefer to use the 'city bloc' metrics: (e.g. Wyżnikiewicz, 1987) or a measure called the Michaeli index, which is defined

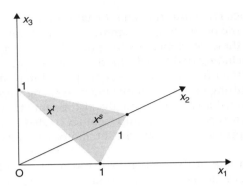

Figure 7.4 Euclidean measure of structural change

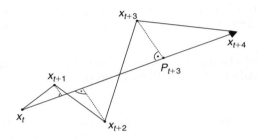

Figure 7.5 Deviations from the direction of change

as $M(t, s) = 100 \times d_M(x^t, x^s)$ (see for example Aiginger, 2002):

$$d_M(x^t, x^s) = \sum_i \left| x_i^t - x_i^s \right|$$

When comparing structural changes across countries or over time one should not forget that the outcome of the analysis may depend on which of the two measures is applied. In other words, if $\vec{v}$ and $\vec{w}$ are two different vectors of structural change, then it might occur that $d_E(\vec{v}) < d_E(\vec{w})$, while $d_M(\vec{v}) > d_M(\vec{w})$.[3] Such an outcome would suggest that the change denoted by $\vec{w}$ is more evenly distributed across branches than that described by $\vec{v}$ (because apparently $\vec{v}$ has more elements close to zero). Both measures have their advantages. While d_E can be applied also to analyse the volatility of structural change, d_M makes it possible to determine the contribution of individual branches to the overall scale of structural change.

Structural change in a given period can be considered stable if throughout the period the industrial structure does not deviate much from the vector defined at the beginning and the end of the period. In Figure 7.5 one can

Table 7.1 Structural change in 1995–2003 according to the Euclidean and the city bloc measures

x	Employment	Nominal sales	Real value added	Nominal value added
$d_E(x_{1995}, x_{2003})$	6.39%	6.09%	8.42%	7.65%
$d_M(x_{1995}, x_{2003})$	38.16%	34.52%	44.95%	41.63%

see structural change over a period of four years. The vector (x_t, x_{t+4}) can be considered to be the direction of change.

Deviation of x_{t+3} from this direction can be defined as the distance between x_{t+3} and vector (x_t, x_{t+4}), which is equal to $d_E(x_{t+3}, p_{t+3})$, where p_{t+3} is the orthogonal projection of x_{t+3} on (x_t, x_{t+4}). Co-ordinates of p_{t+3} can be easily determined using the scalar product of vectors.

It seems likely that the deviation from direction of change will depend on the total scale of change. Therefore in this paper an indicator of relative deviation will be used, which shall be equal to the distance of the given point from the vector of change divided by the length of the vector of change:

$$\delta(x_c; x_a, x_b) = \frac{d_E(x_c, p_c)}{d_E(x_a, x_b)},$$

where (x_a, x_b) is the vector of change and x_c stands for the structure observed within the period (a, b).[4]

Scale and volatility of structural change

We start the presentation of results with the characteristics of the scale of structural change between 1995–2003, followed by analysis of the volatility of the direction of change. We will analyse changes in shares of the 3-digit NACE Rev. 1.1 manufacturing branches, in nominal sales, employment, nominal value added and in value added in constant 1995 prices. Total structural change between 1995–2003 is presented in Table 7.1.

Structural change in Polish manufacturing industry can be assessed as considerable, at least as compared to developments in the EU15. Figure 7.6 illustrates this comparison for the period 1996–2000, for which data for all the countries under consideration were available. Poland experienced the biggest structural changes in all the categories. Note that everywhere employment structure is the variable that changed the least (this applies also to Poland in this particular period). Given that structural change is about uneven growth (or decline), this suggests that industrial branches in a transition country develop at a more uneven pace than is the case in a mature market economy.[5]

Further insights into structural change in Polish manufacturing industry can be obtained from research into the volatility of change, and to this end

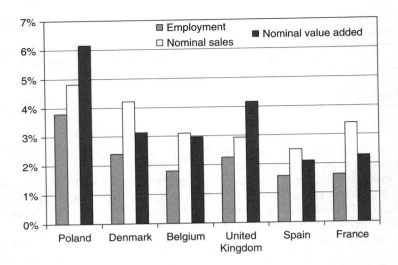

Figure 7.6 Comparative analysis of structural change in Poland and five EU countries 1996–2000

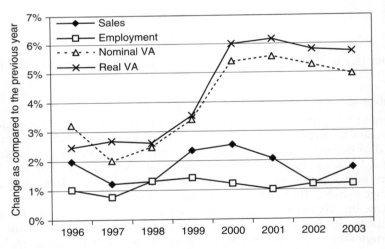

Figure 7.7 Year-on-year structural changes, 1996–2003

year-on-year changes between 1995 and 2003 have been analysed. The result merit some attention (Figure 7.7).

Firstly, year-on-year changes in employment were lower than or at mo equal to such changes in nominal sales throughout the whole period. Beariʳ in mind that the overall structural shift between the beginning and the end the period was bigger for employment than for sales (see Table 7.2) this mean

Table 7.2 Average relative deviation indicator, 1995–2003

x	Employment	Nominal sales	Real value added	Nominal value added
$\frac{1}{7} \sum \delta(x_i\, x_{1995}, x_{2003})$	0.16	0.34	0.52	0.39

Table 7.3 Maximum relative deviation indicator in sub-periods

x	Employment	Nominal sales	Real value added	Nominal value added
$\max[\delta(x_i; x_{1995}, x_{1998})$: $i = 1996, 1997]$	0.25	0.24	0.40	0.40
$\max[\delta(x_i; x_{1998}, x_{2001})$: $i = 1999, 2000]$	0.43	0.98	1.50	1.28
$\max[\delta(x_{2002}; x_{2001}, x_{2003})$: $i = 2003]$	0.38	0.51	1.36	1.20

changes in employment kept more or less the same direction, while year-on-year changes in sales largely offset one another. This finding is confirmed by analysis of the relative deviation indicator. Table 7.2 contains the average values of the indicator between 1995 and 2003.

Secondly, all the variables followed roughly the same scheme of development, which can be characterized by three sub-periods: 'small changes' year-on-year – 'large changes' year-on-year – and 'moderate changes' year-on-year. Initially, year-on-year changes were relatively small, not exceeding 2.6 per cent for value added (both kinds), 1.3 per cent for sales and 1 per cent for employment. However, from 1998 to 1999 structures changed more considerably (for employment it was recorded between 1997 and 1998). The subsequent years saw turbulent changes, reaching 6 per cent for real value added, 2.5 per cent for sales and 1.4 per cent for employment. In 2001 structural changes started to slow down and in the case of sales and employment almost returned to the levels recorded before the acceleration (the slowdown in employment changes started in 2000).

The three stages clearly correspond to the three sub-periods distinguished in the discussion of the macroeconomic framework in section 7.1. Since differences in year-on-year changes over time suggest possible differences in volatility between the sub-periods, we decided to verify this. Indeed, the analysis of the relative deviation indicator for all variables showed that the middle sub-period was the least stable (Table 7.3). In the Appendix we present the lists of branches that were growing/declining in all the sub-periods.

Concluding, the results of this section confirm the hypothesis formulated by Wyżnikiewicz (1987) that structural changes follow a more stable direction when an economy is growing and tend to change direction often in recession.

7.4 Explaining observed developments

As shown in the previous section, in 1995–2003 Poland experienced substantial structural change (in the strict sense), as compared to some Western European countries. In this section we attempt to explain this change. We start from an econometric analysis and then continue with a 'shift and share' analysis of labour productivity.

Econometric analysis

Methodology

The OLS econometric analysis was performed using data for 85 branches of manufacturing industry in 1995 and 2003 (for the list see Table 7.A1 in the Appendix). Dependent variables were the change in the structure of employment and change in the structure of value added (in real terms). Both variables were expressed as ratios of the growth rate in a given branch to the average growth rate in manufacturing. In each model (expressed in log-linear form) we used a uniform set of explanatory variables (in growth terms) which could be grouped into three types, as explained at the beginning of this chapter:

Demand:

- Domestic demand (apparent consumption in Poland).
- External demand (external imports plus internal imports of EU15).

Factor competitiveness:

- Relative unit labour costs (RULC), for example Polish unit labour cost over EU unit labour cost, where unit labour cost (ULC) is defined as the wage–output ratio (in physical unit) and expressed in a common currency.

Competitive performance:

- Share of the domestic market.
- Share of the EU market defined as Polish exports to the EU15 over the internal exports of the EU15.

We expect all parameters to the above variables to have positive signs, except for that for RULC, which should have a negative sign as an indicator of cost competitiveness.

The fourth type of factors of structural change is represented by additional variables reflecting the taxonomic position of those branches under consideration. They are treated as fixed effect factors. We refer to seven branch characteristics:

- Technology level.
- Type of labour skill.

- WIFO multidimensional taxonomic position.
- Concentration level.
- Type of internationalization.
- Level of import penetration ratio.
- Share of foreign-owned companies in output in the beginning of the period.

The first five of them are expressed as sets of binary variables and are based on the following taxonomies:

- Technology level: following the OECD 1997 classification we distinguished four groups of branches: low-tech, medium-low-tech, medium-high-tech and high-tech (Hatzichronoglou, 1997).
- Skill type of labour: following the new WIFO taxonomy of manufacturing industries (Peneder, 1999) we distinguished four groups of branches: low-skilled labour, medium-skilled blue-collar labour, medium-skilled white-collar labour and high-skilled labour.
- The WIFO taxonomy of industries is based on a multidimensional cluster analysis (Peneder, 1999). Following the new WIFO taxonomy we distinguished five groups of branches: mainstream, labour intensive, capital intensive, marketing driven and technology driven.
- Concentration is measured by a quasi-Herfindahl coefficient calculated in terms of employment at the firm level.[6] We distinguished three groups of branches: with high, medium and low scales of concentration.
- Type of internationalization is based on the breakdown of branches by exports to sales ratio and import penetration ratio. We distinguished four groups of branches (Marczewski and Szczygielski, 2005): high export to sales ratio and low import penetration ratio (the group was coined as 'export-dependant'), high export to sales ratio and high import penetration ratio ('internationalized'), low export to sales ratio and high import penetration ratio ('import-dependent'), low export to sales ratio and low import penetration ratio ('non-internationalized').

Additionally, following the findings of industrial organization theory on factors influencing economic performance at the branch level (see for example Rainelli, 1996), we attached to the set of variables describing branch characteristics two more:

- Average import penetration ratio in 1995–2001.
- Average share of foreign-owned companies in output in 1994–96 (Marczewski, 1999).[7]

These two characteristics are represented as continuous variables in the regressions.

For signs of parameters connected with the first five characteristics we do not have any *a priori* expectations. We expect the parameter for the import penetration ratio to have a negative sign, which would reflect the short-term adverse impact of foreign competition on profitability and labour demanded by domestic firms. As concerns the parameter attached to the initial share of the FOC in output, we anticipate that with their bringing in of new technology, organization and often ready-made international networks of suppliers and customers foreign investors should positively contribute to the restructuring process. In this framework foreign competitors are treated as representatives of destructive forces and the FOC as representatives of constructive forces collectively shaping the process.

The econometric analysis was conducted for the whole period under consideration: 1995–2003 and two sub-periods: 1995–98 and 1999–2003.

Regression analysis for the period 1995–2003

The results of the regression analysis for the whole period are presented in Tables 7.4–7.6. In general, we find the same degree of explanation by the chosen set of exogenous variables for changes in employment structure and changes in real value added structure (see the adjusted coefficients of determination R^2). In terms of the four types of factors analysed in this study our findings are as follows:

Demand:

- The impact of domestic demand is statistically very significant (at the 1% significance level) in all regressions.
- EU15 demand has a significant impact only on changes in real value added structure. However, inclusion of the FOC initial share in output to the equation makes even this relationship insignificant.

Competitive performance:

- The share of the domestic market is significant at the 1% level in all regressions.
- The share of the EU15 market has a significant impact only in relation to changes in employment structure.

Factor competitiveness:

- The relative unit labour cost has a significant impact on changes in employment structure, but a positive sign for the estimate suggests the transmission mechanism is not based on changes in output but on changes in labour productivity (compare transmission channels (a) and (b) in

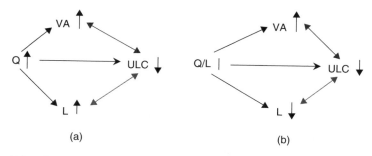

(a)   (b)

Figure 7.8   Alternative transmission channels between employment and ULC

Figure 7.8). On the other hand, the relative ULC negatively effects (though not always significantly) changes in the real value-added structure, which can be interpreted as a competitiveness effect. However, the inclusion of the FOC initial share in output to the equation also makes the latter effect insignificant.

Structural characteristics:

- Technology level (in the OECD definition) is not relevant for the regressions under consideration (see results of F test for exclusion of fixed effects variables).
- Taxonomy of branches by labour skill is also not relevant for all regressions.
- WIFO taxonomy is relevant in the explanation of changes in employment, which is primarily caused by a positive contribution generated by labour-intensive and mainstream branches and a negative one generated by capital-intensive branches.
- The taxonomy of branches by concentration level has no significant influence on the structural change.
- The taxonomy by a type of internationalization shows a significant impact in some cases. Export dependant branches contribute especially positively to the relationship between basic explanatory variables and structural change indicators.
- The import penetration ratio has a significant negative impact on both indicators of structural change.
- The initial share of the FOC in output has a positive impact both on changes in employment and in value added. However, it is significant (even at the 1% level) solely in the latter case.

Concluding the above analysis it is worth noting that the importance of changes in demand as a factor shaping structural change, though high, was not overwhelming. Adjusted R^2 in regressions relating structural change

Table 7.4 The impact of demand, market share and performance measures on structural change indicators (WIFO taxonomy of branches)

Regressor	Change in employment structure		Change in value-added structure	
	(1)	(2)	(4)	(5)
Constant	−0.350**	−0.409**	−0.607**	−0.452**
	(−3.00)	(−3.35)	(−4.76)	(−3.23)
Domestic demand	0.790**	0.786**	0.892**	0.872**
	(10.20)	(11.02)	(10.52)	(10.64)
EU15 demand	0.067	0.071	0.251*	0.240
	(0.63)	(0.68)	(2.17)	(1.99)
Domestic market share	0.671**	0.671**	0.706**	0.737**
	(9.91)	(10.19)	(9.52)	(9.75)
EU15 market share	0.086*	0.087*	0.064	0.069
	(2.11)	(2.28)	(1.42)	(1.56)
Relative unit labour cost	0.327**	0.288*	−0.161	−0.271*
	(3.09)	(2.74)	(−1.39)	(−2.24)
Low skilled labour	0.007		0.182	
	(0.06)		(1.54)	
Medium skilled blue-collar	0.079		0.288*	
	(0.66)		(2.21)	
Medium skilled white-collar	0.005		0.147	
	(0.04)		(1.16)	
Mainstream		0.126		0.028
		(1.18)		(0.23)
Labour intensive		0.129		0.064
		(1.23)		(0.53)
Capital intensive		−0.153		−0.208
		(−1.19)		(−1.40)
Marketing driven		0.093		0.083
		(0.86)		(0.67)
F test for exclusion of fixed effects variables	0.314	2.600*	1.755	1.707
Adjusted R^2	0.707	0.736	0.721	0.723

Notes: The individual coefficient is statistically significant at the * 5% level or ** 1% significance level (*t*-ratios are given in the parentheses under the coefficients); the *F*-statistic tests the exclusion of relevant groups of variables representing fixed effects.

solely to demand variables was equal to 0.254 when explaining changes in employment structure and to 0.314 for changes in value added structure. The role of competitive performance and cost competitiveness was at the least of a similar explanatory power, as adjusted R^2 coefficients for regressions including both demand and competitiveness factors were, respectively, equal to

Table 7.5 The impact of demand, market share and performance measures on structural change indicators (OECD taxonomy of a technological level of branches) and taxonomy of branches by a type of internationalization

Regressor	Change in employment structure			Change in value-added structure		
	(1)	(2)	(3)	(4)	(5)	(6)
Constant	−0.415**	−0.456**	−0.255**	−0.519**	−0.571**	−0.331**
	(−2.85)	(−4.96)	(−3.31)	(−3.20)	(−5.43)	(−3.84)
Domestic demand	0.820**	0.785**	0.809**	0.912**	0.877**	0.900**
	(10.62)	(11.05)	(11.26)	(10.61)	(10.77)	(11.24)
EU15 demand	0.076	0.081	0.134	0.271*	0.275*	0.336**
	(0.65)	(0.81)	(1.29)	(2.09)	(2.40)	(2.91)
Domestic market	0.678**	0.706**	0.631**	0.731**	0.755**	0.674**
share	(9.93)	(10.14)	(9.28)	(9.63)	(9.48)	(8.90)
EU15 market share	0.089*	0.109**	0.085*	0.078	0.093*	0.070
	(2.25)	(2.89)	(2.25)	(1.78)	(2.15)	(1.67)
Relative unit labour	0.323**	0.348**	0.250*	−0.233	−0.183	−0.292*
cost	(2.93)	(3.24)	(2.39)	(−1.90)	(−1.49)	(−2.50)
Low-tech	0.101			0.121		
	(0.80)			(0.86)		
Medium-low-tech	0.030			0.024		
	(0.21)			(0.15)		
Medium-high-tech	0.049			−0.012		
	(0.38)			(−0.08)		
Non-internationalized		0.079			0.113	
		(0.85)			(1.07)	
Internationalized		0.141			0.145	
		(1.75)			(1.57)	
Export dependent		0.305**			0.301**	
		(3.26)			(2.80)	
Import penetration			−0.331*			−0.425*
			(−2.21)			(−2.54)
F test for exclusion of fixed effects variables	0.427	3.671*	4.880*	0.985	2.640	6.471*
Adjusted R^2	0.708	0.741	0.728	0.713	0.730	0.732

Notes: The individual coefficient is statistically significant at the * 5% level or ** 1% significance level (t-ratios are given in the parentheses under the coefficients); the F-statistic tests the exclusion of relevant groups of variables representing fixed effects.

0.714 and 0.713. Adding to the set, variables describing the various structural characteristics of manufacturing branches showed no significant increase in adjusted R^2 coefficients, in general. The only exceptions were type of internationalisation, factor intensity of output, level of import penetration and, especially in the case of value added changes, the FOC early involvement.

Table 7.6 The impact of demand, market share and performance measures on structural change indicators in the 1995–2003 period (taxonomy of branches by concentration level and foreign-owned companies initial share in output)

Regressor	Change in employment structure		Change in value-added structure	
	(1)	(2)	(3)	(4)
Constant	−0.350**	−0.383**	−0.496**	−0.524**
	(−4.27)	(−5.26)	(−5.45)	(−6.70)
Domestic demand	0.797**	0.780**	0.880**	0.850**
	(10.69)	(10.68)	(10.60)	(10.83)
EU15 demand	0.069	0.011	0.264*	0.144
	(0.67)	(0.10)	(2.29)	(1.28)
Domestic market share	0.674**	0.681**	0.736**	0.737**
	(9.75)	(10.57)	(9.56)	(10.65)
EU15 market share	0.088*	0.078*	0.076	0.055
	(2.23)	(2.02)	(1.74)	(1.32)
Relative unit labour cost	0.312**	0.327**	−0.198	−0.190
	(2.93)	(3.25)	(−1.67)	(−1.76)
Low concentration	0.032		0.101	
	(0.43)		(1.23)	
High concentration	0.000		0.084	
	(0.00)		(1.01)	
FOC initial share in output		0.354		0.671**
		(1.92)		(3.39)
F test for exclusion of fixed effects variables	0.116	3.680	0.898	11.475**
Adjusted R^2	0.708	0.724	0.713	0.747

Notes: The individual coefficient is statistically significant at the * 5% level or ** 1% significance level (*t*-ratios are given in the parentheses under the coefficients); the *F*-statistic test the exclusion of relevant groups of variables representing fixed effects.

Regression analysis for sub-periods

In an attempt to capture dynamic elements of the process of structural change we replicated the above econometric analysis for the same set of explanatory variables for two sub-periods: 1995–98 and 1999–2003. The main findings were as follows (see Tables 7.A2–7.A3 in the Appendix).

Demand:

- Domestic demand had a strong positive impact on structural changes in both sub-periods.
- The role of EU15 demand strengthened in the second sub-period, though continued to be statistically insignificant.

Competitive performance:

- The domestic market share made a meaningful positive contribution to structural changes in both sub-periods.
- The role of the EU market share has slightly weakened in the second sub-period, which could mean that the process of Polish manufacturers building up their positions on the EU15 market is almost completed.

Factor competitiveness:

- The role of labour cost competitiveness became more important in the second sub-period, which was reflected by the growing impact of the relative unit labour cost on value added changes.

Structural characteristics:

- The negative impact of import penetration on employment and value added growth disappeared in the second sub-period, which could be interpreted as a symptom of a stabilization of the position of foreign competitors on the domestic market.
- The taxonomy by labour skill became significant both in explaining change in employment and value added in the second sub-period, primarily due to a strong positive impact coming from medium-skilled blue-collar labour.
- Internationalized branches started to show a positive contribution to value added changes during the second sub-period.
- Though levels of concentration showed no significant impact on structural change in both sub-periods we noticed an in-between period change of direction in its influence on value-added structure, with highly concentrated branches contributing positively in the second sub-period.
- The FOC initial share of output had, apparently, a stronger impact on the restructuring process in the first sub-period than in the second. However, it continued to be positive.

Structural change and labour productivity

Methodology

Econometric analysis suggests that those branches that grew more in terms of employment had a better competitive performance but worse cost competitiveness. So, what about labour productivity? Were those branches that increased their share in employment more, or less, productive than those that decreased their shares? The above analysis of structural characteristics makes this problem even less straightforward. On the one hand, the foreign owned companies contributed positively and significantly to employment growth, which could indicate a positive relationship between employment growth and productivity. On the other hand, low import penetration (in the first sub-period) and (in the second sub-period) medium-skilled blue-collar labour intensity were also associated with the increase in employment share, which could imply a negative relationship.

The question of labour productivity is important from the point of view of economic growth, because one would like to know if branches whose role in the economy increases are the more productive ones. On the other hand, as we explained earlier, this question is also important from the labour market perspective.

We will analyse the changes in aggregate apparent labour productivity in manufacturing industry (that is, value added per person employed), employing the 'shift and share' technique based on the following identity (see for example Fagerberg, 1999):

$$\Delta r = \sum \Delta r_i s_i + \sum r_i \Delta s_i + \sum \Delta r_i \Delta s_i$$

where r stands for labour productivity and s_i for the share of the i-th industry in manufacturing employment. Operator Δ denotes the difference in the variable between the base year and the end year, while symbols without Δ – for instance s_i – stand for the value of variables in the base year.

The three components can be interpreted as follows. The first component measures the productivity change 'within industries'. If there is no structural change at all, this is equal to the overall productivity change. Now assume that there is structural change, that is employment in some branches grows/declines faster than in others. In this case the second component measures the impact of these differences in employment growth on productivity, provided there is no productivity growth within industries. The third component combines productivity growth within industries with structural change. While the second term is interpreted as the effect of labour moving to more productive branches, the third one can be regarded as the effect of labour moving to more dynamic industries (Fagerberg, 1999).

Structural change versus productivity growth

Results of the calculations (Table 7.7) are not typical. While the fact that the 'within-growth' component is the biggest is rather normal – this is also the case with most countries in the Fagerberg (1999) study – the negative signs of the two remaining components are not that common.

The negative sign of the second term implies that branches that grew in terms of employment structure had, on average, lower labour productivity than the ones whose share in employment decreased. What is more, given that all the branches increased their labour productivity, a negative dynamic

Table 7.7 Shift and share analysis of the increase in labour productivity 1995–2003 (thousands PLN per person employed, constant 1995 prices), 98 branches

Δr	$\sum \Delta r_i s_i$	$\sum r_i \Delta s_i$	$\sum \Delta r_i \Delta s_i$
28.76	30.77	−1.15	−0.86

shift effect means that branches that grew in employment terms had a lower productivity than those that declined in structural terms.

The occurrence of the negative dynamic shift effect is a confirmation of the econometric analysis findings where we postulate that a transmission between changes in employment and the relative ULC changes works through the opposite direction changes in labour productivity (see Figure 7.8b).

Was that true also for the taxonomy groups of branches? We selected four taxonomies that yielded significant results in the econometric analysis and examined the relationship between structural change in terms of these taxonomies and labour productivity growth. To this end we once again decomposed Δr by splitting the right-hand side of the 'shift and share' identity further into sub-sums according to the taxonomy groups:

$$\sum \Delta r_i s_i = \sum_{J \in T} \sum_{i \in J} \Delta r_i s_i$$

$$\sum r_i \Delta s_i = \sum_{J \in T} \sum_{i \in J} r_i \Delta s_i$$

$$\sum \Delta r_i \Delta s_i = \sum_{J \in T} \sum_{i \in J} \Delta r_i \Delta s_i$$

where T stands for a taxonomy (e.g. by level of concentration) and J for the individual taxonomy groups within this taxonomy (in this case $J \in \{low concentrated, medium concentrated, high concentrated\} = T$). The share of foreign owned companies in output and the import penetration ratio, which were used in the econometric analysis as continuous variables, were converted into taxonomies by dividing industries into three groups of equal size.

The results of our new decompositions are reported in Tables 7.8–7.11. The row labeled 'Total' should contain the same numbers as in Table 7.7; if they are different, then it is the consequence of the fact that some of the taxonomies do not cover all the 3-digit NACE. Rev. 1.1 branches of manufacturing industry. The number of branches covered by each taxonomy is indicated in the respective table heading.

Starting with the role of the share of foreign-owned companies (Table 7.8), we see that branches that early had a high share of FOC grew in terms of

Table 7.8 Shift and share analysis of increase in labour productivity 1995–2003 by FOC taxonomy groups (thousands PLN per person employed, constant 1995 prices), 98 branches

Taxonomy group	Within-growth effect	Static shift effect	Dynamic growth effect	Share in employment	
				1995	2003
Low FOC share	10.85	−2.57	−2.37	38.06%	29,16%
Medium FOC share	7.28	0.10	0.70	31.40%	31,72%
High FOC share	12.64	1.33	0.81	30.53%	39,12%
Total	30.77	−1.15	−0.86		

Table 7.9 Shift and share analysis of increase in labour productivity 1995–2003 by import penetration taxonomy groups (thousands PLN per person employed, constant 1995 prices), 87 branches

	Within-growth effect	Static shift effect	Dynamic growth effect	Share in employment	
				1995	2003
Low import penetration	9.16	0.73	0.92	38.61%	44,62%
Medium import penetration	11.28	−0.95	−0.72	38.08%	33,12%
High import penetration	4.74	0.23	0.24	16.68%	16,99%
Total	25.18	0.01	0.43		

employment. They contributed most to the within growth effect and they contributed positively to the remaining two effects, which means they had both a high labor productivity level in 1995 and a substantial productivity increase. The opposite was the case with 'low FOC', although they also had considerable within productivity growth.

The story is slightly different if we look at import penetration (Table 7.8). Although branches facing low import penetration contributed positively to all three effects, their productivity growth and structural change ('within growth effect') were not the highest. Branches facing medium penetration had a higher within growth effect, but lost shares in employment.

What is worth observing about the developments in the taxonomy groups defined by the character of internationalization (Table 7.10) is the evolution of the non-internationalized group. These industries increased their share in employment, but showed negative static shift and a dynamic shift effect, indicating their relatively low labour productivity level and labour productivity growth. The latter was not the case with export-dependant and import-dependent industries that also grew in terms of employment shares.

Table 7.10 Shift and share analysis of increase in labour productivity 1995–2003 by the character of internationalization (thousands PLN per person employed, constant 1995 prices), 87 branches

	Within-growth effect	Static shift effect	Dynamic growth effect	Share in employment	
				1995	2003
Internationalized	10.67	−0.96	−1.64	31.42%	27,13%
Non-internationalized	6.36	−0.06	−0.20	25.79%	27,08%
Export-dependant	3.64	0.66	1.09	22.82%	25,85%
Import-dependant	4.51	0.37	1.18	15.63%	16,86%
Total	25.18	0.01	0.43		

Table 7.11 Shift and share analysis of increase in labour productivity 1995–2003 by skill-intensity groups (thousands PLN per person employed, constant 1995 prices), 95 branches

	Within-growth effect	Static shift effect	Dynamic growth effect	Share in employment	
				1995	2003
Low-skilled labour	12.83	−1.24	−0.51	47.76%	44,17%
Medium-skilled blue-collar	5.87	0.86	1.07	18.15%	24,09%
Medium-skilled white-collar	9.09	−0.26	−0.85	16.96%	17,88%
High-skilled	2.73	−0.49	−0.56	15.51%	12,25%
Total	30.52	−1.13	−0.85		

Regarding groups defined by labour skill type (Table 7.11), we observed a huge increase in the share of medium-skilled/blue collar-intensive branches, which also resulted in a high static-shift and dynamic-shift effects. Interestingly, branches that were categorized as low skilled by this taxonomy had the biggest 'within' labour productivity growth. However, they also decreased their share in employment.

Although the changes in employment structure between 1995 and 2003 contributed negatively to the growth in labour productivity, this was not always the case when we consider changes in shares of employment of groups in branches defined by some of the taxonomy groups. In particular, it seems that the relative growth of foreign-owned companies (which proved to be significant in the econometric analysis) contributed positively to productivity growth. But, apparently, other factors that drove structural changes contributed negatively to this, and these factors were ultimately stronger.

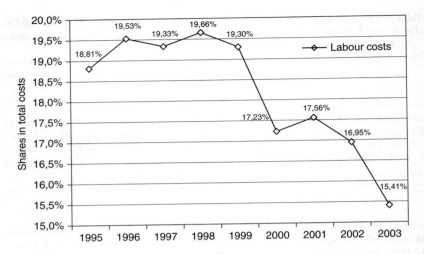

Figure 7.9   Labour intensity of manufacturing production in 1995–2003 (share of labour costs in total costs)

Structural change versus labour-market developments

From the labour market perspective, the question is if the rise in the capital-labour ratio observed by labour economists was homogenous across industries. As previous research (Bukowski, 2005) shows, the Polish labour market has experienced two shocks in the course of the last decade: one at the end of 1998, beginning of 1999 and the other in 2000–01. It has been claimed that 'Poland ... experienced a significant increase in structural unemployment and, as a result, a long lasting shift in the capital/labour ratio in the economy' (Bukowski, 2005, p. 28). The last point is also supported by our data: if one measures the labour intensity of manufacturing production by the share of labour costs in total costs, then one sees two abrupt declines following one year after the labour market shocks described in Bukowski *et al.* (see Figure 7.9).[8]

Consequently, the second question we would like to ask is: was the observed shift in the capital–labour ratio homogenous across branches or was it a question of relative growth in more capital intensive industries in terms of employment structure. We will assume that more capital intensive industries are also the ones with higher labour productivity.

Table 7.7 would suggest that the capital–labour shift in manufacturing was rather homogenous across industries and was not caused by structural change (if we assume that more productive industries are also more capital intensive ones). However, this was different in the short-term. Both labour–market shocks were echoed in the positive and relatively big static shift effects (see Table 7.12). In 1998–99 almost the entire growth in productivity was due to structural change.

Table 7.12 Year-on-year shift and share analysis, 1995–2003

	Within-growth effect	Static shift effect	Dynamic growth effect	Total
1995–1996	2.27	0.04	0.01	2.32
1996–1997	5.88	0.16	0.00	6.04
1997–1998	2.36	−0.13	−0.34	1.89
1998–1999	−0.33	1.14	−0.11	0.70
1999–2000	4.60	−0.81	−0.09	3.70
2000–2001	4.58	−0.17	−0.01	4.40
2001–2002	3.97	0.23	−0.92	3.28
2002–2003	7.49	−0.90	−0.14	6.45

Most likely the less productive industries reacted faster to the unfavourable conditions and cut employment immediately, while in the more productive industries this process was distributed over a few years.

7.5 Conclusions

The intensity of structural change in Polish manufacturing was high in international terms in the period under consideration, despite the fact that the radical reforms of the early 1990s had already been completed. We identified two serious external shocks accelerating the restructuring process – in 1998/1999 and 2001/2002. Among the forces shaping the process we distinguished demand factors, competitive performance, factor competitiveness and the structural characteristics of branches. Apparently, the most important among them were changes in domestic demand and domestic market share. Labour-cost competitiveness had a standard positive impact on value-added changes. However, its influence on changes in employment was in the opposite direction. We interpret this finding in terms of a negative relation between changes in employment and labour productivity (the negative dynamic shift effect), which is a rather rare phenomenon in developed market economies but which is seen quite often in transforming economies. In general, the structural characteristics of branches were not so important in the process. The exceptions to this were type of internationalization, factor intensity of output, level of import penetration and – especially in the case of value-added changes – the share of foreign own companies in output. Analysing the dynamics of the process we recognized an increasing role of cost competitiveness and certain branch characteristics (especially labour skills and type of internationalization) and a decreasing role of import competition as factors influencing structural change. These tendencies seem to support the view that Polish manufacturing is eventually approaching the stage of a mature market economy.

Appendix

Table 7.A1   List of the analysed NACE 3-digit level manufacturing branches. Branches that were included in the regression analysis are marked with an 'R'; branches that have increased or decreased their shares in manufacturing employment in all three sub-periods (1995–98, 1998–2001, 2001–03) are marked with a '+' or a '−' respectively; 'o' denotes branches which showed no evident developments

NACE code	*NACE category*	*Included in the regression analysis*	*Increase or decline in all 3 sub-periods*
151	Production, processing, preserving of meat, meat products	R	+
152	Processing and preserving of fish and fish products	R	o
153	Processing and preserving of fruit and vegetables	R	o
154	Manufacture of vegetable and animal oils and fats	R	o
155	Manufacture of dairy products	R	o
156	Manufacture of grain mill products, starches and starch products	R	−
157	Manufacture of prepared animal feeds	R	
158	Manufacture of other food products	R	+
159	Manufacture of beverages	R	o
160	Manufacture of tobacco products		−
171	Preparation and spinning of textile fibres	R	−
172	Textile weaving	R	−
173	Finishing of textiles		+
174	Manufacture of made-up textile articles, except apparel		o
175	Manufacture of other textiles	R	o
176	Manufacture of knitted and crocheted fabrics	R	−
177	Manufacture of knitted and crocheted articles		−
181	Manufacture of leather clothes	R	o
182	Manufacture of other wearing apparel and accessories	R	−
183	Dressing and dyeing of fur; manufacture of articles of fur	R	o
191	Tanning and dressing of leather	R	−
192	Manufacture of luggage, handbags and the like, saddler	R	−
193	Manufacture of footwear	R	−
201	Sawmilling and planning of wood, impregnation of wood	R	o

Table 7.A1 (Continued)

NACE code	NACE category	Included in the regression analysis	Increase or decline in all 3 sub-periods
202	Manufacture of veneer sheets; manufacture of plywood, laminboard, particle board, fibre board and other panels and boards	R	+
203	Manufacture of builders' carpentry and joinery	R	+
204	Manufacture of wooden containers	R	o
205	Manufacture of other products of wood; manufacture of articles of cork, straw and plaiting materials	R	+
211	Manufacture of pulp, paper and paperboard	R	–
212	Manufacture of articles of paper and paperboard	R	+
221	Publishing	R	+
222	Printing and service activities related to printing	R	o
231	Manufacture of coke oven products		o
232	Manufacture of refined petroleum products	R	–
233	Processing of nuclear fuel	R	o
241	Manufacture of basic chemicals	R	–
242	Manufacture of pesticides and other agro-chemical products	R	–
243	Manufacture of paints, varnishes and similar coatings, printing ink and mastics	R	+
244	Manufacture of pharmaceuticals, medicinal chemicals and botanical products	R	+
245	Manufacture of soap, detergents, cleaning, polishing	R	+
246	Manufacture of other chemical products	R	–
247	Manufacture of man-made fibres	R	–
251	Manufacture of rubber products	R	+
252	Manufacture of plastic products	R	+
261	Manufacture of glass and glass products	R	+
262	Manufacture of non-refractory ceramic goods other than for construction purposes; manufacture of refractory ceramic products	R	o
263	Manufacture of ceramic tiles and flags	R	+
264	Manufacture of bricks, tiles and construction products	R	o
265	Manufacture of cement, lime and plaster	R	–
266	Manufacture of articles of concrete, plaster, cement	R	
267	Cutting, shaping and finishing of stone	R	+
268	Manufacture of other non-metallic mineral products	R	o

(Continued)

Table 7.A1   (Continued)

NACE code	NACE category	Included in the regression analysis	Increase or decline in all 3 sub-periods
271	Manufacture of basic iron and steel and of ferro-alloys (ECSC)	R	−
272	Manufacture of tubes		−
273	Other first processing of iron and steel and production of non-ECSC ferro-alloys		−
274	Manufacture of basic precious and non-ferrous metals	R	−
275	Casting of metals		
281	Manufacture of structural metal products	R	+
282	Manufacture of tanks, reservoirs and containers of metal; manufacture of central heating radiators and boilers	R	+
283	Manufacture of steam generators, except central heating hot water boilers	R	−
284	Forging, pressing, stamping and roll forming of metal; powder metallurgy		+
285	Treatment and coating of metals; general mechanical engineering		+
286	Manufacture of cutlery, tools and general hardware	R	o
287	Manufacture of other fabricated metal products	R	+
291	Manufacture of machinery for the production and use of mechanical power, except aircraft, vehicle and cycle engines	R	o
292	Manufacture of other general purpose machinery	R	o
293	Manufacture of agricultural and forestry machinery	R	−
294	Manufacture of machine-tools	R	o
295	Manufacture of other special purpose machinery	R	−
296	Manufacture of weapons and ammunition	R	o
297	Manufacture of domestic appliances n.e.c.	R	−
300	Manufacture of office machinery and computers		o
311	Manufacture of electric motors, generators and transformers	R	o
312	Manufacture of electricity distribution and control apparatus	R	o
313	Manufacture of insulated wire and cable	R	+
314	Manufacture of accumulators, primary cells and primary batteries	R	o

Table 7.A1   (Continued)

NACE code	NACE category	Included in the regression analysis	Increase or decline in all 3 sub-periods
315	Manufacture of lighting equipment and electric lamps	R	o
316	Manufacture of electrical equipment n.e.c.	R	+
321	Manufacture of electronic valves and tubes and other electronic components	R	−
322	Manufacture of television and radio transmitters and apparatus for line telephony and line telegraphy	R	o
323	Manufacture of television and radio receivers, sound or video recording or reproducing apparatus and associated goods	R	o
331	Manufacture of medical and surgical equipment and orthopaedic appliances	R	o
332	Manufacture of instruments and appliances for measuring, checking, testing, navigating and other purposes, except industrial process control equipment	R	o
333	Manufacture of industrial process control equipment		−
334	Manufacture of optical instruments, photographic equipment		o
341	Manufacture of motor vehicles	R	−
342	Manufacture of bodies (coachwork) for motor vehicles; manufacture of trailers and semi-trailers	R	o
343	Manufacture of parts, accessories for motor vehicles	R	+
351	Building and repairing of ships and boats	R	o
352	Manufacture of railway, tramway locomotives, rolling stock	R	o
353	Manufacture of aircraft and spacecraft	R	o
354	Manufacture of motorcycles and bicycles	R	o
355	Manufacture of other transport equipment n.e.c.	R	o
361	Manufacture of furniture	R	+
362	Manufacture of jewellery and related articles	R	o
363	Manufacture of musical instruments	R	−
364	Manufacture of sports goods	R	o
365	Manufacture of games and toys	R	o
366	Miscellaneous manufacturing n.e.c.	R	o

Table 7.A2   The impact of demand, market share and performance measures on structural change indicators in the 1995–1998 sub-period (WIFO taxonomy of branches)

Regressor	Change in employment structure		Change in value-added structure	
	(1)	(2)	(3)	(4)
Constant	−0.187 (−1.93)	−0.258** (−2.71)	−0.285* (−2.42)	−0.046 (−0.41)
Domestic demand	0.485** (5.51)	0.476** (5.96)	0.878** (8.19)	0.807** (8.61)
EU15 demand	−0.027 (−0.41)	−0.049 (−0.76)	−0.015 (−0.19)	−0.074 (−0.98)
Domestic market share	0.849** (5.64)	0.770** (5.12)	0.828** (4.52)	0.782** (4.43)
EU15 market share	0.145* (2.26)	0.136* (2.23)	0.180* (2.30)	0.219** (3.04)
Relative unit labour cost	0.276 (1.96)	0.279* (2.05)	−0.154 (−0.90)	−0.291 (−1.82)
Low-skilled labour	−0.040 (−0.54)		0.072 (0.81)	
Medium skilled blue-collar	−0.055 (−0.64)		0.020 (0.19)	
Medium skilled white-collar	−0.028 (−0.35)		0.119 (1.21)	
Mainstream		0.070 (1.00)		−0.114 (−1.39)
Labour intensive		0.025 (0.34)		−0.124 (−1.46)
Capital intensive		−0.056 (−0.66)		−0.288** (−2.90)
Marketing driven		0.070 (0.95)		−0.021 (−0.25)
F test for exclusion of fixed effects variables	0.161	1.117	0.788	3.085*
Adjusted R^2	0.442	0.463	0.573	0.617

Notes: The individual coefficient is statistically significant at the * 5% level or ** 1% significance level (t-ratios are given in the parentheses under the coefficients): the F-statistic tests the exclusion of relevant groups of variables representing fixed effects.

Table 7.A3 The impact of demand, market share and performance measures on structural change indicators in the 1995–98 sub-period (OECD taxonomy of the technological level of branches and taxonomy of branches by a type of internationalization)

Regressor	Change in employment structure			Change in value-added structure		
	(1)	(2)	(3)	(4)	(5)	(6)
Constant	−0.225*	−0.249**	−0.171**	−0.096	−0.238*	−0.128
	(−2.06)	(−3.19)	(−2.68)	(−0.74)	(−2.51)	(−1.65)
Domestic demand	0.490**	0.506**	0.546**	0.891**	0.877**	0.952**
	(5.98)	(6.37)	(6.94)	(9.14)	(9.09)	(9.95)
EU15 demand	−0.030	−0.032	−0.011	−0.043	−0.016	0.008
	(−0.45)	(−0.51)	(−0.19)	(−0.54)	(−0.20)	(0.11)
Domestic market share	0.791**	0.645**	0.600**	0.769**	0.588**	0.478*
	(5.18)	(4.04)	(3.83)	(4.22)	(3.03)	(2.51)
EU15 market share	0.145*	0.154*	0.127*	0.212**	0.241**	0.193**
	(2.36)	(2.55)	(2.19)	(2.90)	(3.28)	(2.74)
Relative unit labour cost	0.294*	0.287*	0.327*	−0.227	−0.218	−0.155
	(2.16)	(2.19)	(2.54)	(−1.40)	(−1.37)	(−0.99)
Low-tech	0.001			−0.071		
	(0.01)			(−0.71)		
Medium-low-tech	0.006			−0.133		
	(0.07)			(−1.23)		
Medium-high-tech	−0.043			−0.190		
	(−0.53)			(−1.98)		
Non-internationalized		0.055			0.049	
		(0.81)			(0.60)	
Internationalized		−0.072			−0.075	
		(−1.37)			(−1.17)	
Export dependent		0.055			0.134	
		(0.85)			(1.70)	
Import penetration			−0.296**			−0.413**
			(−2.73)			(−3.13)
F test for exclusion of fixed effects variables	0.328	2.086	7.474**	2.068	2.794*	9.811**
Adjusted R^2	0.446	0.482	0.501	0.593	0.603	0.619

Notes: The individual coefficient is statistically significant at the * 5% level or ** 1% significance level (t-ratios are given in the parentheses under the coefficients): the F-statistic tests the exclusion of relevant groups of variables representing fixed effects.

Table 7.A4 The impact of demand, market share and performance measures on structural change indicators in the 1995–98 sub-period (taxonomy of branches by concentration level and foreign-owned companies initial share in output)

Regressor	Change in employment structure		Change in value-added structure	
	(1)	(2)	(3)	(4)
Constant	−0.213*	−0.264**	−0.227*	−0.271**
	(−2.92)	(−4.05)	(−2.55)	(−3.48)
Domestic demand	0.456**	0.432**	0.826**	0.777**
	(5.82)	(5.44)	(8.64)	(8.16)
EU15 demand	−0.046	−0.047	−0.018	−0.047
	(−0.69)	(−0.75)	(−0.23)	(−0.63)
Domestic market share	0.756**	0.813**	0.716**	0.771**
	(5.16)	(5.90)	(4.01)	(4.67)
EU15 market share	0.139*	0.117	0.216**	0.171*
	(2.31)	(1.95)	(2.95)	(2.37)
Relative unit labour cost	0.265	0.313*	−0.224	−0.168
	(1.96)	(2.39)	(−1.36)	(−1.06)
Low concentration	0.040		0.103	
	(0.82)		(1.71)	
High concentration	−0.040		−0.004	
	(−0.79)		(−0.06)	
FOC initial share in output		0.249		0.440**
		(1.99)		(2.93)
F test for exclusion of fixed effects variables	1.254	3.951	1.991	8.563**
Adjusted R^2	0.464	0.480	0.586	0.613

Notes: The individual coefficient is statistically significant at the * 5% level or ** 1% significance level (*t*-ratios are given in the parentheses under the coefficients); the *F*-statistic tests the exclusion of relevant groups of variables representing fixed effects.

Table 7.A5   The impact of demand, market share and performance measures on structural change indicators in the 1999–2003 sub-period (WIFO taxonomy of branches)

Regressor	Change in employment structure		Change in value-added structure	
	(1)	(2)	(3)	(4)
Constant	−0.087	−0.023	−0.264**	−0.240*
	(−1.03)	(−0.30)	(−2.67)	(−2.55)
Domestic demand	0.713**	0.683**	0.768**	0.722**
	(9.27)	(9.07)	(8.50)	(7.82)
EU15 demand	0.081	0.063	0.149	0.115
	(1.14)	(0.88)	(1.78)	(1.30)
Domestic market share	0.454**	0.478**	0.653**	0.657**
	(8.07)	(8.29)	(9.87)	(9.30)
EU15 market share	0.094**	0.115**	0.058	0.071
	(2.65)	(3.22)	(1.40)	(1.64)
Relative unit labour cost	0.230*	0.168	−0.274**	−0.285*
	(2.63)	(1.80)	(−2.66)	(−2.49)
Low-skilled labour	0.027		0.056	
	(0.36)		(0.63)	
Medium skilled blue-collar	0.218*		0.233*	
	(2.56)		(2.33)	
Medium skilled white-collar	0.070		0.002	
	(0.87)		(0.03)	
Mainstream		−0.006		0.062
		(−0.07)		(0.67)
Labour intensive		0.063		0.123
		(0.85)		(1.36)
Capital intensive		−0.203*		−0.045
		(−2.25)		(−0.41)
Marketing driven		−0.037		0.027
		(−0.48)		(0.29)
F test for exclusion of fixed effects variables	4.029*	3.075*	3.682*	1.048
Adjusted R^2	0.611	0.608	0.627	0.590

Notes: The individual coefficient is statistically significant at the * 5% level or ** 1% significance level (*t*-ratios are given in the parentheses under the coefficients); the *F*-statistic tests the exclusion of relevant groups of variables representing fixed effects.

Table 7.A6 The impact of demand, market share and performance measures on structural change indicators in the 1999–2003 sub-period (OECD taxonomy of a technological level of branches and taxonomy of branches by a type of internationalization)

Regressor	Change in employment structure			Change in value-added structure		
	(1)	(2)	(3)	(4)	(5)	(6)
Constant	0.005	−0.054	−0.020	−0.229*	−0.231**	−0.183*
	(0.05)	(−0.80)	(−0.31)	(−2.18)	(−2.79)	(−2.39)
Domestic demand	0.694**	0.689**	0.677**	0.735**	0.740**	0.719**
	(8.43)	(9.32)	(8.48)	(7.62)	(8.07)	(7.71)
EU15 demand	0.065	0.061	0.071	0.122	0.126	0.122
	(0.86)	(0.88)	(0.96)	(1.39)	(1.47)	(1.40)
Domestic market share	0.467**	0.532**	0.464**	0.660**	0.719**	0.659**
	(7.73)	(9.03)	(7.57)	(9.32)	(9.85)	(9.19)
EU15 market share	0.107**	0.134**	0.110**	0.063	0.082	0.066
	(2.85)	(3.91)	(2.98)	(1.43)	(1.93)	(1.53)
Relative unit labour cost	0.257*	0.340**	0.235*	−0.243*	−0.166	−0.268*
	(2.53)	(3.59)	(2.42)	(−2.04)	(−1.42)	(−2.36)
Low-tech	−0.008			0.075		
	(−0.09)			(0.72)		
Medium-low-tech	−0.040			0.033		
	(−0.43)			(0.30)		
Medium-high-tech	0.033			0.078		
	(0.34)			(0.69)		
Non-internationalized		−0.020			0.026	
		(−0.32)			(0.32)	
Internationalized		0.160**			0.168*	
		(2.65)			(2.25)	
Export dependent		0.228**			0.169	
		(3.31)			(1.97)	
Import penetration			0.030			0.007
			(0.27)			(0.05)
F test for exclusion of fixed effects variables	0.408	5.874**	0.075	0.271	2.348	0.003
Adjusted R^2	0.557	0.634	0.562	0.577	0.609	0.584

Notes: The individual coefficient is statistically significant at the * 5% level or ** 1% significance level (t-ratios are given in the parentheses under the coefficients); the F-statistic tests the exclusion of relevant groups of variables representing fixed effects.

Table 7.A7 The impact of demand, market share and performance measures on structural change indicators in the 1999–2003 sub-period (taxonomy of branches by concentration level and foreign-owned companies initial share in output)

Regressor	Change in employment structure		Change in value-added structure	
	(1)	(2)	(3)	(4)
Constant	−0.019	−0.084	−0.179*	−0.257**
	(−0.30)	(−1.28)	(−2.34)	(−3.33)
Domestic demand	0.677**	0.682**	0.712**	0.727**
	(8.47)	(8.84)	(7.65)	(8.01)
EU15 demand	0.074	0.058	0.110	0.108
	(0.97)	(0.80)	(1.23)	(1.27)
Domestic market share	0.453**	0.459**	0.672**	0.656**
	(7.39)	(7.92)	(9.43)	(9.64)
EU15 market share	0.109**	0.104**	0.067	0.060
	(2.94)	(2.90)	(1.56)	(1.43)
Relative unit labour cost	0.213*	0.216*	−0.239*	−0.281**
	(2.20)	(2.39)	(−2.13)	(−2.66)
Low concentration	0.014		−0.005	
	(0.25)		(−0.08)	
High concentration	−0.021		0.059	
	(−0.36)		(0.89)	
FOC initial share in output		0.286*		0.302
		(2.18)		(1.96)
F test for exclusion of fixed effects variables	0.174	4.748*	0.548	3.845
Adjusted R^2	0.558	0.586	0.584	0.603

Notes: The individual coefficient is statistically significant at the * 5% level or ** 1% significance level (*t*-ratios are given in the parentheses under the coefficients); the *F*-statistic tests the exclusion of relevant groups of variables representing fixed effects.

Notes

1 Data on REER come from the IMF.
2 However one should be somewhat cautious with this interpretation, considering that the value of d_E can be bigger than 100% (the maximal value is $\sqrt{2}$)
3 For instance consider $\vec{v} = x^2 - x^1$ and $\vec{w} = y^2 - y^1$, where $x^1 = y^1 = (1, 0, 0)$, $x^2 = (0.45, 0.25, 0.30)$ and $y^2 = (0.5, 0.5, 0)$.
4 In the notation of Figure 7.5, $\delta(x_{t+3} ; x_t , x_{t+4}) = \frac{d_E(x_{t+3} , p_{t+3})}{d_E(x_t , x_{t+4})}$
5 For a brief analysis of differences in structural changes occurring *within* the post-socialist group of countries see Campos and Coricelli (2002). They compare two groups of countries: the CEEB (Central and Eastern European countries including the Baltic states, plus the Balkan countries) and the CIS countries (Confederation of Independent States).

6   Inputs for our estimates of quasi-Herfindahl coefficients were the F-01 statistics of the Central Statistical Office and the list of Poland's 1,500 biggest companies in 2002 published by the 'Rzeczpospolita' daily. We assumed that each industry consisted of (a) firms from the 1,500 list, and (b) of the remaining firms, whose number and total employment we knew thanks to F-01. To calculate quasi-Herfindahl coefficients we assumed that the (b) group firms were all of equal size in terms of employment. While realizing the deficiency of this measure, we believe that it is satisfactory for creating a taxonomy for distinguishing three large equal-sized groups.

7   We treat this variable as an indicator of the early engagement of foreign investors in the restructuring process.

8   One might wonder if the falls in labour intensity observed in 2000 and 2003 were not a merely statistical effect caused by replacing permanent employment with self-employment. This has not been the case in manufacturing, however, because declines in the shares of labour costs were not reflected in a simultaneous increase in shares in outsourcing costs.

References

Aiginger, K. (2000) 'Speed of Change and Growth of Manufacturing', in M. Peneder, K. Aiginger, G. Hutschenreiter and M. Marterbauer (eds), *Structural Change and Economic Growth*. Wien: WIFO (Austrian Institute of Economic Research).

Boni, M. (ed.) (2004) 'Elastyczny rynek pracy w Polsce. Jak sprostać temu wyzwaniu?' (An Elastic Labour Market for Poland. How to Face the Challenge?), Warsaw: Zeszyty BRE-Bank-CASE no. 73.

Bukowski, M. (ed.) (2005) 'Employment in Poland 2005', Ministry of Economy and Labour (www.mgip.gov.pl).

Campos, N.F. and F. Coricelli (2002) 'Growth in Transition: What We Know, What We Don't, What We Should', *Journal of Economic Literature*, 40(3): 793–836.

Chenery, H.B. and L. Taylor (1968) 'Development Patterns, Over Countries and Over Time', *Review of Economics and Statistics*, 50(4): 391–416.

Corden, W.M. (1997) *Trade Policy and Economic Welfare*. Oxford: Clarendon Press.

Czyżewski, A.B. and W.B. Orłowski (2000) 'Czynniki zmian struktury wytwarzania PKB, przemysłu i usług w latach 1992–98' (Factors of Change of the GDP, industry and services structures in 1992–98), in A. Lipowski op. cit. (2000).

Fagerberg, J. (1999) 'Specialization and Growth: World Manufacturing Productivity 1973–90' mimeo, Centre for Technology, Innovation and Culture University of Oslo, Oslo.

European Commission (2004) *Facing the Challenge. The Lisbon Strategy for Growth and Unemployment* ['The Kok Report']. Luxembourg: Office for Official Publications of the European Communities.

Hatzichronoglou, T. (1997) *Revision of the High Technology Sector and Product Classification*. Paris: OECD.

Kuznets, S. (1971) *Economic Growth of Nations: Total Output and Production Structure*. Cambridge, Mass.: Harvard University Press.

Lipowski, A. (1998) *Towards Normality. Overcoming the Heritage of Central Planning Economy in Poland in 1990–94*, Warsaw: CASE – Center for Social and Economic Research and Adam Smith Research Center.

Lipowski, A. (ed.) (2000) *Struktura gospodarki transformującej się. Polska 1990–1998 i projekcja do roku 2010* (Structure of an economy under transition. Poland in

1990–98 and a forecast until 2010). Warsaw: Institute of Economics, Polish Academy of Science.

Marczewski, K. (1999) 'Foreign Trade, Industrial Growth and Structural Changes in Poland', Warsaw: Foreign Trade Research Institute Discussion Paper no. 75.

Marczewski, K. and K. Szczygielski (2005) 'Process of Structural Change in Polish Manufacturing between 1995–2003. Characteristics and Factor', Warsaw: Foreign Trade Research Institute Discussion Paper no. 88.

Peneder, M. (1999) 'Intangible Investment and Human Resources. The New WIFO Taxonomy of Manufacturing Industries', Vienna: WIFO.

Rainelli, M. (1996) *Ekonomia przemysłowa* (Industrial Economics). Warsaw: Wydawnictwo Naukowe PWN (translated from French).

Royuela-Mora, V. (2005) 'Monitorowanie celów Strategii Lizbońskiej' (Monitoring Lisbon Strategy Goals), in B. Błaszczyk and K. Szczygielski (eds), *Strategia Libońska na półmetku: oczekiwania a rzeczywistość* (The Lisbon Strategy at Midterm: Expectations and Reality), Warsaw: CASE Reports no. 58.

Wyżnikiewicz, B. (1987) *Zmiany Strukturalne w gospodarce. Prawidłowości i ograniczenia* (Structural Changes in Economy: Regularities and Limitations). Warsaw: Polskic Wydawnictwa Ekonomicrne.

8
Structural Change, Productivity and Performance: Evidence from Irish Manufacturing

Mary O'Donnell

8.1 Introduction

This chapter examines two specific aspects of structural change not previously investigated for Irish manufacturing for the period before and after Ireland's accession to the European Community (EC) in 1973. The first issue of interest is the relationship between structural change and labour productivity growth. Productivity is the fundamental determinant of difference in living standard across countries and across regions within a country (Tang and Wang, 2004). Over the longer term, productivity growth is the only way to sustain improvements in living standards or quality of life (Krugman, 1994). The prevailing economic structure of a country is one determinant of its overall level of income and productivity. Economic growth depends importantly on the ability of a country to continuously shift its resources to dynamic sectors in response to technological change and shifts in consumer demand (Harberger, 1998). This adjustment process is linked to structural change; that is, the reallocation of resources from one economic activity to another. The impact of structural change on growth has been the focus of much attention (see for example Salter, 1960; Kaldor, 1966; Kuznets, 1979; Kendrick, 1984). Fagerberg (1999) notes that the growth accounting literature has also emphasized structural change as a major impetus to growth (Denison, 1967; Young, 1995). However, he also notes that the emphasis in much of this research has been on the effects of shifts from agriculture to services, rather than the effects of structural change within manufacturing. Recent efforts that have concentrated on examining the impact of structural change within manufacturing on productivity growth include Fagerberg (2000), Timmer and Szirmai (2000), Scarpetta *et al.* (2000), Peneder (2002), European Commission (2003) and Havlik (2005). In the Irish context, Ruane and Ugur (2004) have investigated the origins of productivity growth in Irish manufacturing; our research here differs from theirs in a number of respects. Firstly, their paper uses plant-level data while ours uses more aggregated industry-level data. Secondly, the focus of their paper is the 1991–99 period; we are interested here in specifically examining the relationship between structural change and labour-productivity growth for the pre and post-accession periods, as well as the more recent 1995–2002 period. The objective of our research is to estimate the degree to which industry structures and the reallocation of resources within manufacturing have contributed to labour-productivity growth and to investigate this issue at a more detailed sectoral level than any previous study for Irish manufacturing.

The second issue of interest is the relationship between structural change and performance in Irish manufacturing in the pre-accession, post-accession and 1995–2002 periods. To capture structural change we calculate the shares of each sector in output, value added, employment and investment in each period. We also examine the growth rates in output, value added, employment and investment for each sector in each period. For 1995–2002, we have data on exports and turnover (sales) that we include in the analysis for that time period. We calculate these growth rates based on three-year averages for the 1968–73, 1973–78 and 1995–2002 periods.[1] We use three performance indicators as follows. Firstly, profitability, measured as value-added less labour costs as a proportion of output; secondly, labour productivity, measured as value added per person employed; and finally, the value added intensity of production, measured by value added as a proportion of output. Frequently, industrial policy in Ireland and elsewhere has referred to 'moving up the value chain' or shifting towards higher value added activities; thus by including this measure we can examine how growth is related to value added. Our motivation for including these measures of growth and performance is to examine the following specific hypotheses:

1 Is there a relationship between relative growth and relative performance; that is, do sectors that experience relatively higher growth also have relatively higher profitability, labour productivity and value added as a proportion of output levels?

2 Is there a relationship between relative growth and relative improvements in performance; that is, do sectors which experience relatively higher growth also have relatively larger increases in profitability, labour productivity, and value added as a proportion of output?

3 Do sectors which perform well in one area also perform well in other areas; that is, do sectors which have relatively higher labour productivity, also have relatively higher profitability and value added as a proportion of output?

4 Finally, is there a relationship between relative size of sectors and relative performance; that is, do relatively larger sectors also have relatively

higher profitability, labour productivity and value added as a proportion of output?

We calculate the rank of each sector for shares, growth rates and the performance indicators as a basis for Spearman rank correlations. We also investigate in greater detail, through the use of panel data analysis, two specific hypotheses. Firstly, focusing on the issue of productivity, we investigate the relationship between productivity and performance to examine which performance indicators best help explain productivity levels. Secondly, we investigate to what extent is there a relationship between the size of sectors, and the performance of sectors; that is, which performance indicators have the strongest influence on the size of sectors. While the Spearman rank correlations are useful in terms of indicating significant pairwise relationships, the use of panel data econometric techniques allows us to examine these hypotheses in a more precise way.

Our data for the pre-accession period cover 40 sectors, for the post-accession period 69 sectors and for the 1995–2002 period 59 sectors.[2] All data are taken from the Central Statistics Office Census of Industrial Production. Our research here differs from the existing evidence[3] on structural change in manufacturing as the relationship between structural change and performance has not previously been examined for Irish manufacturing. Furthermore, we examine these issues specifically for the pre-accession and post-accession periods as well as 1995–2002, and our analysis is conducted at a more detailed sectoral level that many existing studies.

8.2　Methodology

To assess the contribution of structural change to labour productivity growth,[4] we use a shift-share methodology pioneered by Fabricant (1942) and which has been previously used to investigate this issue. While the conceptual and empirical shortcomings of this methodology have been extensively reviewed by Savona (2003). Havlik (2005) notes that the shift-share analysis provides a convenient tool for investigating how aggregate growth is linked to differential growth of labour productivity at the sectoral level, and to the reallocation of labour between industries.

We define aggregate labour productivity in manufacturing as a weighted sum of sectoral labour productivity, where the weights are equal to sectoral employment shares, as follows:

$$\sum_{i=1}^{n} LP_i = \sum_{i=1}^{n} \left[\frac{Q_i}{N_i} \frac{N_i}{\sum N_i} \right] \tag{8.1}$$

where LP_i represents labour productivity level in industry i; Q, value added; N, Employment; i, industry ($i = 1, \ldots, n$).

Following the methodology used in Fagerberg (2000), Timmer and Szirmai (2000) and Peneder (2002), using equation (8.1), the growth in aggregate labour-productivity levels at time 0 and time t can be decomposed into three separate effects as follows:

$$\frac{LP_t - LP_0}{LP_0} = \underbrace{\frac{\sum_{i=1}^{n} (S_{ti} - S_{0i})LP_{0i}}{LP_0}}_{I} + \underbrace{\frac{\sum_{i=1}^{n} (S_{ti} - S_{0i})(LP_{ti} - LP_{0i})}{LP_0}}_{II} + \underbrace{\frac{\sum_{i=1}^{n} (LP_{ti} - LP_{0i})S_{0i}}{LP_0}}_{III}$$

(8.2)

where S_i is the share of industry i in total employment, $S_i = \frac{N_i}{\sum_{i=1}^{n} N_i}$.

The first term, I, is called the 'static effect'. It is calculated as the sum of relative changes in the allocation of labour across industries between the base year and the final year, weighted by the value of the sector's labour productivity in the base year and divided by labour productivity in the base year. This term is positive (negative) if industries with high levels of productivity attract more (less) labour resources and hence increase (decrease) their share of total employment. Havlik (2005) remarks that industries with high levels of productivity, usually also have high capital intensity.

The second term, II, is the 'dynamic effect', calculated as the interaction of changes in employment shares and changes in labour productivity of individual industries, divided by labour productivity in the base year. If industries increase both labour productivity and their share of total employment, the combined effect is a positive contribution to overall productivity growth. This interaction term becomes larger the more resources shift towards industries with fast productivity growth. This term will be negative if industries with fast growing labour productivity could not maintain their shares in total employment and will be larger the more industries with high productivity growth are faced with declining employment shares. As industry branches differ not only in terms of productivity levels but also in terms of productivity growth rates, resources reallocation has both static and dynamic effects and this distinction between the two terms in equation (8.2) is useful.

The first two terms thus reflect structural change involving employment shifts from those industries with lower labour-productivity growth and levels. Following Peneder (2002), Savona (2003) and Timmer and Szirmai (2000) we use the sign on the static and dynamic shift terms to test the following hypotheses. First, the structural bonus hypothesis of industrial growth posits that during the process of economic development, economies upgrade from activities with relatively low labour-productivity levels to industries with relatively higher labour-productivity levels, with a consequent positive relationship between structural change and growth resulting from the reallocation of labour favouring industries with higher levels of labour productivity. The structural bonus hypothesis thus corresponds to an expected positive contribution of the static shift effect to aggregate growth in labour productivity, that is:

$$\frac{\sum_{i=1}^{n} (S_{ti} - S_{0i})LP_{0i}}{LP_0} > 0 \tag{8.3}$$

Secondly, Baumol's (1967) structural burden hypothesis postulates that employment shares shift away from progressive industries towards industries with lower growth of labour productivity, that is:

$$\frac{\sum_{i=1}^{n} (S_{ti} - S_{0i})(LP_{ti} - LP_{0i})}{LP_0} < 0 \tag{8.4}$$

The final term in equation (8.2) is calculated as the sum of the growth of labour productivity in each branch, weighted by the initial share of each branch in total employment. This reflects the contribution of labour productivity growth within individual industries to aggregate labour productivity growth and is termed the 'within-growth effect' or 'intra-sectoral effect'.

The finding of a negligible or negative contribution from structural change to labour-productivity growth does not mean that structural changes are not important (OECD, 2004a). Peneder (2002) and Havlik (2005) both observe that shift share analysis often fails to reveal substantial direct contributions of structural change to aggregate growth; this can be due to the fact that the effects of shifts in employment shares of industries with high and low levels of productivity, as well as high and low rates of productivity increases, may net out at the aggregate level. Thus looking at the decomposition of labour productivity only from an aggregate level hides important structural changes at the industry level. For this reason, in addition to identifying the relationship between structural change and productivity growth for total manufacturing, we also examine:

- the contribution to each sector's labour productivity growth from each of the terms in the shift-share equation, and
- the contribution of each sector to each of the individual terms in the shift-share equation.

To examine the relationship between structural change and performance we use Spearman rank correlations as well as panel data analysis.

8.3 Results

Structural change and labour productivity

We firstly examine the aggregate results for each period to see the propor-tion of labour productivity explained by each of the effects in equation (8.2) and these are presented in Table 8.1. We note first the predominance of the within-growth effect in explaining aggregate labour-productivity growth in Irish manufacturing in all periods; that is, the overwhelming part of labour-productivity growth is due to productivity growth within individ-ual industries. The relative importance of the contribution of productivity growth within individual industries has however declined over time and was relatively more important in the pre-accession period than either the post-accession or 1995–02 periods. Consequently, the role of structural change in explaining labour productivity growth has increased in importance over time. For the pre-accession period the transfer of resources from low product-ivity to high productivity industries, or from low productivity growth to high productivity growth industries does not appear to have been an important factor in aggregate labour productivity growth. While the sign on the two structural terms are positive for the pre-accession period, we can accept the structural bonus hypothesis and reject the structural burden hypothesis, but the combined effects at just 2.2 per cent of total labour productivity growth in Irish manufacturing are small.

For the post-accession period, structural changes were relatively more important in contributing to aggregate labour-productivity growth, with shifts to industries with relatively higher productivity growth rates being more important than the shift into industries with relatively higher produc-tivity levels. Again here, while we accept the structural bonus and reject the structural burden hypotheses, the magnitude of the contribution of the static shift effect at just 2.9 per cent of total productivity growth is relatively

Table 8.1 Labour-productivity growth explained by each effect

	Proportion of total (%)			
	Static shift effect	*Dynamic shift effect*	*Within-growth effect*	*Total*
1968–73	1.8	0.4	97.7	100.0
1973–78	2.9	7.8	89.2	100.0
1995–02	8.1	16.6	75.3	100.0
Actual % changes				
1968–73	1.96	0.47	103.7	106.1
1973–78	5.2	14.0	159.5	178.8
1995–02	9.9	26.3	83.8	120.0

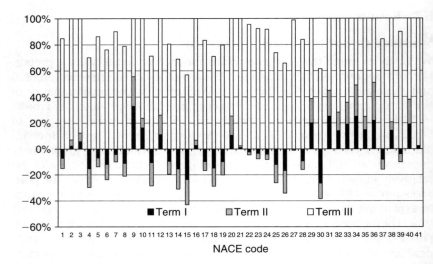

Figure 8.1 Contribution of 'three effects' to labour-productivity growth in each sector: pre-accession

small. However, there are significant differences between the pre and post accession periods and the more recent 1995–2002 period. Here we see that almost a quarter of total labour-productivity growth has been due to structural change in manufacturing; given the sign on the static shift effect, we accept the structural bonus hypothesis for this period; the shift of resources into sectors with relatively higher productivity levels has provided a boost to aggregate labour productivity growth in this period. We reject the structural burden hypothesis given the positive sign on the dynamic shift effect for this period. The increasing importance of Irish manufacturing industries with relatively higher labour-productivity growth rates has contributed positively to overall labour-productivity growth.

To summarize, we accept the structural bonus hypothesis and reject the structural burden hypothesis for all periods; the relative contribution of structural change to sectors with higher productivity levels and growth rates has increased in importance over time in terms of its effect on labour-productivity growth rates in Irish manufacturing, with the shift to sectors with relatively higher labour-productivity growth rates relatively more important than the shift to sectors with relatively higher labour productivity levels.

Next, we present some details on the relative contribution of structural change in each industry to labour-productivity growth in each sector. Figures 8.1–8.3 set out the proportion of labour-productivity growth in each sector due to each of the terms in equation (8.2) for each period where term I represents the static effect, term II represents the dynamic effect and term III

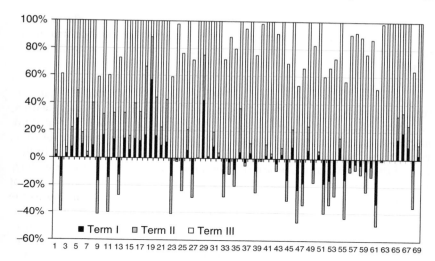

Figure 8.2 Contribution of three effects to labour productivity growth in each sector: post-accession

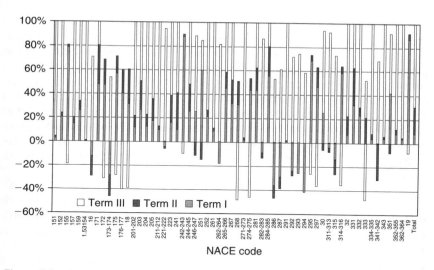

Figure 8.3 Contribution of three effects to labour productivity growth in each sector: 1995–2002

represents the intra-sectoral effect, as specified in equation 8.2. The final bar in each figure represents total manufacturing. As noted by Havlik (2005) and Peneder (2003), relatively small aggregate effects may hide considerable variations across industries. This is certainly the case for Ireland in the pre-accession period (Figure 8.1). While the static and dynamic effects overall were relatively small, across industries there were substantial contributions from each of these effects in terms of labour-productivity growth within sectors.

In many ways, these figures serve to confirm what we already know with regard to structural change in Irish manufacturing; that is, that over time labour-intensive traditional sectors such as clothing, textiles, leather, footwear and so on have declined in relative importance while more capital-intensive, high-tech sectors have increased in relative importance over time. While these figures are interesting in the sense that they give us an indication of the relative contribution of structural changes to labour-productivity growth within each branch of industry, they do not give any indication of the relative importance of those individual branches in contributing to the individual effects within overall labour-productivity growth. We have summarized the sectors which made the largest and smallest contribution to overall labour productivity growth in each period in Table 8.2. This table underscores the importance of looking behind the aggregate figures to examine labour productivity growth at a disaggregated level in order to understand and identify the sectoral forces instrumental in driving labour productivity growth in Irish manufacturing.

These results illustrate a number of interesting points regarding labour-productivity growth in Irish manufacturing over time. Firstly, the relative importance of the top five sectors in driving overall labour-productivity growth has increased over time. In the pre-accession period, the five largest contributors to labour-productivity growth collectively accounted for 37 per cent of the 106 per cent total growth, or about one-third. In the post-accession period, the top five sectors accounted for 60 per cent of the total 180 per cent increase in labour productivity. However, in contrast to the pre-accession and post-accession periods, for 1995–2002 we see the top five sectors accounting for 100 per cent of the 120 per cent growth, or about 80 per cent of the total.

Secondly, these figures illustrate the increasing importance of individual sectors in driving overall labour-productivity growth. For the pre-accession period, miscellaneous manufacturing accounted for just over 11 per cent of the total 106 per cent growth; for the post-accession period, chemicals accounted for just over 23 per cent of total growth of 179 per cent, but for the more recent period, we find that basic chemicals contributed a phenomenal 60 per cent of the total 120 per cent growth. Thus over time Ireland has become increasingly reliant on individual sectors in determining labour productivity growth.

Thirdly, we observe differences across the three time periods in terms of the sectors which made the smallest contribution to overall labour productivity growth, and in particular between the pre and post-accession periods and the more recent period. Collectively the smallest contributors to growth

Table 8.2 Contribution to actual labour-productivity growth rates

	Rank	Sector	Overall	Static effect	Dynamic effect	Within effect
Pre-accession						
Top 5	1	Miscellaneous mfg	10.6	2.0	2.0	6.6
	2	Metal trades	7.7	1.5	1.3	5.0
	3	Brewing, malting	6.7	−1.7	−2.8	11.2
	4	Chemicals, drugs	6.2	1.2	1.2	3.8
	5	Concrete, cement	5.8	0.8	0.8	4.1
	Total		37.0	3.9	2.5	30.6
Bottom 5	40	Soap, detergents	0.1	−0.1	−0.1	0.3
	39	Leather	0.1	−0.1	−0.1	0.3
	38	Margarine, cooking fats	0.3	0.0	0.0	0.2
	37	Linen, cotton	0.3	−0.5	−0.4	1.2
	36	Railroad equipment	0.5	0.0	−0.1	1.0
	Total		1.3	−0.7	−0.6	2.9
Post-accession						
Top 5	1	Pharmaceuticals, chemicals	22.6	2.0	7.0	13.6
	2	Dairy products	11.1	0.2	0.3	10.6
	3	Miscellaneous foodstuffs	10.1	0.5	3.2	6.4
	4	Brewing, malting	8.3	−0.4	−0.5	9.2
	5	Non-metallic mineral products	8.2	0.3	0.4	7.6
	Total		60.3	2.6	10.4	47.4
Bottom 5	69	Mfg pulp, paperboard	0.0	−0.3	−0.1	0.4
	68	Mfg fur/fur goods	0.0	0.0	−0.1	0.1
	67	Leather	0.1	−0.1	−0.1	0.2
	66	Silk, flax, jute	0.1	−0.3	−0.3	0.7
	65	Misc mfg industries	0.2	0.0	−0.2	0.4
	Total		0.4	−0.8	−0.8	2.0
1995–2002						
Top 5	1	Basic chemicals	61.7	6.3	18.9	36.5
	2	Pharmaceuticals	12.3	3.2	2.8	6.4
	3	Reproduction recording media	10.6	1.7	2.4	6.5
	4	Fruit/vegetables/misc foods	9.1	0.0	0.0	9.0
	5	Medical/surgical equip	7.4	2.4	2.3	2.8
	Total		101.1	13.6	26.4	61.2
Bottom 5	62	Office machinery	−4.0	−1.1	0.3	−3.1
	61	Misc chemicals	−2.2	−0.7	0.3	−1.8
	60	Clothing	−0.5	−0.8	−0.7	1.0
	59	Mfg rubber products	−0.5	−0.4	0.1	−0.2
	58	Dairy products	−0.3	−0.4	0.0	0.1
	Total		−7.5	−3.4	0.0	−4.0

accounted for just over one per cent for the pre-accession period and 0.4 per cent for the post-accession period. The contrast with the 1995–2002 period is stark in that for the first time we see a negative contribution to overall labour-productivity growth amounting to a drag of 7.5 per cent of the total.

Regarding the individual sectors that have been important and significant in driving labour-productivity growth, these have been a mix of traditional and high-tech sectors in the pre and post-accession periods. However, for the 1995–2002 period these are entirely the foreign-dominated high-tech sectors. For the sectors making the smallest contribution to labour productivity growth these are dominated by traditional sectors in the pre and post-accession periods, but for the 1995–2002 periods we see a mix of high-tech and traditional sectors, with sectors such as dairy and chemicals appearing alongside each other. Most interesting for this period, however, is the presence of the office machinery sector on this list which contributed the largest drag on labour productivity growth, driven mainly by a negative within effect for this sector rather than by the negative structural effects.

In each period, as with the aggregate results, the within-effect explains the lions share of overall labour-productivity growth for the largest and smallest contributors. For the largest contributors, the static and dynamic effects are positive in all periods, with the exception of the brewing sector in the pre and post-accession periods where the structural effects were negative due to a decline in its share of employment. Furthermore, the sector making the largest contribution to overall labour-productivity growth also made the relatively largest contribution to the structural terms, accounting for about half or more of the static and dynamic shift effects amongst the top five sectors. For the smallest contributors, for the pre and post-accession periods, generally the contribution of these sectors to overall labour-productivity growth was reduced due to the negative static and dynamic structural effects; thus although these sectors managed to increase labour productivity over these periods as indicated by the positive within effect, they experienced a decline in their shares which resulted in negative structural effects. More recently, the characteristics of labour productivity growth differ for the smallest contributors in that for the first time over the three periods we see sectors exhibiting a decline in labour productivity as reflected in the negative within effect; again, this is notable in the office machinery sector as well as in miscellaneous chemicals. In terms of the dynamic shift effect, for the 1995–2002 period this was positive but small for all sectors except clothing indicating that all these sectors suffered a decline in employment shares as well as a decline in labour-productivity levels over the period.

Structural change and performance: Spearman rank correlations

The first hypothesis we examine through the use of Spearman rank correlations is whether there is a relationship between relative growth and relative performance; that is, do sectors that experience relatively higher growth also

Table 8.3 Correlation coefficients between the rank of growth and the rank of performance

		Output	Value added (VA)	Employment	Investment	Turnover	Exports
(VA − LC)/Y	1968–73	0.14	0.06	0.07	0.12		
	1973–78	0.30*	0.34**	0.22	0.01		
	1995–2002	0.42**	0.38**	0.25	0.31*	0.43**	0.22
VA/Emp	1968–73	0.32*	0.40**	0.27	0.20		
	1973–78	0.44**	0.43**	0.39**	0.05		
	1995–2002	0.40**	0.27*	0.26*	0.29*	0.40**	0.20
VA/Y	1968–73	0.05	−0.07	−0.08	0.17		
	1973–78	0.07	0.04	−0.07	0.04		
	1995–2002	0.15	0.20	0.04	0.13	0.17	0.08

Notes: * significant at 5% level; ** significant at 1% level.

have relatively higher profitability, labour productivity and value added as a proportion of output levels? These correlation coefficients thus relate to the rank of performance and the rank of growth and are given in Table 8.3.[5]

Firstly we note that for all periods, there is no significant association between relative growth in output, value added (VA), employment, investment, turnover and exports, and the relative value-added intensity of production. Thus sectors with relatively higher growth were not necessarily the sectors which also had relatively higher value added as a proportion of output in either the pre, post-accession or more recent 1995–2002 period. Secondly, with regard to profitability, for the pre-accession period, there is no significant correlation between relative growth and relative profitability across sectors. However, for the post-accession period, sectors that experienced relatively higher growth in value added also experienced relatively higher profitability ratios. This positive correlation coefficient is significant at the 1 per cent level. Output growth was also correlated with profitability, but only at the 5 per cent significance level. For the 1995–2002 period, the relatively higher growth in output, value added and turnover were all significantly and positively correlated with profitability at the 1 per cent level with the correlation coefficients on all these variables of a similar magnitude. Sectors which achieved relatively higher growth in these variables also had relatively higher profitability ratios. Interestingly, growth in employment, investment or exports was not significantly correlated at the 1 per cent level with profitability in any period.

Finally, for labour productivity in the pre-accession period only relative growth in value added was significantly correlated with relative labour-productivity levels; thus sectors which experienced relatively higher growth in output, employment or investment were not necessarily the sectors with relatively higher labour-productivity levels. However, the relationship between growth and productivity changes in the post-accession period, with significant positive correlations between relative growth in output, value added and employment at the 1 per cent level. This relationship changes again for the 1995–2002 period, with significant correlation only between relative labour productivity and relative growth in output at the one per cent significance level, although value added, employment and investment are significant at 5 per cent; generally the magnitude of the significant correlation coefficients are similar in all three periods.

Overall, with regard to the relationship between relative growth and relative performance, we note that given that the correlations are not constant over time indicating that the nature of the relationship between relative growth and relative labour productivity and profitability levels over time is dynamic rather than static in nature. Growth in investment was the only variable which was not significantly correlated at 1 per cent with any of the performance variables in any period.

The second set of correlations we examine are for relative growth and relative performance; that is, do sectors which experience relatively higher growth also experience relatively larger improvements in profitability, labour productivity and the value-added intensity of production. These correlation coefficients are given in Table 8.4.

For profitability, we see no significant correlations between relative growth in any of the structural variables and relative improvements in profitability in the pre-accession period. For the post-accession and 1995–2002 periods, only sectors which experienced relatively higher growth in value added also experienced relatively greater improvements in profitability ratios, as indicated by the positive coefficient significant at one per cent in these periods. This would seem to indicate that relative improvements in profitability are driven by growth in value added rather than by growth in any of the other structural variables.

Relative growth in labour productivity is also significantly and positively correlated with relative growth in value added at the 1 per cent level in all periods; in addition to this, for the pre-accession period, it is also associated with relatively higher growth in output, but only at the 5 per cent level. For the more recent 1995–2002 period, relative growth in output, turnover and exports were also all positively correlated with relative growth in labour productivity, but the magnitude of the correlation coefficients are weaker than that for value added in all periods.

For value added as a proportion of output, while there are no significant correlations for the post-accession or 1995–2002 periods, we see strong and positive significant correlations for the pre-accession period. In particular, sectors which experienced relatively large increases in the value added intensity of production also experienced relatively faster growth in output, value

Table 8.4 Correlation coefficients between the rank of growth and the rank of the growth of performance

		Output	Value added (VA)	Employment	Investment	Turnover	Exports
(VA − LC)/Y	68–70 vs 71–73	−0.04	0.23	−0.23	−0.01		
	73–75 vs 76–78	0.15	0.44**	−0.04	−0.14		
	95–97 vs 00–02	0.01	0.39**	0.05	0.00	0.11	0.11
VA/Emp	68–70 vs 71–73	0.39*	0.57**	−0.07	0.21		
	73–75 vs 76–78	0.32	0.50**	−0.07	−0.08		
	95–97 vs 00–02	0.33**	0.59**	0.12	0.22	0.34**	0.36**
VA/Y	73–75 vs 76–78	0.69**	0.82**	0.65**	0.15		
	68–70 vs 71–73	−0.27	0.13	−0.17	−0.03		
	95–97 vs 00–02	−0.15	0.29*	0.00	0.07	−0.13	−0.08

Notes: * significant at 5% level; ** significant at 1% level.

added and employment and the magnitude of these correlations are the strongest of all significant coefficients in this table. As for the first set of correlations we examined, the fact that we observe variations in the significant correlations for all periods, with the exception of value added and labour productivity which was significant in all periods, this indicates that the structural variables important for improvements in performance have not been constant over time. Furthermore, we note that as in the pre accession period, overall in the post-accession period there were no significant correlations between investment and any of the performance indicators.

The third set of correlations we examine are for the rank of share and rank of performance indicator. We wish to see whether there is any association between the relative size of sectors in terms of their relative contribution or share in output, value added, employment, investment or exports, and their relative performance in terms of labour productivity, profitability or value added intensity of production. These are presented in Table 8.5.

Firstly, overall, there appears to be a weak association between the relative size of sectors and the relative value-added intensity of production. We find that only in the pre-accession period did relatively larger sectors,

Table 8.5 Correlation coefficients between the rank of shares with the rank of performance indicator

	Period	Output	Value added (VA)	Employment	Investment	Turnover	Exports
(VA − LC)/Y	1968–73	−0.08	0.27	−0.12	0.32*		
	1973–78	−0.07	0.17	0.02	0.19		
	1995–02	0.52**	0.63**	0.44**	0.53**	0.52**	0.50**
VA/Emp	1968–73	0.35*	0.27	0.13	0.29		
	1973–78	0.52**	0.45**	0.09	0.52**		
	1995–02	0.75**	0.78**	0.56**	0.73**	0.75**	0.70**
VA/Y	1968–73	−0.33*	0.07	−0.09	0.18		
	1973–78	−0.23	0.07	0.07	−0.08		
	1995–02	0.12	0.27	0.16	0.16	0.13	0.10

Notes: * significant at 5% level; ** significant at 1% level.

in this case in terms of their relative share of output, also have relatively higher value added as a proportion of output. However this was significant at the 5 per cent level and we find no significant correlations at the 1 per cent level in any period.

For the pre-accession period, there are no significant correlations at 1 per cent level between relative size and relative performance in terms of profitability or labour productivity, although we do find association at 5 per cent level between relative size in terms of share of investment and profitability, and in terms of output and labour productivity. Relatively larger sectors in terms of output, value added and investment also had relatively higher labour productivity in the post-accession period and this relationship between relative size and relative labour productivity appears to have strengthened over time with significant positive correlations between labour productivity and all variables at the 1 per cent level for the 1995–2002 period. Relatively larger sectors in terms of value added, output, sales, investment, exports and employment had relatively higher labour productivity levels, although we note that the coefficient for employment share is the weakest. Furthermore, the relationship between relative size and relative performance has strengthened over time given the magnitude of the significant coefficients for the more recent period as compared to the previous periods.

To see whether sectors which had relatively high labour productivity also had relatively high profitability or value added intensity of production, we found the correlation between the ranks of the performance indicators with each other and these correlations are presented in Table 8.6. As with the other correlations, again here there are differences between the three periods with regard to sectors which performed relatively well across the various performance indicators. Sectors which had relatively higher labour productivity

Table 8.6 Correlation coefficients between the ranks of performance indicators

	VA/PPE	VA/Y
1968–73		
(VA – LC)/Y	0.27	0.60**
VA/PPE		−0.26
1973–78		
(VA – LC)/Y	0.29**	0.01
VA/PPE		0.10
1995–02		
VA – LC/Y	0.76**	0.66**
VA/PPE		0.29**

Notes: * significant at 5% level; ** significant at 1% level.

in the post-accession and 1995–2002 periods also had relatively higher profitability ratios, as indicated by the positive and significant coefficients at the 1 per cent level, with the strength of correlation being much stronger for the more recent 1995–2002 period. While there is no relationship between relative labour productivity and relative value-added intensity of production in the pre and post-accession periods, we do find that it is significantly positively correlated at the 1 per cent level for the 1995–2002 period. Finally, while we find no significant correlation between the relative value-added intensity of production and relative profitability for the post-accession period, for the pre-accession and 1995–2002 periods sectors with relatively higher value added intensity also had relatively higher profitability ratios as indicated by the significant coefficients which were of a similar magnitude in both periods.

Overall, the correlations indicate the following stylized facts. Relatively higher growth in investment was not associated with relatively higher performance or relatively larger improvements in labour productivity, profitability or the value-added intensity of production. The lack of significance of investment may be due to the fact that the investment figures in the Census of Industrial Production do not include 'greenfield' investment; that is, they only record investment once plants are up and running and so overall tend to underestimate the true level of investment undertaken in Irish manufacturing. There appears to be no association with relative growth and the value added intensity of production in any period and there appears to be no association with relative growth and relative changes in the value–added intensity of production in the post-accession and 1995–2002 periods. Sectors that experienced relatively large changes in value added also experienced relatively large improvements in profitability since EC accession. Relative growth in value added was also important in all periods for improvements in labour productivity; relative growth in other variables was also associated

Table 8.7   Regression analysis, productivity and performance

	Pre-accession		Post-accession		1995–2002	
	Coefficient	*P-value*	*Coefficient*	*P-value*	*Coefficient*	*P-value*
VA/Y	9.54	0.09	25.22	0.23	1.41	0.07
VA − LC/Y	12.10	0.19	30.39	0.38	−1.17	0.14
I/PPE	1.75	0.00**	1.74	0.00**	3.10	0.00**
I/Y	−100.84	0.00**	−326.71	0.00**	−4.00	0.04*
Industry	0.25	0.91	7.84	0.19	−1.07	0.40
Constant	44,96	0.80	−812.75	0.32	−17.33	0.07
Wald χ^2	1483.00	0.00**	746.3	0.00**	6883.00	0.00**
R^2	0.78		0.83		0.92	
n	240		402		168	

Note: ** significant at 1% level.

with relative growth in labour productivity in the 1995–2002 period, but value added was the most important. There is no association between relative sectoral size and relative value added intensity of production at the 1 per cent level in any period and there is a stronger association between relative size and relative performance in the 1995–2002 period than either pre-or post-accession, but this relationship is weaker for employment than for the other structural variables.

Labour productivity and performance: panel-data analysis

Focusing specifically on the issue of productivity, we firstly investigate the relationship between productivity and performance to examine which performance indicators best help explain productivity levels. Our measure of productivity is value added per person employed. For performance we use profitability, measured as value added less labour costs as a proportion of output, and the value-added intensity of production, measured as value added as a proportion of output. To capture the possible influence of investment on productivity we also include investment per person employed and investment as a proportion of output as explanatory variables in the regression. The results from this regression with value added per person employed as the dependent variable are presented in Table 8.7.

We note firstly the Wald Chi-squared test for each period indicating that the regressions are significant, and the coefficient of determination, R-squared for each period indicates that value added per person employed is well-explained by the explanatory performance variables included in the model. Furthermore, the relationship between performance and productivity has been stable over time in that the same variables are significant in each period. Investment per employee has a significant positive impact on productivity levels in all

Table 8.8 Regression analysis, performance and size: output

	Pre-accession		Post-accession		1995–02	
	Coefficient	P-value	Coefficient	P-value	Coefficient	P-value
VA/Y	−0.0003	0.00**	−0.0007	0.00**	0.00	0.90
VA − LC/Y	0.001	0.00**	0.0004	0.04	0.005	0.32
VA − LC/PPE	−0.00001	0.00**	0.00	0.61	−0.0001	0.00**
Y/PPE	0.000002	0.00**	0.00	0.83	0.0005	0.00**
I/PPE	0.00003	0.00**	0.000003	0.01**	0.001	0.00**
I/Y	−0.0017	0.00**	−0.0008	0.00**	−0.001	0.00**
Constant	0.015	0.01**	0.03	0.00**	−0.01	0.56
Wald χ^2	205.5	0.00**	107.8	0.00**	8259.0	0.00**
r^2	0.47		0.21		0.91	
n	240		408		168	

Note: ** significant at 1% level.

periods, with the magnitude of the coefficient for the more recent 1995–2002 period stronger than for the pre-and post-accession periods. Interestingly, investment as a proportion of output is also statistically significant at the 1 per cent level for the pre-and post-accession periods and at the 5 per cent level for the 1995–2002 period; the negative sign on the coefficient indicates that sectors with relatively higher labour productivity levels tended to have relatively lower investment as a proportion of output. This may appear counterintuitive but can be explained by the fact that while sectors that had relatively higher labour productivity levels may not have had the relatively highest investment as a proportion of output, the actual value of investment was greater, as reflected in the higher levels of investment per employee. This suggests that it is not the proportion of output invested which is important for labour productivity levels, but the actual amount. The actual and fitted values, the scaled residuals and the correlogram of the residuals for each period indicated that the fitted values from the regression equations are in each case are close to the actual values, that the scaled residuals fall either side of zero and that the equations do not suffer from autocorrelation.

The second hypotheses that we wish to investigate is to what extent is there a relationship between the size of sectors, and the performance of sectors; that is, which performance indicators have the strongest influence on the size of sectors. Our investigation focuses on three measures of size, the share of output, value added and employment. For performance, we include profitability as a proportion of output, as well as per person employed, value added intensity of output, investment per employee and investment as a proportion of output. We also included output per person employed as an additional measure of productivity. The results from the regression with output as the dependent variable are set out in Table 8.8.

Overall, for the pre-accession period, the share of output is more strongly associated with performance than share in either value added or employment. For the post-accession period, again share in output is most strongly associated with performance, with no significant association between size in terms of employment or value added and performance. For the most recent 1995–2002 period, size in terms of output and value added, but not employment, is associated with better performance, with the magnitude of the coefficients on value added stronger than those for output.

We find that all three regressions are significant as indicated by the Wald Chi-squared test. The coefficient of determination is highest for the more recent 1995–2002 period at 91 per cent, and is much lower for the pre- and post-accession periods at 47 per cent and 21 per cent respectively. The relationship between relative performance and the relative size of sectors in terms of the share of output has not been constant over the three periods, as indicated by differences in the significant variables in each period, but the sign on the significant variables were constant across all periods. We note, however, the relatively weak magnitude of all significant coefficients in all periods. For the pre-accession period, all performance variables included in the regression were significant at the 1 per cent level. Sectors with larger shares of output had relatively higher profitability, output per employee, and investment per employee, but relatively lower value added as a proportion of output, profit per employee and investment as a proportion of output. For the post-accession period, only investment per employee had a significant positive impact on sectoral size at the 1 per cent level, with profitability also significant at the 5 per cent level. Value added as a proportion of output and investment as a proportion of output were negative and significant at the 1 per cent level indicating that relatively small sectors tended to have relatively higher value-added intensity and investment intensity. For the 1995–2002 period, higher output per employee and investment per employee, and lower profit per employee and investment as a proportion of output, were associated with relatively larger shares in output. Again the plots from each regression indicated that the fitted values in each case are close to the actual values, that the scaled residuals fall either side of zero and that the equations do not suffer from autocorrelation. The results for value added as a performance measure are presented in Table 8.9.

The table indicates that all three regressions are significant at the 1 per cent level, but the R-squared statistic is low for the pre-and post-accession periods. For the pre-accession period, only profitability and investment intensity were positively associated with share in value added, while sectors with relatively higher investment intensity tended to have relatively lower shares in value added. For the post-accession period, there is no significant relationship between relative size and relative performance in terms of share of value added as indicated by the lack of significant coefficients for any of the individual performance indicators. The strongest relationship between

Table 8.9 Regression analyses, performance and size: value added

	Pre-accession		Post-accession		1995–2002	
	Coefficient	P-value	Coefficient	P-value	Coefficient	P-value
VA/Y	−0.014	0.60	−0.009	0.72	0.08	0.02*
VA − LC/Y	0.14	0.00**	0.035	0.14	0.007	0.85
VA − LC/PPE	−0.0009	0.09	0.00	0.08	−0.01	0.00**
Y/PPE	0.00	0.17	0.00	0.20	0.01	0.00**
I/PPE	0.002	0.00**	0.0002	0.14	0.31	0.00**
I/Y	−0.11	0.01**	−0.05	0.05*	−0.27	0.00**
Constant	0.12	0.92	1.02	0.34	−3.20	0.00**
Wald χ^2	32.6	0.00**	33.82	0.00**	1773.0	0.00**
r^2	0.21		0.23		0.90	
n	240		408		168	

Note: ** significant at 1% level.

Table 8.10 Regression analysis performance and size: employment

	Pre-accession		Post-accession		1995–2002	
	Coefficient	P-value	Coefficient	P-value	Coefficient	P-value
VA/Y	−0.01	0.65	0.01	0.61	0.01	0.84
VA − LC/Y	0.12	0.02*	−0.009	0.69	0.009	0.83
VA − LC/PPE	−0.001	0.01**	0.00	0.34	−0.008	0.03*
Y/PPE	0.00	0.29	0.00	0.32	0.004	0.03*
I/PPE	0.0018	0.00**	0.0003	0.08	0.02	0.20
I/Y	−0.10	0.09	−0.05	0.03*	−0.04	0.47
Constant	0.01	0.13	1.33	0.16	1.81	0.36
Wald χ^2	13.82	0.05*	9.76	0.21	90.90	0.00**
r^2	0.10		0.02		0.18	
n	240		408		168	

Notes: * significant at 5% level; ** significant at 1% level.

size in terms of share of value added and performance is for the more recent 1995–2002 period, where sectors with relatively larger shares in value added had relatively higher output per employee and investment per employee, but relatively lower profit per employee and investment as a proportion of output.

Finally, the results for employment as a performance measure are presented in Table 8.10.

The table shows that in the pre-accession period, higher profitability per employee was associated with relatively smaller shares in employment at the 1 per cent level, with relatively higher profitability positively associated with shares in employment at the 5 per cent level, and with higher investment per employee at the 1 per cent level. For the post-accession and 1995–2002 periods, the relationship between size and performance is weaker overall as indicated by the lack of significant coefficients at the 1 per cent level, although investment as a proportion of output was significant at the 5 per cent for the post-accession period and profit and output per employee also significant at the 5 per cent level for 1995–2002.

8.4   Summary and policy implication

This chapter has analysed at a detailed sectoral level structural change in the period before and after Ireland's accession to the European Community (EC) in 1973, namely 1968–73 and 1973–78 as well as the more recent 1995–2002 period. The first issue we examined was the relationship between structural change and labour productivity growth. We accepted the structural bonus hypothesis and rejected the structural burden hypothesis for all periods. We can conclude that the relative contribution of structural change to sectors with higher productivity levels and growth rates has increased in importance over time in terms of its effect on labour-productivity growth rates in Irish manufacturing, with the shift to sectors with relatively higher labour-productivity growth rates being relatively more important than the shift to sectors with relatively higher labour productivity levels. The relatively small contribution of structural change to labour-productivity growth at an aggregate level does, however, mask considerable variation across sectors and structural changes are important in explaining labour-productivity growth at a sectoral level across Irish manufacturing in all periods we examined. In addition to this, individual sectors have become increasingly important over time in driving overall labour-productivity growth within Irish manufacturing. The results may be due to the involvement of a relatively small number of foreign dominated high tech sectors in driving Irish labour-productivity growth, particularly in recent years.

The second issue we examined was the relationship between growth and trade performance by calculating Spearman rank correlations between the performance indicators and growth of output, value added, employment, investment, turnover and exports. These correlations served to illustrate that growth in the various structural variables does not have a uniform impact upon the performance measures. In addition to this, the differences between the different periods, indicates that these relationships are not constant and are dynamic in nature. Previous commentators noted that accession did not have a major impact on the structural changes in Irish manufacturing due to a large part to the Anglo Irish Free Trade Agreement in 1965 and the outward looking industrial policy in place since the late 1950s. But the fact that we observed differences in the significant correlations for the pre-and post-accession periods indicates that the relationship between growth and performance was affected by accession and the dynamics of this relationship has changed over time as reflected in the additional significant correlations for the 1995–2002 period.

Finally, we conducted a panel-data analysis to examine which performance indicators best help explain labour productivity and size in terms of shares in output, value added and employment. Our results showed that the relationship between performance and productivity has been stable over time in that the same variables are significant in each period. Investment per employee has a significant positive impact on productivity levels in all periods, with the magnitude of the coefficient for the more recent 1995–2002 period stronger than for the pre-and post-accession periods. Investment as a proportion of output was also statistically significant for all periods, although weaker for the more recent 1995–2002 period than for the pre-and post-accession periods. In terms of the importance of individual performance indicators in explaining the size of sectors, overall, for the pre-accession period, the share of output was more strongly associated with performance than share in either value added or employment. For the post-accession period, again share in output was most strongly associated with performance, with no significant association between size in terms of employment or value added and performance. For the most recent 1995–2002 period, size in terms of output and value added, but not employment, was associated with better performance, with the magnitude of the coefficients on value added stronger than those for output.

The aspects of structural change in Irish manufacturing we examined in different periods serve to highlight the critical importance of Irish industrial policy and the role of foreign direct investment in driving structural changes in manufacturing and overall labour productivity growth. Ruane and McGibney (1991) notes that the key elements of this policy have been consistency with a single apolitical policy for over 40 years, the gradual abandonment of attempts to protect declining industry, sensible selectivity of sectors, financial and fiscal based incentives, investment in education and infrastructure and appropriate macro policies. The key policy instruments in attracting FDI included a low corporate tax rate and grants designed to promote investment, influence company location and incentivise company behaviour.

The support structure to attract FDI was also important. In particular, the Irish Industrial Development Authority (IDA) which concentrates exclusively on FDI has been recognized as one of the most effective proactive national investment promotion organizations (White, 2000). Other locational advantages which were important in attracting FDI included a highly skilled English speaking labour force, relatively low wages and social partnership agreement on wage moderation (Krugman, 1994). However, while the forces of industrial policy and FDI have been constant over time, the individual sectors which have driven structural changes and contributed to labour productivity growth have not remained static. Irish manufacturing is still undergoing substantial structural changes reflecting the evolving and dynamic nature of industrial development in manufacturing.

The experience of Ireland indicates that investment in labour both in terms of skills and education as part of labour-market flexibility policies should be an important focus for policies to improve productivity. Ireland itself faces challenges in this regard and there is scope for raising the quality of education as well as improving completion rates in education. Increased expenditure on education is one way in which this could be achieved, as it has been noted by the OECD (2004b) that Ireland's spending of 3 per cent of GDP on education gave it a ranking of 27th out of 30 industrial countries. There is also scope for Irish policy to focus on upgrading the skills of those already at work through increased training. With regard to industrial policy, the Irish experience indicates there is clearly a role for effective industrial development agencies as well as effective export promotion. Ireland's experience and success in attracting foreign direct investment is evidence of the potentially positive impact on the economy; but Ireland can be faulted for its relative overemphasis on foreign firms to the detriment of indigenous firms, especially in the 1970s and 1980s. This suggests that in learning from Ireland's experience, countries should seek to develop both the foreign and indigenous sectors of manufacturing. On the issue of foreign direct investment, there is also the related question of whether policy should target certain sectors. While Ireland's current policy has been successful in this regard, the difficulty for other countries in pursuing such a policy is the challenge of identifying specific industries to target. Porter (2000) notes that direct targeting is only likely to succeed when a country possesses investment driven national advantage, although when implemented properly can significantly influence the bases of competitive advantage; to move an economy to innovation driven advantage requires a shift to more indirect forms of government assistance to support effort by any industry and so governments have an important role at that stage of encouraging the development of skills or technologies that are important in a substantial number of industries.

Appendix

Table 8.A1   Description of UNISIC codes (1968–73)

Sector

1	Bacon factories
2	Slaughtering, preparation and preserving of meat
3	Creamery, butter, cheese, condensed milk, chocolate crumb, ice cream and other edible milk products
4	Canning of fruit and vegetables and manufacture of preserves, jams, jellies etc.
5	Grain milling and animal feeding stuffs
6	Bread, biscuit and flour confectionary

(Continued)

Table 8.A1   (Continued)

Sector	
7	Manufacture and refining of sugar
8	Manufacture of cocoa, chocolate and sugar confectionery
9	Misc food preparation (incl canning and preserving of fish)
10	Margarine, compound cooking fats and butter blending
11	Distilling, malting and brewing
12	Aerated and mineral waters
13	Tobacco
14	Woollen and worsted (excl clothing)
15	Linen and cotton spinning, weaving and manufactures
16	Jute, canvas, rayon, nylon, cordage and misc textile manufactures
17	Hosiery
18	Boot and shoe
19	Clothing
20	Manufacture of made up textile goods except apparel
21	Manufactures of wood and cork except furniture
22	Manufacture of furniture and fixtures: brushes and brooms
23	Manufacture of paper and paper products
24	Printing, publishing and allied trades
25	Fellmongery, tanning and dressing of leather
26	Manufacture of leather and leather substitutes
27	Fertilisers
28	Oils, paints, inks and polishes
29	Chemicals and drugs
30	Soap, detergents and candles
31	Glass and glassware, pottery, china and earthenware
32	Structural clay products, asbestos goods, plaster, gypsum and concrete products, slate, cement
33	Metal trades (excl mach & transp equip)
34	Manufacture and assembly of machinery (excl electrical equip)
35	Manufacture of electrical machinery, apparatus and appliances
36	Ship and boat building and repairing
37	Manufacture of railroad equipment
38	Assembly, construction and repair of mechanically propelled road and land vehicles
39	Assembly, construction and repair of vehicles other than mechanically propelled road and land vehicles
40	Miscellaneous manufacturing industries

Table 8.A2   Description of 3-digit NACE codes (1973–78)

	NACE code	Sector
1	14	Mineral oil refining and processing of petroleum derivatives
2	22	Production and preliminary processing of metals

(*Continued*)

Table 8.A2 (Continued)

	NACE code	Sector
3	241–6	Manufacture of non-metallic mineral products (excl glass and ceramic goods)
4	247	Manufacture of glassware
5	248	Manufacture of ceramic goods
6	251	Manufacture of basic industrial chemicals (including fertilisers)
7	255	Manufacture of paints, varnishes and printing inks
8	256–7	Manufacture of pharmaceuticals and of chemical products mainly for industrial and agricultural purposes
9	258	Manufacture of soap, synthetic detergents, perfume and toilet preparations
10	259–60	Manufacture of other chemical products (including man made fibres)
11	311	Foundries
12	312	Forging, pressing and stamping of metals
13	313	Secondary transformation, treatment and coating of metals
14	314	Manufacture of structural metal products
15	315	Boilermaking, manufacture of tanks etc
16	316–19	Manufacture of finished metal articles and other metal workshop products
17	32	Mechanical engineering
18	33	Office and data processing machinery
19	341	Manufacture of insulated wires and cables
20	342/347–8	Manufacture of electrical machinery and lighting equipment, and assembly and installation of electrical equipment
21	343	Manufacture of electrical apparatus for industrial use, including batteries and accumulators
22	344	Manufacture of equipment for telecommunications, electronic recording etc
23	345	Radio and television receiving sets, sound reproducing and recording equipment
24	346	Domestic electrical appliances
25	351–3	Manufacture and assembly of motor vehicles, including parts and accessories
26	361	Shipbuilding
27	362	Manufacture of railway rolling stock
28	363–5	Manufacture of cycles, motor cycles, aerospace equipment and other transport equipment
29	37	Instrument engineering
30	411	Margarine and other prepared fats and oils
31	412	Slaughtering and preserving of meat
32	413	Manufacture of dairy products
33	414	Processing and preserving of fruit and vegetables
34	415	Processing and preserving of edible fish and other sea food
35	416	Grain milling
36	417–8/423	Misc foodstuffs

(Continued)

Table 8.A2   (Continued)

	NACE code	Sector
37	419	Bread, biscuit and flour confectionery
38	420	Manufacture and refining of sugar
39	421	Manufacture of cocoa, chocolate and sugar confectionery
40	422	Manufacture of animal and poultry foods
41	424	Spirit and distilling and compounding
42	425–426/428	Manufacture of wine, cider and soft drinks
43	427	Brewing and malting
44	429	Manufacture of tobacco
45	431	Wool industry
46	432	Cotton industry
47	433–5	Silk, flax and jute industries
48	436	Knitting industry
49	437/9	Textile finishing and misc textile industries
50	438	Manufacture of carpets, linoleum and other floor coverings
51	441	Tanning and dressing of leather
52	442	Manufacture of products from leather and leather substitutes
53	451	Manufacture of footwear
54	453–4	Manufacture of ready-made clothing and accessories (excl knitwear)
55	455	Manufacture of household and other textile goods
56	456	Manufacture of furs and fur goods
57	461–2	Sawing and processing of wood and manufacture of semi-finished wood products
58	463	Manufacture of carpentry and joinery components
59	464–5	Manufacture of wooden containers and other wood manufactures (except furniture)
60	466	Articles of cork, straw etc; brushes and brooms
61	467	Manufacture of wooden furniture
62	471	Manufacture of pulp, paper and board
63	472	Processing of paper and board
64	473–4	Printing, publishing and allied industries
65	481–2	Manufacture of rubber products (including retreading tyres)
66	483	Processing of plastics
67	491	Manufacture of articles of jewellery, etc
68	494	Manufacture of toys and sports goods
69	492–493/495	Miscellaneous manufacturing industries

Notes

1 While it would have been preferable to analyse real changes, the lack of availability of industry deflators at the level of disaggregation used here means that all values reported are in nominal terms.

2 Unfortunately, as the three different time periods involve three different classification systems, UNISIC, NACE and NACE Rev.1, direct comparability of ranks of sectors across the three different time periods was not possible.

3   See, for example, Barry and Hannan (1996), Barry and Bradley (1997), Barry (1999a), Barry *et al.* (1999b), Boylan (1984), Croughan (1984), Fitzpatrick and Kelly (1985), McAleese, (1977), McAleese and Foley (1991), O'Malley (1985), O'Sullivan, (2000), Ruane and Görg (1996, 1997), Ruane and McGibney (1991), Walsh and Whelan (1999).
4   While it would have been preferable to examine the issue of total factor productivity growth, the lack of data on capital stock at the industry level prevent us from doing so.
5   For brevity we do not report the *t*-statistics here.

References

Barry F. and Hannan, A. (1996) 'Education, Industrial Change and Unemployment in Ireland', Working Paper WP 96/18, Centre for Economic Research, University College, Dublin.

Barry F. and J. Bradley (1997) 'FDI and Trade: the Irish Host-Country Experience', *Economic Journal*, 107: 1798–811.

Barry, F. (1999a) 'FDI and Industrial Structure in Ireland, Spain, Portugal and the UK: Some Preliminary Results', Paper presented to the Annual Conference on the European Economy, ESEG, Lisbon, December 1999.

Barry, F., J. Bradley and E. O'Malley (1999b) 'Indigenous and Foreign Industry: Characteristics and Performance', in F. Barry (ed.), *Understanding Ireland's Economic Growth*. Basingstoke: Palgrave Macmillan.

Baumol, W. (1967) 'Macroeconomics of Unbalanced Growth: The Anatomy of Urban Crises', *American Economic Review*, 57: 415–26.

Boylan, T.A. (1984) 'The Drive to Industrialise', in L. Ryan (ed.), *Irish Industry in the Eighties*. Dublin: Confederation of Irish Industry.

Central Statistics Office, *Census of Industrial Production*. Dublin: Stationery Office, various years.

Croughan, D. (1984) 'Irish Industry Today', in L. Ryan (ed.), *Irish Industry in the Eighties*. Dublin: Confederation of Irish Industry.

Denison, E. (1967) *Why Growth Rates Differ*. Washington, DC: Brookings Institute.

European Commission (2003) *Employment in Europe 2003: Recent Trends and Prospects*. Brussels: European Commission DG Employment and Social Affairs.

Fabricant, S. (1942) *Employment in Manufacturing 1899–1939*. New York: National Bureau of Economic Research.

Fagerberg, J. (1999) Specialization and Growth: World Manufacturing Productivity 1973–1990, mimeo, Centre for Technology, Innovation and Culture, University of Oslo, Oslo.

Fagerberg, J. (2000) 'Technological Progress, Structural Change and Productivity Growth: A Comparative Study', *Structural Change and Economic Dynamic*, 11: 393–411.

Fitzpatrick, J. and J.H. Kelly (1985) 'Industry in Ireland: Policies, Performance and Problems', in J. Fitzpatrick and J. Kelly (eds), *Perspectives on Irish Industry*. Dublin: Irish Management Institute.

Foley, A. (1991) 'Interpreting Output Data on Overseas Industry', in A. Foley and D. McAleese (eds), *Overseas Industry in Ireland*. Dublin: Gill & Macmillan.

Harberger, A. (1998) 'A Vision of the Growth Process', *American Economic Review*, 88: 1–32.

Havlik, P. (2005) 'Structural Change, Productivity and Employment in the New EU Member States', WIIW Research Report no. 313, The Vienna Institute for International Economics Studies, Vienna.

Kaldor, N. (1966) *Causes of the Slow Rate of Growth in the United Kingdom*. Cambridge: Cambridge University Press.

Kendrick, J. (1984) *International Comparisons of Productivity and Causes of the Slowdown*. Massachusetts: Ballinger.

Krugman, P. (1994) *The Age of Diminished Expectations*. Cambridge, Mass.: MIT.

Kuznets, S. (1979) 'Growth and Structural Shifts', in W. Galenson (ed.), *Economic Growth and Structural Change in Taiwan: The Postwar Experience of the Republic of China*. London: Cornell University Press.

McAleese, D. (1977) 'A Profile of Grant-Aided Industry in Ireland', *Publication Series Paper*, 5, The Industrial Development Authority, Dublin.

McAleese, D. and A. Foley (1991) 'The Role of Overseas Industry in Industrial Development', in A. Foley and D. McAleese (eds), *Overseas Industry in Ireland*. Dublin: Gill and Macmillan.

OECD (2004a) *Structural Change and Growth: Trends and Policy Implications*. Directorate for Science, Technology and Industry. Paris: OECD.

OECD (2004b) *Education at a Glance*. Paris: OECD.

O'Malley, E. (1985) 'The Performance of Indigenous Industry: Lessons for the 1980s', in J. Fitzpatrick and J. Kelly (eds), *Perspectives on Irish Industry*. Dublin: Irish Management Institute.

O'Sullivan, M. (2000) 'Industrial Development in Ireland: A New Beginning?', in J.W. O'Hagan (ed), *The Economy of Ireland: Policy and Performance of a European Region*. Dublin: Gill and Macmillan.

Peneder, M. (2002) 'Structural Change and Aggregate Growth', *WIFO Working Paper no. 182*, Austrian Institute of Economic Research, Vienna.

Porter, M. (2000) *The Competitive Advantage of Nations*. London. Macmillan.

Ruane, F. and H. Görg (1996) 'Aspects of Foreign Direct Investment in Irish Manufacturing since 1973: Policy and Performance', *Journal of the Statistical and Social Inquiry Society of Ireland*, xxvii: 37–87.

Ruane., F and H. Görg (1997) 'The Impact of Foreign Direct Investment on Sectoral Adjustment in the Irish Economy', *National Institute Economic Review*, 160: 76–86.

Ruane, F., and A. McGibney (1991) 'The Performance of Overseas Industry' 1973–89, in A. Foley and D. McAleese (eds), *Overseas Industry in Ireland*. Dublin: Gill & Macmillan.

Ruane, F. and A. Ugur, (2004) 'Labour Productivity and Foreign Direct Investment in Irish Manufacturing Industry: A Decomposition Analysis', *IIS Discussion Paper no. 27*, Trinity College, Dublin.

Salter, W. (1960) *Productivity and Technical Change*. Cambridge: Cambridge University Press.

Savona, M. (2003) 'Structural Change and Macroeconomic Performance: The Structural Bonus Hypothesis in Services', mimeo, Science and Technology Policy Research, Freeman Centre, University of Sussex.

Scarpetta, S., A. Bassanini, D. Pilat and P. Schreyer, (2000) 'Economic Growth in the OECD Area: Recent Trends at the Aggregate and Sectoral Level', Economics Department Working Paper no. 248, OECD, Paris.

Tang, J. and W. Wang (2004) 'Sources of Aggregate Labour Productivity Growth in Canada and the United States', *Canadian Journal of Economics*, 37: 421–44.

Timmer, M. and A. Szirmai, (2000) 'Productivity Growth in Asian Manufacturing: The Structural Bonus Hypothesis Examined', *Structural Change and Economic Dynamics*, 11: 371–92.

Walsh, P.P. and C. Whelan (1999) 'The Importance of Structural Change in Industry for Growth', *Journal of the Statistical and Social Inquiry Society of Ireland*, xxix: 1–32.

White, P. (2000) 'The IDA: Keys to Success', in R MacSharry and P White (eds), *The Making of the Celtic Tiger*. Dublin: Mercier Press.

Young, A. (1995) 'The Tyranny of Numbers: Confronting the Statistical Realities of the East Asian Growth Experience', *Quarterly Journal of Economics*, 110: 641–80.

9
What Drives Trade Specialization in the New EU Member States?
Dora Borbély

9.1 Introduction

European Union (EU) enlargement creates a wider single market, which stimulates structural adjustment and economic specialization. These impulses are expected to be part of the driving forces for structural change in the European economies, and for changes in their competitiveness, which are reflected in changes in relative factor prices and technological upgrading.

One may expect accelerated structural change in the Central and East European accession countries (AC) to have been taking place since the middle of the 1990s as the effects of systemic transformation and EU accession have stimulated a dynamic adjustment process, including a shift in specialization in particular countries and regional trade orientation towards the EU, trade liberalization and rising foreign direct investment (FDI) inflows from EU countries. The process should be accompanied by shifts in revealed comparative advantage. It is therefore clear that major changes in sectoral specialization in Western Europe will reflect major changes in the competitiveness of the new member states (NMS).

This explains the increasing interest in analysing foreign trade patterns, in particular export specialization, within the EU market, and it is here that this chapter makes a contribution. It aims at analysing the determinants of export specialization patterns of the NMS. The chapter is organized as follows: section 9.2 gives an overview on trade specialization patterns at a two-digit level in the NMS3: the Czech Republic, Hungary and Poland. In order to find out the determinants of these trade specialization patterns section 9.3 presents the results of a dynamic panel estimation, while section 9.4 draws some policy conclusions.

9.2 Trade specialization patterns in the Czech Republic, Hungary and Poland

The following analysis makes use of a Revealed Comparative Advantage (RCA) Index (Balassa, 1965), carried out at a disaggregated level for three AC with the focus on trade with the EU15 countries. For the whole analysis of the manufacturing sector, data at a 2-digit-level are used.[1] Data are classified according to NACE Rev.1.1, and the list of product groups can be found in the Appendix.

There is a wide range of modifications of the original RCA commonly used in the economic literature,[2] and the specialization indicator used here is a modification of the classical RCA index. This modification is often referred to as relative export shares; it reveals the relative comparative advantage of an industry within a country by comparing the share of that particular industry in the country's total exports to the share of that industry in total world exports at a certain point in time. Since we are interested in the question as to whether an AC has a comparative advantage as compared to the EU15, we take the respective country's exports to the EU15 instead of total exports worldwide, and intra-EU15 exports instead of worldwide exports. The modified RCA-Balassa for a specific industry k in country i is defined as follows:

$$RCA_{ik}^{modified} = \frac{\left(\dfrac{x_{ik}}{\sum\limits_{k=1}^{n} x_{ik}}\right)}{\left(\dfrac{x_{jk}}{\sum\limits_{k=1}^{n} x_{jk}}\right)}$$

where x stands for exports of the AC and j for the EU15. The modified RCA-Balassa has a minimum value of 0 and a maximum value of infinity. If $RCA_{ik} > 1$, country i has a comparative advantage in that industry k compared to the EU15. If $RCA_{ik} < 1$, there is a comparative disadvantage of country i in industry k. Instead of exports one could also use different variables, such as patents or value added.

Figures 9.1–9.3 show the modified RCA indices for three NMS. The horizontal line at 1 (on the left-hand scale) indicates the border between comparative advantage and disadvantage. The vertical lines indicate the border between the different industries classified according to the OECD taxonomy (OECD, 1987). At the same time, one should take a closer look at unit export values (UEV), whose development over time indicates the ability of a country to obtain adequate – if possible higher – prices on world markets. The black line shows the UEV, which is measured in euros per unit (kg) of exports of the respective 2-digit industry in 2003, the grey line is the UEV for 1993.

Figure 9.1 makes it clear that some very high and some very low technology-intensive products play the most important role in Hungary's EU exports. RCAs exceed unity in two labour-intensive product groups, apparel (18) and leather products (19), with UEVs of 30 and €17/kg respectively. However, RCAs were declining throughout the 1990s in these and in other labour

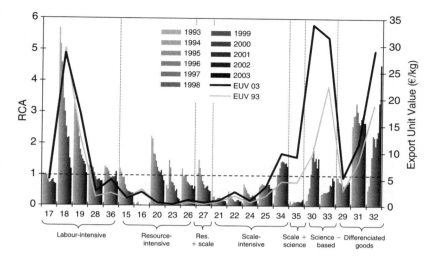

Figure 9.1 Hungary: RCA of exports 1993–2003 and UEV 1993 and 2003
Source: EC (2004), own calculations.

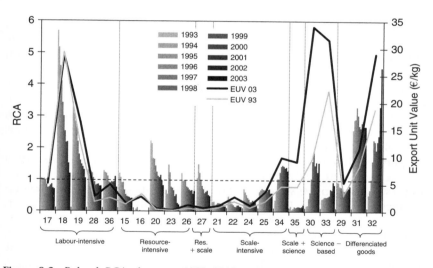

Figure 9.2 Poland: RCA of exports 1993–2003 and UEV 1993 and 2003
Source: EC (2004), own calculations.

and resource-intensive – low and medium technology – product groups. In contrast, RCAs were rising and exceeded unity in the differentiated goods' sectors, especially electrical machinery and apparatus (31) and in radio, television and communication equipment (32) industries. Here, UEVs rose

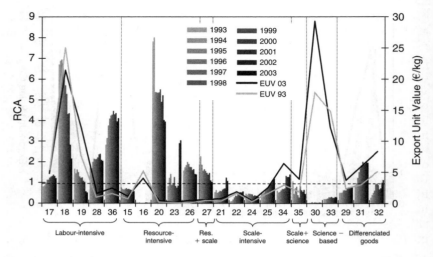

Figure 9.3   Czech Republic: RCA of exports 1993–2003 and UEV 1993 and 2003
Source: EC (2004), own calculations.

between 1993 and 2003 reaching roughly 10 and €30/kg, respectively, in 2003. In most of the other product groups, especially in resource and scale intensive industries, which mostly belong to medium technologies, both RCAs and UEV are rather low. One exception might be the manufacturing of motor vehicles (34), where Hungary had a comparative advantage throughout the second half of the 1990s with steadily rising RCAs and an UEV of €10/kg in 2003. Furthermore, there is a comparative advantage in one science-based product group, namely office machinery and computers (30), where UEV rose considerably between 1993 and 2003.

Figure 9.2 shows the respective diagram for Poland. Most industries with a relative comparative advantage compared to the EU15 belong to the labour and resource-intensive sectors, meaning they are positioned rather low on the technology ladder. The highest RCAs are yielded in apparel (18), furniture (36) and wood and wood products (20). However, especially for the latter two, UEVs are extremely low at far below €5/kg. The value of 1 kg of exports in apparel is considerably higher at roughly €20. In most of the scale-intensive, science-based and differentiated goods' sectors Poland still has a comparative disadvantage, although many RCAs in these sectors seem to have a tendency to increase. Thus, rubber and plastic products (25), motor vehicles (34) and especially electrical machinery and apparatus (31) had reached levels of RCA exceeding unity by 2003. Among these categories, UEV are the highest in the science-based sector, with up to €30/kg in 2003; however, especially in the science-based sector, Poland's comparative disadvantage is very distinct.

A similar tendency is visible in the Czech Republic (Figure 9.3) as in Hungary. Many of the RCAs in the lower technology sectors were declining and many in the higher technology-intensive sectors were rising in the time period considered in the analysis. At the same time, rather strong comparative advantages can be found all along the technology ladder. UEVs are similar to the other two countries analysed so far, especially to Poland. Comparative advantages can be found mainly in the labour intensive, resource intensive and also in the differentiated goods' sectors. Within the labour-intensive category, apparel (18) with a UEV of more than €30/kg was losing its comparative advantage, as was leather products (19), which had a UEV of less than €15/per kg. There was a very sharp decline of RCAs as well as of UEV within the resource-intensive category, where UEV were extremely low in 2003. Similar to the other accession countries, the Czech Republic also had a relative comparative disadvantage in science-based product groups, although UEVs grew considerably from €12/kg in 1993 to almost €35/kg in 2003.[3]

9.3 Determinants of export specialization in the six new member states: a dynamic panel analysis

Several factors play a major role in explaining export specialization patterns. They mainly depend on the production structure of an economy, which again is dependent on factor endowments (for example labour and capital) and factor prices, according to the Traditional Trade Theory. Other theoretical models, such as New Trade Theory models, stress the importance of distance and explain why intra-industry trade exists. In addition, interregional demand differences and trade costs are emphasized by the New Economic Geography theories. Newer theories show the major role played by investments, especially foreign direct investments, innovation and technological development. In this section we will analyse the impact of different variables on the sectoral modified RCAs, as shown in detail in the previous sections. Unfortunately, such a sectoral analysis is strongly restricted by data availability for Central and Eastern European countries (CEEC). Even if data are available from different sources, one has to control for mismatch in the data. To minimize such measurement and incomparability problems it is advisable to use not too many different data sources.

Data

The choice of exogenous variables for explaining the modified RCAs is unfortunately strongly influenced by the restrictions that the (lack of) data availability imposes. Since the main focus of this analysis is industry level, some severe data availability restrictions appear. The dependent variable is the modified RCAs, as already used in the first part of this chapter, which can also be termed the relative export share of industries on the EU15 market (European Commission, 2004).

Sectoral industrial production is expected to be one of the most robust explanatory variables. Ignoring pure trade with final products, exported products are usually generated domestically, thus they appear in sectoral industrial output. It is reasonable to assume that an increase in sectoral industrial production will lead to a rise in the relative export position. Hence the expected coefficient factor is positive. In this analysis we use nominal industrial production for 22 NACE 2-digit level manufacturing industries in six NMS, provided from the WIIW Industrial Database Eastern Europe (2004).

Wage differentials are one of the main driving forces for the European division of labour, thus enhancing export specialization patterns in CEECs. Especially for labour-intensive industries, high-wage countries from Western Europe see the possibilities to adjust. They can either relocate the labour-intensive part of their production to a lower wage country, for example in CEECs (that is offshoring), and whose mechanisms would be included in the FDI variable, or such a company can buy parts or intermediate products from a lower wage country and import them. Such outsourcing enhances the exports of the respective lower wage country, for example in Eastern Europe. From a European perspective, the greater the wage differential between West and East, the greater the incentives for outsourcing and the stronger the enhancing effect for the CEEC exports towards Western Europe. In this analysis we use relative wages to capture wage differentials. More precisely we use average nominal monthly wages in euro per employee for the CEECs, provided by the WIIW (2004) and relate them to average nominal monthly wages in Euros in the aggregate of 12 Euroland countries. The wages for the individual Euroland countries are published in the OECD's STAN Industrial Database (2005), whereas the aggregate for the 12 countries is calculated by the author using nominal GDP weights from 2000. By definition, a rise in the CEECs wage lowers the wage differential, more precisely it raises our variable, the relative wage share, which hampers the relative export shares of the CEECs. Thus we expect this variable's factor to be negative.

Furthermore, in the basic specification of our regression we expect the impact of UEV (European Commission, 2004) to appear with a positive sign. As in the previous section UEV is measured in euros per unit (kg) of exports. If one manages to raise the value of one unit of one's exports, for most products this tends to be a sign for an increase in quality. For some products, however, such as high-quality clothing (for example down jackets), a decline in the weight implies a rise in quality. Also for products with very fast technological development, such as the computer industry, there is a general tendency for lowering prices while increasing quality at the same time. Although these effects are not captured by the export unit value variable, for the total of 22 industries we expect to see a positive correlation between UEV and modified RCAs.

So far we have introduced all the variables used in the baseline specification of the panel setting. As indicated above, our panel comprises six new member states (all new members from transition countries except for the Czech Republic and Slovakia),[4] 22 industries, and 11 years, 1993–2003 which gives a number of potential maximum observations of $6 \times 22 \times 11 = 1452$. Besides data problems, the choice of estimation method is also difficult and will be dealt with in the next part of this chapter.

Methodology

Since we are interested in explaining the dynamics of specialization patterns, the lagged dependent variable should be included as an explanatory variable in the regression. Such a dynamic panel-data model might be estimated with a Least Squares Dummy Variables (LSDV) estimator, which renders, however, biased results (Baltagi, 2001). A better alternative is the use of a Generalized Method of Moments (GMM) estimation, which is advisable for smaller t dimensions.

We will use the so-called 'system GMM' estimator by Blundell and Bond (1998), which fits the two related dynamic panel-data models well. The first is the Arellano–Bond (1991) estimator, which is often called the 'difference GMM'. While taking the first difference of the equation the individual fixed effects are removed, which eliminates a potential source of omitted variable bias in the estimation. At the same time predetermined variables become dependent. The authors develop a GMM estimator, which treats the model as a system of equations, one for each time period. The only difference between the equations is the use of their set of instruments. The dependent and predetermined variables in first differences are instrumented with lags of their own levels. However, as the literature shows, lagged levels are often bad instruments for first differences. Exogenous variables enter the instrument matrix in first differences with one column per instrument.

Here the second model steps in, an extended version of a model by Arellano and Bover (1995), further developed by Blundell and Bond (1998), and called the 'system GMM' estimator. Arellano and Bover show that the efficiency of the estimator can be raised by adding the original equations in levels to the system, thus having additional moment conditions. In these equations, in levels, predetermined and dependent variables are instrumented with lags of their own first differences. Bludell and Bond develop the necessary assumptions for this model augmentation and test it with Monte Carlo simulations.

Furthermore, the 'system GMM' is available as a one- and a two-step estimator. The two-step estimator is asymptotically more efficient, but at the same time its standard errors are often downward biased (Arellano and Bond, 1991; Blundell and Bond, 1998). However, this is controlled for in the used two-step 'system GMM' estimation. A finite-sample correction is available for the two-step covariance matrix, as described by Windmeijer (2000), which dramatically improves the accuracy, as shown in Monte Carlo simulations.

Table 9.1   Determinants of export specialization in total manufacturing Arellano–Bond dynamic panel-data estimation, two-step system GMM results

Group variable: cross	Number of obs = 935
Time variable: time	Number of groups = 122
Number of instruments: 34	Obs per group: min = 3
$F(5,121) = 278.96$	Avg = 7.66
Prob > $F = 0.000$	max = 9

Dep.var: ln $rcamod_t$	Coef.	Corr. Std. error	t	$P > \|t\|$	95%	conf. interval
ln $rcamod_{t-1}$	0.774	0.039	19.38	0.000	0.695	0.853
ln ip_{t-1}	0.116	0.035	3.30	0.001	0.046	0.187
ln UEV	0.040	0.022	1.79	0.075	−0.004	0.085
ln $wagerel$	−0.100	0.059	−1.69	0.094	−0.218	0.017
$dlab$	0.242	0.062	3.89	0.000	0.119	0.366
constant	0.152	0.147	1.03	0.303	−0.139	0.444

Hansen test of overidentification restrictions: chi2(28) = 33.39 Prob > chi2 = 0.222
Arellano–Bond test for AR (1) in first differences: $z = -2.13$ pr > $z = 0.033$
Arellano–Bond test for AR (2) in first differences: $z = 1.31$ pr > $z = 0.189$

Notes: List of variables: *rcamod* – modified RCA; *ip* – industrial production; *UEV* – unit export value; *wagerel* – relative wage; *dlab* – dummy variable for labour-intensive industries.

Therefore the two-step estimator, which is used here, is more efficient than the one-step estimator in the 'system GMM'.

Thus the estimated model has the following form:

$$\Delta y_{i,t} = \alpha \Delta y_{i,t-1} + \beta \Delta X_{i,t} + \Delta \varepsilon_{i,t}$$

where y stands for the RCAs, X is the vector of the above mentioned exogenous variables, and finally there is the error term. i indicates the cross-section dimension, which is a combination of countries and industries.

Estimation results

The basic specification of the model includes those variables that have been explained in more detail above. Dummy variables for the different groups of industries as described by the OECD – such as labour, resources, scale intensive, science-based and differentiated goods – are also included in the basic specification. However, the only dummy with a significant impact is the one for labour-intensive industries. Table 9.1 shows the results for total manufacturing.

Due to the already mentioned data unavailability, only 935 observations could be realized from the potentially available 1,452 in the basic specification. However, the results are meaningful. As expected, the lagged dependent variable is highly significant with a positive sign, indicating that a 1 per cent increase (decline) in the modified RCA of the previous period leads to an increase (decline) of the RCA in the current period by 0.77 per cent. Thus there is an adjustment process of RCAs in the time dimension. Also, the sectoral industrial production has a positive impact on RCAs, and this impact is the most distinctive for one-year lagged industrial output. Accordingly, a 1 per cent rise in output results in a 0.11 per cent increase in the RCA a year later. As a matter of course, the coefficient for industrial production is much lower than the coefficient for the lagged dependent variable. The expected positive influence of the UEV as an indicator for the quality of exports could – with an error probability of 7 per cent – also be proved. A 1 per cent increase in the UEV brings about a 0.04 per cent rise in the relative export share. However, since this coefficient is rather low one can also see from Table 9.1 that the 95 per cent confidence interval includes negative values for the coefficient of the unit export value. As indicated earlier, dummy variables for the five OECD industry groups are also included. The only dummy variable to prove to be significant is the one for labour-intensive industries. This shows that the relative export shares in the labour-intensive industries are still significantly higher than the RCAs in the other industries. Although RCAs are clearly declining in the labour-intensive industries in some new member states, such as Hungary, a strong specialization in those industries is still present. This result remains robust even if one runs the regression without Poland, which shows one of the highest RCAs in the labour-intensive industries among the six countries considered in the analysis.

Finally, with an error probability of 9 per cent, relative wages in new member states play an important role in determining comparative export advantages. A 1 per cent rise in the relative wage of NMS, which corresponds to a decline in the wage differential, implies a 0.1 per cent decline in the sectoral RCA covering all 22 industrial sectors. This is some proof for the widespread expectation that the comparative advantages of the NMS result to some extent from the fact that they have sufficiently lower wages than in Western European EU countries. At the same time one should not over-out that the 95 per cent confidence interval includes negative coefficient values. At the end of the Table 9.1 some tests are included to assess the validity of the specification. The Hansen test rejects the hypothesis of over-identifying restrictions. That means that the instruments as a group appear as exogenous. Furthermore, the Arellano–Bond test for the auto-correlation of the first and second orders delivers the expected results. The way the model is constructed implies that one should find first order auto-correlation in the regression. However, second order auto-correlation should be avoided, since this would imply that the instruments for the lagged dependent variable are not exogenous. Both auto-correlation tests deliver the correct and expected results for our basic specification.

Table 9.2   Determinants of export specialization for labour-intensive industries Arellano–Bond dynamic panel-data estimation, two-step system GMM results

Group variable: cross			Number of obs $= 221$			
Time variable: time			Number of groups $= 29$			
Number of instruments: 27			Obs per group: min $= 5$			
$F(4, 28) = 568.62$			Avg $= 7.62$			
Prob $> F = 0.000$			max $= 9$			

Dep.var: $\ln$ $rcamod_t$	Coef.	Corr. Std. error	t	$P > |t|$	95%	conf. interval
$\ln$ $rcamod_{t-1}$	0.914	0.123	7.43	0.000	0.662	1.166
$\ln$ ip_{t-1}	0.123	0.079	1.55	0.132	−0.039	0.285
$\ln$ UEV	0.011	0.059	0.19	0.852	−0.109	0.132
$\ln$ $wagerel$	−0.172	0.041	−4.21	0.000	−0.256	−0.088
Constant	0.251	0.331	0.76	0.454	0.427	0.930

Hansen test of overidentification restrictions: chi2(22) $= 25.95$ Prob $>$ chi2 $= 0.254$
Arellano–Bond test for AR (1) in first differences: $z = -2.54$ pr, $> z = 0.011$
Arellano–Bond test for AR (2) in first differences: $z = -1.15$ pr $> z = 0.248$

It is worth testing the robustness of our results for sub-samples by excluding some countries, industries or years. Since the number of years and also of countries is already very limited the most reasonable, and from an economic point of view the most interesting, appears to be to run the regression for specific industries or groups of industries. In particular the impact of relative wages and maybe also of UEV may differ among industries. Therefore below we run the basic regression for the five labour-intensive industries alone, according to the OECD classification, which include manufacture of textiles, of apparel, leather, luggage, handbags and footwear, fabricated metal products and manufacture of furniture. The results are shown in Table 9.2.

First of all, the number of observations declines to 221 if one excludes all non-labour-intensive manufacturing industries. Still, all tests on the validity of the specification indicate no problem. Note that the number of instruments has also been reduced. The lagged dependent variable is still highly significant, the coefficient is even closer to unity than in the respective estimation for all industries, indicating lower adjustment dynamics. At the same time the impact of lagged industrial production – though displaying roughly the same coefficient – is not significant. Interestingly, the coefficient for the UEV has turned out to be insignificant, indicating that competition on the EU15 market in labour-intensive products is not to any great extent influenced by quality competition. Finally, and this is the most important part of this exercise, the impact of relative wages on comparative advantage

Table 9.3 Determinants of export specialization for high-technology industries Arellano–Bond dynamic panel-data estimation, two-step system GMM results

Group variable: cross			Number of obs $= 258$			
Time variable: time			Number of groups $= 34$			
Number of instruments: 27			Obs per group: min $= 3$			
$F(4, 33) = 142.48$			Avg $= 7.59$			
Prob $> F = 0.000$			max $= 9$			

Dep.var: ln *rcamod*$_t$	Coef.	Corr. Std. error	t	P > |t|	95%	conf. interval
ln *rcamod*$_{t-1}$	0.426	0.059	7.19	0.000	0.305	0.547
ln *ip*$_{t-1}$	0.486	0.092	5.25	0.000	0.298	0.675
ln *UEV*	0.274	0.072	3.77	0.001	0.126	0.422
ln *wagerel*	0.064	0.143	0.45	0.695	−0.228	0.356
constant	1.341	0.442	3.18	0.003	0.482	2.201

Hansen test of overidentification restrictions: chi2(22) $= 22.15$ Prob $>$ chi2 $= 0.451$
Arellano–Bond test for AR (1) in first differences: z $= -1.76$ pr $>$ z $= 0.078$
Arellano–Bond test for AR (2) in first differences: z $= -0.01$ pr $>$ z $= 0.989$

in labour-intensive industries is significant, with an error probability of less than 1 per cent. Also, the coefficient is clearly higher, as in the estimation for total manufacturing. For labour-intensive industries a 1 per cent increase in relative wages results in a 0.17 per cent decrease in comparative advantages. This must be perfectly in line with the Heckscher–Ohlin theorem, which focuses on the importance of relative endowments in shaping foreign trade patterns.

In the next step we only consider the upper end of the technology ladder and do the basic regression just for science-based and differentiated goods. According to the OECD classification these include manufacture of office machinery and computers, of medical precision and optical instruments, of machinery and equipment, of electrical machinery and apparatus and manufacture of radio, television and communication equipment and apparatus. The results are displayed in Table 9.3.

The number of observations in the high-technology groups at 258 is very similar to the labour-intensive industries regressed before. Also here, the Hansen test for over-identifying restrictions, as well as both the Arellano–Bond tests for AR(1) and AR(2) indicate no problem in the estimation; the results clearly correspond to prior expectations. The lagged dependent variable and lagged industrial production show a highly significant positive sign. Thus a 1 per cent increase in the RCA in the previous period results in a 0.42 per cent higher RCA in the current period; and a 1 per cent increase in the industry output in the previous year brings about a 0.48 per cent higher RCA in the current period. For high-technology industries, UEV as indicators for quality matter a lot. This is shown in the highly significant and positive coefficient for the UEV. A rise in the UEV by 1 per cent improves the revealed comparative advantage in high-technology industries by 0.27 per cent. It seems that in these industries competitiveness is much more influenced by quality differences than in lower technology industries. Advancing comparative advantages in science-based and differentiated goods apparently depend to a great extent on the ability of upgrading quality. Given the fast technological change and tough competition in these industries this finding is to a large extent reasonable. So are the findings on the impact of relative wages on comparative advantages in high-technology industries, which is basically non-existent. The coefficient is not significant, indicating that wages do not play an important role for export advantages in these industries.

In the next step we modify the basic specification by adding other exogenous variables that are expected to have an impact. The results are briefly summarized.

Relative labour productivity

First of all we look at labour productivity, which is measured as sectoral industrial output in million euros per employee in NMS in relation to the same measure in the Euroland. Output for CEECs is provided by the WIIW (2004) in national currencies and has been converted into euros using annual average exchange rates to the euro published by Eurostat. The number of employees on a sectoral level is also provided by WIIW (2004). Output for Euroland is taken from the OECD STAN Industry Database (2005), as is also the case for the number of employees. Again, Euroland is calculated using GDP shares in 2000. Using this measure one might at first sight expect a positive coefficient in explaining revealed comparative advantages. If labour productivity in NMS rises, assuming Euroland productivity remains stable, relative productivity rises, which in turn would be expected to enhance comparative advantages. However, we find that labour productivity is strongly correlated with wages. Thus, if productivity rises, wages rise, and this has a negative effect on RCA. Therefore the expected factor of labour productivity on RCA is negative. As a matter of course we drop wages from the equations.

The empirical model does not reveal a significant negative effect of labour productivity on RCA, neither for total manufacturing nor for high-tech industries. However, for labour-intensive industries a rise in productivity of 1 per cent results in a decline of RCA by 0.14 per cent, with a significance level of 99 per cent.

Unit labour costs

It is not only wages and labour productivity that might play an important role in explaining comparative advantages, but also relative unit labour costs.

These are calculated as the ratio of wages to productivity. The intuitive impact of relative unit labour costs would appear, however, to be negative since a rise would deteriorate the competitiveness, especially, of labour-intensive industries. On the other hand, since wages and productivity are strongly correlated in our sample, one might expect that there is no movement between these two variables and no explanatory power left in the data. Indeed, the regression results including relative unit labour costs show no significant impact of them in any of the three samples. The other coefficients remain robust, but since there is no additional information provided by the estimations, the results are not reported.

Foreign direct investment

It seems clear that foreign direct investment is an important factor driving economic development in CEECs. FDI stock in million euros is provided from the WIIW FDI Database (2005), while GDP in million euros is taken from Eurostat. However, before running the estimation several problems appear. Sectoral FDI data as a percentage of GDP as described above are not only correlated with RCAs, the dependent variable of the panel, but also with several exogenous variables of the basic specification, such as relative wages, UEV and even with industrial output. In order to bring some clarity to the situation we chose to run the dynamic panel regression for RCAs and FDI only. The results show no contemporary correlation for any of the three samples. For high-tech industries the one-year lagged FDI has a small, but significant, impact. For labour-intensive industries, however, the boosting effect of FDI on RCA is highly significant (with coefficients of 0.019–0.024) for both the contemporary and the lagged influence.

Research and development

Finally we analyse the impact of R&D expenditure on RCA. R&D expenditure aggregated at the level of the firm for NACE 2-digit-level industries is available for the CEECs from Eurostat. The data is given in million euros. The explanatory variable in our model additionally controls for the size of the sector by relating R&D expenditures to GDP. Furthermore, the R&D variable shows a strong and significant correlation with industrial production. We therefore drop industrial production as an explanatory variable. The dynamic panel estimation with an R&D-extended basic specification reveals no significant influence of the simultaneous R&D variable either for the total sample or for the two sub-samples. As for the first lag of R&D as an explanatory variable we find no significant correlation for total manufacturing and for labour-intensive industries. We do, however, find a significant coefficient for the high-technology industries. A 1 per cent increase in the R&D to GDP ratio results in a 0.065 per cent higher RCA one year later. This seems to underline the importance of research and development for higher technology industries, which one would expect from theoretical and practical considerations. It also seems reasonable that research and development expenditure materializes with some time lag.

9.4 Summary and policy conclusions

Considering the dynamic development of RCAs we find that Poland exports mainly low and some medium technology (or labour-intensive) products to the EU15. The Czech Republic, however, shows clear specialization patterns in the field of medium and even high-technology products, while in Hungary we also find export specialization in some very-low-technology products in the 1990s.

Concerning the determinants of export specialization we can summarize the results as follows:

- Firstly, industrial production, especially with a time lag of one year, plays a very important role in explaining comparative advantage. This is valid across all the 22 two-digit manufacturing industries considered.
- NMS are still significantly more strongly specialized in labour-intensive industries and thus have a significantly higher comparative advantage in the labour-intensive industries as compared to all the other industries.
- UEV plays an important role in explaining comparative advantages. This is valid in a cross-sectoral perspective, but especially for science-based and differentiated goods industries, which are situated at the upper end of the technology ladder. Furthermore, UEV seems to play hardly any role for labour-intensive industries.
- Relative labour productivity and relative wages are highly correlated, showing that rises in labour productivity are to a great extent reflected in wage increases.
- Relative wages strongly determine comparative advantages, not only for labour-intensive industries, but even on a cross-industrial basis. For high technology industries relative wages turn out to hardly matter at all.
- FDI is strongly correlated both with labour productivity and industrial production. A contemporary impact on comparative advantages is only found for labour intensive industries. With a time lag of one year FDI stock has a positive impact both on labour-intensive and on high-tech industries. For labour intensive industries FDI even displays export-enhancing effects after two years.
- The contemporary positive impact of research and development expenditure is found for total manufacturing. For high-technology industries the export enhancing effects seem to unfold only after one or two years. For labour-intensive industries no significant impact is found.

Bearing in mind the results of the previous analysis, one of the main policy conclusions is to highlight the importance of an investor-friendly economic environment. Policy-makers should clearly focus on attracting foreign direct investment in diversified industries. This can be done by political and legal security, as well as an adequate tax system. The positive impact of foreign direct investment on the development of foreign trade specialization has clearly been empirically indicated.

Although the NMS have witnessed relatively favourable economic development in the past decade, especially Poland, but to a lesser extent also Hungary and the Czech Republic still show rather high – and in some cases stubborn – unemployment rates. Initially it seemed that labour markets in the NMS would benefit from outsourcing and offshoring from Western European companies, which is undeniable. However, as European integration proceeds, firms in NMS themselves face considerable pressure for outsourcing internationally, especially from Asian countries, such as China. Given high sustained unemployment rates in many NMS, one must be worried about unemployment problems. Jobless growth could be one of the new problems in the NMS. To the extent that the mass unemployment problem contributes to social and political conflicts as well as political radicalization, high long-term unemployment could contribute to political destabilization which in turn would raise the political risk premium and weaken growth in the long run. Therefore two policy conclusions should be drawn. Firstly, policy-makers have to put emphasis on upgrading human capital formation by increasing the quality and quantity of education and training activities, which will be important to enhance productivity and to encourage the creation of new firms, which often not only create new jobs but contribute to overall flexibility and innovativeness. Secondly, it is inevitable that policy-makers stimulate innovations and thus enhance the quality of products to gain competitiveness on international markets. Underlying econometric analysis shows the positive influence of UEV on RCA, thus showing that a higher quality product can better be placed on international (especially European) markets, than a low-quality product. Therefore quality upgrading by enforcing innovativeness is one of the main ingredients of successful economic policy in CEECs.

Also, the positive impact of research and development expenditure on comparative advantages in foreign trade were shown empirically. However, also from a theoretical and a political perspective it is clear that national R&D programmes are likely to generate a positive effect on economic development and on the competitiveness of countries and industries. However, due to cross-border benefits through international technology spillovers there is some risk that national policymakers will cut incentives for R&D expenditures, causing them to decline, since it can be expected that positive external effects of innovation would not be fully internalized in the EU. Shifting more funds in R&D to the supranational policy level might not be a reasonable way to cope with the problem. Due to the weakness of the European Commission's political control and the established budgetary priorities for agriculture and structural funds we cannot expect an efficient EU innovation policy. However, the EU could be quite useful in innovation policy, in particular by regular analysis of innovation dynamics in EU countries and in the regions of the EU. More transparency could generate stronger incentives towards adequate national policy reforms.

To conclude, for policy-makers in NMS it is advisable to emphasize education and R&D support in the course of European integration and worldwide globalization, as well as to enforce the creation and maintenance of an investor-friendly economic and political environment.

Appendix

Table 9.A1   NACE Rev. 1.1. Classification (in parts)

D	Manufacturing
15	Manufacture of food products and beverages
16	Manufacture of tobacco products
17	Manufacture of textiles
18	Manufacture of wearing apparel; dressing and dyeing of fur
19	Tanning and dressing of leather, manufacture of luggage, handbags, saddlery, harness and footwear
20	Manufacture of wood and of products of wood and cork, except furniture;
21	Manufacture of pulp, paper and paper products
22	Publishing, printing and reproduction of recorded media
23	Manufacture of coke, refined petroleum products and nuclear fuel
24	Manufacture of chemicals and chemical products
25	Manufacture of rubber and plastic products
26	Manufacture of other non-metallic mineral products
27	Manufacture of basic metals
28	Manufacture of fabricated metal products, except machinery and equipment
29	Manufacture of machinery and equipment n.e.c.
30	Manufacture of office machinery and computers
31	Manufacture of electrical machinery and apparatus n.e.c.
32	Manufacture of radio, television and communication equipment and apparatus
33	Manufacture of medical, precision and optical instruments, watches and clocks
34	Manufacture of motor vehicles, trailers and semi-trailers
35	Manufacture of other transport equipment
36	Manufacture of furniture, manufacturing n.e.c.

Notes

1 Data are extracted from the COMEX database of the European Commission.
2 The original RCA shows the export/import share of an industry as compared to the export/import share of an economy.
3 For a more detailed and extended analysis including a convergence analysis see Borbély (2004a, 2004b).
4 Data on industrial production and wages are not available at the two-digit level for these two countries and therefore they drop out of the panel.

References

Arellano, M. and S. Bond (1991) 'Some Tests of the Specification for Panel Data: Monte Carlo Evidence and an Application to Employment Equations', *Review of Economic Studies*, 58(2): 277–97.
Arellano, M. and O. Bover (1995) 'Another Look at the Instrumental Variable Estimation of Error-Components Models', *Journal of Econometrics*, 68: 29–51.
Balassa, B. (1965) 'Trade Liberalization and Revealed Comparative Advantage', *The Manchester School*, 33: 99–123.
Baltagi, B.H. (2001) *Econometric Analysis of Panel Data*, 2nd edn. Chichester: John Wiley & Sons.
Blundell, R.W. and S. Bond (1998) 'Initial Conditions and Moment Restrictions in Dynamic Panel Data Models', *Journal of Econometrics*, 87(1): 115–43.
Borbély, D. (2004a) 'EU Export Specialization Patterns in Selected Accession Countries', EIIW Working Paper no. 116, Wuppertal.
Borbély, D. (2004b) 'Competition Among Accession and Cohesion Countries: Comparative Analysis of Specialization within the EU Market', EIIW Working Paper no. 122, Wuppertal.
European Commission (2004) 'Intra- and Extra-EU Trade', COMEXT Annual Database, CD-Rom Supplement 2.
OECD (1987) *Structural Adjustment and Economic Performance*. Paris: OECD.
OECD (2005) STAN Industrial Database, Paris: OECD.
WIIW (The Vienna Institute for International Economic Studies) (2004) *Industrial Database Eastern Europe*, CD-ROM, June 2004.
WIIW FDI Database (2005) *Database on Foreign Direct Investment in Central, East and Southeast Europe*, CD-ROM, May 2005.
Windmeijer, F.A.G. (2000) 'A Finite Sample Correction for the Variance of Linear Two-Step GMM Estimator', Institute for Fiscal Studies, Working Paper series 00/19, London.

10
Specialization and Integration of Accession Countries into the EU Market: An Alternative View
Michael Brandmeier

10.1 Introduction

Changes in specialization within the European Union (EU) market naturally occur in an economic integration process like the EU's integration eastwards. The latest EU integration process differs in two important aspects from former EU enlargements. Firstly, the new EU member states (NMS) are former socialist countries with long years of experience in planning their economies and then transforming them into market economies. Secondly, the competitive advantage of the NMS lies in their very low labour costs and relatively highly educated labour force. Both describe the reasons for changes in export specialization in East Europe (EE) and the different export-promoting strategies in the region compared to Central Europe (CE). In EE one finds the lowest labour costs and mainly labour-intensive production, such as outward processing trade (OPT) in textiles and clothing. In CE the foreign trade structure is comparatively more diversified and more similar to the EU15.

In Chapter 9, Borbély focused on two questions: firstly, what are the trade specialization patterns in the NMS? Secondly, which factors play a major role in explaining these export specialization patterns? Borbély (2004b) shows the key shifts in sectoral developments and changing RCA indicators in exports to the EU15: Poland and the Czech Republic compete mainly with Portugal and Greece in lower and middle quality goods and Hungary is a competitor of Spain and Ireland in some higher quality goods.

Confirming the empirical analysis in Brandmeier (2005), Borbély (2004c) found that cohesion countries – Portugal, Greece, Spain and Ireland – and the accession countries (AC) – Hungary, Poland and the Czech Republic – mainly compete in labour and resource-intensive industries, with relatively low technology input. Inflows of foreign direct investment (FDI) mainly from Germany, Holland, Austria and the United States to the Czech Republic, Hungary and Poland promote the capability of these countries to act as competitive suppliers on the EU15 market (Brandmeier, 2005, p. 280). Borbély (2004b, p. 55) focuses her attention on the fact that 'Hungary to a greater and

Poland to a less extent converge to the EU15 export specialisation patterns, as do the cohesion countries.'

This chapter is organized as follows. After outlining various methodological aspects of using RCA values and unit values (section 10.2) we focus on the trade specialization process in the context of the factor content of several sectors (section 10.3). It is very interesting to see how the shares of export volumes of several factor content groups have changed over time. We discuss the results of the dynamic panel analysis of the determinants of export specialization in section 10.4, while section 10.5 concludes.

10.2 Methodological aspects

In empirical analysis of foreign trade it is common to use the concept of Revealed Comparative Advantage Values (RCA values). RCA values show whether a single industry in one country exports relatively more than it imports from another country in comparison with the export/import ratio of all industries. RCA values serve as an indicator of competitiveness if one conceives of this ratio as a means of observing how a higher share of a foreign market sector is successfully acquired.

In Chapter 9, Borbély defines, accordingly, a modified RCA export/import ratio where x_{ik} signifies the exports of the acceding country i in a specific industry k, and j stands for the EU15. The author has interpreted this as a ratio of export shares, which reveals the relative comparative advantage of an industry within a country by comparing the share of that industry in intra-EU15 exports:

$$RCA_{ik}^{\text{modified}} = \frac{\left[\dfrac{x_{ik}}{\sum\limits_{k=1}^{n} x_{ik}}\right]}{\left[\dfrac{x_{jk}}{\sum\limits_{k=1}^{n} x_{jk}}\right]}$$

Using the OECD taxonomy of factor intensity groups in Chapter 9, Borbély is interested in those factor intensity groups with the highest export shares compared with intra-EU15 export patterns.

It is possible to fix the convergence of one country's industry by using the deviations in the export patterns of EU15-intra trade. This information gives a hint as to whether the trade structure is becoming more similar to EU15-intra trade. It also highlights the comparative advantage of those industries of the AC – signified by high RCA values – in comparison with the EU15 average. In another way of using RCA values, in empirical trade analysis, the total exports and imports of one country can be used to determine its trade structure and to reveal the comparative advantage of several of its industries. Before discussing the empirical results of changes in export specialisation patterns the key aspects of using and interpreting RCA values and unit values (UV) are discussed briefly.

RCA values as an indicator for export specialization patterns

RCA values, calculated from the Standard Industrial Trade Classification (SITC), do not indicate that the sources of economic growth are the most important conditions for the economic convergence processes of countries with lower national incomes per capita. Only the RCA values classified by factor content and the classification of economic activities in the European Community (NACE) allow one to make statements on the factors which drive outstanding RCA values, because they give information about the competitive position of a single industry in one country with similar factor content intensities. The definition of a taxonomy group according to NACE Rev.1 2-digit classification is not very precise, because such groups of industries heterogeneously consist of industries with different factor content intensities (Neven, 1995, pp. 53–7).

Unit values as an indicator of different quality of export and import goods

According to Aiginger (1997, p. 572), the unit exports value (UEV) is defined as nominal sales divided into some quantity measure, usually the kilogram. This definition is flexible enough to include also unit values of imports or of domestic production. The UV can be interpreted as average costs if the economic profits are zero or are 'much more a sign of quality or of the efficient use of material than of price' (Aiginger, 1997, p. 573). An increasing UV indicates that production shifts from a low-quality to a high-quality sub-segment. A product segment is signified by quality differences if positive net exports are combined with increasing UV. Homogenous products are indicated if positive net exports and decreasing unit values coincide.

Aiginger (1997, p. 585) did not interpret UEV as 'prices' or 'quality', and the author discriminated between 'quality-dominated markets' (UV exp < UV imp $\rightarrow$ Q exp > Q imp) and 'price elastic markets' (UV exp < UV imp $\rightarrow$ Q exp > Q imp) (*ibid.*, p. 574). For example, the 18 three-digit industries in the machinery sector (roughly SITC 7) were classified as quality-dominated, but only three industries (clothing, leather and pottery) were in all 18 of the OECD countries definitely classified by Aiginger (1997, p. 582) as price-dominated, as well as the 'majority of the electrical machinery sectors [which] are driven by price differences'.[1] The author also counters the view that UEVs are the final and only means of discriminating between competition in a market classified as 'price-elastic' and 'quality-dominated'.

These aspects have to be kept in mind when conclusions are drawn from motions of UV. They only give information on the change in the standard deviations of RCA values – interpreted as the relative export share of each country compared to the EU15 – at the beginning and the end of the period in each of the 22 sectors. Nothing is said about in which sectors the relative export shares of CE and South Europe countries are the highest.

Empirical results of foreign trade specialization on the EU market

The overall results of the comparative analysis of the AC3 and cohesion countries concerning foreign trade and the factors determining their future structural adjustment can be summarized as follows:

Borbély (2004a) found that all 10 EU countries showed converging patterns if 3-digit-level industries are considered. Only the Czech Republic, Italy and Slovenia diverged from the EU15 export specialization pattern. Secondly, at the more disaggregated industry level, the labour and resource-intensive industries showed a relatively strong increase in concentration. The β-concentration in trade patterns is higher the greater the positive regression coefficient β of first-order auto-regression (AR) (1) of RCA values in individual sectors is across countries and over time. Borbély (2004a) asserted from this that there is a strong tendency towards de-specialization at the intra-country cross-sectoral level.

Borbély (2004a) also found that β-specialization dominates the picture. This means that initial trade patterns (RCA values) change over time in both directions. Therefore, most countries moved closer to the EU15 average export specialization patterns in the period 1993–2001. The export pattern of Hungary moved more closely to the EU15 export specialization pattern than that of Poland. Surprisingly, the Czech Republic had a rather static export pattern and diverged from the EU15 average pattern (Borbély 2004a, p. 24), despite its relatively high degree of economic integration through inflow channels for foreign direct investment (FDI) and its comparatively high export/GDP ratio (see Figures 10.1 and 10.2).

The Heckscher–Ohlin–Samuelson model (HOS model) postulates that comparative advantages caused by different factor endowments are responsible for increasing trade, especially in labour-intensive industries. In the past, cohesion and accession countries had considerably high comparative advantages in labour and resource-intensive production lines. Their relatively low unit labour costs (ULC) lead to the concentration of labour-intensive production sequences in South and East Europe instead of in the former traditional production sites of textiles (NACE code 17) and clothing (NACE code 18) in Germany and in Holland (Flanders).

Borbély (2004d, p. 15) found that Poland only exported (in NACE Rev.1.1: 18, 20, 28, 35, 36) more manufactured goods[2] to the EU15 than it imported from these countries in the period 1995 until 2001 in a handful of branches.

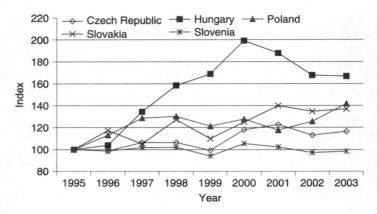

Figure 10.1   Import/GDP ratio of five CECs (1995 = 100)

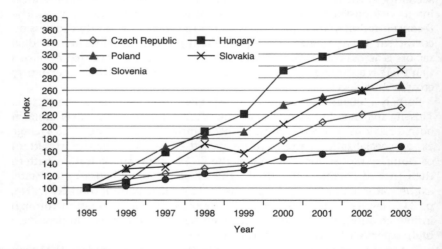

Figure 10.2   Import growth of five CECs
Source for Figures 10.1 and 10.2:   WIIW Research Report no. 266, June 2000, table 8, since 1999; data from Eurostat Luxembourg. Basic year for index is 1995, own calculations.

The opposite is true for the Czech Republic (NACE Rev.1.1: 18, 26, 28, 30, 31, 34, 35, 36). Hungary had a more diversified export specialization pattern.

In Borbély (2004b) the following key shifts in sectoral developments were found:

- Competition between the cohesion countries (Portugal and Greece) and the AC (Poland and the Czech Republic) concentrated on labour and

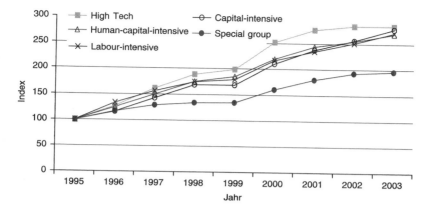

Figure 10.3 Exports of 4 CEECs to EU15 according to factor intensities
Notes: The CEECs are the Czech and Slovak Republics, Hungary and Poland.
Source: Eurostat, Luxembourg, own calculations.

resource-intensive industries. This result complies with the hypothesis of the HOS model. Moreover, the de-specialization in the EU25 in Borbély 2004–6, fig. 1) goes along with the increase in RCA Values in increasing numbers of industries in Central and East European countries (CEECs) foreign trade with Germany and the EU15. This first result is confirmed by empirical research on the export specialization of four CEECs (see Figure 10.3).

- Borbély (2004b) clearly showed β-de-specialization in the EU25 for the period 1993–2001 as well as σ-de-specialization. The latter means that the variance of the actual RCA values in $t_1 = 2001$ and of the initial RCA values in $t_0 = 1993$ are decreasing over time.

Most of the industries show a decreasing variance over time if the number of countries in the sample is increasing (Borbély, 2004b). The exceptions are the labour-intensive manufacture of fabricated metal products (28), and the resource-intensive fabrication of products of wood and cork (20). Especially the manufacture of other transport equipment (motor vehicles are not included) shows the export specialization of the three countries in CE in this sector in comparison with the EU15 export specialization pattern. This second result is also consistent with the fact that mainly the four CEC – Poland, Hungary, the Slovak and Czech Republic – evince stable comparative advantages in labour-intensive industries (see Figure 10.3).

The ACs are in intense competition in the labour and resource-intensive industries not only with the cohesion countries in Southern Europe, but also with northern and western EU countries such as France,

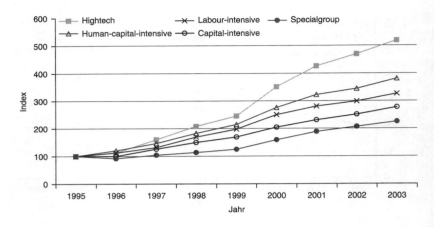

Figure 10.4 Imports of 4 CEECs in EU15 according to factor intensities
Notes: The four CEECs are the Czech and Slovak Republics, Hungary and Poland.
Source: Eurostat, Luxembourg, own calculations.

Belgium/Luxembourg, Netherlands, Denmark, Germany, Ireland and the UK (see Neven, 1995, for details). First of all, the NMS are succeeding in exporting labour and resource-intensive products because of their overwhelmingly low labour costs, making it cheaper for multinational firms to outsource those product lines with low technology input. Later on, modern production sites are completed by local vocational education and research centres to improve the product quality and decrease the innovation costs.

The empirical fact of booming exports in a few manufacturing industries of several factor intensity groups confirms the hypothesis of the new trade theory and New Economic Geography (see Krugman and Venables, 1995, 1996; Markusen and Venables, 1998), that the production of differentiated goods in non-perfect markets leads to fragmentation of the whole production process across different countries because of falling trading and transport costs. However, other reasons seem to be more relevant than transport costs, for example adequate supply policy, combined with the labour force's minimum human capital endowments. This additionally explains the concentration of export growth and export volume of only five CEC (the Czech Republic, Hungary, Poland, Slovakia and Slovenia), because these countries are still more attractive for foreign direct investors than the countries in East Europe with very low labour costs.

Figures 10.1 to 10.4 show that Hungary has had the highest real export growth rates since 1998, although it also possesses the largest export/GDP ratio. Economic growth theory would postulate a larger potential for the growth rate if the export potential were lower. In order to make the different countries more amenable to comparison it is useful to calculate the import/GDP ratio as an indicator of the openness of the country or its ability to foster better relations with foreign investors (see Figure 10.1).

The import growth rate signals the dynamic evolution of these relations because the fragmentation of production lines of – for example – German firms goes hand in hand with increasing volumes of intermediate goods for further processing in the AC. These often supplemental products are destined for other countries or for re-import to Germany.

The slowest import growth rate of the five AC (the Czech Republic, Hungary, Poland, Slovakia and Slovenia) was in Slovenia. In 1999 there is a break in the trend of the growth rate. Excluding Slovenia the import growth index of all four countries increased astonishingly strongly. In the case of Hungary it jumped about 80 index points in comparison with the preceding year, 1999 (see Figure 10.2).

Looking at the export specialization patterns of the four AC (the Czech and Slovak Republic, Hungary and Poland), it is amazing to see that exports of high-tech-intensive branches were rising most strongly (see Figure 10.3). This special group consists mainly of sectors in the food-processing industries. The growth rates of human-capital-intensive, labour-intensive and capital-intensive exports are converging.

The fact that exports and imports according to factor intensities are mutually dependent is confirmed by the same development for corresponding growth rates (see Fig.10.3 and 10.4). The difference is in the broader dispersion, showing that the export specialization pattern is more uniform than the import specialization pattern for three factor-intensity groups and across these five countries.

Table 10.1 shows the differences between the import and export share in each factor-intensity group for each AC. We see that the differences between import and export shares are negative but diminishing in the technology and human-capital-intensive groups and positive and quite stable in the labour-intensive groups. The tables in the Appendix show the RCA values for each of the four AC, according to NACE Rev.1 classification.

In the Slovak Republic the labour-intensive producing industries are less-integrated with the EU15, because EU15 imports are considerably lower than in Hungary. In 2003, the difference between EU15 imports and EU15 exports is −1.19 percentage points in Hungary.

Figure 10.5 shows the competition position of the four CEECs in EU15 trade. The RCA value of labour-intensive producing industries is very stable and always between 0.4 and 0.6. Notice that the four AC gain more of the contestable market share in high-tech industries: the RCA value increases from –0.5 in 1995 to over –0.2 in 2003, but is still negative. Labour-intensive industries clearly count as export industries in the AC. The same is true for capital-intensive industries, but with deteriorating RCA values. The capital-intensive industries are signified by relatively high inputs of capital and

Table 10.1 Difference between EU15 imports and EU15 exports of each factor-intensity group for Bulgaria, Czech Republic, Hungary, Poland, Slovakia and Slovenia (in per cent points)

FI class	Czech Republic			Hungary		
	1995	1999	2003	1995	1999	2003
High and medium tech.	−7.00	−11.05	−2.25	−7.94	−0.16	11.25
Human-capital-intensive	−10.11	−5.38	−5.28	−6.62	−9.43	−11.87
Labour-intensive	8.17	16.09	8.15	6.57	4.85	−1.19
Capital-intensive	9.86	3.46	1.59	9.10	5.65	3.17
Special group (food processing industry)	−1.44	−2.35	−1.82	−2.93	−1.62	−2.14

FI class	Bulgaria			Slovenia		
	1995	1999	2003	1995	1999	2003
High and medium tech.	−0.55	−14.19	−12.78	−7.38	−6.78	−9.35
Human-capital-intensive	−15.66	−8.32	−9.25	−8.83	−7.82	−8.86
Labour-intensive	8.54	19.86	19.32	17.17	18.69	17.50
Capital-intensive	14.55	6.59	1.74	−2.08	−3.12	1.53
Special group (food processing industry)	−5.46	−1.72	−0.78	−0.05	0.13	0.86

FI class	Poland			Slovakia		
	1995	1999	2003	1995	1999	2003
High and medium tech.	−12.23	−13.75	−10.16	−4.97	−8.85	−7.71
Human-capital-intensive	−2.77	−4.11	1.49	−13.12	−10.76	−10.62
Labour-intensive	22.19	18.02	13.42	17.26	32.00	35.55
Capital-intensive	−2.59	2.77	−0.93	−3.40	11.41	−17.23
Special group (food processing industry)	−3.50	−2.81	−2.98	2.95	−1.37	−1.07

Note: The four CEE countries are the Czech and Slovak Republics, Hungary and Poland.
Source: Eurostat, Luxembourg; own calculations.

relatively high employment of less-qualified workers in comparison to the labour-intensive industries.

To summarize the analysis in this section, the following three aspects of the export specialization patterns of the AC have to be kept in mind. The hypothesis of HOS theory that differences in factor endowment explain export specialization patterns is confirmed by the above analysis. Moreover, de-specialization in the EU25 in Figure 10.1 is in line with the increase in RCA values in increasing numbers of industries in terms of the CEECs' foreign trade with Germany or the EU12. The specialization pattern according to factor intensities is signified by exports and imports being mutually dependent

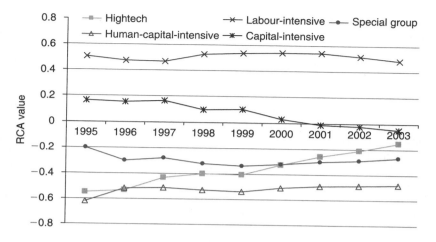

Figure 10.5 RCA values of 4 CEECs in EU15 trade according to factor intensities
Source: Eurostat, Luxembourg. The four CEE countries are the Czech and Slovak Republics, Hungary and Poland. Classification according to Neven (1995), own calculations.

and the German foreign trade with AC concentrated on Poland, the Czech Republic, Slovakia and Hungary.

The AC are in a tough competition in labour and resource-intensive industries not only with the cohesion countries in Southern Europe but also with northern and western EU countries such as France, Belgium/Luxembourg, Netherlands, Denmark, Germany, Ireland and the UK.

The next section focuses on the determinants of export specialization patterns. Firstly, we briefly summarize the main results of Chapter 9. The author has completed the convergence analysis by estimating a dynamic panel analysis to determine the main factors of foreign trade specialization on the EU market, and these results are supplemented by a change in the observation view point. By calculating a metric indicator we quantify the quantity of outsourcing volume and the main determinants of these imports from Central Europe.[3] Although the methodology and data source are different to Borbély (2005a), the analysis could be interpreted as a supplement to the former analysis because it locates the specific factors that boost or hinder export specialization in a large country located in the centre of the enlarged EU.

10.3 Empirical results of the main determinants of export specialization on the EU and German markets for intermediate goods

In Chapter 9, Borbély found that the most important factors driving comparative advantages in trade are sectoral industrial production, unit export values (UEV), FDI, R&D and low relative wages as compared to EU15 countries.

In section 10.2 we criticized the use and interpretation of RCA values as a measure of competitiveness, if they are highly aggregated and not classified by factor intensities. Using RCA values as a dependent variable in a dynamic panel analysis with a cross-section dimension has the advantage that we can easily interpret the independent variables as factors supporting or hindering comparative advantage in one of six AC (excluding the Czech Republic and Slovakia) and one of 22 industrial sectors.

Unsurprisingly, sectoral industrial production in the six AC is positively related with the RCA values, because a part or all of the domestic production volume will probably be destined for export. In Chapter 9, Borbély calculates the impact of sectoral industrial production on RCA: a 1 per cent rise in output brings about a 0.11 per cent increase in the RCA value. The quality aspects are factored in by using UEV as an independent variable; the UEV are defined as the export value in euro per kg. Borbély shows that a 1 per cent increase in the UEV implies a 0.04 per cent increase in the relative export share. Therefore, one can conclude that a 1 per cent higher increase in the value of exports in comparison with the overall weight of exports positively promotes the relative export share in a cross-section dimension. By dividing the sample according to factor intensities the author showed that the UEV are not significant for labour-intensive industries (textiles, wearing apparel, leather, metal products and furniture).

Table 10.2 gives the impression that the part of industrial intermediate production with a foreign origin is very high and has increased steadily in Germany. For 2004, the German Federal Statistical Office presented foreign trade data showing that the Czech Republic, Poland and Hungary exported more goods to Germany than the United States did. Poland outnumbered Irish exports to Germany. Spain exported only about €300 million more than the Czech Republic. These figures demonstrate that the bilateral foreign trade volumes between the ACs in Central Europe and Germany are considerable. Therefore it is important to calculate the factors driving import growth in German manufacturing.

The share of imports of total intermediate goods increased between 1995 and 2000 by 7.8 percentage points and amounted to 38.5 per cent. The sectoral distribution of this import volume is decisive in localizing its determinants.

The dependent variable of the following regression is defined as:[4]

$$Outs - CE_{i,t} = \frac{z_{i,t} \cdot 100}{\sum_{j}^{n} y_{ij,t} + m_{i,t}}$$

Table 10.2 Intermediate goods in German manufacturing

	1995 bn €	2000 bn €	Annual change at average in per cent
Intermediate goods, total	639.3	824.1	5.8
domestic origin	490.7	580.4	3.7
foreign origin	148.6	243.7	12.8
Imports in per cent of[a]	23.2	29.6	5.5
Manufacturing goods	390.1	506.4	6.0
domestic origin	270.5	311.3	3.0
foreign origin	119.6	195.1	12.6
Imports in per cent of[a]	30.7	38.5	5.1
Services	171.3	226.0	6.4
domestic origin	165.7	215.7	6.0
foreign origin	5.6	10.3	16.8
Imports in per cent of[a]	3.3	4.5	7.3
Other goods	77.9	91.7	3.5
domestic origin	54.5	53.5	−0.4
foreign origin	23.4	38.2	12.6
Imports in per cent of[a]	30.0	41.7	7.8

Notes: Figures calculated with actual prices; [a] share of imports in total intermediate goods.
Source: German Federal Statistical Office, time-series service, specialist series, no. 18, vol. 2.

where $Z_{i,t}$ = indicator for imports of intermediate goods from five countries of Central Europe (CE = Czech Republic, Hungary, Poland, Slovakia, Slovenia) of a single output branch i at time t; $y_{ij,t}$ = in Germany produced intermediate goods for each input sector j being destined for the output branch i at time t; $m_{i,t}$ = total German imports of intermediate goods being destined for the output branch i at time t; and t = 1995, 1996,..., 2000.

Tables from 10.3 and 10.5 show the results of estimating the outsourcing volume (variable Outs-CE). In the first specification of the cross section and cross-country regression equation the ratio of FDI/GDP, wage share and labour-productivity differences across sectors and between Germany and Central Europe are included. The relative wage level is defined as the ratio of the average monthly wage for each country and sector relative to the corresponding average monthly wage rate in Germany. The FDI/GDP ratio signifies the openness of the country in CE for foreign investors and its ability to attract FDI. Labour-productivity differences across countries should explain positively the comparative advantage of a single export sector. In Chapter 9, Borbély assumes that an increase in labour productivity will negatively influence the relative export share because productivity rises if wages have been increased. This has not always been the case; labour productivity could also increase if the return of capital investment in the

Table 10.3 Estimation of outsourcing volume with FDI share of GDP in NMS – dependent variable: outsourcing volume (specification 1)

Specification 1	Non standardized coefficient		Co-linearity statistic	
	Coefficient B	Standard error	Tolerance	VIF
(Constant)	−0.094	0.432		
FDI / GDP	0.088**	0.016	0.428	2.336
Production structure	−0.005	0.008	0.803	4.245
Payroll share in production costs	0.105**	0.015	0.236	4.245
Relative labour productivity (CE / GER)	−0.018**	0.003	0.784	1.275
Trend	−0.035	0.032	0.512	1.951
R&D spending	1.117	0.895	0.986	1.014
labour productivity (manufacturing = 100 %)	0.000	0.001	0.527	1.897

Notes (specification 1):   observation number = 900; dependent variable, outsourcing volume; ** significant at 1% level; *significant at 5% level; F-test: F value = 27.639 **; coefficient of determination $R^2 = 0.199$; VIF = Variance Inflation Factor.
Sources: Comext foreign trade statistics; WIIW Industrial Database 6/2004, own calculations according to data files comprising Germany, Czech Republic, Slovak Republic, Poland, Hungary and Slovenia.

past is reflected in a rise of output amount per man hour. Increases in the pay roll may follow later if workers with special skills are scarcely available in the local labour market. Borbély assumes a negative relationship between unit labour costs and RCA and found no significant impact if labour productivity is included. Therefore, unit labour costs do not additionally explain relative export shares, if sectoral labour productivity is included in the regression.

Exercising normal distribution test of residuals (Jarque–Bera test) we get the result that both classical assumptions have to be rejected: ($JB = 500.4 > \chi^2_2(0.95) = 5.99$). Testing the homogeneity of the variance of residuals (the Wald test) leads to the rejection of this assumption too:

$$W = 900 \cdot 0.081 = 72.9 : \chi^2_9\text{-distributed with 9 degrees of freedom.}$$

$$W = 72.9 > \chi^2_9(0.95) = 16.92.$$

Having rejected a normal distribution of residuals and homogeneity of their variance, one has to take care in interpreting the coefficients of the regression.

Table 10.4 Estimation of outsourcing volume with FDI share of GDP in NMS – dependent variable: outsourcing volume (specification 2)

Specification 2	Non standardized coefficient		Co-linearity statistic	
	Coefficient	Standard error	Tolerance	VIF
(Constant)	0.452	0.156		
FDI / GDP	0.074**	0.011	0.833	1.201
Payroll share on production costs	0.105**	0.008	0.874	1.144
Unit labour costs (Manufacturing = 100)	−0.096	0.0625	0.233	4.285
Relative labour costs share (CE/GER)	−0.013*	0.005	0.799	1.252
Trend	−0.021	0.037	0.604	1.655
R&D-spending	0.033	0.0305	0.994	1.006

Notes (specification 2): observation number = 900; dependent variable, outsourcing volume;
** significant at 1% level; * significant at 5% level; F test: F value = 63.630**; coefficient of determination: $R^2 = 0.176$.
Sources: Comext foreign trade statistics, WIIW Industrial Database 6/2004, own calculation according to data files comprising Germany, Czech Republic, Slovak Republic, Poland, Hungary and Slovenia.

The FDI/GDP share explains the significantly positive outsourcing volume, and this is confirmed by the results of Borbély (2005b, p. 14) showing that FDI has a boosting effect on relative export shares in the AC.

For German manufacturing industries lower monthly wages in Central Europe are all important in making location decisions, especially if the percentage of labour costs of total production costs are high (instrument variable: payroll share).

To check the robustness of the regression equation we replace the FDI/GDP share with country dummy variables. Only the dummy variable for the Slovak Republic is significantly negatively correlated with the outsourcing volume across sectors and five countries.

Exercising the test of normal distribution of residuals (Jarque–Bera test) and the test of homogeneity of the variance of residuals (the Wald test) one must state that both classical assumptions have to be rejected:

$$W = 111.6 > \chi^2_{11}(0.975) = 21.92$$
$$JB = 379.94 > \chi^2_2(0.95) = 5.99$$

The coefficient of the variable 'relative labour cost share' is −0.024 and weakly significant ($\alpha = 5\%$). Checking the robustness of the coefficient

Table 10.5 Estimation of outsourcing volume with country-specific dummy variables – dependent variable: outsourcing volume (specification 3)

Specification 3	Non standardized coefficient		Co-linearity statistic	
	B	Standard error	Tolerance	VIF
(Constant)	−0.562	0.404		
Payroll share on Production costs	0.102**	0.011	0.402	2.488
Labour costs share (CEE/GER)	−0.024*	0.012	0.141	7.095
R&D-Spending	0.569	0.896	0.967	1.034
Czech Republic	0.125	0.120	0.594	1.684
Hungary	0.061	0.128	0.564	1.775
Slovakia	−0.805**	0.135	0.511	1.956
Slovenia	−1.467**	0.260	0.137	7.301
Labour productivity CEE (Manufacturing = 100)	0.00003	0.001	0.585	1.708

Notes (specification 3): observation number = 900; dependent variable, outsourcing volume; ** significant at 1% level; * significant on 5% level; F test; F value = 29.906 **; coefficient of determination: $R^2 = 0.212$.
Sources: Comext foreign trade statistics, WIIW Industrial Database 6/2004, own calculation according to data files comprising Germany, Czech Republic, Slovak Republic, Poland, Hungary and Slovenia.

became insignificant if we included country dummies in the regression instead of a linear trend variable (Table 10.5).

We have assumed that the relative labour productivity should decrease if the increased sectoral labour productivity in Germany is compared against the assumed stable values in CEEC. Then we would expect, theoretically, that the imports of particular labour-intensive intermediate goods (outsourcing volume) should increase, because rising labour productivity could be signified by relatively high labour costs. In contrast with the results of Borbély (Chapter 9) we do not find a significant impact of the relative wage level on German imports from CE in both specifications. The share of monthly wages in CE relative to German wages cannot significantly explain the movement of imports from CE destined for a special output sector in German manufacturing.

To sum up the second part of the empirical analysis, exports of labour-intensive industries were boosted by FDI inflow and the quality of export products – measured by unit values – is only relevant for human-capital-intensively producing industries. For the case of Germany we do not confirm the result of the dynamic panel estimation in Borbély that wage level differences have a significant impact on German outsourcing volume from

CE; instead of the wage level the sectoral labour productivity differences significantly explain the outsourcing volume.

10.4 Conclusions

Besides the details the following main conclusions can be drawn:

- The comparative advantages of the EU15 in human-capital-intensive goods and high-tech-intensive goods (science-based industries) are still positive but eroding.
- The comparative advantages of Central Europe in labour-intensive goods continue to be positive. But we also have to take into consideration that sharp competition between acceding and cohesion countries is accompanied by increasing import pressures from low and middle technology-intensive and almost labour-intensively-manufactured mass production from Far East countries like China.
- Hungary is in comparison to Poland the more competitive country because it has the more diversified export structure and faces competition from Spain and Ireland in some higher quality goods (human-capital-intensive goods). Poland and the Czech Republic have a quite similar export specialization pattern and compete with Portugal and Greece in the lower and middle-quality segment. Calculating RCA values for foreign trade with the EU15 we see similar high values in resources (coal and ore production) and labour-intensive production (mainly manufacturing of furniture and wood as well as production of transport equipment).
- The amount of relative export shares are boosted by foreign direct investment. FDI helps to improve labour productivity in Central Europe (see the relatively more diversified export structure in Hungary), and the export growth potential also comprises more technology-intensive products because intra-firm trade will strongly increase if multinational firms outsource the production of relatively more human-capital-intensive intermediate goods to plants in Central Europe.
- For the competitiveness of European industries the capability of firms to innovate their products very quickly is essential to secure relative export shares in contestable markets. Therefore the economic policy of governments has to focus on creating investment-friendly environments for firms. It has to support training of the labour force to obtain better employment opportunities in European industries that are producing increasingly intensively in human capital terms.

Appendix

Table 10.A1   Comparative advantages and disadvantages of Hungary in foreign trade with the EU15

Description of classification	1995	1999	2003
Positive RCA values in foreign trade with EU15 in 2003			
Manufacture of tobacco products	−0.46	−3.70	3.96
Manufacture of coke, refined petroleum products	1.15	1.02	1.63
Manufacture of radio, television	−0.18	0.27	0.90
Manufacture of other transport equipment	−2.16	−1.03	0.59
Manufacture of office machinery and computers	−0.70	0.54	0.57
Manufacture of wood and of products of wood	1.21	0.88	0.51
Manufacture of wearing apparel, dressing and dyeing of fur	1.20	1.01	0.49
Manufacture of food products and beverages	1.09	1.15	0.47
Manufacture of furniture	0.15	0.06	0.41
Manufacture of electrical machinery and apparatus n.e.c.	0.32	0.34	0.35
Manufacture of machinery and equipment n.e.c.	0.14	0.36	0.10
Tanning and dressing of leather, manufacture of luggage	0.17	0.04	0.04
Manufacture of motor vehicles, trailers and semi-trailers	−0.46	0.22	0.03
Negative RCA values in foreign trade with EU15 in 2003			
Mining of metal ores	−3.70	−1.24	−4.61
Extraction of crude petroleum and natural gas	1.96	−1.32	−3.94
Mining of coal and lignite	−3.18	−1.12	−2.34
Other mining and quarrying	−0.55	−1.06	−1.48
Manufacture of pulp, paper and paper products	−2.00	−1.09	−1.04
Publishing, printing and reproduction of recorded media	−0.84	−1.09	−0.86
Manufacture of chemicals and chemical products	−0.40	−0.65	−0.63
Manufacture of other non-metallic mineral products	−0.31	−0.52	−0.53
Manufacture of textiles	−0.82	−0.86	−0.49
Manufacture of rubber and plastic products	−0.41	−0.55	−0.43
Manufacture of fabricated metal products, except machinery	−0.24	−0.53	−0.39
Manufacture of basic metals	0.77	−0.03	0.30

Source: Eurostat Luxemburg, own calculations.

Table 10.A2   Comparative advantages of Poland in foreign trade with the EU15

NACE Rev.1	Description of classification	1995	1999	2003
	Positive RCA value in foreign trade with EU15 in 2003			
CA 10	Mining of coal and lignite; extraction of peat	8.25	6.48	5.01
DN36	Manufacture of furniture	1.46	1.81	1.73
DD20	Manufacture of wood and of products of wood	2.38	2.04	1.55
DB18	Manufacture of wearing apparel, dressing and dyeing of fur	2.19	1.73	1.46

(*Continued*)

Table 10.A2   (Continued)

NACE Rev.1	Description of classification	1995	1999	2003
DF23	Manufacture of coke, refined petroleum products	0.73	2.23	0.79
CB13	Mining of metal ores	−0.10	1.99	0.64
DL31	Manufacture of electrical machinery and apparatus n.e.c.	0.07	0.31	0.44
DM34	Manufacture of motor vehicles, trailers and semi-trailers	−0.27	0.10	0.40
DA 15	Manufacture of food products and beverages	0.07	0.24	0.36
DJ27	Manufacture of basic metals	1.39	0.66	0.30
DM35	Manufacture of other transport equipment	1.08	1.54	0.23
DJ28	Manufacture of fabricated metal products, except machinery	0.28	0.44	0.15
DE22	Publishing, printing and reproduction of recorded media	1.87	−0.25	0.11
DI26	Manufacture of other non-metallic mineral products	0.35	0.04	0.08
DL32	Manufacture of radio, television	−0.51	0.85	0.01
Negative RCA values in foreign trade with EU15 in 2003				
DA 16	Manufacture of tobacco products	−2.94	−1.00	−4.38
DL30	Manufacture of office machinery and computers	−2.93	−2.73	−2.79
CA 11	Extraction of crude petroleum and natural gas	−6.27	−5.47	−1.41
DG24	Manufacture of chemicals and chemical products	−0.67	−1.05	−1.20
DL33	Manufacture of medical, precision and optical instruments	−1.81	−1.33	−0.89
DK29	Manufacture of machinery and equipment n.e.c.	−1.35	−1.07	−0.81
DB17	Manufacture of textiles	−1.31	−0.69	−0.74
DC19	Tanning and dressing of leather, manufacture of luggage	0.36	0.52	−0.58
DE21	Manufacture of pulp, paper and paper products	−0.80	−0.57	−0.39
CB14	Other mining and quarrying	1.16	0.00	−0.32
DH25	Manufacture of rubber and plastic products	−1.00	−0.45	−0.31

Source: Eurostat Luxemburg, own calculations.

Table 10.A3   Comparative advantages and disadvantages of the Czech Republic in foreign trade with the EU15

NACE Rev.1	Description of classification	1995	1999	2003
Positive RCA values in foreign trade with EU15 in 2003				
CA 10	Mining of coal and lignite; extraction of peat	8.48	6.67	5.99
CB13	Mining of metal ores	−1.29	−4.51	1.57
DD20	Manufacture of wood and of products of wood	2.05	1.41	1.17
DN36	Manufacture of furniture	0.60	0.77	0.92
DL30	Manufacture of office machinery and computers	−1.00	−1.02	0.50

(Continued)

Table 10.A3   (Continued)

DM35	Manufacture of other transport equipment	0.41	0.35	0.44
CA11	Extraction of crude petroleum and natural gas	1.18	−0.06	0.40
DM34	Manufacture of motor vehicles, trailers and semi-trailers	−0.15	0.59	0.30
DI26	Manufacture of other non-metallic mineral products	0.86	0.64	0.30
JDJ28	Manufacture of fabricated metal products, except machinery	0.34	0.39	0.28
DJB18	Manufacture of wearing apparel, dressing and dyeing of fur	0.86	0.77	0.27
DL31	Manufacture of electrical machinery and apparatus n.e.c.	−0.09	0.17	0.22
DE22	Publishing, printing and reproduction of recorded media	−0.39	−0.15	0.14
DL32	Manufacture of radio, television	−0.74	−0.64	0.03
DJ27	Manufacture of basie metals	0.66	0.18	0.00
Negative RCA values in foreign trade with EU15 in 2003				
DA 16	Manufacture of tobacco products	−4.80	−5.46	−9.90
DG24	Manufacture of chemicals and chemical products	−0.32	−0.82	−1.01
DA15	Manufacture of food products and beverages	−0.74	−0.62	−0.73
DL33	Manufacture of medical, precision and optical instruments	−0.96	−0.73	−0.72
DE21	Manufacture of pulp, paper and paper products	−0.05	−0.53	−0.50
DC19	Tanning and dressing of leather, manufacture of luggage	0.46	0.06	−0.44
DF23	Manufacture of coke, refined petroleum products	0.42	−0.52	−0.32
DH25	Manufacture of rubber and plastic products	−0.29	−0.19	−0.21
CB14_	Other mining and quarrying	0.98	0.10	−0.19
DK29	Manufacture of machinery and equipment n.e.c.	−0.58	−0.21	−0.07
DB17	Manufacture of textiles	0.12	−0.11	−0.03

Source: Eurostat Luxemburg, own calculations.

Table 10.A4   Comparative advantages and disadvantages of Slovakia in foreign trade with the EU15

NACE Rev.l	Description of classification	1995	1999	2003
Positive RCA values in foreign trade with EU15 in 2003				
CA 11	Extraction of crude petroleum and natural gas	−0.65	−2.85	1.81
DB18	Manufacture of wearing apparel, dressing and dyeing of fur	1.68	1.52	1.25
DD20	Manufacture of wood and wood products	1.57	1.51	0.89
DE22	Publishing, printing and reproduction of recorded media	0.13	0.44	0.88
DF23	Manufacture of coke, refined petroleum products	0.92	0.22	0.71

(*Continued*)

Table 10.A4 (Continued)

NACE Rev.1	Description of classification	1995	1999	2003
DC19	Tanning and dressing of leather, manufacture of luggage	0.54	0.66	0.68
DN36	Manufacture of furniture	0.64	0.40	0.62
DM34	Manufacture of motor vehicles, trailers and semi-trailers	−0.26	0.50	0.59
DM35	Manufacture of other transport equipment	1.25	0.53	0.23
DJ27	Manufacture of basic metals	0.71	0.77	0.06
Negative RCA values in foreign trade with EU15 in 2003				
CA 10	Mining of coal and lignite; extraction of peat	2.68	−2.46	−3.65
DL33	Manufacture of medical, precision and optical Instruments	−2.18	−1.97	−1.61
DA 15	Manufacture of food products and beverages	−1.42	−1.11	−1.14
DB17	Manufacture of textiles	−1.07	−1.02	−1.02
DG24	Manufacture of Chemicals and chemical products	−0.01	−0.67	−0.86
DL30	Manufacture of office machinery and computers	−3.23	−0.29	−0.84
DK29	Manufacture of machinery and equipment n.e.c.	−1.00	−0.6	−0.56
DL32	Manufacture of radio, television	−1.33	−0.98	−0.52
DJ28	Manufacture of fabricated metal products, except machinery	0.34	−0.22	−0.5
CB13	Mining of metal ores	2.80	−2.01	−0.35
DH25	Manufacture of rubber and plastic products	−0.11	−0.54	−0.33
DE21	Manufacture of pulp, paper and paper products	0.70	−0.23	−0.24
CB14	Other mining and quarrying	0.74	0.18	−0.19
DI26	Manufacture of other non-metallic mineral products	1.25	0.48	−0.14
DL31	Manufacture of electrical machinery and apparaturs n.e.c.	−0.37	0.33	−0.07

Source: Eurostat Luxembourg, own calculations.

Notes

1 The 18 OECD countries consist of 12 EU members, the USA, Canada, Japan, Hungary, Poland and the Czech Republic.
2 Manufactured goods are classified according to the Classification of Economic Activities in the European Community (NACE Rev. 1.1 classification) and encompass manufacture from food products and beverages (code 15) until recycling (code 36).
3 Imports of Central Europe are defined as the sum of German imports from the Czech Republic, Hungary, Poland, Slovakia and Slovenia.
4 We use the input–output tables of the German Federal Statistical Office to calculate the share of imported intermediate goods needed for the production process in each German manufacturing output sector.

References

Aiginger, K. (1997) 'The Use of Unit Values to Discriminate between Price and Quality Competition', *Cambridge Journal of Economics*, 21: 571–92.

Borbély, D. (2005a) 'Foreign Trade Specialization on the EU Market: Dynamics, Determinants and Competitiveness', European Institute for International Economic Relations at the University of Wuppertal, November, mimeo.

Borbély, D. (2005b) 'Determinants of Foreign Trade Specialization Patterns and Policy Conclusions', deliverable 5.6, European Institute for International Economic Relations at the University of Wuppertal, August, mimeo.

Borbély, D. (2004a) 'Comparative Analysis of 3 Accession Countries on Potential and Direction of Future Structural Adjustment after Integration with the EU and Factors Determining Those Adjustments', Deliverable no. 5.4 prepared for the project on 'Changes in Industrial Competitiveness as a Factor of Integration: Identifying Challenges of the Enlarged Single European Market', European Institute for International Economic Relations at the University of Wuppertal, October, mimeo.

Borbély, D. (2004b) 'EU15 Export Specialization Patterns of Selected Accession and Cohesion Countries', Discussion Paper, European Institute for International Economic Relations at the University of Wuppertal, October.

Borbély, D. (2004c) 'Comparative analysis of Changes in Specialization within the EU Market and Conclusions', Deliverable no. 5.3 prepared for the project on 'Changes in Industrial Competitiveness as a Factor of Integration: Identifying Challenges of the Enlarged Single European Market', European Institute for International Economic Relations at the University of Wuppertal, June, mimeo.

Borbély, D. (2004d) 'Draft Reports on Evolution of Specialization Patterns in Exports of the 3 Accession Countries to the EU', Deliverable no. 5.2 prepared for the project on 'Changes in Industrial Competitiveness as a Factor of Integration: Identifying Challenges of the Enlarged Single European Market', European Institute for International Economic Relations at the University of Wuppertal, March, mimeo.

Brandmeier, M. (2005) 'Die ökonomische Integration der mittelosteuropäischen Länder – Außenhandel, Outsourcing, Direktinvestitionen und Unternehmenskooperationen' (Economic Integration of the Central and Eastern European Countries Foreign Trade, Outsourcing, Foreign Direct Investments, and Enterprise). Köln: Cooperations Lohmar.

German Federal Statistical Office (2004), time series service, no. 18, vol. 2.

Krugman, P. and A.J. Venables (1996) 'Integration, Specialization and Adjustment', *European Economic Review*, 40: 959–67.

Krugman, P. and A.J. Venables (1995) 'Globalization and the Inequality of Nations', *Quarterly Journal of Economics*, cx (4): 857–80.

Markusen, J.R. and A.J. Venables (1998) 'Multinational Firms and the New Trade Theory', *Journal of International Economics*, 46: 183–203.

Neven, D. (1995) 'Trade Liberalization with Eastern Nations: How sensitive?' in R. Fini and R. Portes (eds), *European Union Trade with Eastern Europe: Adjustment and Opportunities*. London: CEPR, pp. 19–60.

WIIW (The Vienna Institute for International Economic Studies) (2000) *WIIW Research Report*, no. 266, Vienna, June.

WIIW Industrial Database (2004) no. 6.

11
Policy Implications for New and Old Member States of the EU

Jorge Núñez Ferrer and David Kernohan

11.1 Introduction

The issue of competitiveness of the new member states (NMS) and the implications of enlargement for the European Union (EU) as a whole and individual member states is very complex. This chapter starts with a definition of competitiveness and then discusses the factors influencing competitiveness in the Central and East European Countries (CEECs) and particularly in the three NMS of the Czech Republic, Hungary and Poland (referred to in this chapter as NMS3 for three new members). It further summarizes the results of studies on the impact of government policies on the competitiveness of these countries during the years of transition and accession up to 2003. After the results of the studies on these countries have been presented, the chapter discusses the implications for the EU15, in particular the impact on their industrial competitiveness in terms of benefits and challenges.

After presenting the results of the changes in competitiveness in Europe and their implications, we draw policy conclusions. Policy actions on industrial competitiveness may be taken at national or EU level; understanding the positive and negative implications of specific policy interventions is very important, as the national or sectoral interests can clash severely with an optimum EU policy. Policy coordination between the EU and the member states as well as amongst the latter is very important to avoid the parallel existence of incompatible policies.

11.2 Defining competitiveness and its alternative dimension for the new member states

What about 'Competitiveness and some of its effects in an enlarged Europe'? The term competitiveness does not have a universally accepted definition.

For a firm, it is often defined as its ability to stay in the market at competitive prices. At national level, competitiveness is considered 'the ability of a nation's economy to make rapid and sustained gains in living standards (*Global Competitiveness Report*, 1996) or 'the ability of an economy to provide its population with high rising standards of living and high rates of employment on a sustainable basis' (European Commission, 2001). Competitiveness is also defined in terms of foreign trade performance, deeply intertwined with the theories of comparative advantage.

Since this chapter concentrates on policy implications for the EU, the European Commission's definition of competitiveness will be used. The term 'economy' rather than nation is useful, as the competitiveness of the EU is the outcome of the economic activity of the member states combined. The use of the terms 'employment' and 'sustainable' in the definition has important policy implications, as it indicates a strategic path influencing the selection of objectives at EU level. Competitiveness policies should not only aim at GDP growth, but should pay attention to employment effects and the long-term sustainability of the policies. The EU should thus include wider welfare considerations.

Competitiveness in the European Union is a particularly complex and controversial matter, especially with the recent enlargement process. The NMS bring with their accession a large increase in the labour force but also a lower reservation wage and a lower capital endowment (per capita) compared to the (old) EU15. The labour force of the NMS is also generally well-educated. In terms of EU competitiveness, this is good news. EU industries can take advantage of the lower wage costs and increase their competitiveness in world markets. However, in the older member states, an improvement in the overall competitiveness of the EU is not universally welcomed. While all member states potentially benefit from an enlarged market, in the shorter run the NMS can become strong competitors in particular sectors or geographical areas. The increased competitiveness of the EU as a whole may be accompanied by decreased 'competitiveness' and the decline of some industries in certain regions within the EU.

Industrial location is likely to change as a result of the changes in the member states' comparative advantage. The increased labour mobility between the old and the new member states also generally reduces the reservation wages in all member states. While it increases the competitiveness of the EU economy, it may cause the living standards of some groups of workers in the old member states to decline. In any case, the process induces change, which requires all members of the EU to adapt. While hardly any economist would doubt that the overall impact on the EU is positive, some might show concern over the impacts in individual member states, especially those showing structural rigidities (see Davis and Weinstein, 2002 and Weinstein, 2002, for possible negative impacts of labour migration). As the reactions to the proposed EU directive on the liberalization of services has shown, there is sometimes strong political resistance for these same reasons.

The overall welfare of the EU can be expected to increase if the NMS allow EU companies to open new operations or relocate all or part of their operations to the NMS, especially when one uses the diminishing marginal returns to consumption concept, which states that an additional € of income has a higher value for lower income groups. In this case, an increase in the income of workers in the NMS will result in higher consumption which exceeds the loss in the consumption caused by the same fall in income in the higher income countries.

11.3 Importance of the industrial sector in CEECs

The future of the industrial sector in the NMS is particularly important for these countries. During the communist period of central planning, the industrial sector (and particularly heavy industry) was a central pillar of the economy. The production of this heavy industry was, however, inefficient and out of line with needs and demand. The end of central planning brought the collapse of large sections of industry and an important restructuring process. Despite the changes, however, the industrial sector has remained both an important contributor to employment and an important sector of the economy. In both areas, the values are in most cases higher than in the EU15. The average gross value added (GVA) of the industrial sector in the eight new members from Central and Eastern Europe was 26.3 per cent and share of employment 24.01 per cent compared with 18.3 per cent and 21.2 per cent EU-14,[1] which was respectively (Table 11.1 lists the results).

It is rare for an old EU15 country to exceed a 20 per cent share of employment, while for the NMS it is rare if they do not. In GVA terms, the difference is not so marked, even if for the EU15 the share is slightly lower. Considering the smaller size of the economies of the NMS and their larger share in employment, there is a clear indication that productivity in the industrial sectors is still low compared to the EU15.

This analysis also indicates that if there were to be a convergence in productivity, the industrial sector, even if it developed still further, will most likely show no increase in employment; indeed, reductions are more likely. Given the large manpower involved in structural improvements in a country, there is a risk that when the construction boom starts to recede, there could also be a reduction in employment. Furthermore, in most countries a further move of labour out of the agricultural sector is expected. Consequently, the future unemployment situation in these countries will depend on the services sector. The prosperity of this sector will in turn depend on the economic growth of the country, which in the industrial sector can only be fostered through high technology and capital-intensive industries. The

Table 11.1 Share of employment and GVA of the industrial sector (excluding building and construction), 2003

Countries	Share of GVA	Share of employment	Countries	Share of GVA	Share of employment
Belgium	19.87%	15.23%	Malta	22.17%	n/a
Czech Rep	31.58%	30.72%	NL	18.85%	12.94%
Denmark	20.11%	16.07%	Austria	22.82%	16.50%
Germany	24.39%	21.24%	Poland	24.49%	21.15%
Estonia	21.51%	25.07%	Portugal	19.25%	n/a
Greece	13.88%	15.92%	Slovenia	30.15%	29.48%
Spain	18.65%	17.84%	Slovakia	26.47%	26.16%
France	18.75%	15.62%	Finland	25.10%	19.71%
Ireland	31.83%	16.72%	Sweden	22.94%	17.28%
Italy	21.58%	22.76%	UK	19.50%	13.89%
Cyprus	12.21%	11.07%	Bulgaria	25.52%	n/a
Latvia	17.20%	18.85%	Romania	31.42%	25.48%
Lithuania	24.82%	20.69%	EU15	21.20%	18.40%
Lux	10.63%	17.72%	CEEC 8	26.30%	24.01%
Hungary	25.42%	25.66%			

Source: AMECO database.

policy implications here are fairly clear, and are in line with the need to develop higher value-added industrial output, while facilitating the development of the service sector, even without the boost from the EU's Services Directive.

11.4 Factors affecting industrial competitiveness in the new member states

The competitiveness performance of the NMS during the accession process indicates several important trends. First, the countries have undergone a restructuring process whereby old inefficient industries have either been closed or modernized. A first wave of foreign direct investment (FDI) has concentrated on taking over the domestic market which the old industries covered. New, more export-oriented industries developed later, often in direct competition with established industries in the EU.

Borbély (2005) describes how the accession economies were characterized at the beginning of the transition to a market economy by a low share of technologically advanced industries in production and exports compared to the EU. The transformation of the economy has caused large adjustments in the structure of the industrial sectors, shifting the trade pattern of the NMS3 towards the EU. The share of exports of the middle to high technology sectors increased over time (from 1993 to 2001). While Poland and the Czech

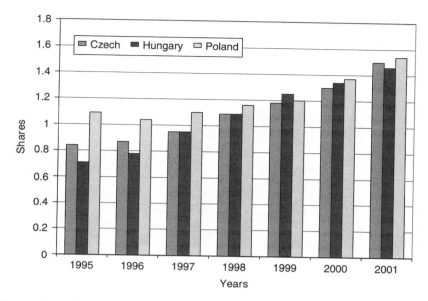

Figure 11.1 Share of NMS3 in the EU25 internal exports
Source: Wziątek-Kubiak and Magda (2005).

Republic still compete in lower- to middle-quality products with Greece and Portugal, Hungary has started competing with middle- to high-quality and technology products of Ireland and Spain.

Wziątek-Kubiak and Magda (2005) show that the share of EU25 internal exports for the NMS3 has increased steadily in the last few years (Figure 11.1), and, furthermore, the three countries account for most of the exports (Figure 11.2). Between 1996–2001 the Czech Republic, Hungary and Poland captured an increasing part of the increment of the EU-intra export of the 10 NMS. In 2001 their share in the total NMS export to EU15 amounted to 77.3 per cent. Their export to the EU15 in the EU25-intra export increased from 2.7 per cent to 4.7 per cent, that is by as much as 67 per cent. This increase was at the costs of other NMS, as well as some EU producers.

It is interesting to note that the Czech and Hungarian export markets are developing faster than Poland's. In fact, Poland is slower in adapting to higher-value products. According to Wziątek-Kubiak and Magda, this lag can be attributed to Poland's higher unit labour cost compared with the other two countries.

Despite the increased competition, the analysis of Wziątek-Kubiak and Magda (2005) concludes that the sectors in which the NMS3 have been competing with the EU15 were already under restructuring. The enlargement accelerated the restructuring but did not provoke the restructuring of EU

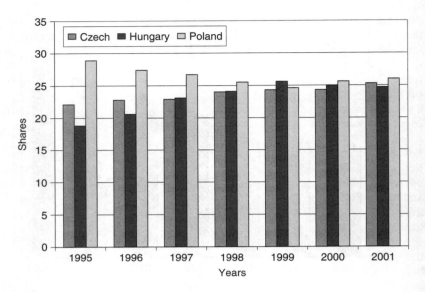

Figure 11.2   Share of NMS3 in exports of AC10 to EU15
Source: Wziątek-Kubiak and Magda (2005).

industries. Strong EU industries have taken over the markets of the weak
NMS3 industries, accelerating their restructuring in turn. Overall the enlargement has been speeding up improvements in efficiency on both sides.

Foreign direct investment

There are strong links between trade, FDI, innovation and competitiveness,
which are of great relevance to the region. FDI in Central and Eastern Europe
has been strong and increasing, despite a general worldwide decline during
2001 and 2002. These countries managed an increase of 15 per cent during
the same period, as the region provided a stable investment area.

The first stage of the transition to a market economy was characterized
by market-seeking FDI, used to buy underdeveloped non-tradable sectors,
such as utilities, transport, communications, trade, financial intermediation
and other services. The main motive was to exploit the first-mover advantage to supply the domestic market. This contributed in the first instance to
an increase in tariff barriers, as large companies negotiated higher domestic protection for the sector they were investing it. Thus the most advanced
accession countries, like the NMS3, negatively affected the trade balance in
the first decade of transformation, rather than improving it (Barry, 2002).

The situation has been gradually changing as FDI has shifted to develop
export-oriented industries in these countries. However, the process is still in

development. Several studies have shown that an important share of trade flows was caused by intra-industry trade of the investors, with roughly the same export to import ratio. Market-seeking investors, however, import more than they export, thus having a negative impact on the current account. The results of this project agree with the accumulating evidence that 'related-party trade' (or foreign-affiliate trade) of MNCs (multinational companies) is a very important component of trade and dominates trade between OECD countries (Hamilton and Quinlan, 2004).

A growing FDI sector in the most advanced acceding countries (Czech Republic, Hungary, Poland, Slovakia and Slovenia) increasingly targets logistical centres and R&D. Paradoxically, however, this FDI is small in volume, because most of these investments are directed to call centres, headquarters and back offices, which need little investment. Nevertheless, new greenfield investment is important to compensate for the reduction in FDI inflows due to the initial privatization process.

A result to be noted is that, despite the predictions of traditional trade theories that the NMS would concentrate on labour and resource intensive branches of industry, there is a shift towards higher technology and capital-intensive sectors. In fact, one of the key factors for NMS' growth now and in the future is their ability to compete in the higher value-added segment of the market.

FDI is an essential input to improving productivity growth across sectors, but the composition of FDI is also very important, because it influences the relative prices of tradables. Whether FDI flows are directed to the tradable or the non-tradable sectors is a macroeconomic policy issue, as it affects balanced growth and employment. In fact, evidence shows that the success of a country in promoting growth through FDI flows depends on the type of FDI that is attracted.

Labour and labour productivity

The ability of the labour market to adapt to the changes in the economy is also a crucial factor in the development of a country's competitiveness. A key to a successful transformation of the economy in the post-socialist countries has been labour mobility and transferable skills, to allow the restructuring of the economy away from the predominance of heavy industry and the primary sectors.

There have been important shifts in employment and the value-added structures of the economic sectors in the new NMS3, but the developments have not always been comparable. Hungary and the Czech Republic have managed a better transformation of the economy than Poland. The restructuring of the labour market has been weaker in Poland, with a large share of the workforce still in the primary sector and a large pool of unemployed unskilled workers. This is likely to remain the single most important barrier in Poland's growth path. Lagging behind also are countries such as Lithuania and especially the most recent members Bulgaria and Romania.

Productivity studies clearly indicate that labour productivity in the Czech and Hungarian cases is higher: even if Poland's labour productivity has risen more proportionally, the start is on a lower base. In fact, even in industry, the decline in the 1990s has halted and in Hungary it has even started to rise, indicating that CEECs such as Hungary are attractive locations for the industrial sector. In the Czech Republic, productivity in industry increased between 1997 and 2003 by 86 per cent, while employment in the sector fell by 9.6 per cent. The most dramatic changes have been seen in the automotive sector with productivity rising by 149 per cent and the competitiveness of the sector in the EU25 has increased by 232 per cent over the same period (Filipova *et al.*, 2005).

The countries where labour restructuring has been slowest also show the lowest productivity growth. According to Stephan (2000), as long as their employment structures do not align with the structure in the EU, their labour productivity will not rise above 50 per cent of the EU average.

Studies by Furmańska-Maruszak (2005) indicate that unit labour costs are one of the single most important variables in determining the competitiveness of products from the NMS3 in the EU15. Results indicate that the most successful combination is high-value production with low unit labour costs, which is not surprising since external competition is strong in the lower value-added production across sectors. The NMS also suffer from the competitive pressures of the emerging large Asian developing economies. This international competition reduces the ability of the NMS to compete in the EU in the lower value-added labour-intensive sectors. While proximity has a value, the margin is limited due to advances in transport and telecommunications.

Structural determinants for growth and competitiveness

According to Gros and Suhrcke (2000), the speed of development of a functioning market economy with growth potential depends also on the physical infrastructure available. Business development is hampered by infrastructure bottlenecks and thus higher transaction costs. As the ability to absorb advanced technology is also considered an important factor for the development of an economy, advanced infrastructures are needed to operate more effectively.

Countries in Central and Eastern Europe benefited from the fact that central planning had developed infrastructure more than the wealth of these countries would warrant, compared to other countries of similar economic size. This has certainly assisted FDI flows and growth. In terms of infrastructure in relation to income, the NMS are already in a good position. One way to estimate the adequacy of the infrastructure in the new member countries relative to their income is to run the following cross-section regression using data from around 120 countries:[2]

$$Indicator_i = \alpha + \beta GNPpc_i + \phi CEE8 + \gamma SEE + \eta CIS + \varphi ASEAN + \varepsilon_i, \quad (11.1)$$

with i as the country-subscript and '*Indicator*' as one of the infrastructure density indicators used here. The explanatory variables are, first, per capita income measured at PPP (*GNPpc*) plus a series of dummy variables; CEE8 stands for the new Central and East European member countries, SEE for South-Eastern Europe, that is the Balkans, CIS for the countries of the former Soviet Union (except the Baltic states) and ASEAN for members of the Association of South-East Asian Nations. The inclusion of the latter is a useful check on whether this group of high-growth countries stands out in terms of infrastructure. 'ε' is an error-term. All variables – except the dummy variables – are in natural logarithms so that the coefficients can be interpreted as elasticities.

The two indicators used here (the only ones available for a large number of countries) are:

- the quality of the road network (proxied by the length of all paved roads as a share in surface area[3]); and
- the density of the rail network (in km per surface area).

The results are clear-cut: Table 11.2 shows that both indicators are closely related to income per capita, as one would expect. The key result for the present context is, however, that the dummy variable for the new member countries is in both cases positive, large and highly significant. Hence one can decisively reject the hypothesis that the new member countries do not have adequate infrastructure for their level of income. This does not indicate that the level is excessive or adequate in itself, but it is higher than in countries with a similar economic size.

Table 11.2   Regression results – infrastructure link to GNP

	GNP per capita PPP	CEE8	SEE	CIS	ASEAN	R2
Paved road network (% of all roads)[a]	1.20**** (12.9)	1.50*** (2.8)	1.21**** (9.5)	1.57**** (8.5)	0.44 (0.9)	0.80
Rail network (km per surface area)[a]	0.71**** (11.3)	1.42**** (11.4)	1.34**** (11.4)	1.08**** (4.8)	−0.97**** (−2.8)	0.73

Notes: [a]Additional explanatory variable: population density, 118 observations (1999 data). Estimation results are heteroskedasticity-consistent. The symbols: *** and **** indicate coefficients that are significant at the 1 per cent and 0.1 per cent levels, respectively. All variables are in logarithms. All standard errors are corrected.
Source: Gros and Suhrcke (2000).

It is interesting that the dummy variables for all transition countries are positive. The heavy investment in physical infrastructure under the central planning system has apparently left a legacy in terms of the part of infrastructure that depreciates very slowly, like roads and rail networks. Finally, the dummy variable for the ASEAN group of countries is not significantly different from zero. High growth does not seem to be closely associated with a high density of infrastructure. The point estimates for the dummy variables suggest that the new member countries have a rail network that is approximately twice as extensive as one would expect.

Against this point of view one might argue that the proper measure of the need for more infrastructure is the degree to which the current stock of public capital constitutes a brake on growth (as opposed to being adequate for the current level of income). One way to check whether this is the case is to look at the intensity of the use of the currently available road and rail infrastructure in the NMS. As there is no absolute standard or capacity limit in this area, all one can do is to compare infrastructure use in the old and the new member countries from Central and Eastern Europe. The available data are quite limited, but three indicators are available for the two main modes of transport (railways and roads).

The two indicators presented in Table 11.3 (with data for the year 2000) show a mixed picture. The number of persons carried by railways could double in some of the NMS before the existing network would approach the degree of capacity utilisation of the current EU15. Constructing new railway lines for passengers is thus not a high priority. (Upgrading existing lines might be necessary, but this is much cheaper than constructing new lines.) In terms of freight transport, railway usage is somewhat higher in two out of the three larger new member countries shown in Table 11.3. But this is probably mostly a reflection of the still excessive importance of heavy industry in these countries (especially coal and steel in Poland). As their economies continue to modernize, the relative importance of railway transport, whose comparative advantage is in large volumes of heavy goods, will decline, as everywhere else, in favour of the more flexible road transport. In addition,

Table 11.3   Capacity on rails and roads

	Freight (in TKM) per km railway line	Passengers (in PKM) per km railway line	Passenger cars per km road
EU15 average	1.6	1.9	53.6
Czech Republic	1.9	0.8	27.1
Hungary	1.1	1.3	10.9
Poland	2.4	1.1	24.4
Turkey	1.1	0.7	11.0

Source: Gros and Suhrcke (2000).

the figures do not give any indication if the rail links are located according to today's needed links.

One straightforward indicator to measure the need for more roads is the number of cars per km of existing road. The data reported in the table for the year 2000 show a similar result as for railways: there is ample free capacity in most new member countries. Congestion due to insufficient infrastructure is thus much more a problem for the EU15 than for most candidate countries. As for railways, one can argue that the quality of the road network in the new member countries is lower than in the EU15, but given the large difference in the density this difference in quality would have to be huge to compensate for the 2:1, sometimes 5:1 difference in motor vehicle density. Moreover, as argued above, it is much cheaper to improve and upgrade existing roads than to construct new ones.

It is thus difficult to argue that public infrastructure is their main impediment to growth, and hence it is questionable that the candidates need more public investment relative to their income. However, the network of roads and rail may not fit the new economic structures, as industrial location has shifted in many cases. It indicates, however, that NMS should take care to do the necessary based 'on the existing stock', rather than neglecting the present potential.

Public investment and growth

Within the EU one actually does not find any correlation between public investment and growth in GDP. Ireland, by far the fastest growing economy of the EU over the last decades, has a somewhat below-average ratio of public investment to GDP. One crude method of gauging the impact of public investment on growth is to look at the correlation between growth in real GDP and the share of GDP spent on general government investment. If one takes decade averages to iron out business-cycle fluctuations, one finds the following: the correlation is negative or close to zero for the 1970s and 1990s. Only for the 1980s does one find a small positive correlation, which is however, due to the special case of Luxembourg. The growth literature in general has also not found a strong impact of publicly financed infrastructure investment on growth.

Nevertheless, the quality of infrastructures is below the standards of EU member states and still presents a barrier to development. A large effort to upgrade the infrastructure accrues to the governments of these countries, which have inherited weak economies and a difficult budgetary situation. In fact, in the first years after liberalization, the infrastructure of many countries suffered deterioration rather than an improvement. This trend has been reversed and the infrastructure is quickly being updated due to the increased growth of the economies combined with foreign aid, for which the EU is an important source.

However, as the highly varying quality of the impacts of the EU structural operations have shown in the EU (or even lack of visible impact on growth), careful planning of the priorities and objectives for the investments in infrastructure is needed. Section 6.3 develops this issue further.

Governance

Governance is another key element for development and competitiveness, not least because it is a strong determinant for FDI. The impressive development performance of the NMS since the early 1990s, has been strongly influenced by the quality of governance. The EU accession process has allowed the candidate countries to anchor their policies to EU standards, the *Acquis Communautaire*, which have been a prerequisite for admission to the EU. It is interesting to note that all countries that have embarked seriously on the accession process have seen impressive economic growth.

Applicant countries that have been laggards in improving governance, such as Bulgaria and Romania, have seen much weaker developments. Turkey is an even stronger case, as it is a solid market economy which has applied for accession to the EU but has not introduced the necessary governance rules. The lack of prudential supervision and corruption, amongst other causes, have affected severely the growth performance of this economy. During the decade 1995 to 2005, the country has been affected by various crises and per capita income declined in real and nominal terms between 1995 and 2001 (Ameco database).

Despite the impressive progress realized in many aspects of the structural and institutional framework, a lot needs to be done in most new member countries. Derviş *et al.* (2005) provide an analysis. The starting point is measured by data that reflect the situation at the turn of the century and show the distance between the new (and aspiring members like Turkey) and the old EU15 in the field of quality of governance. Table 11.4 shows the data on six different indicators of the quality of domestic economic governance obtained from the World Bank. The scores broadly reflect the level of development. The new members come out well-below the EU15 average (higher values mean a better performance; that is, more control of corruption, a more effective government, and so on), but there is also considerable variability among the new (and perspective) member states in all of the indicators used here. Romania and Bulgaria have similar values to Turkey.

Table 11.5 provides a brief statistical analysis of the same data by normalizing each variable to make the range comparable and then making a comparison with the old EU15. For example, the value of −2.7 in the column 'control of corruption' means that if one compares the average new members from Central and Eastern Europe to the EU15, the value is almost three standard deviations below the EU15 mean. In statistical terms this would be called an 'outlier', that is a value that is so far from the average that it should be considered belonging to a different set. In general, any entry above 2 in the

Table 11.4   Indicators of the quality of governance

Country	Country2	Control of corruption	Government effectiveness	Political stability	Regulatory quality	Rule of law	Voice and accountability
EU15	Mean	1.70	1.67	1.15	1.57	1.58	1.42
	STDEV	0.52	0.43	0.31	0.26	0.42	0.20
EU27							
Bulgaria	Mean	−0.17	−0.06	0.56	0.62	0.05	0.56
Estonia	Mean	0.66	0.78	0.98	1.35	0.8	1.05
Hungary	Mean	0.6	0.78	1.08	1.21	0.9	1.17
Poland	Mean	0.39	0.61	0.71	0.67	0.65	1.11
Romania	Mean	−0.34	−0.33	0.42	0.04	−0.12	0.38
Turkey	Mean	−0.38	−0.2	−0.61	0.08	0	−0.47

Source: Derviş *et al.* (2005).

Table 11.5   Summary statistics for indicators of the quality of governance

Country		Control of corruption	Government effectiveness	Political stability	Regulatory quality	Rule of law	Voice and accountability
EU27	Mean	1.1	1.2	1.0	1.3	1.2	1.2
	STDEV	0.8	0.7	0.3	0.5	0.6	0.3
Average CEEC normalised EU15		−2.7	−2.7	−0.9	−2.8	−2.5	−2.5
Turkey normalized EU27		−1.9	−2.0	−4.8	−2.6	−1.8	−5.1
Turkey normalized EU15		−4.0	−4.3	−5.8	−5.8	−3.8	−9.3

Source: Derviş *et al.* (2005).

lower part of Table 11.5 should be considered as showing that the country, or group of countries, is far away from the norm. Thus the table shows that the average value of indicators for the new members from Central and Eastern Europe is far away from the EU15 values in all categories except political stability (where the value is only 0.9). If one compares Turkey to the EU27, one sees that the distance separating Turkey from the EU27 was about as large as the distance that separates the CEECs from the EU15. This implies that when compared to averages of the enlarged EU, Turkey – before the reforms of the last three years – was in a class of its own with respect to the low quality of indicators measuring the quality of governance that have been quantified.

While the quality of domestic governance is undoubtedly low, one might ask whether this does not represent simply the level of development of the country. Poorer countries in general have weaker institutions, and maybe these institutions will improve as income grows and the country develops.

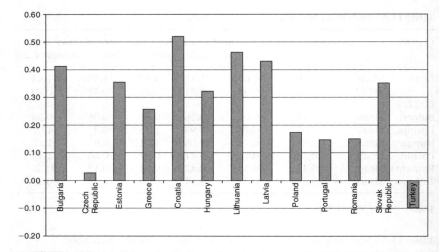

Figure 11.3 Change in composite quality of government indicator, 1996–2002
Notes: Higher value means a better performance.
Source: World Bank (2002).

This is indeed what seems to have happened over the last years as documented in Figure 11.3. The general improvement one observes for the NMS (before they actually became members) occurred during a period that was dominated by accession negotiations. In this narrow sense there has thus been an improvement of 'competitiveness' in the new member countries. The opening of membership negotiations with Turkey could thus provide a similar impetus for improvement in the quality of governance in that country.

Exchange-rate dynamics

One principal concern in the area of exchange rates is the possibility of risks stemming from an imbalanced exchange-rate regime. Particularly problematic is the aim of the NMS, in joining EMU, to enter the ERM II first. This is equivalent to a strong currency peg. Pegging the exchange rate to a foreign currency runs the risk of causing imbalances between the real and nominal exchange rates. A pegged currency also suffers from possible excessive foreign currency volatility. The studies undertaken (Vincentz, 2004; Welfens, 2005; Welfens and Borbély, 2004) analyse the exchange-rate implications for competitiveness. Gros *et al.* (2002) also concentrate on the macroeconomic implications of exchange-rate imbalances and EMU accession.

During the early 1990s, a lively discussion took place on whether the 'Club Med' currencies were overvalued. There was no general agreement because the judgement depended, as usual, on the indicator and the base period used. The two indicators most often used to measure competitiveness are (and were then) the real exchange rate deflated by the Consumer Price Index (CPI) and by Unit Labour Costs (ULC). These two usually give different indications.

In the case of Spain, it was argued that there was no need for a large exchange-rate adjustment because there was no real overvaluation – but only if one used ULC as the competitiveness indicator and 1980 as the base period. Not surprisingly, this was the position taken by the authorities. A similar argument was used in the case of Italy, where there was also a large discrepancy between the ULC and the CPI-based measures.

The NMS and other CEE candidates present a very similar picture. Depending on the base period and the indicator chosen, it can be argued that their currencies are overvalued by a very small margin or, on the contrary, by a very large one. In the case of the Czech Republic, Hungary and Estonia the potential overvaluation is relatively small across most indicators and base periods. Poland and Lithuania report much higher levels of real appreciation. In Romania, the CPI deflated exchange rate indicates a considerable overvaluation, whereas the ULC-based one points to an undervaluation. In the future, further trend real appreciation of candidate countries' currency is expected. Strong appreciations have occurred especially in the Czech Republic (from December 2001 to April 2002 by more than 10 per cent), Poland and also in Hungary (after the country widened the Forint fluctuation band).

The argument that the CEE currencies cannot be overvalued because exports of most of the candidate countries keep growing fast was also used in the case of Spain, where exports had actually doubled in dollar terms in the five years prior to 1992. This is typical of countries that have recently opened up to trade, such as the transition countries today or Spain in 1992, when it dismantled its last tariffs within the, then, EC. In such cases both exports and imports tend to grow strongly, whatever the exchange rate, more and more sectors are exposed to international competition.[4]

These data suggest that sooner or later an exchange-rate adjustment might be needed.[5] What does this imply for the exchange-rate policies pursued by these countries? For example, during the pre-accession period Poland and the Czech Republic officially followed a floating exchange rate, accompanied by domestic inflation targets. They are thus in a different situation than Spain and Italy in the early 1990s, which were members of a fixed exchange-rate adjustment, the ERM. In theory, an exchange-rate adjustment could thus come about gradually and without disruption.

However, experience has shown that large exchange-rate adjustments almost always lead to some disruption in financial markets. This was the case even for Spain, which in 1992 had actually a rather large amount of room for manoeuvre under the ERM (Spain had margins of +/−6 per cent). A sudden large depreciation usually forces the central bank to increase interest rates to limit the domestic inflationary pressures that would otherwise worsen inflation. Moreover, the terms-of-trade shock (deriving from the depreciation) in combination with higher interest rates might initially lead to a contraction in demand (as in Italy and Spain). This in turn puts pressure on the budget, leading to higher deficits; which then might undermine confidence and thus aggravate the depreciation.

But, such a negative spiral does not need to develop. The case of Greece shows that a smooth 'glide path' to EMU is possible. But it could be potentially dangerous for the candidate countries operating flexible exchange-rate regimes to enter into an ERM-type arrangement that would tie their currencies to the euro before they have a clearer view of whether the current exchange rate levels are sustainable in the long run. The case of Greece, which successfully engineered a one-step surprise devaluation is instructive in this regard.

However, the real appreciation which is a natural consequence of the transition and catching-up process does not necessarily have to be damaging for the candidate countries. If it comes through the Balassa-Samuelson effect it does not imply any loss of international competitiveness. Moreover, real appreciation may also reflect further trade integration and elimination of non-quality related price differences. And lastly, it may generate pressure on the exporters to increase their productivity and improve performance and thus eventually lead to an increase in competitiveness. Figure 11.4 demonstrates that despite the considerable real appreciation, competitiveness (measured by real unit labour costs) has even increased in some of the candidate countries relative to the EU.

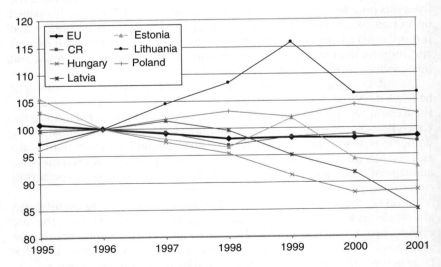

Figure 11.4   Real unit labour costs $(1996 = 100)$
Source: Gros *et al.* (2004).

Nominal convergence à la Maastricht

The ultimate condition for membership in EMU is to achieve a certain degree of nominal convergence with the other members as stipulated by the Maastricht criteria. The EU institutions have so far made it clear that the criteria will have to be fully adhered to by the candidate countries in their run up to monetary union.

The motivation behind the formulation of the Maastricht convergence test was threefold. First, the EU countries wanted to create a stable low-inflationary, growth-friendly environment and hence the stress put on the level of inflation and interest rates. Second, the founders of EMU wanted to eliminate the risk of free-riding behaviour and thus they introduced the conditions limiting the size of budget deficits and the government debt. And eventually, the conditions regarding exchange rates were intended to test the stability of the currency in question and the appropriateness of the level of exchange rate *vis-à-vis* the other ERM countries.

Despite the fact that the Maastricht criteria had been heavily criticized, they proved, at least in terms of the stabilization of the public finances, rather successful. Indeed the EU countries managed in the run-up to EMU to bring the public deficits under control and those with a substantial government debt succeeded in bringing it down to more acceptable levels. Hence, as a consequence it can be expected that the current eurozone countries, together with the ECB and the European Commission will insist on 'stringent'[6] adherence to the wording of the criteria. But many economists in this context call for some tailoring of the criteria so that they are more suited to the candidates' specific situation (Pelkmans *et al.*, 2000; Halpern and Wyplosz, 2001; Buiter and Grafe, 2002). They voice concerns that attempts to comply with the criteria in a relatively short time might prove to be destabilizing for the CEECs and could potentially lead to a real divergence instead of catch up.[7] The latest softening of the budget deficit rules will not affect the NMS, as the entry criteria are the same.

There are some inherent features of the candidate economies that make it difficult for them, if not impossible, to comply with the criteria in the short to middle term, but at the same time do not pose a risk to their overall stability and thus do not contradict their membership in the eurozone. An attempt to fulfil the criteria in a relatively short time might undermine the process of real convergence and potentially lead to a divergence. Thus an early entry into the eurozone, which most of the CEE candidates wish to achieve, would be endangered and the consequent economic disruptions might have an adverse impact on the incumbent member states themselves.

Most objections and warnings are directed to the criteria concerning price stability, budget balance and exchange rate stability. Hence we deal with these now.

The Balassa–Samuelson effect

The candidate countries have in most cases a rather impressive record in bringing down inflation rates. Today, all of the countries have managed to achieve single-digit inflation rates and forecasts indicate that in the coming years the stabilization of price-level growth will continue. However, as is also apparent from the forecasts, inflation is expected to decline only modestly and stay at higher levels than those common in the EU and also the eurozone. This might have potentially important implications regarding the timing and strategy of accession of the candidate countries to EMU.

When looking for the causes of this sort of inflation inertia, one has to resort to the theoretical framework of the Balassa–Samuelson (B–S) effect to explain the trend appreciation of the real exchange rates in terms of productivity differentials in the tradable and non-tradable sectors of an economy.[8]

The catching-up process in the candidate countries can be characterized by the trend appreciation of their real exchange rates. Why is that so? The labour productivity in the candidate countries rises in most cases at a higher pace compared to the EU economies, and the large gap in price and productivity levels between the CEE candidates and the EU countries coupled with strong FDI inflows indicate that the faster productivity growth might be preserved in the future as well. However, the high degree of trade integration implies that most of the increases are experienced in the tradable sector. The non-tradable sector benefits from increases in productivity only to the extent that non-traded goods and services enter the production of the traded goods as intermediate inputs thus facing indirect competition. As the marginal product of labour in the tradable sector increases and prices are kept stable, due to international competition, wages in the sector also tend to rise.

The basic assumption of the model is that wages in the economy tend to be equalized. First, there exists, though in reality somewhat limited, labour mobility between the sectors and thus workers would move to better paid jobs in the tradable sector thus generating pressure towards equalization. And further, trade unions also tend to make sure that the wage developments in the whole economy are more or less synchronized (Halpern and Wyplosz, 2001). Thus, the increase in wages in the tradable sector results in equivalent increases in the non-tradable sector. However, the profitability of the non-traded sector facing rising wages and limited productivity increases cannot be retained without upward adjustment of prices of non-traded goods and services. Hence inflation in the non-traded sector tends to overtake inflation in the traded sector (see Appendix).[9]

At this point it is important to stress that the B–S effect is an equilibrium phenomenon which naturally occurs when an economy experiences economic growth. Through an adjustment in relative prices in the economy, an appreciation of the real exchange rate is achieved. Therefore, higher inflation generated by this process is in no way a threat to the monetary stability of a country, or its international competitiveness, and thus there is no need to counteract it by economic policies.

It is of course important to know what the magnitude of the effect might be, or whether it occurs at all. A number of recent papers have found evidence in favour of the B–S hypothesis.[10] Pelkmans *et al.* (2000) estimate that the inflation differential generated by the B–S effect might amount to between 3.5 per cent and 4 per cent, and Halpern and Wyplosz (2001) arrived at a similar estimate of about 3.5 per cent. Sinn and Reutter (2001) also report high levels of inflation which might be compatible with the B–S effect. According to their estimates the candidate countries might have inflation rates that are higher, by between 3 per cent to 7 per cent, than those in Germany – a country with the smallest difference between productivity in the tradable and non-tradable sectors. Coricelli and Jazbec (2001) estimated the possible size of the effect for 19 transition countries and arrived at a conclusion that under the assumption of a yearly rate of real convergence between the transition countries and the EU of 2 per cent, the B–S effect will result in real exchange rate appreciation of about 1 per cent. The estimates of the UNO (2001) vary between 2 per cent and 2.2 per cent, while the Deutsche Bundesbank (2001) arrived at estimates of 1.9 per cent to 2.6 per cent.

Welfens (2005) confirms that the B–S effect is of importance; for Poland in particular the effective real exchange rate was more than twice the nominal value in 2002 (see Fig. 11.5). With the Poland strongly committed to entry into the euro, this imbalance can have serious consequences for Poland's growth in the future.

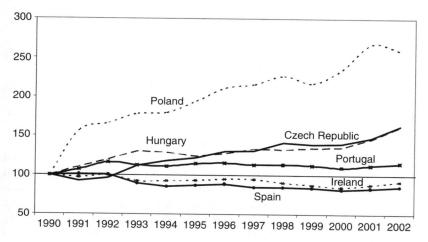

Figure 11.5 Real effective exchange rate (p/ep^*) dynamics in selected EU countries in 1990–2002 (1990 = 100)
Source: Welfens (2005).

These numbers show large differences which are due to the different methods applied, various sizes of the samples and the periods covered. Many are subject to various reservations regarding the very short time periods used in estimations which in addition were characterized by large structural changes. Also the division between the tradable and non-tradable sectors is hard to determine in practice. As a result, studies use various techniques which make the results incomparable. Moreover, the estimates of the impact of the B–S effect on the CPI inflation might be further distorted as most of the studies use a GDP value-added distinction which can be considerably different (Durjasz, 2001). Moreover, some of the assumptions on which the estimates are based, such as full labour mobility and resulting wage equalization, can in reality be violated to some extent which leads to an overestimation of the overall impact of the B–S effect.

Even when taking into account these reservations, it is obvious that the B–S effect can play an important role. The estimated values in most cases exceed the 1.5 per cent limit given by the Maastricht inflation criteria. From this point of view, insisting on a strict adherence to the criteria seems to be capable of generating economic crises rather than achieving the desired stabilization of the EMU candidate countries. If new member states wish to adopt the euro in the shortest possible time, as many of them have already proclaimed, it will be forced to suppress the inflation under the stipulated limit which could mean generating recession. Of course, it can be argued that the effect will have a decreasing tendency in time, but given the large differences in economic levels between the CEE candidates and the EU and thus also productivity, it seems improbable that the gap would close sufficiently until the desired '€-day' for some of them, such as 2009. Welfens (2005) also considers that the fixing of the exchange rate can be detrimental, because non tradable price will be increasing in the long term, and keeping inflation under the Maastricht criteria will be difficult.

The inflation problem could certainly be solved, at least temporarily, with the help of flexible exchange rates. The undesired, in the light of Maastricht criteria, inflation differential could be compensated for by proportional nominal appreciation of the exchange rate. This might, however, be in breach of the criteria concerning the stability of exchange rates within ERM II. The relatively wide ±15 per cent band could soon appear uncomfortably tight and an adjustment might be needed (Halpern and Wyplosz, 2001). However, it is noteworthy that this would be an upward adjustment whereas the inflation criterion only speaks of unilaterally decided devaluation. The reasoning behind the Balassa-Samuelson logic would thus advocate for more flexibility regarding the upward adjustments. This would only be a temporary solution and after the entry into the eurozone the change in relative prices would be needed anyway. As a result inflation differentials will persist.

Moreover, some of the new members have deprived themselves of this possibility by fixing their exchange rates in a form of conventional pegs or currency boards. Therefore, the appreciation of the real exchange rate can be achieved solely through changes in relative prices. These countries then have little possibility to limit overall inflation without resorting to price controls and generating recession at least in some sectors of their economies. From this point of view, an adjustment in the Maastricht criteria would be desirable without running the risk of damaging the commitment to price stability in the eurozone (Buiter and Grafe, 2002). The EU and member countries' officials have so far been opposed to such proposals, arguing a principle of an equal approach to all countries.[11] However, it is worth noting that no official intervention into the wording of the Treaty would be necessary as the quantification of the criteria is done in a separate protocol (Pelkmans *et al.*, 2000).

The general conclusion one can draw from this partial survey is that the B–S effect exists. Therefore, if the inflation criterion remains without changes, the candidate countries that want an early membership at a fixed exchange rate will have to accept a period of reduced growth in order to reduce inflation temporarily. This might not be needed if they engineer the appropriate appreciation just before joining. But at any rate they will have to accept higher inflation later if the catch up continues. The key question is how much. The earlier estimates were quite high in this respect. However, new evidence trying to disentangle the relative importance of various factors on the inflation differentials is somewhat more modest as far as the absolute values of expected B–S effects are concerned.

Anyway, if the candidate countries decide not to push too much and wait, with the introduction of the euro one good year might help them to get under the magical limit and they would be 'in' (Szapary, 2000; Pelkmans *et al.*, 2000). This could, however, take somewhat longer than they would wish and could also bring along all the negative aspects of unfulfilled expectations including financial market volatility, reverse capital flows and increased pressure on their currency. On the other hand, such an approach would require longer-term sound fiscal and monetary policies which would generally support the overall stability.

The NMS face a difficult political trade-off: either implement restrictive policies to squeeze inflation during the qualification period for EMU, or accept a delay in being able to join the euro. Gros *et al.* (2002) also warn that capital mobility and 'fixed but adjustable' exchange rates are difficult to manage, but this is the situation these countries will face while in the ERM II. They recommend tailoring the convergence criteria to the needs of these candidates to EMU.

11.5 Government policies in the NMS3

Hashi (2004) has analysed the effectiveness of government interventions to assist the business sector since the start of transition. The NMS3 countries have used state-aid mechanisms extensively. The arguments for the use of state aid in the transition counties were based first on the needs of facilitating the process of transformation and systemic change. As time evolved arguments based on correction of 'market failures' or infant industry considerations have been used to continue the wide use of state-aid tools; these have been tax incentives, subsidies or other interventions in the form of subsidized loans, grants and other investment schemes.

The analysis shows a rather weak or negative impact in these countries. The three countries appear to have often suffered from the political failures of rent-seeking, regulatory capture and interest-group pressure often present in government intervention. Furthermore, while state aid is a common and politically easy action, it is often not the most effective. Due to the difficulty of identifying the full costs and benefits of externalities to the policy, state aid has potentially harmed more than assisted the economy.

An important intervention in these countries has been associated with assistance to the growth of small and medium-sized enterprises (SMEs). While these have been correctly identified as an important motor for development, financial support is not the only mean to assist their development. Heavy entry barriers imposed by the state discourage the entry of entrepreneurs and these are important in the countries studied.

In the initial years of transition the state intervened heavily with state-aid tools to 'rescue and restructure' ailing industries. This support has, according to Hashi (2004) or also Balcerowicz and Sobolewski (2005), not been successful, delaying rather than assisting restructuring and drawing resources from other sectors to do so. Industrial policy in this period was dominated by political considerations, which were especially strong during the difficult and unstable initial period of transformation. Resources were being diverted to cover running costs of loss-making firms with little or no effect on competitiveness.

The EU imposed in the association agreements an obligation to eliminate distorting subsidies, bringing state aid in line with EU rules. This has forced a reduction of incompatible state aids, but the process has been uneven and difficult. Still today, due to the large number of schemes in place in these countries, regulatory bodies are unable to verify compliance. It is interesting to note that while most state aid in the EU is horizontal, that it is open to all businesses fulfilling certain requirements, state aids in the NMS3 are still dominated by sectoral aid.

Interesting to note is that state aid in the form of tax exemptions; deferrals and soft loans and guarantees have particularly benefited multinational companies. State aid has been used to attract FDI and foreign companies rather than assist local companies. This is a case of intergovernmental competition and as far as it relocates operations from one EU country to another based solely on tax considerations, it is of no net benefit to the EU. There is evidence that tax considerations are only one of a number of reasons for FDI in the countries. Tax concessions when excessive will not affect the decision of

MNCs to operate in the country, causing just a loss in corporate tax revenues for the government.

The studies also show several weaknesses in state-aid schemes used for regional development, and one of the main tools used has been the creation of Special Economic Zones (SEZs). Studies for Poland suggest (Kryńska, 2000) that economic zones with their preferential tax schemes attracted operations from other regions rather than creating new ventures, strongly reducing any employment benefits expected.

An econometric model on the impact of state aid on competitiveness was performed by Hashi (2004) and indicated that state aid has negligible or negative effects on the overall competitiveness of the economies, while labour productivity and thus investment in human capital have in general had significant impact on competitiveness.

However, Ambroziak (2005) challenges the present general position that state aids have to be horizontal, and argues that targeted specific state aids can have a better potential, and that the focus should be on better state aid rules and controls. He argues that the effectiveness of horizontal state-aid is not proven to be better. While the second argument is valid due to the limited empirical evidence of horizontal aid effectiveness, the first is questionable. In theory, if the government had superior information about the needs of companies and markets and were also operating altruistically and impartially, specific state aids could well be the most effective option. However, the track record of failures, vested interest and the ability of interest groups to capture rents gives sufficient evidence that while the horizontal aids have not been proven to be effective, specific aids granted by the state have generally been proven ineffective.

11.6 Policy implications for the EU15 and new member states

This chapter has highlighted the factors affecting a balanced growth and competitiveness of the industrial sector in the NMS. FDI, human capital, appropriate labour-market policies, infrastructures, entry barriers and governance, fiscal and exchange-rate policies, all play a role in the developments of competitiveness in the industrial sector. The speed and the success of transforming the industrial sector into a competitive and growth-contributing sector will depend on the interplay of the different factors. Many of the variables are highly influenced by government policies, positively as well as negatively.

Sectoral policies towards horizontal state aid and FDI promotion

Evidence suggests that state-aid policies are overall damaging rather than assisting competitiveness of the industrial sector, because these, even if benefiting a specific sector, are drawing resources which could be used with a better impact elsewhere. The opportunity costs are high. The shift from sec-toral state-aid support to horizontal measures should be continued, in line with EU support measures.

Horizontal state-aid based on criteria to promote entrepreneurship, such as for SMEs, should ensure that selection criteria target those ventures which are not only economically sustainable, but which for reasons of their location or other characteristics are not able to draw the financial resources from the private financial sector. State support should not substitute the private sector where it operates effectively, but target market failure where it occurs.

These countries should show more restraint in producing tax-based incen-tives for regional development. The impact of these is distortive and generally weaker than expected. Instead, they should consider, as a first stage of assis-tance to SMEs, the reduction of the bureaucratic burden and heavy charges affecting SMEs through institutional reform. This can be more effective than state-aids and has been widely discussed in the literature. The World Bank has dedicated special attention to this issue, reporting important implications of the barriers to entry and other state imposed burdens on businesses (World Bank, 2002).

Human capital

One of the clearest messages of the studies is that the economic development of the countries will depend to an important extent on the more advanced technological sectors, which requires an increase in the quality of human cap-ital and thus labour productivity. Basing growth on cheap labour-intensive industries is not a correct strategy for encouraging convergence with the EU economy. Labour-market policies fostering labour mobility and transferable skills are primordial to a successful development of the countries and their industries.

The new countries should focus principally on the human-capital devel-opment measures that the European Social Fund (ESF) provides, avoiding an emphasis on simple financial transfers for the long-term unemployed. The employment policy has to be proactive. Given the number of unemployed and particularly the young unemployed, training and skill-developing job placements should be a priority.

Infrastructure

Infrastructure is an important element in the development of a country, as it reduces the transaction costs for doing business. The EU Structural Funds have been conceived mainly to create the necessary environment for businesses to develop, but badly planed infrastructure can cause that large investment to have no effect on the competitiveness of industries or long-run growth of the economy. Infrastructures are also subject to the law of diminishing returns to the investment and additions of infrastructure do not *per se* attract investments.

Careful planning of the infrastructure developments ensuring effective links between suppliers and markets is necessary. A careful analysis of the needs and potential of each country and its regions in necessary to draw maximum benefit from the infrastructure developed. The quality of the National Development Plans and the associated Operational Programmes for the EU Structural Funds are a key element in the development of successful aid strategies. The NMS should ensure that the driving force behind the strategy is efficient allocation of resources, rather than a mere exercise of ensuring a prompt absorption of the EU funds. Given the size of the support relative the government financial capacity, the efficient use of the Structural Funds is important.

Public financing for infrastructure investment should be limited where possible. Given the changes in financial markets that have taken place over the last decade it is now generally recognized that most infrastructure projects could also be financed and sometimes even operated with substantial private-sector involvement. Major projects, such as motorways, are already undertaken on a mainly private-sector basis in the NMS. The merit of letting the private sector run at least some parts of what is traditionally subsumed under infrastructure is apparent in the telecommunications sector. It is interesting to note that despite running large budget deficits until the early 1980s which led to a large build up of public debt, supposedly justified by the need for public investment, growth in Ireland only started to 'take off' when this policy was abandoned and the deficits sharply reduced.

All in all, there should thus be no presumption that the candidates would need to run large deficits on the grounds that they have a stronger need for infrastructure investment.

Governance

One of the key elements that have attracted FDI to the region is the governance improvement achieved. Kinoshita and Campos (2004) have shown that for the NMS, variables such as external liberalization, the rule of law and quality of the bureaucracy have been the most potent predictors of FDI. The accession process to the EU has introduces changes in the quality of institutions, increasing investor confidence. However, as the banking crisis in the Czech Republic has shown, further steps in improving prudential supervision is needed. An efficient and functioning bureaucracy and legal system are important prerequisites for further investment attraction. The quality of the domestic institutions is considered a key determinant of growth.

Exchange rate and monetary union

Section 4.5 analysed the exchange-rate implications for competitiveness based on the possible imbalances caused by the so-called Balassa–Samuelson effect. This effect can affect the real exchange rate and inflation in the NMS.

However, NMS have announced their intention to join the euro as soon as possible, based on the expected benefits of a reduction in transaction costs for businesses and the positive signal it gives to the financial market about the stability of the currency – hoping in turn to attract more FDI.

Officials from the EU are, however, calling for caution, as entry into the EMU is accompanied by the Maastricht criteria for membership which will require the new members to bring down the inflation differential while keeping a stringent fiscal discipline. Given the present situation in these countries and the Balassa–Samuelson effects, this is a sub-optimal policy approach. While the repercussions are not critical, the trade-off between the benefits of EMU membership have to be weighted against the implications of an adjustment that will be costly, like any disinflation policy is in the short term. Gros *et al.* (2002) consider that the Maastricht criteria on nominal exchange-rate convergence are not in line with the needs of the member states.

The NMS face a difficult political trade-off: either implement restrictive policies to squeeze inflation during the qualification period for EMU, or accept a delay in being able to join the euro.

Gros *et al.* (2002) also warn that capital mobility and 'fixed but adjustable' exchange rates are difficult to manage, but this is the situation these countries will face while in the ERM II. They recommend tailoring the convergence criteria to the needs of these candidates to EMU.

11.7   Policy implications for the EU member states

The enlargement process brings opportunities for the EU15, as the market increases, but also introduces changes into the EU capital and labour markets and a possible competition with some growing industries of the CEECs. Some of these changes will cause some adaptation and restructuring in the EU15. This is due to the rising potential of the NMS to compete in the same product groups as older member states.

As these countries are still largely producing low to medium-technology products, they appear to be potential competitors to the EU cohesion countries and cause trade and welfare losses to them (Baldwin 1994; Baldwin *et al.*, 1997; Emerson and Gros, 1998; Egger and Katena, 2003). The early studies by Baldwin and Emerson and Gros have pointed to a competitive disadvantage for Portugal, directly clashing in its major items of production of textiles and clothing with the competitive sectors of the accession countries. The top exports from Portugal – clothing, mechanical vehicles, electrical goods and footwear – are sectors in which the transition countries also strongly developing, that is the labour-intensive low and medium-technology sectors.

Boberly (2005) analyses trade between the EU15 and the 10 acceding NMS, and trade between the NMS3 and the EU15. The result show that some industrial sectors at the core of the EU face crowding-out effects, although Greece and partially Spain is also facing competitive risks, while Portugal shows surprisingly no competitive disadvantage. In any case the trade vulnerability analysis shows that the implications are not heterogeneous for all member states.

The studies show that while multinational companies of the EU15 member states have benefited from the increase in trade with the new members and by relocating some operations to them, some sectors will have to restructure, including a number of 'sensitive' sectors according to the EU, either due to their vulnerability or strategic importance.

Governments of the EU have shown increasing concern in the last decade over the competitiveness of their industrial sector and their economy in general. EU member states have hoped that the increasing size of the internal market would increase growth rates in the EU without the need for difficult and unpopular structural changes. The increase in size of the single market, while increasing economic opportunities for Europe may increase the need for fundamental reforms in member states.

Studies have shown that policies to subsidize sectors in decline do not generally improve their prospects but simply delay their restructuring, causing longer periods of decline and a harder adjustment in the end (Hoshi, 2004). The area in which the member states can give an important contribution to competitiveness is by improving the business environment in the EU, by improving the regulatory framework. Various member states have an unfriendly business environment and reducing their bureaucratic and often excessive tax and social contributions could give a first spur to the economy.

In addition, labour-market policies in many member states do not encourage the necessary adjustments to the capacity of the workforce. This rigidity creates disincentives for companies to hire workers and can discourage the operations of companies in areas undergoing rapid change, such as high-tech industries. Less rigid and more active unemployment and training schemes are required to facilitating the economic adjustment of enterprises to the increasingly changing market environment.

Member states' commitment to education and R&D investment has to increase; these are key for economic development. An important factor to unleash the innovation potential is introducing a system of finance based on competitive tendering and excellence. Links between industries and research centres should be fostered.

As proposed by the European Commission (COM 487 final, p.16), countries and regions should provide a strategic reference document defining the objectives and priority actions, and this strategic framework should outline the actions necessary and member states should ensure that the objectives are effectively reached. It is necessary that member states deliver on actions they have committed themselves to follow such as the Lisbon strategy.

Member states' industrial policies should be geared towards creating the necessary physical environment for industries to develop and prosper.

Infrastructure is an important reference point. Investment can be concentrated in developing centres of excellence, ensuring that their location is logical. The location of firms, provision of infrastructures and other key elements should be based on a well-integrated strategy, such as the strategic reference framework mentioned above.

Industrial policy based on state-aid, tax incentives or other forms of soft-credit concessions should be limited and, if used, based on stringent criteria and for a strictly limited period of time. These should also not replace the private financial markets where available. Assistance should always aim at restructuring and adapting industries to new challenges and not sustain their losses.

In the single market, actions to support domestic industries should not be undertaken with the aim of artificially undercutting competitors from other member states. This is already an obligation under EU competition law, but the stringency of its application is variable.

Finally, one of the main barriers for competitiveness in Europe is the underdeveloped services market. The growth potential of Europe lies to a large extent in developing this sector. Gros *et al.* (2004) clearly indicate that too much capital in the EU is immobilized in the declining sectors (mainly industry) and too little in growing sectors. It is important to mention this even if the study is centred on industrial competitiveness. It is also interesting that the free movement of industrial goods is a reality, while services are largely land-locked. A competitiveness policy centred on assistance to industry risks being detrimental if it comes at the expense of investment in growing sectors. The relevant opportunity costs have to be considered seriously. Improving the service sector, which is a large employer and an important sector for the overall economy and for industry, can bolster the overall competitiveness. Industry and services are not independent, but interdependent. A better service growth also bolsters overall demand.

Member states should find the courage to free up trade barriers in the services sector, which the European Commission proposed with the Services Directive (COM(2004) 2 final/3). This move is overdue, as lack of progress is contrary to single-market aspirations. In aggregate, 60 to 70 per cent of the EU's economic activity depends on the services sector, and thus limiting the free provision of services undermines prospects for growth and competitiveness. There will undoubtedly be transitory adjustment periods, but improved services provision in the EU will benefit the competitiveness of Europe across the board.

As section 11.4 illustrated, future employment creation in the NMS will largely depend on the development of services. This is also true for the rest of the EU, but the scale of potential labour restructuring needs is a particular challenge for the new members. Without a strongly developing services sector there is a risk of mounting unemployment.

11.8 Policy implications for the EU

The European Union has shown concern over the general weaknesses in competitiveness in the EU. This is reflected in the policy proposals of the EU in the Financial Perspectives [COM (2004) 101 final] and the subsequent Communication [COM(2004)187 final] and the calls for better policy coordination in the Treaty establishing a European Constitution (Articles I-15 and I-17). While these proposals have positive aspects, the way these are implemented in practice will have a large impact on their effectiveness in promoting industrial competitiveness.

The European Commission has rightly pinpointed the economic weaknesses hampering the reaping of the full benefits of the internal market. To fully exploit the single market the fragmented national systems in many economic areas have to be removed. Furthermore, commitments by the member states to work towards EU actions, such as the Lisbon strategy fail to be followed up by the member states.

The free provision of services is a crucial element for enhancing growth and competitiveness in Europe, and this report underlines the importance to renew the efforts to implement the Services Directive.

The studies have revealed that before considering any state intervention in support of the industrial sector, the EU could already achieve advances by pushing for the reduction in the non-tariff barriers which still exist. But these trade barriers are not the only item undermining EU growth. There is a certain lack of transnational cooperation which leads innovation and industrial structures to be more fragmented than they should be. The EU can play a role in improving cooperation here.

The EU should put pressure to increase macroeconomic, labour and fiscal policy coordination, especially in the eurozone. The ECB can lead a dialogue (Gross *et al.*, 2004) on non-inflationary sustainable growth policies. While macroeconomic policies in the member states should reflect their circumstances, policy conflicts and inconsistency between the member states and EU objectives should be minimized.

The European Commission's request for more policy coordination is understandable, but there are limits to this process. One-size-fits-all approaches to macroeconomic policy, based on bureaucratic assessments, are a risky approach. There is, however, a case for reinforcing the role of strategies and the enforcement of their implementation when countries commit themselves to an objective, such as the Lisbon strategy.

There is evidence that an appropriate level of infrastructures is necessary to develop the economic potential of the NMS, improving the economic environment for the industrial sector. Some of the new countries still require important investments. However, neither the 'absorption capacity' of a country nor the level of aid, indicators often used as proxies for a countries development capacity, are sufficient to predict success in developing the national or regional economy.

The economic and industrial development of a country depends on an appropriate mix of policies and investments. Structural Fund operations, if wisely allocated, can create necessary market signals for enterprises. However, development is created neither by decree nor by accumulating infrastructure in specific areas alone. It is thus of paramount importance that the structural investments are based on a sound overall economic analysis and strategy, ensuring that the size and direction of the funds invested are in relation with the real endogenous potential of the areas assisted.

The European Commission should ensure that development plans and Operational Programmes are not only drafted to be able to successfully absorb the funds offered by the European Union, but that the strategies underlying the use of EU aid are sound and robust. To do so the European Commission should reinforce the *ex ante* economic evaluation capacity, as well as the subsequent monitoring and *ex post* evaluation. This is especially important in the NMS where a substantial share of government funds for investment and development are linked to co-financing EU operations. The National Development Plan documents and the Operational Programmes ensuing from it thus become the main development strategy of the country. Given this situation, the Commission should ensure that EU assistance is appropriate and coherent. It is also important to understand the macroeconomic policy context of the country, to ensure that investments are not aimed to develop sectors which fail to develop due to policy failure rather than lack of investment. The work by Hoshi (2004) has clearly described such cases.

This might create conflicts of competence, due to the subsidiarity principle, in the preparation of plans and place limits to the Commission's competences. The Commission and member states may disagree on the strategies. It is thus important to create an improved dialogue between the member states and the Commission, as well as a better guidance of the objectives of the funds.

The EU has failed to agree on a strong financial intervention by the European budget to promote investments in R&D, while this is considered a key factor for European economic development. It is important that the member states increase their support for innovation, as this is one of the few fields where Europe still has a certain competitive edge in the world market. Subsidies are, however, not the only action possible; some member states should also improve their internal market by reducing the bureaucratic and tax burden on companies.

The policy competences of the EU cannot by themselves propel European competitiveness; full participation of the member states is crucial. Economic strategies approved by member states have to be followed and enforced, which is not currently the case. The EU needs also to further develop the strategic character of its budget interventions, moving away from the simple redistribution and 'absorption capacity' of funds more towards efficiency and results-driven approaches, across all policies.

11.9 Conclusions

This chapter has discussed the main challenges for the NMS and for the old EU15 that the further developments of the industrial sector bring. The principal message emerging from the papers discussed is that industrial competitiveness in the NMS will depend on the level of innovation and their capacity to develop high-technology products. The results of the studies discourage a heavy intervention by the state as this has not been successful in the past and often damages rather than assists the economic development of the country. The state should, rather, aim to ensure that the investment climate in the country is positive. Furthermore, the decline of the agricultural sector, combined with a rise in productivity in industry along with a reduction over time of the building and construction sectors, is likely to put pressure on the labour market. Hence, the development of the services sector is crucial for these countries.

But efforts and changes are not only required from the NMS. The development of the services sector in Europe holds the key to improving European competitiveness in general. For the NMS this has a particular relevance, but there is also a need for the old members of the EU to adapt, restructure their labour markets and implement the revised Lisbon strategy. This chapter, and the book as a whole, recommend improving the business environment in the member states and completing the single market for services by implementing the services directive to allow the EU to develop its economic potential.

Appendix

The Balassa–Samuelson effect

The evolution of the real exchange rate due to the Balassa–Samuelson effect can easily be depicted by several equations. The real exchange rate can be written as:

$$s_r = \varepsilon + \pi^* - \pi$$

where ε is the rate of expected depreciation of the nominal exchange rate, π and π^* are the inflation rates (based on the CPI index) in the transition country and eurozone, respectively. The overall inflation rate can be decomposed to inflation rate in the traded sector and inflation rate in the non-traded sector, π^T and π^N, respectively. Also in this case the asterisk will denote the eurozone. α will be the share of the tradables in the CPI index and its composition is assumed to be the same in the transition country and the eurozone.
Thus,

$$\pi = \alpha\pi^T + (1 - \alpha)\pi^N \text{ and } \pi^* = \alpha\pi^{T^*} + (1 - \alpha)\pi^{N^*}$$

From this it follows that:

$$s_r = \varepsilon + \alpha\pi^{T*} + (1 - \alpha)\pi^{N*} - \alpha\pi^{T} + (1 - \alpha)\pi^{N}$$

Due to the international arbitrage it must hold that the inflation rate of domestic tradable goods is equal to the inflation of the eurozone tradable goods plus expected rate of depreciation. Therefore,

$$\pi^{T} = \pi^{T*} + \varepsilon$$

Then we can find that:

$$s_r = -(1 - \alpha)\left[(\pi^{N} - \pi^{T}) - (\pi^{N*} - \pi^{T*})\right]$$

From this it follows that the real exchange rate will appreciate if the difference between the excess inflation in the domestic non-tradable sector over the tradable sector is larger than that in the eurozone. And the higher differences in productivity levels in the transition countries compared to the eurozone indicate that it will probably be the case. The gap between the GDP per capita levels in the candidate countries and their EU partners is very wide. Thus there is large potential for catching-up and productivity increases.

Notes

1 Excluding Portugal, for which no data were available.
2 For more details, see Gros and Suhrcke (2000).
3 For similar evidence on the cross-country relationship between road infrastructure and income, see Querioz and Gautman (1992) and Ingram and Li (1997). For the rail–income relationship, see also Canning (1999).
4 For an analysis of the experience of transitions countries see De Broeck and Slek (2001).
5 For further discussion of the potential for real appreciation in the transition economies see Halpern and Wyplosz (2001).
6 Stringent in a sense that no formal changes to the criteria will be allowed. The interpretation of the criteria in the case of the incumbent EMU members was however a different story as a rather flexible approach was adopted. From this point of view one could also expect a relatively benevolent approach towards the present candidates (or at least the candidate countries can use this fact in negotiations on entry). However, one also needs to bear in mind that this time the situation will be to a certain extent different. It can be assumed that the EMU membership of the current candidate countries will not be such a politically predominated issue as was the launch of the EMU in 1999 and therefore more attention to the economic aspects will likely be devoted. This is also indicated by the rather cautious, if not discouraging, stance of the ECB in terms of timing of the entry into the eurozone.
7 Note that the EU uses the same line of reasoning but arrives at completely different conclusions: the enlargement of the eurozone to the East should be postponed rather than adapting the criteria.

8 Another reason might be the still considerably high share of goods and services in the consumer basket whose prices are not fully determined by the free market forces (in Poland the share is estimated at almost 15% (Durjasz, 2001). This might be due to direct regulation or structural weaknesses. The case of regulated prices will not be further dealt with, as it is reasonable to expect that the prices will have been deregulated by the time the candidate countries enter the EU/EMU.

9 The magnitude of the effect also depends on the demand-side effects. Rising increased productivity leads through increasing income and wealth to increases in consumption. If the demand for non-traded goods and services, as it is usually assumed because of their 'superior' character, rises at a higher speed than the demand for non-traded good, the price increases might be even further reinforced.

10 Typically, these studies have used econometric techniques to detect the existence of long-run relationships (co-integration) between relative price levels and relative productivity. In this framework, the direction of the applied studies has been twofold. A first class of studies focuses on the relationship between long-run changes in relative prices and productivity differentials across countries, while others analyse the link between the productivity differentials and inflation differentials across sectors within countries. The general conclusion of the first approach is that there is evidence of a relationship between the evolution of the relative price levels across countries and that of productivity differentials. Following the second approach, a clear causality between productivity growth in the traded-goods sector and inflation in the non-traded-goods sector has been identified. Indeed, recent studies show that, while some of the more restrictive assumptions of the hypothesis are not supported by the data, there is still clear evidence that the B–S effect has been at work within the euro area.

11 This is after all not that surprising as the EU institutions do not even take into account the impact of the B–S effect on the interest rates differentials in the eurozone (see Sinn and Reutter, 2001).

References

Ambroziak, A.A. (2005) 'State Aid as an Instrument for Reinforcing Competitiveness of Polish Undertakings. Necessity for Retargeting of the Granted Aid?', paper presented at the final conference of the project on 'Changes in Industrial Competitiveness as a Factor of Integration: Identifying Challenges of the Enlarged Single European Market' CEPS, 25–6 November, Brussels.

Balcerowicz, E. and M. Sobolewski (2005) 'Competitiveness of the Polish Manufacturing Sector: Does Government Policy Matter?', paper presented at the final conference of the project on 'Changes in Industrial Competitiveness as a Factor of Integration: Identifying Challenges of the Enlarged Single European Market', CEPS, 25–6 November, Brussels.

Baldwin, R. (1994) *Towards an Integrated Europe*. London: Centre for Economic Policy Research (CEPR) and Cambridge University Press.

Baldwin, R., J. Francois and R. Portes (1997) 'The Costs and Benefits of Eastern Enlargement: The Impact on the EU and Central Europe', *Economic Policy*, 24: 125–76.

Barry, F.G. (2002) 'EU Accession and Prospective FDI Flows to CEE Countries: A View from Ireland', in R. E. Lipsey (ed.), *Real and Monetary Aspects of FDI in Industrial Countries*. Deutsche Bundesbank/Springer Verlag.

Borbély, D. (2005) 'Foreign Trade Specialization on the EU Market: Dynamics, Determinants and Competitiveness', paper presented at the final conference of the project on 'Changes in Industrial Competitiveness as a Factor of Integration: Identifying Challenges of the Enlarged Single European Market', CEPS, 25–6 November, Brussels.

Buiter, W. and C. Grafe (2002) 'Patching up the Pact: Some Suggestions for Enhancing Fiscal Sustainability and Macroeconomic Stability in an Enlarged European Union', CEPR Discussion Paper no. 3496, Centre for Economic Policy Research, London.

Canning, D. (1999) Infrastructure's contribution to aggregate output, World Bank Policy Research Paper no. 2246, World Bank, Washington, D.C.

Coricelli, F. and B. Jazbec (2001) 'Real Exchange-Rate Dynamics in Transition Economies', CEPR Discussion Paper no. 2869, Centre for Economic Policy Research, London.

Davis, D.R. and D.E. Weinstein (2002) 'Technological Superiority and the Losses From Migration', NBER Working Paper no. 8971, National Bureau of Economic Research, Cambridge, MA, June.

Derviş, K., M. Emerson, D. Gros and S. Ülgen (2005) 'The European Transformation of Modern Turkey', CEPS Paperback, Centre for European Policy Studies, Brussels.

Deutsche Bundesbank (2001) 'Monetary Aspects of the Enlargement of the EU', *Monthly Report*, October.

Durjasz, P. (2001) 'How to balance real and nominal convergence? The case of Poland', paper presented at the East–West Conference of the Austrian National Bank, Vienna, 5–6 November.

Egger, P. and K. Kratena (2003) 'A Tale of Competition between Eastern and Southern Europe', Review of Word Economics, *Weltwirtschaftliches Archiv*, 139(1).

Emerson, M. and D. Gros (1998) 'Impact of Enlargement, Agenda 2000 and EMU on Poorer Regions, The Case of Portugal', CEPS Working Document no. 125, Centre for European Policy Studies, Brussels.

European Commission (2001) 'European Competitiveness Report 2001', Eur-Op.

European Commission (2002a) 'Communication from the Commission on Streamlining the Annual Economic and Employment Policy Coordination cycles', COM(2002) 487 final.

European Commission (2002b) 'Proposal for a Directive of the European Parliament and the Council on services in the internal market', COM (2004) 2(03).

European Commission (2004a) 'Communication from the Commission to the Council and the European Parliament – Financial Perspectives 2007–2013', COM(2004) 487 final.

European Commission (2004b) 'Communication from the Commission to the Council and the European Parliament on Building our common Future – Policy challenges and Budgetary means of the Enlarged Union 2007–2013', COM(2004) 101 final.

Filipová, L., G. Jaromír and M. Šimek (2005) 'Impact of Changes in Competitiveness on Czech Labour Market Developments', paper presented at the final conference of the project on 'Changes in Industrial Competitiveness as a Factor of Integration: Identifying Challenges of the Enlarged Single European Market', CEPS, 25–6 November, Brussels.

Furmańska-Maruszak A. (2005) 'Labour cost versus labour market development. Empirical evidence for Polish, the Czech Republic and Hungarian manufacturing', paper presented at the final conference of the project on 'Changes in Industrial Competitiveness as a Factor of Integration: Identifying Challenges of the Enlarged Single European Market', CEPS, 25–6 November, Brussels.

Global Competitiveness Report (1996) Geneva: World Economic Forum.

Gros, D. and M. Suhrcke (2000) 'Ten Years After: What is so special about Transition Countries?', HWWA Discussion Paper no. 86, Hamburg.

Gros, D. with N. Thygesen, M. Castelli, T. Mayer, J. Jimeno and R. Perotti. (2002) 'The euro at 25, Special Report of the CEPS Macroeconomic Policy Group', Centre for European Policy Studies, Brussels, December.

Gros, D. with N. Thygesen, M. Castelli, T. Mayer, J. Jimeno and R. Perotti (2004) 'Breaking the Reform Deadlock', 6th Annual Report of the CEPS Macroeconomic Policy Group, Centre for European Policy Studies, Brussels.

Halpern, L. and C. Wyplosz (2001) 'Economic Transformation and Real Exchange Rates in the 2000s: The Balassa–Samuelson Connection', paper commissioned by the Secretariat of the United Nations Economic Commission for Europe and published as Chapter 6 in *Economic Survey of Europe* no. 1, UN/ECE, Geneva, September.

Hamilton, D. and J. Quinlan (2004) 'Partners in Prosperity: The Changing Geography of the Transatlantic Economy', Centre for Transatlantic Relations, Johns Hopkins University, Washington, D.C.

Hashi, I. (2004) 'The Comparative Analysis of State Aid and Government Policy in Poland, Hungary and the Czech Republic', Warsaw: CASE-Foundation (Centre for Social and Economic Research).

Kinoshita, Y. and N.F. Campos (2004) 'Why Does FDI Go Where it Goes? New Evidence from the Transitional Economies', CEPR Discussion Paper no. 3984, Centre for Economic Policy Research, London.

Kryńska, E. (2000) *Polskie Specjalne Strefy Ekonomiczne* (Polish Special Economic Zones). Warsaw: Wydawnictwo Naukowe Scholar.

Pelkmans, J., D. Gros and J. Núñez Ferrer (2000) 'Long-run Economic Aspects of the European Union's Eastern Enlargement', Working Document, Netherlands Scientific Council for Government Policy (WRR), The Hague.

Querioz, C. and S. Gautman (1992) 'Road infrastructure and economic development: Some diagnostic indicators', World Bank Policy Research Working Paper no. 921, World Bank, Washington, DC.

Sinn, H-W and M. Reuter (2001) 'The Minimum Inflation Rate for Euroland', NBER Working Paper no. 8085, National Bureau of Economic Research, Cambridge, MA.

Stephan, J. (2000) 'EU-Integration and Development Prospects of CEECs. The Productivity-Gap and Technological Structural Change', Papers 112, American University in Cairo: Economics and Political Sciences.

Szapary, G. (2000) 'Maastricht and the choice of exchange rate regime in transition countries during the run-up to EMU', NHB Working Paper no. 7, National Bank of Hungary, Budapest.

Vincentz, V. (2004) 'A Note on Relative Prices, Investment and Productivity', contribution prepared for the project on 'Changes in Industrial Competitiveness as a Factor of Integration: Identifying Challenges of the Enlarged Single European Market', mimeo.

Weinstein, D.E. (2002) 'Migration for the Benefit of All', *International Labour Review*, 141(3).

Welfens, P.J.J. (2005) 'Impact of the Real Exchange Rate on Trade, Structural Change and Growth', paper presented at the final conference of the project on 'Changes in

Industrial Competitiveness as a Factor of Integration: Identifying Challenges of the Enlarged Single European Market', Brussels: CEPS, 25–6 November.

Welfens, Paul J.J. and D. Borbély (2004) 'Exchange Rate Developments and Stock Market Dynamics in Transition Countries: Theory and Empirical Analysis', paper prepared as part of the 5th Framework Programme 'Changes in Industrial Competitiveness as a Factor of Integration: Identifying Challenges of the Enlarged Single European Market', EIIW, Wuppertal, Germany.

World Bank (2002) *Transition – The First Ten Years*. Washington, DC: World Bank.

Wziatek-Kubiak, A. and I. Magda (2005) 'Differentiation of changes in competitiveness among Polish manufacturing industries', CASE Studies and Analysis no. 314. http://www.case.com.pl/upload/publikacja_plik/9939339_ sa314.pdf.

Index